Presidential Elections Since 1789

Third Edition

Congressional Quarterly Inc.
1414 22nd Street, N.W.
Washington, D.C. 20037

Congressional Quarterly Inc.

Congressional Quarterly Inc., an editorial research service and publishing company, serves clients in the fields of news, education, business and government. It combines specific coverage of Congress, government and politics by Congressional Quarterly with the more general subject range of an affiliated service, Editorial Research Reports.

Congressional Quarterly was founded in 1945 by Henrietta and Nelson Poynter. Its basic periodical publication was and still is the *Congressional Quarterly Weekly Report,* mailed to clients every Saturday. A cumulative index is published quarterly.

CQ also publishes a variety of books including college political science texts, public affairs paperbacks and reference volumes. The latter include the *CQ Almanac,* a compendium of legislation for one session of Congress that is published each spring, and *Congress and the Nation,* a record of government for a presidential term that is published every four years.

The public affairs books are designed as timely reports to keep journalists, scholars and the public abreast of developing issues, events and trends. They include such recent titles as *Regulation: Process and Politics,* the fourth edition of *The Washington Lobby* and the third edition of *Dollar Politics.*

College textbooks, prepared by outside scholars and published under the CQ Press imprint, include such recent titles as *Goodbye to Good-time Charlie: The American Governorship Transformed, Second Edition,* and *Interest Group Politics.*

In addition, CQ publishes *The Congressional Monitor,* a daily report on current and future activities of congressional committees. This service is supplemented by *The Congressional Record Scanner,* an abstract of each day's *Congressional Record,* and *Congress in Print,* a weekly listing of committee publications. CQ also publishes newsletters including *Congressional Insight,* a weekly analysis of congressional action, and *Campaign Practices Reports,* a bi-monthly update on campaign laws and developments.

CQ conducts seminars and conferences on Congress, the legislative process, the federal budget, national elections and politics, and other current issues. CQ Direct Research is a consulting service that performs contract research and maintains a reference library and query desk for clients.

Editorial Research Reports covers subjects beyond the specialized scope of Congressional Quarterly. It publishes reference material on foreign affairs, business, education, cultural affairs, national security, science and other topics of news interest. Service to clients includes a 6,000-word report four times a month, bound and indexed semi-annually. Editorial Research Reports publishes paperback books in its field of coverage. Founded in 1923, the service merged with Congressional Quarterly in 1956.

Library of Congress Cataloging in Publication Data

Main entry under title:

Presidential elections since 1789.

    Bibliography: p.
    Includes index.
    1. Presidents — United States — Election — History — Statistics.   I. Congressional Quarterly, inc.
JK524.P68 1983   324.973   83-1864
    ISBN 0-87187-268-4

Editor: Margaret C. Thompson
Associate Editor: John L. Moore
Contributors: Rhodes Cook, Christopher Buchanan, Edna Frazier-Cromwell, Robert E. Healy, Larry Light, Warden Moxley
Cover Design: Richard A. Pottern
Graphics: Belle T. Burkhart

Contents

Editor's Note. This third edition of *Presidential Elections Since 1789* updates the first and second editions to include facts and figures on the 1980 presidential elections, which saw Republican candidate Ronald Reagan sweep to a landslide victory over incumbent Democratic President Jimmy Carter. First published in 1975, the book contains information on American presidential elections that heretofore had been widely scattered in numerous sources not readily available to the general reader or researcher. Following a summary of the careers of men who became president, the book traces the electoral process, beginning with a relatively new phenomenon, the presidential primary, initiated in 1912. Tables provide returns for all candidates who ran in primaries. The next chapter traces the development of party nominating conventions and contains a comprehensive list of nominees for all parties since 1831, the first year national nominating conventions were held. A discussion of voting trends and turnout follows, along with tables displaying the national plurality of the leading popular vote candidate and state-by-state breakdowns of vote totals and percentages for major candidates. Minor candidate returns are provided in a separate section. The last chapter deals with the origins and development of the Electoral College, the uniquely American system of electing presidents. Maps and tables display all presidential Electoral College results since 1789. An appendix includes a biographical directory of presidential and vice presidential candidates, texts of constitutional provisions and major statutes relating to presidential elections and a bibliography. The general index provides quick access to information contained throughout the book.

Introduction

For a long while before the appointed time has come, the [presidential] election becomes the important and, so to speak, the all engrossing topic of discussion. Factional ardor is redoubled, and all the artificial passions which the imagination can create in a happy and peaceful land are agitated and brought to light. The President, moreover, is absorbed by the cares of self-defense. He no longer governs for the interest of the state, but for that of his re-election; he does homage to the majority, and instead of checking its passions, as his duty commands, he frequently courts its worst caprices.

As the election draws near, the activity of intrigue and the agitation of the populace increase; the citizens are divided into hostile camps, each of which assumes the name of its favorite candidate; the whole nation glows with feverish excitement; the election is the daily theme of the press, the subject of private conversation, the end of every thought and every action, the sole interest of the present. It is true that as soon as the choice is determined, this ardor is dispelled, calm returns, and the river, which had nearly broken its banks, sinks to its usual level; but who can refrain from astonishment that such a storm should have arisen?

—Alexis de Tocqueville, 1835

As one reads this description 147 years later, Tocqueville's astute observations of the American political landscape seem just as incisive and pertinent to the 1980 presidential elections as they were when he made them. But although the politics, motivations and emotions underlying presidential election campaigns have remained constant, changes in the mechanisms of the battle for the presidency have occurred gradually over the decades.

One of the first and most important developments came about in the early part of the 19th century as more and more states chose presidential electors by popular vote rather than by the state legislatures and the electors be-

came bound by party loyalty rather than voting according to personal preference. During the early years of the Republic, the parties had created an informal nominating device for choosing a president: a caucus of each party's members in Congress. From 1796 until 1824, congressional caucuses (when a party had enough representatives to form one) chose almost all the candidates for president; the electors then chose from the party nominees. Only twice, in 1800 and 1824, as a result of a failure of any candidate to receive a majority of electoral votes, were presidential elections decided by the House of Representatives, and even in those two cases political parties were instrumental in the election of the president. By 1832 all states except Maryland and South Carolina held statewide elections to choose slates of electors pledged to vote for the parties' presidential candidates.

The trend to democratization of the presidential nominating process, as evidenced by the expansion of suffrage and increased importance of the popular vote for president, led to creation of the national nominating convention. The convention system was initiated by the Anti-Masons in 1831 and subsequently was adopted by the major parties before the end of the decade.

The birth of the national nominating convention was a milestone in the evolution of the presidential nominating process. In his book, *Politics, Parties and Pressure Groups* (1964), political scientist V. O. Key Jr. summarized some of the major forces that brought about the rise of the convention system: "The destruction of the caucus represented more than a mere change in the method of nomination. Its replacement by the convention was regarded as the removal from power of self-appointed oligarchies that had usurped the right to nominate. The new system, the convention, gave, or so it was supposed, the mass of party members an opportunity to participate in nominations. These events occurred as the domestic winds blew in from the growing West, as the suffrage was being broadened, and as the last vestiges of the early aristocratic leadership were disappearing. Sharp alterations in the distribution of power were taking place, and they were paralleled by the shifts in methods of nomination."

The establishment of the national convention solidified the two-party system. Unlike the Founding Fathers, who were suspicious of competitive parties, some political leaders in the late 1820s and 1830s favorably viewed the

1

existence of opposing parties. One of the most prominent of these men, Martin Van Buren, a leading organizer of Democrat Andrew Jackson's 1828 election victory, had written in 1827: "We must always have party distinctions...."

20th Century Changes

By the 1900s presidential campaigns had undergone another significant transformation as candidates began to campaign more and more on their own behalf.

At the same time the delegate selection process was revolutionized by the birth of the presidential primary election, in which delegates were elected directly by the voters. Initiated in Florida in 1904, the presidential primary by 1912 was used by 13 states. In his first annual message to Congress the following year, President Woodrow Wilson advocated the establishment of a national primary to select presidential candidates: "I feel confident that I do not misinterpret the wishes or the expectations of the country at which the voters of the several parties may choose their nominees for the presidency without the intervention of nominating conventions." Wilson went on to suggest the retention of conventions for the purpose of declaring the results of the primaries and formulating the parties' platforms.

Before any action was taken on Wilson's proposal, the progressive spirit that spurred the growth of presidential primaries died out. Not until after World War II, when widespread pressures for change touched both parties, especially the Democratic, was there a rapid growth in presidential primaries. The most dramatic surge occurred in the 1970s. Twenty-three primaries were held in 1972, 30 in 1976 and 37 in 1980 (including the District of Columbia and Puerto Rico). While only about 40 percent of the delegates were elected from primaries to the Democratic and Republican conventions in 1968, about three quarters of the delegates in 1980 were the product of primary elections.

As presidential campaigns have grown longer, the elimination of candidates has come earlier. It used to be that most candidates remained in the race until the convention. But not since 1952 has a Democratic or Republican convention taken more than one ballot to nominate a president. During the opening round of the 1976 primaries, for example, six Democratic candidates withdrew from the field, while Georgia Gov. Jimmy Carter hurdled to the front of the pack. At the same time, Republican candidate Ronald Reagan was nearly knocked out of the GOP race by a series of early primary losses. An upset victory in North Carolina rescued his flagging campaign but was insufficient to stop incumbent Republican President Gerald R. Ford's momentum.

Elections 1980

The 1980 primaries concluded in a manner nearly the reverse of 1976. In 1976 Jimmy Carter wrapped up the Democratic nomination in the final week of the primary season, while Republican candidate Reagan and President Ford battled on to the Republican convention. Four years later, Reagan became the almost certain nominee early in the primary campaigns, while Carter — although holding more than enough delegates to win the nomination — continued to face challenges from his principal Democratic opponent, Sen. Edward M. Kennedy, D-Mass., up to, and even during, the party's convention in August.

The end result of the long 1980 presidential campaign was a landslide victory for Reagan. Official returns gave the Republican nominee an absolute majority of the popular vote and an 8,417,992 vote (or a 7 percentage point) lead over Carter.

By carrying 44 states, Reagan's Electoral College advantage was even more pronounced. He won 489 electoral votes to just 49 for Carter, who carried only six states and the District of Columbia. Carter campaign managers had feared that independent candidate John B. Anderson, R-Ill., would draw the support of enough liberal Democrats to deny the president re-election. However, Anderson did not win any states. Even if Carter had won every vote that went to Anderson, Reagan still would have carried a majority of states, winning more than 300 electoral votes. Only 270 were needed for victory.

In rejecting Carter, voters for the second consecutive election turned their backs on an embattled incumbent to elect a challenger promising a fresh approach to government and a dynamic new brand of leadership. But unlike the close contest in 1976 in which Carter narrowly defeated Ford, the results in 1980 were emphatic. Since the Civil War, only two presidents — William Howard Taft in 1912 and Herbert Hoover in 1932 — had been denied re-election by larger popular vote margins than Carter.

Taft was crippled by the Republican Party split that produced the Bull Moose candidacy of Theodore Roosevelt. Taft finished third in the 1912 election, 19 percentage points behind Democratic winner Woodrow Wilson. Hoover unsuccessfully sought a second term in the midst of the Depression and was beaten by Democrat Franklin D. Roosevelt by 18 percentage points. Still, Hoover won more electoral votes (59) than Carter, who was the first Democratic incumbent president denied re-election since 1888. In that election Grover Cleveland was ousted by Republican Benjamin Harrison even though Cleveland ran ahead in the popular vote.

Carter's defeat underscored the Democrats' difficulty in winning presidential elections. Since the end of World War II, the Republicans had won five elections to the Democrats' four. But only twice — in 1964 and 1976 — had the Democratic candidate drawn a majority of the popular vote. Carter's percentage of the vote dropped below his 1976 share in every state by at least 2 percentage points. In nearly half the states it declined by at least 10 percentage points. Reagan easily carried every region of the country, including the keystones of Carter's triumph four years before — the industrial Northeast and the president's native South.

A variety of public opinion polls showed an unusually large number of undecided voters in the final weeks of the campaign. In addition, many Americans apparently did not vote. Only about 54 percent of the nation's voting age population of 160.5 million went to the polls, marking the fifth consecutive election that the presidential turnout had declined. The 1980 figure was less than 1 percentage point below the 1976 turnout rate of 54.4 percent, but it was the lowest turnout since 1948.

Is the Election Process Too Long?

Many participants in the present presidential election process view it as a time-consuming and expensive system laden with liabilities and political hazards. Campaigns are increasingly being conducted in a media fishbowl that leaves little room for mistakes. There is little doubt that the visible, public side of campaigns has grown longer. As of June 1979 there were seven major announced candidates for president. By contrast, in June 1975 there were six; in June 1971, one (George McGovern, D-S.D.); and in June 1967, none.

Observers have pointed out that the intense scrutiny may force candidates to shy away from the detailed discussion of issues, reducing the campaign to a long endurance contest that fatigues both the candidates and the voters. According to 1980 Democratic National Committee Chairman John C. White, the result has been lower and lower turnouts. "Candidates are seeking attention and are creating contrived crises," he contended. "By the time we elect a president, the people and the candidates are worn out."

White also argued that the long campaign cut into the president's ability to govern. "At some time, with this many primaries, the president must turn away from his duties" to campaign, he said.

Critics of the lengthy election campaign are in general agreement that a reduction in the number of primaries would shorten the process. They argue that without the large quantity of primaries there would be less incentive for the candidates to conduct such long campaigns.

Moreover, some states have discovered on their own that primary elections are not the bonanza that they expected. Many had hoped that a primary would attract glamorous candidates and focus media attention on their states. But many of the small states that switched from caucuses to primaries in the 1970s have been disappointed. Their presidential primaries drew little attention and, when operated on a different date from the primary election for state offices, proved to be expensive.

About This Book

The choosing of a president has evolved into one of the most dramatic political events in the United States and, perhaps, in the world. Every four years for almost 200 years, the country has been offered a hectic nominating process based on rhetoric, partisan maneuvering and character analysis as ambitious politicians vie for the nation's top prize.

Since 1789 Americans have gone to the polls 49 times to elect a president. The history of those elections has been the subject of countless volumes, monographs, dissertations and articles in academic journals. Nevertheless, it is difficult to find a single book that comprehensively and succinctly covers the basic facts and figures on the Electoral College, popular returns, presidential primaries, nominations of minor party candidates and biographical data on presidential candidates.

Presidential Elections Since 1789, first published in 1975, contains information on American presidential elections that heretofore had been widely scattered in numerous sources not readily available to the general reader or researcher. It includes popular vote returns for president, obtained from the Historical Archive of the Inter-University Consortium for Political Research (ICPR) at the University of Michigan. Congressional Quarterly has updated this material and added data on the 1976 and 1980 presidential elections to produce a third edition of this comprehensive reference book.

Following a summary of the careers of men who became president ("Roads to the Presidency"), the book traces the electoral process, beginning with a relatively new phenomenon, the presidential primary. An introductory section contains a historical discussion of the origins and development of primaries followed by tables of primary election returns since 1912.

The next chapter traces the development of party nominating conventions and the evolution of their functions. It describes the delegate selection process, credentials disputes, convention rules and the adoption of party platforms. The comprehensive list of party nominees since 1831, the first year national nominating conventions were held, includes nominations of minor candidates — some of whom did not even receive popular votes. For example, on page 72 can be found the nominations in 1872 by the People's Party of the first woman candidate for president, Victoria Claflin Woodhull, and the first black candidate for vice president, Frederick Douglass.

After the parties have selected their nominee, the presidential campaign gathers momentum, culminating on the Tuesday next after the first Monday in November (a date established in 1845), when voters go to the polls to cast their ballots. Although formally choosing presidential electors rather than the president himself, the focus of public attention is on the popular vote returns. This section of the book contains material on the popular vote, with an introductory section briefly describing voting trends and turnout, the broadening franchise, voting behavior and party affiliation. The material is presented in a readily readable format displaying the national plurality of the leading popular vote candidate, state-by-state breakdowns of votes, percentages and pluralities and national vote totals and percentages for each candidate. The scope of this material can best be appreciated by noting that the figures in the returns range from the record high of 47,170,179 votes cast for Richard Nixon in 1972 to the single vote cast for Andrew Gump in South Carolina in 1924.

The last chapter of the book deals with the constitutional origins and historical development of the Electoral College, the uniquely American system of electing presidents. The section details complex and little-known methods used in the various states through the first third of the 19th century to choose presidential electors, recounts historical anomalies in the functioning of the Electoral College and discusses reasons why a state's electoral votes have frequently been divided among several candidates. It covers the two occasions when a president was elected by the House of Representatives, explains procedures for counting and challenging electoral votes in Congress and describes the famous Tilden-Hayes contest in 1877. The section concludes with a discussion of instances of presidential disability and the ratification of the 25th Amendment to the Constitution. Maps and tables display all presidential Electoral College results since 1789. Vice presidential electoral votes appear at the end of the section. The popular vote returns for president up through 1972 were obtained from ICPR. The 1976 and 1980 figures were compiled by Congressional Quarterly from the final, official reports of the secretaries of state and the District of Columbia Board of Elections.

The appendix includes a biographical directory of presidential and vice presidential candidates. Texts of constitutional provisions and amendments, major statutes and rules relating to presidential elections are also included.

The general index provides quick access to information contained throughout the book and is also itself a source of information. For example, the index entry for Herbert Hoover indicates that Hoover received votes in presidential primaries in the years 1920, 1928, 1932, 1936 and 1940 and was a presidential nominee in 1928 and 1932.

Presidents and Vice Presidents of the United States

President and Political Party	Born	Died	Age at inauguration	Native of—	Elected from—	Term of Service	Vice President
George Washington (F)*	1732	1799	57	Va.	Va.	April 30, 1789-March 4, 1793	John Adams
George Washington (F)			61			March 4, 1793-March 4, 1797	John Adams
John Adams (F)	1735	1826	61	Mass.	Mass.	March 4, 1797-March 4, 1801	Thomas Jefferson
Thomas Jefferson (D-R)	1743	1826	57	Va.	Va.	March 4, 1801-March 4, 1805	Aaron Burr
Thomas Jefferson (D-R)			61			March 4, 1805-March 4, 1809	George Clinton
James Madison (D-R)	1751	1836	57	Va.	Va.	March 4, 1809-March 4, 1813	George Clinton
James Madison (D-R)			61			March 4, 1813-March 4, 1817	Elbridge Gerry
James Monroe (D-R)	1758	1831	58	Va.	Va.	March 4, 1817-March 4, 1821	Daniel D. Tompkins
James Monroe (D-R)			62			March 4, 1821-March 4, 1825	Daniel D. Tompkins
John Q. Adams (N-R)	1767	1848	57	Mass.	Mass.	March 4, 1825-March 4, 1829	John C. Calhoun
Andrew Jackson (D)	1767	1845	61	S.C.	Tenn.	March 4, 1829-March 4, 1833	John C. Calhoun
Andrew Jackson (D)			65			March 4, 1833-March 4, 1837	Martin Van Buren
Martin Van Buren (D)	1782	1862	54	N.Y.	N.Y.	March 4, 1837-March 4, 1841	Richard M. Johnson
W. H. Harrison (W)	1773	1841	68	Va.	Ohio	March 4, 1841-April 4, 1841	John Tyler
John Tyler (W)	1790	1862	51	Va.	Va.	April 6, 1841-March 4, 1845	
James K. Polk (D)	1795	1849	49	N.C.	Tenn.	March 4, 1845-March 4, 1849	George M. Dallas
Zachary Taylor (W)	1784	1850	64	Va.	La.	March 4, 1849-July 9, 1850	Millard Fillmore
Millard Fillmore (W)	1800	1874	50	N.Y.	N.Y.	July 10, 1850-March 4, 1853	
Franklin Pierce (D)	1804	1869	48	N.H.	N.H.	March 4, 1853-March 4, 1857	William R. King
James Buchanan (D)	1791	1868	65	Pa.	Pa.	March 4, 1857-March 4, 1861	John C. Breckinridge
Abraham Lincoln (R)	1809	1865	52	Ky.	Ill.	March 4, 1861-March 4, 1865	Hannibal Hamlin
Abraham Lincoln (R)			56			March 4, 1865-April 15, 1865	Andrew Johnson
Andrew Johnson (R)	1808	1875	56	N.C.	Tenn.	April 15, 1865-March 4, 1869	
Ulysses S. Grant (R)	1822	1885	46	Ohio	Ill.	March 4, 1869-March 4, 1873	Schuyler Colfax
Ulysses S. Grant (R)			50			March 4, 1873-March 4, 1877	Henry Wilson
Rutherford B. Hayes (R)	1822	1893	54	Ohio	Ohio	March 4, 1877-March 4, 1881	William A. Wheeler
James A. Garfield (R)	1831	1881	49	Ohio	Ohio	March 4, 1881-Sept. 19, 1881	Chester A. Arthur
Chester A. Arthur (R)	1830	1886	50	Vt.	N.Y.	Sept. 20, 1881-March 4, 1885	
Grover Cleveland (D)	1837	1908	47	N.J.	N.Y.	March 4, 1885-March 4, 1889	Thomas A. Hendricks
Benjamin Harrison (R)	1833	1901	55	Ohio	Ind.	March 4, 1889-March 4, 1893	Levi P. Morton
Grover Cleveland (D)	1837	1908	55			March 4, 1893-March 4, 1897	Adlai E. Stevenson
William McKinley (R)	1843	1901	54	Ohio	Ohio	March 4, 1897-March 4, 1901	Garret A. Hobart
William McKinley (R)			58			March 4, 1901-Sept. 14, 1901	Theodore Roosevelt
Theodore Roosevelt (R)	1858	1919	42	N.Y.	N.Y.	Sept. 14, 1901-March 4, 1905	
Theodore Roosevelt (R)			46			March 4, 1905-March 4, 1909	Charles W. Fairbanks
William H. Taft (R)	1857	1930	51	Ohio	Ohio	March 4, 1909-March 4, 1913	James S. Sherman
Woodrow Wilson (D)	1856	1924	56	Va.	N.J.	March 4, 1913-March 4, 1917	Thomas R. Marshall
Woodrow Wilson (D)			60			March 4, 1917-March 4, 1921	Thomas R. Marshall
Warren G. Harding (R)	1865	1923	55	Ohio	Ohio	March 4, 1921-Aug. 2, 1923	Calvin Coolidge
Calvin Coolidge (R)	1872	1933	51	Vt.	Mass.	Aug. 3, 1923-March 4, 1925	
Calvin Coolidge (R)			52			March 4, 1925-March 4, 1929	Charles G. Dawes
Herbert Hoover (R)	1874	1964	54	Iowa	Calif.	March 4, 1929-March 4, 1933	Charles Curtis
Franklin D. Roosevelt (D)	1882	1945	51	N.Y.	N.Y.	March 4, 1933-Jan. 20, 1937	John N. Garner
Franklin D. Roosevelt (D)			55			Jan. 20, 1937-Jan. 20, 1941	John N. Garner
Franklin D. Roosevelt (D)			59			Jan. 20, 1941-Jan. 20, 1945	Henry A. Wallace
Franklin D. Roosevelt (D)			63			Jan. 20, 1945-April 12, 1945	Harry S Truman
Harry S Truman (D)	1884	1972	60	Mo.	Mo.	April 12, 1945-Jan. 20, 1949	
Harry S Truman (D)			64			Jan. 20, 1949-Jan. 20, 1953	Alben W. Barkley
Dwight D. Eisenhower (R)	1890	1969	62	Texas	N.Y.	Jan. 20, 1953-Jan. 20, 1957	Richard M. Nixon
Dwight D. Eisenhower (R)			66		Pa.	Jan. 20, 1957-Jan. 20, 1961	Richard M. Nixon
John F. Kennedy (D)	1917	1963	43	Mass.	Mass.	Jan. 20, 1961-Nov. 22, 1963	Lyndon B. Johnson
Lyndon B. Johnson (D)	1908	1973	55	Texas	Texas	Nov. 22, 1963-Jan. 20, 1965	
Lyndon B. Johnson (D)			56			Jan. 20, 1965-Jan. 20, 1969	Hubert H. Humphrey
Richard M. Nixon (R)	1913		56	Calif.	N.Y.	Jan. 20, 1969-Jan. 20, 1973	Spiro T. Agnew
Richard M. Nixon (R)			60		Calif.	Jan. 20, 1973-Aug. 9, 1974	Spiro T. Agnew Gerald R. Ford
Gerald R. Ford (R)	1913		61	Neb.	Mich.	Aug. 9, 1974-Jan. 20, 1977	Nelson A. Rockefeller
Jimmy Carter (D)	1924		52	Ga.	Ga.	Jan. 20, 1977-Jan. 20, 1981	Walter F. Mondale
Ronald Reagan (R)	1911		69	Ill.	Calif.	Jan. 20, 1981-	George Bush

*Key to abbreviations: (D) Democrat, (D-R) Democrat-Republican, (F) Federalist, (N-R) National Republican, (R) Republican, (W) Whig

SOURCE: Joseph Nathan Kane, *Facts About the President*, revised edition, 1976

Roads to the Presidency

Most presidents have come to the White House with long public careers behind them, but there have been notable exceptions. Zachary Taylor's only career was the Army; he went straight from the service to the White House.

In the 19th century, men changed public jobs frequently as they prepared for the presidency. James Madison, Thomas Jefferson and Andrew Jackson each held nearly a dozen public posts before reaching the White House. In recent years, however, presidents have done fewer things. Gerald R. Ford, for example, had held no public position except U.S. representative. But he was a representative for 25 years.

The field of candidates for the 1980 presidential nomination continued a trend that first appeared in the 1976 campaign — the re-emergence of governors as leading contenders in the nomination sweepstakes.

For 16 years, starting with John F. Kennedy's ascension from the Senate to the White House in 1960 until 1976, senators dominated presidential compaigns. During that time every single major party nominee was a senator or former senator.

That represented an about-face from earlier times. In the 36 years before Kennedy, the two major parties nominated only one man who ever served in the Senate. And that man, Harry S Truman, was already president when he was nominated.

While there was no shortage of senators in the 1976 campaign it was the governors that attracted the most attention. Former California Governor Ronald Reagan came close to depriving incumbent Gerald R. Ford of the Republican presidential nomination. The Democratic nominee, former Georgia Governor Jimmy Carter, faced a dramatic last-minute challenge from the governor of California at the time, Jerry Brown.

Carter, Reagan and Brown were candidates again in 1980. Former Texas Governor John Connally, who had joined the field of those seeking the Republican nomination, dropped out of the race March 9.

The fact that Carter and Reagan emerged as the Democratic and Republican nominees was consistent with the fads and trends through American history that have marked the public's ideas about the proper training for a president.

A look backward to the 18th century shows just how often the fashion has changed. The nation has never made up its mind what background a president ought to have.

Paths of Glory

The earliest tradition developed around the secretary of state. The secretary of state was considered the preeminent Cabinet officer and thus the most important man in the executive branch after the president. Washington's first secretary of state was Thomas Jefferson. Although Jefferson left the Cabinet early in Washington's second term, he went on to become leader of the newly formed Democratic Republican Party and its candidate for president in 1796, 1800 and 1804. Losing to John Adams in 1796, Jefferson came back to win four years later.

In turn, Jefferson's secretary of state, James Madison, won the presidency in 1808. Madison had been a close ally of Jefferson's in the political struggles of the 1790s and served throughout Jefferson's two presidential terms as secretary of state (1801-09). During his first term as president, Madison appointed fellow Virginian James Monroe as his secretary of state. And following in what was rapidly becoming a tradition, Monroe went on to the presidency in 1816, serving two terms (1817-25).

Throughout Monroe's terms, the secretary of state was John Quincy Adams, son of former President John Adams. When Monroe's second term was nearing its end, five major candidates entered the race to succeed him. Three were Cabinet officers, including Adams.

None of the four remaining candidates (one had withdrawn) managed to acquire a majority in the Electoral College and the House then chose Secretary of State Adams.

Adams was the last secretary of state to go directly from his Cabinet post to the White House. After him, only two secretaries of state made it to the White House at all — Martin Van Buren, who was secretary of state from 1829 to 1831 and president from 1837 to 1841, and James Buchanan, who served as secretary of state under President James K. Polk (1845-49) and as president from 1857 to 1861.

Two other institutions died at approximately the same time as the Cabinet tradition — the Virginia dynasty and "King Caucus." After the four Virginians who occupied the presidency during the first 36 years of the Republic — Washington, Jefferson, Madison and Monroe — there have been no presidents elected who were both born in and made their careers in the state. John Tyler was a Virginian, but succeeded to the presidency from the vice presidency in 1841 and was not renominated. Three other presidents were born in Virginia but made their careers elsewhere — William Henry Harrison, Zachary Taylor and Woodrow Wilson.

"King Caucus" was a derogatory reference to the congressional party caucuses that met throughout the early 1800s to designate presidential nominees. During its heyday, the Washington-centered mentality of the caucus had virtually guaranteed that Cabinet officers should be among those most often nominated by the party in power. But the caucus came under attack as being undemocratic and unrepresentative, and ceased to function as a presidential nominating mechanism after 1824. It was replaced by the national conventions, bodies which are not connected with Congress and which have never met in the national capital.

Men on Horseback

The next cycle of American politics, from the presidency of Andrew Jackson (1829-37) to the Civil War, saw a variety of backgrounds qualify candidates for the presidency. One of the most prevalent was the military. Andrew Jackson, who ran in 1824 (unsuccessfully), 1828 and 1832, was a general in the War of 1812, gaining near-heroic stature by his defeat of the British at the Battle of New Orleans in January 1815. Like most military officers who have risen to the presidency, however, Jackson was only a part-time military man. As a politician, Jackson had served in the U.S. House during George Washington's presidency and in the Senate during John Adams' administration, as well as later, under Monroe and John Quincy Adams. Only Presidents Taylor, Grant and Eisenhower were career military officers.

Other candidates during this era who were or had been military officers included William Henry Harrison, a Whig candidate in 1836 and 1840; Zachary Taylor, the Whig nominee in 1848; Winfield Scott, the 1852 Whig candidate; Franklin Pierce, the Democratic nominee in 1852, and John Charles Fremont in 1856, the Republican Party's first presidential candidate. Thus, from 1824 through 1856, all but one presidential election featured a major candidate with a military background.

Like Jackson, Harrison had a mixed military and political career. A member of a distinguished Virginia family, Harrison was the son of a signer of the Declaration of Independence. He served in Congress during the John Adams administration and again under Madison, Monroe, and John Quincy Adams. In between, he battled the Indians and the British during the War of 1812.

Taylor and Scott were both career military men who led conquering armies in the Mexican War. Pierce also had a command in the Mexican War, although he had been primarily a politician, with service in both the House and the Senate during the 1830s and 1840s. Fremont was famous as an explorer as well as for a dashing military campaign through California during the Mexican War. Later, he was an early U.S. senator from California (1850-51).

The smoldering political conflicts of the 1840s and 1850s probably contributed to the naming of military men for the presidency. Generals had usually escaped involvement in national politics and had avoided taking stands on the issues that divided the country — slavery, expansion, the currency and the tariff. In 1840, for example, the Whigs adopted no platform or statement of principles, simply nominating Harrison and assuming his personal popularity

plus the resentments against the incumbent Democratic administration of Martin Van Buren would suffice for Whig victory. They were right.

Later on, the nature of the Civil War almost automatically led at least one of the parties to choose a military officer as presidential standard-bearer every four years. To have been on the "right" side during the war — fighting to save the union and destroy slavery — was a major political asset in the North and Middle West, where tens of thousands of war veterans were effectively organized in the Grand Army of the Republic (GAR). The GAR became part of the backbone of the Republican Party during the last third of the 19th century.

Consequently, it became customary for Republicans to have a Civil War officer at the head of their ticket. With the exception of James G. Blaine in 1884, every Republican presidential nominee from 1868 to 1900 had served as an officer in the Union Army during the Civil War. Blaine, who had spent the Civil War years as a Maine state legislator and a member of the U.S. House, lost the election.

Of all the Republican nominees, however, only Grant was a professional military man. The others — Rutherford B. Hayes in 1876, James A. Garfield in 1880, Benjamin Harrison in 1888 and 1892 and William McKinley in 1896 and 1900 — were civilians who volunteered for service in the Civil War. Two of them — Hayes and Garfield — were elected to the House while serving in the Army. At the time of their presidential nominations, Hayes was governor of Ohio, Garfield was minority leader of the U.S. House and a senator-elect, Harrison was an ex-senator from Indiana and McKinley was a former governor of Ohio.

The Democrats, who had been split over the war, had few prominent military veterans to choose from. Only twice between 1860 and 1900 did the Democrats pick a Civil War officer as their nominee. In 1864, during the Civil War, the Democrats nominated Gen. George B. McClellan, the Union military commander who had fallen out with President Lincoln. And in 1880, Gen. Winfield Scott Hancock of Pennsylvania was the Democrats' choice.

The Empire State

Otherwise, Democrats tended to favor governors or former governors of New York. Their 1868 nominee was Horatio Seymour, who had been governor of New York in 1853-55 and again 1863-65. In 1876 they chose Samuel J. Tilden, New York's reform governor who was battling Tammany Hall. And in 1884, Grover Cleveland, another New York reform governor, captured the Democratic nomination. He went on to become the first Democrat to win the White House in 28 years. Cleveland was again the Democratic nominee in 1888 and 1892.

Besides being the most populous state, New York was a swing state in presidential politics. During the period from Reconstruction through the turn of the century, most Southern states voted Democratic, while the Republicans usually carried Pennsylvania, the Midwest and New England. A New Yorker appeared as the nominee for president or vice president of at least one of the major parties in every single election from 1868 through 1892.

This general tradition was maintained through the candidacy of Thomas E. Dewey, Republican governor of New York, in 1948. Only twice between 1868 and 1948 was there no New Yorker on the national ticket of at least one of the major parties — for president or vice president.

Once, in 1944, both major party presidential nominees, Democrat Franklin D. Roosevelt and Republican Dewey, were selected from New York.

Since 1948, however, the only New Yorker to be nominated by a major party for president or vice president was Rep. William E. Miller, R-N.Y. (1951-65), the Republican vice presidential nominee in 1964. Eisenhower in 1952 and Nixon in 1968 were technically residents of New York, but they were generally identified with other states. Gerald R. Ford's vice president, Nelson Rockefeller, was a former governor of New York, but he was appointed to the vice presidency. He was not asked to be on the ticket when Ford ran in 1976.

Another major swing state in the years from the Civil War through the First World War was Indiana. And in most elections, a prominent Indianan found his way onto one of the major party's national tickets. In the 13 presidential elections between 1868 and 1916, an Indianan appeared 10 times on at least one of the major parties' national tickets. However, since 1916 only one Indianan, Wendell Willkie in 1940, has been a major party's nominee.

The Governors

From 1900 to 1956, Democrats tended to favor governors for the presidential nomination, a trend that may be making a comeback. Democratic governors who received their party's presidential nomination included Woodrow Wilson of New Jersey in 1912, James M. Cox of Ohio in 1920, Alfred E. Smith of New York in 1928, Franklin D. Roosevelt of New York in 1932 and Adlai E. Stevenson of Illinois in 1952.

During the same period, 1900 to 1956, Republican presidential nominees had a wide variety of backgrounds. There were two Cabinet officers (Secretary of War William Howard Taft in 1908 and Secretary of Commerce Herbert Hoover in 1928), a Supreme Court justice (Charles Evans Hughes in 1916), a U.S. senator (Warren G. Harding in 1920), two governors (Alfred M. Landon of Kansas in 1936 and Thomas E. Dewey of New York in 1944 and 1948), a private lawyer (Wendell Willkie in 1940) and a general (Eisenhower in 1952 and 1956). Calvin Coolidge of Massachusetts, the 1924 nominee, and Theodore Roosevelt of New York, the 1904 nominee, both of whom succeeded to the presidency from the vice presidency, had been governors of their respective states. As noted, both Carter and

Reagan in 1980 had been governors.

Curiously, the two world wars did not produce a plethora of military candidates for the presidency. The only general besides Eisenhower who made a strong bid for a presidential nomination was Gen. Leonard Wood, who had commands in the Spanish-American War and the First World War. Wood led on five ballots at the 1920 Republican national convention before losing out on the 10th ballot to Warren G. Harding. Otherwise, only a few military men have even been mentioned for the presidency in the 20th century — most notably Gen. Douglas MacArthur in the 1940s and 1950s — and they got little support at national conventions.

Former Vice Presidents

A sudden change took place in 1960 with the nomination of Kennedy, a senator, and Nixon, a former senator and sitting vice president. It was the first time since 1860 and only the second time in the history of party nominating conventions that an incumbent vice president was chosen for the presidency (the others were Democrat Martin Van Buren in 1836 and John C. Breckinridge, the choice of the Southern Democratic faction in 1860). And it was only the second time in the 20th century that an incumbent U.S. senator was nominated for the presidency (Republican Warren G. Harding was the first, in 1920). In the 19th century the phenomenon was also rare, with National Republican Henry Clay in 1832, Democrat Lewis Cass in 1848 and Democrat Stephen A. Douglas in 1860 the only incumbent senators nominated for president by official party conventions. Republican James A. Garfield was a senator-elect at the time of his election in 1880.

The nomination of Nixon, like the nomination of Kennedy, was a sign of things to come. Beginning in 1960 the vice presidency, like the Senate, became a presidential training ground. Vice President Hubert H. Humphrey was chosen by the Democrats for president in 1968. Vice President Spiro T. Agnew (R 1969-73) was the leading contender for the 1976 Republican presidential nomination before his resignation in October 1973. Even defeated vice presidential nominees have been considered for the nomination — witness Henry Cabot Lodge Jr. of Massachusetts in 1964, Edmund S. Muskie of Maine in 1972, Sargent Shriver of Maryland in 1976, and Bob Dole of Kansas in 1980.

Presidential Primaries

Presidential primaries originated as an outgrowth of the progressive movement in the early 20th century. Progressives, populists, and reformers in general at the turn of the century were fighting state and municipal corruption. They objected to the links between political bosses and big business and advocated returning the government to the people.

Part of this "return to the people" was the inauguration of primary elections, wherein candidates for office would be chosen by the voters of their party rather than by what were looked upon as boss-dominated conventions. It was only a matter of time before the idea spread from state and local elections to presidential contests. Since there was no provision for a nationwide primary, state primaries were initiated to choose delegates to the national party conventions (delegate selection primaries), and to register voters' preferences on their parties' eventual presidential nominees (preference primaries).

Florida enacted the first presidential primary law in 1901. The law gave party officials an option of holding a party primary to choose any party candidate for public office, as well as delegates to the national conventions. However, there was no provision for placing names of presidential candidates on the ballot — either in the form of a preference vote or with information indicating the preference of the candidates for convention delegates.

Impact of Progressive Movement

Wisconsin's progressive Republican politician, Gov. Robert M. La Follette, gave a major boost to the presidential primary following the 1904 Republican national convention. It was at that convention that the credentials of La Follette's progressive delegation were rejected and a regular Republican delegation was seated from Wisconsin. Angered by what he considered his unfair treatment, La Follette returned to his home state and began pushing for a presidential primary law. The result was the Wisconsin law of 1905 providing for the mandatory direct election of national convention delegates. The law, however, did not include a provision for indicating delegate preference for presidential candidates.

Pennsylvania closely followed Wisconsin (in 1906) with a statute providing that each candidate for delegate to a national convention could have printed beside his name on the official primary ballot the name of the presidential candidate he would support at the convention. However, no member of either party exercised this option in the 1908 primary.

La Follette's sponsorship of the delegate selection primary helped make the concept part of the progressive political program. The growth of the progressive movement rapidly resulted in the enactment of presidential primary laws in other states.

The next step in presidential primaries — the preferential vote for president — took place in Oregon. There, in 1910, Sen. Jonathan Bourne, R (1907-13), a progressive Republican colleague of La Follette (then a senator), sponsored a referendum to establish a presidential preference primary, with delegates legally bound to support the winner of the preference primary.

By 1912, with Oregon in the lead, 12 states had enacted presidential primary laws that provided for either direct election of delegates, a preferential vote, or both. The number had expanded to 26 states by 1916.

Primaries and Conventions

The first major test of the impact of presidential primary laws — in 1912 — demonstrated that victories in the primaries did not ensure a candidate's nomination at the convention. Former President Theodore Roosevelt, campaigning in 12 Republican primaries, won nine of them, including a defeat of incumbent Republican President William Howard Taft in Taft's home state of Ohio. Roosevelt lost only three — to Taft by a narrow margin in Massachusetts and to La Follette in North Dakota and in La Fol-

Sources

James W. Davis. *Presidential Primaries: Road to the White House.* New York: Thomas Y. Crowell Co., 1967.

Richard M. Scammon. *America Votes 1956-57.* New York: The Macmillan Co., 1958. *America Votes 4,* Pittsburgh: University of Pittsburgh Press, 1962. *America Votes 6, America Votes 8, America Votes 10, America Votes 12.* Washington, D.C.: Congressional Quarterly Inc., 1966, 1970, 1973, 1977; *America Votes 14,* Washington, D.C., Elections Research Center, 1981.

Types of Primaries and Procedures

Presidential primaries consist of two basic types. One is the presidential preference primary in which voters vote directly for the person they wish to be nominated for president. The second type is the delegate selection primary in which voters elect delegates to the national conventions.

States may use various combinations of these methods:

• A state may have a preference vote but choose delegates at party conventions. The preference vote may or may not be binding on the delegates.

• A state may combine the preference and delegate selection primaries by electing delegates pledged or favorable to a candidate named on the ballot. However, under this system, state party organizations may run unpledged slates of delegates.

• A state may have an advisory preference vote and a separate delegate selection vote in which delegates may be listed as either pledged to a candidate, favorable or unpledged.

• A state may have a mandatory preference vote with a separate delegate selection vote. In these cases, the delegates are required to support the preference primary winner.

For those primaries in which the preference vote is binding upon delegates, state laws may vary as to the number of ballots through which delegates at the convention may remain committed.

Most primary states hold presidential preference votes, in which voters choose among the candidates who have qualified for the ballot in their states. Although preference votes may be binding or non-binding, in most states the vote is binding on the delegates, who either are elected in the primary itself or chosen outside of it by a caucus process, by a state committee or by the candidates who have qualified to win delegates.

Delegates may be bound for as short as one ballot or as long as a candidate remains in the race. National Democratic rules require delegates to be bound for one ballot unless released by the candidate that they were elected to support.

Until 1980 the Republicans had a rule requiring delegates bound to a specific candidate by state law in primary states to vote for that candidate at the convention regardless of their personal presidential preferences. That rule was repealed at the July 1980 convention.

There are a variety of ways in which delegates from primary states are allocated to candidates.

Most of the methods are based on the preference vote — proportional representation, statewide winner-take-all (in which the candidate winning the most votes statewide wins all the delegates), congressional district and statewide winner-take-all (in which the high vote-getter in a district wins that district's delegates and the high vote-getter statewide wins all the at-large delegates) or some combination of the three. Still another method is the selection of individual delegates in a "loophole" primary. Then the preference vote is either non-binding, or there is no preference vote at all — the case in 1980 with the Republican primaries in New York, Mississippi and the District of Columbia.

In the proportional representation system, the qualifying threshold for candidates to win delegates can vary.

In 1980 Democratic rules set the threshold in congressional districts at a range of 15 to 25 percent of the vote but generally no lower than 15 percent, and for statewide at-large delegates and an expanded 10 percent "bonus" group of party and elected officials who were delegates at 15 to 20 percent of the statewide vote.

The Republicans allow the primary states to set their own thresholds, which in many states in 1980 were lower than the Democrats'. In Massachusetts, for example, a GOP candidate had to receive only 2.4 percent of the vote in order to win a delegate.

In nearly half the primary states, major candidates are placed on the ballot by the secretary of state or a special nominating committee. The consent of the candidate is required in only three states — Kentucky, Michigan and North Carolina.

Elsewhere, candidates must take the initiative to get on the ballot. The filing requirements range from sending a letter of candidacy to election officials — the case in Puerto Rico — to filing petitions signed by a specified number of registered voters and paying a filing fee — the case in Alabama.

On many primary ballots, voters have the opportunity to mark a line labeled "uncommitted" if they do not prefer any of the candidates. In 1976 an "uncommitted" line appeared on the ballot in more than a dozen primary states. Few voters marked it in the early primaries, but later it was used by supporters of Democrats Hubert Humphrey, Minn., and Edmund G. Brown Jr., Calif., to show support for them. Humphrey never entered the race, while Brown launched his drive too late to make the ballot in most primaries.

Democrats require states to set their filing deadlines 30 to 90 days before the election. Delegates must declare presidential preference or uncommitted status. Republicans have no deadline and delegates are not required to declare preference.

lette's home state of Wisconsin.

Despite this impressive string of primary victories, however, the Republican National Convention rejected Roosevelt in favor of Taft. The Republican National Committee, which organized the convention, and the convention's credentials committee, which ruled on contested delegates, both were dominated by Taft supporters. Moreover, Taft was backed by many state organizations, especially in the South, where most delegates were chosen by caucuses or conventions dominated by party leaders.

On the Democratic side, the primaries were more closely connected with the results of the convention. New Jersey Gov. Woodrow Wilson and Speaker of the House Champ Clark of Missouri were closely matched in total primary votes, with Wilson only 29,632 votes ahead of Clark. Wilson emerged with the nomination after a long struggle with Clark at the convention.

Likewise in 1916, Democratic primary results foreshadowed the winner of the nomination. However, Wilson was then the incumbent president and had no major opposition for renomination. But once again Republican presidential primaries had little to do with the nominating process at the convention. The eventual nominee, U.S. Supreme Court Justice Charles Evans Hughes, won only two primaries.

In 1920 presidential primaries did not play a major role in determining the winner of either party's nomination. Democrat James M. Cox, the eventual nominee, ran in only one primary, his home state of Ohio. Most of the Democratic primaries featured favorite son candidates or write-in votes. And at the convention, Democrats took 44 ballots to make their choice.

Similarly, the main entrants in the Republican presidential primaries that year failed to capture their party's nomination. Sen. Warren G. Harding of Ohio, the compromise choice, won the primary in his home state but lost badly in Indiana and garnered only a handful of votes elsewhere. The three leaders in the primaries — Sen. Hiram Johnson, of California, Gen. Leonard Wood of New Hampshire and Illinois Gov. Frank O. Lowden — all lost out in the end.

Revival of Interest

After the first wave of enthusiasm for presidential primaries in the 1910s, interest waned. By 1935 eight states had repealed their presidential primary laws.

The diminution of reform zeal during the 1920s and the preoccupation of the country with Depression in the 1930s and war in the 1940s appeared to have been leading factors in this decline. Also, party leaders were not enthusiastic about primaries; the cost of conducting them was relatively high, both for the candidates and the states; many primaries were ignored by presidential candidates; and there was often low voter participation.

But after World War II, interest picked up again. Some politicians with presidential ambitions, knowing the party leadership was not enthusiastic about their candidacies, entered the primaries to try to generate a bandwagon effect. In 1948, Harold Stassen, Republican governor of Minnesota from 1939 to 1943, entered Republican presidential primaries in opposition to the Republican organization and was able to make some dramatic headway before losing to Gov. Thomas E. Dewey, R, of New York in Oregon. And in 1952 Tennessee Sen. Estes Kefauver, D (1949-63), riding a wave of public recognition as head of a Senate Organized Crime Investigating Committee, challenged Democratic Party leaders by winning several primaries, including an upset of President Truman in New Hampshire. The Eisenhower-Taft struggle for the Republican Party nomination that year also stimulated interest in the primaries.

Sen. John F. Kennedy, D-Mass., in 1960, Sen. Barry M. Goldwater, R-Ariz., in 1964, Richard M. Nixon, R, in 1968, Sen. George S. McGovern, D-S.D., in 1972, and Georgia Gov. Jimmy Carter, D, in 1976 — all party presidential nominees — were able to use the primaries to show their vote-getting and organizational abilities.

With the growing demand for political reform in the 1960s and early 1970s, the presidential primaries became more popular as a route to the nomination. The revival of the old progressive reformist faith that primaries would allow the people to choose their own leaders made participation in primaries almost mandatory for anyone seeking a presidential nomination. By 1976 26 states plus the District of Columbia held some variation of the presidential preference primary. Also, in Alabama, New York and Texas, delegates to the national party conventions were elected in primaries, but none of these states provided for a specific expression statewide of presidential preference by the voter.

Primary Growth, Turnout

With a record 37 presidential primaries in 1980, the opportunity for mass participation in the nominating process was greater than ever before. But as in 1976 it was the voters in the early primary states who had the most impact. As the number of primaries has grown, the importance of the early ones has increased.

There were seven more primaries in 1980 than in 1976, with Connecticut, Kansas, Louisiana, Mississippi (Republicans only), New Mexico, Puerto Rico and South Carolina (Republicans only) joining the flock. The more than three dozen primaries were compressed into a 14-week period with most of the later elections scheduled on the same dates. As a result, it was New Hampshire and other early primary states such as Massachusetts, Florida and Illinois that were the focus of attention.

Presidential campaigns have grown so long that the first indications of candidate strength no longer were occurring in New Hampshire but in the myriad straw polls and public opinion surveys that were taken in the year before the election. Consequently, said Republican consultant Lance Tarrance, the early primaries have been transformed from "harbingers" to "determinants."

One of the major factors in the growth of primaries has been the belief that they would greatly increase mass participation in the nominating process.

But reality has not matched expectations. There were six more preference primaries in 1976 than 1972, but the nationwide turnout for Democratic contests increased by less than 200,000 votes (16 million to 16.2 million votes). The turnout for Republican primaries was up by nearly 3.8 million from 1972 to 1976, but in 1972 President Richard Nixon faced negligible opposition for the GOP nomination.

The turnout for the 1980 preference primaries was a record 32.3 million voters, compared to 26.4 million in 1976. But the figure is somewhat deceptive because more primaries were held in 1980 than ever before. The Republican primary turnout barely kept pace with the rate of population growth, while the Democratic primary turnout sagged noticeably.

Between 1976 and 1980 the national voting age population grew by about 7 percent. Comparing turnout totals for primaries that were held both in 1976 and 1980, the 1980 Republican primary turnout increased 7.7 percent from 1976, while the Democratic primary turnout in 1980 decreased 5.7 percent.

The 1980 primaries had a much lower rate of participation than the 1976 general election or even the 1978 midterm elections. Based on July 1979 voting age population estimates from the Census Bureau, only 24 percent of the eligible population in the primary states voted in either the Democratic or Republican preference primaries. In no 1980 primary did a majority of the state's voting age population participate.

Primaries and 1980 Elections

President Jimmy Carter and Republican Ronald Reagan were the clear winners of the long 1980 primary season.

Although Carter received a bare majority of the cumulative Democratic primary vote, he amassed a plurality of nearly 2.7 million votes over his major rival, Sen. Edward M. Kennedy, D-Mass.

With no opposition in the late primary contests, Reagan emerged as a more one-sided choice of GOP primary voters. He finished nearly 4.6 million votes ahead of George Bush, who withdrew from the race May 26.

Carter and Reagan built up large early leads with a series of landslide primary victories in the South and industrial Midwest. Reagan ran best in closed primaries, where only Republican voters could participate. Carter was strongest in open primaries, where crossover voting was permitted. The president drew the support of 51 percent of the nearly 20 million voters who cast ballots in the Democratic primaries. He won 24 of the primary contests to 10 for Kennedy. Reagan won 28 preference primaries to Bush's six, although 11 of Reagan's primary triumphs came after Bush had withdrawn.

Both Carter and Reagan benefited significantly from their parties' delegate allocation systems. They won a far higher percentage of delegates than their comparable share of primary votes.

While Carter received 51 percent of the combined popular vote in the Democratic preference primaries, he garnered 58 percent of the primary state delegates. The disparity was even greater on the Republican side, where Reagan's 60 percent share of the GOP preference vote translated into 78 percent of his party's primary state delegates.

Both front-runners were aided by victories in winner-take-all contests. There were more of them on the Republican side, where they are permitted by party rules. Winner-take-all elections are prohibited under Democratic rules, but Illinois and West Virginia were granted exemptions to retain "loophole," or district winner-take-all primaries in 1980. Carter won in both states. *(Primary procedures, types, box, p. 10)*

Proposals for Reform

Despite the growing use of primaries however, the existing system came under considerable criticism. The critics often cited the length of the primary season (nearly twice as long as the general election campaign), the expense, the physical strain on the candidates and the variations and complexities of state laws as leading problems of presidential primaries.

To deal with these problems, several states in 1974-75 discussed the feasibility of creating regional primaries, in which individual states within a geographical region would hold their primaries on the same day. Supporters of the concept believed it would reduce candidate expenses and strain and would permit concentration on regional issues.

The idea achieved some limited success when two groups of states — one in the West and the other in the South — decided to organize regional primaries in 1976 in each of their areas. However, the two groups both chose the same day, May 25, to hold their primaries, thus defeating one of the main purposes of the plan by continuing to force candidates to shuttle across the country to cover both areas. The Western states participating in the grouping were Idaho, Nevada and Oregon; the Southern states were Arkansas, Kentucky and Tennessee.

Attempts were also made in New England to construct a regional primary. But jealousy on the part of New Hampshire for its first-in-the-nation primary and hesitancy by the other New England state legislatures defeated the idea. Only Vermont joined Massachusetts, on March 2, in holding a simultaneous presidential primary.

In 1980 limited regional primaries were held again in several areas of the country — on March 4 in New England (Massachusetts and Vermont), on March 11 in the Southeast (Alabama, Florida and Georgia), and on May 27 in the South (Arkansas and Kentucky) and the West (Idaho and Nevada).

Other approaches to changing the primary system have been attempted at the national level. National reform proposals included a single nationwide primary, standardization of the date of primaries to shorten the campaign season, and a law mandating a regional primary system.

Since 1911 hundreds of bills have been introduced in Congress to reform the presidential primary system. The largest quantities were introduced in sessions after the 1912, 1952 and 1968 nominating campaigns. All three campaigns produced the feeling among many voters that the will of the electorate, as expressed in the primaries, had been thwarted by national conventions. But since 1911 the only legislation enacted by Congress concerned the presidential primary in the District of Columbia. Rarely did primary reform legislation even reach the hearing stage.

Presidential Primary Returns, 1912-1980

The main source for the primary returns from 1912 through 1952 was James W. Davis' *Presidential Primaries: Road to the White House* (Copyright © by Harper & Row, Publishers, Inc. Reprinted by Permission of the Publisher).

Congressional Quarterly has supplemented Davis' material with the following sources: Louise Overacker's *The Presidential Primary*, the source used by Davis for the 1912-1924 returns; "Presidential Preference Primaries, 1928-1956," a 1960 Library of Congress study by Walter Kravitz; Paul Davis, Malcolm Moos and Ralph Goldman, *Presidential Nominating Politics in 1952*, the Johns Hopkins Press, 1954; the offices of the secretaries of state; and state handbooks and newspapers. All statistics and footnotes are from Davis, unless otherwise indicated.

The basic source for the primary returns from 1956 through 1980 was Richard M. Scammon's *America Votes* series. All statistics and footnotes are from Scammon, unless otherwise indicated.

Figures in the following charts represent one of three types of votes:

● Votes cast directly for a presidential candidate.

● Votes cast for delegates whose candidate preference was indicated on the ballot.

● Votes cast for unpledged delegates. (Included in the "unpledged" category were delegates designated on the ballot as "uninstructed" and "no preference.")

For the delegate-at-large vote in 1912-1924 primaries, Overacker listed the average vote for delegates at large. For the 1928-1952 delegate-at-large vote, Davis listed the highest vote received by any one delegate at large. Congressional Quarterly followed Davis' style for subsequent years.

Percentages in the following tables have been calculated to two decimal points and then rounded; 0.05 percent appears as 0.1 percent. Therefore, columns of percentages do not always total 100 percent. Presidential candidates, primary winners, favorite sons, members of Congress and prominent national and state political figures are included in the state-by-state primary results; others receiving votes are listed in the footnotes.

1912 Primaries

Republican	Votes	%	Democratic	Votes	%
March 19 North Dakota					
Robert M. LaFollette (Wis.)	34,123	57.2	John Burke (N.D.)[1]	9,357	100.0
Theodore Roosevelt (N.Y.)	23,669	39.7			
William H. Taft (Ohio)	1,876	3.1			
March 26 New York[2]					
April 2 Wisconsin					
LaFollette	133,354	73.2	Woodrow Wilson (N.J.)	45,945	55.7
Taft	47,514	26.1	Champ Clark (Mo.)	36,464	44.2
Roosevelt	628	.3	Others	148	.2
Others	643	.4			
April 9 Illinois					
Roosevelt	266,917	61.1	Clark	218,483	74.3
Taft	127,481	29.2	Wilson	75,527	25.7
LaFollette	42,692	9.8			
April 13 Pennsylvania					
Roosevelt	282,853[3]	59.7	Wilson	98,000[3]	100.0
Taft	191,179[3]	40.3			
April 19 Nebraska					
Roosevelt	45,795	58.7	Clark	21,027	41.0
LaFollette	16,785	21.5	Wilson	14,289	27.9
Taft	13,341	17.1	Judson Harmon (Ohio)	12,454	24.3
Others	2,036	2.6	Others	3,499	6.8

13

	Republican			**Democratic**	
	Votes	%		Votes	%

April 19   Oregon

Roosevelt	28,905	40.2	Wilson	9,588	53.0
LaFollette	22,491	31.3	Clark	7,857	43.4
Taft	20,517	28.5	Harmon	606	3.3
Others	14	—	Others	49	.3

April 30   Massachusetts

Taft	86,722	50.4	Clark	34,575	68.9
Roosevelt	83,099	48.3	Wilson	15,002	29.9
LaFollette	2,058	1.2	Others	627	1.2
Others	99	.1			

May 6   Maryland

Roosevelt	29,124	52.8	Clark	34,021	54.4
Taft	25,995	47.2	Wilson	21,490	34.3
			Harmon	7,070	11.3

May 14   California

Roosevelt	138,563	54.6	Clark	43,163	71.5
Taft	69,345	27.3	Wilson	17,214	28.5
LaFollette	45,876	18.1			

May 21   Ohio

Roosevelt	165,809	55.3	Harmon	96,164	51.7
Taft	118,362	39.5	Wilson	85,084	45.7
LaFollette	15,570	5.2	Clark	2,428	1.3
			Others	2,440	1.3

May 28   New Jersey

Roosevelt	61,297	56.3	Wilson	48,336	98.9
Taft	44,034	40.5	Clark[4]	522	1.1
LaFollette	3,464	3.2			

June 4   South Dakota

Roosevelt	38,106	55.2	Wilson[5]	4,694	35.2
Taft	19,960	28.9	Clark[5]	4,275	32.0
LaFollette	10,944	15.9	Clark[5]	2,722	20.4
			Others	1,655	12.4

TOTALS

Roosevelt	1,164,765	51.5	Wilson	435,169	44.6
Taft	766,326	33.9	Clark	405,537	41.6
LaFollette	327,357	14.5	Harmon	116,294	11.9
Others	2,792	.1	Burke	9,357	1.0
			Others	8,418	.9
	2,261,240			974,775	

1. Burke was the "favorite son" candidate, according to the North Dakota secretary of state.
2. Primary law optional in 1912. Republicans elected pledged delegates but figures not available.
3. Unofficial figures.
4. Write-in.

5. No presidential preference. Three sets of delegates ran: one labelled "Wilson-Bryan" which came out openly for Wilson: one "Wilson-Clark-Bryan" which became identified with Clark: one Champ Clark which was accused by the Clark people of being a scheme to split the Clark vote. The "Wilson-Clark-Bryan" list polled 4.275 and the Champ Clark list 2.722. The delegates were given to Wilson by the convention.

1916 Primaries

	Republican			Democratic		
	Votes	%			Votes	%
March 7 Indiana						
Charles W. Fairbanks (Ind.)[1]	176,078	100.0	Woodrow Wilson (N.J.)		160,423	100.0
March 14 Minnesota						
Albert B. Cummins (Iowa)	54,214	76.8	Wilson		45,136	100.0
Others	16,403	23.2				
March 14 New Hampshire						
Unpledged delegates	9,687	100.0	Wilson		5,684	100.0
March 21 North Dakota						
Robert M. LaFollette (Wis.)	23,374[2]	70.4	Wilson		12,341	100.0
Others	9,851[2]	29.6				
April 3 Michigan						
Henry Ford (Mich.)	83,057	47.4	Wilson		84,972	100.0
William A. Smith (Mich.)	77,872	44.4				
William O. Simpson (Mich.)	14,365	8.2				
April 4 New York						
Unpledged delegates	147,038	100.0	Wilson		112,538	100.0
April 4 Wisconsin						
LaFollette[1]	110,052	98.8	Wilson		109,462	99.8
Others	1,347	1.2	Others		231	.2
April 11 Illinois						
Lawrence Y. Sherman (Ill.)[1]	155,945	90.2	Wilson		136,839	99.8
Theodore Roosevelt (N.Y.)[3]	15,348	8.9	Others		219	.2
Others	1,689	1.0				
April 18 Nebraska						
Cummins	29,850	33.7	Wilson		69,506	87.7
Ford	26,884	30.3	Others		9,744	12.3
Charles E. Hughes (N.Y.)[3]	15,837	17.9				
Roosevelt[3]	2,256	2.5				
Others	13,780	15.6				
April 21 Montana						
Cummins	10,415	89.9	Wilson		17,960	100.0
Others	1,173	10.1				
April 25 Iowa						
Cummins	40,257	100.0	Wilson		31,447	100.0
April 25 Massachusetts						
Unpledged delegates at large[4]	60,462	57.3	Wilson		19,580	100.0
Roosevelt[4]	45,117	42.7				
April 25 New Jersey						
Roosevelt[3]	1,076	73.7	Wilson		25,407	100.0
Hughes[3]	383	26.3				

Republican   # Democratic

	Votes	%		Votes	%

April 25   Ohio

Theodore E. Burton (Ohio)[1]	122,165	86.8	Wilson	82,688	97.2
Roosevelt[3]	1,932	1.4	Others	2,415	2.8
Ford[3]	1,683	1.2			
Hughes[3]	469	.3			
Others	14,428	10.3			

May 2   California

Unpledged delegates	236,277	100.0	Wilson	75,085	100.0

May 16   Pennsylvania

Martin G. Brumbaugh (Pa.)[1]	233,095	86.3	Wilson	142,202	98.7
Ford[3]	20,265	7.5	Others	1,839	1.3
Roosevelt[3]	12,359	4.6			
Hughes[3]	1,804	.7			
Others	2,682	1.0			

May 16   Vermont

Hughes[3]	5,480	70.0	Wilson	3,711	99.4
Roosevelt[3]	1,931	24.6	Others	23	.6
Others	423	5.4			

May 19   Oregon

Hughes	56,764	59.8	Wilson	27,898	100.0
Cummins	27,558	29.0			
Others	10,593	11.2			

May 23   South Dakota

Cummins	29,656	100.0	Wilson	10,341	100.0

June 6   West Virginia

[5]   [5]

TOTALS

Unpledged delegates	453,464	23.6	Wilson	1,173,220	98.8
Brumbaugh	233,095	12.1	Others	14,471	1.2
Cummins	191,950	10.0			
Fairbanks	176,078	9.2		1,187,691	
Sherman	155,945	8.1			
LaFollette	133,426	6.9			
Ford	131,889	6.9			
Burton	122,165	6.4			
Hughes	80,737	4.2			
Roosevelt	80,019	4.2			
Smith	77,872	4.0			
Simpson	14,365	.7			
Others[6]	72,369	3.8			
	1,923,374				

1. Source for names of "favorite son" candidates: The New York Times.
2. Source for vote breakdown: North Dakota secretary of state.
3. Write-in.
4. No presidential preference vote but one set of delegates at large was for Roosevelt and the other set unpledged.

5. Figures not available. Republican winner was Sen. Theodore E. Burton (R Ohio) and Democratic winner was Woodrow Wilson. according to The New York Times.
6. In addition to scattered votes, "others" includes Robert G. Ross who received 5,-506 votes in the Nebraska primary; Henry D. Estabrook who received 9,851 in the North Dakota primary and 8,132 in the Nebraska primary.

1920 Primaries

	Republican			Democratic		
	Votes	%		Votes	%
March 9 New Hampshire					
Leonard Wood (N.H.)[1]	8,591	53.0	Unpledged delegates[1]	7,103	100.0
Unpledged delegates	5,604	34.6			
Hiram Johnson (Calif.)[1]	2,000	12.3			
March 16 North Dakota					
Johnson	30,573	96.1	William G. McAdoo (N.Y.)[2]	49	12.6
Leonard Wood[2]	987	3.1	Others[2]	340	87.4
Frank O. Lowden (Ill.)[2]	265	.8			
March 23 South Dakota					
Leonard Wood	31,265	36.5	Others	6,612	100.0
Lowden	26,981	31.5			
Johnson	26,301	30.7			
Others	1,144	1.3			
April 5 Michigan					
Johnson	156,939	38.4	McAdoo	18,665	21.1
Leonard Wood	112,568[3]	27.5	Edward I. Edwards (N.J.)	16,642	18.8
Lowden	62,418	15.3	A. Mitchell Palmer (Pa.)	11,187	12.6
Herbert C. Hoover (Calif.)	52,503	12.8	Others	42,000	47.5
Others	24,729	6.0			
April 6 New York					
Unpledged delegates	199,149	100.0	Unpledged delegates	113,300	100.0
April 6 Wisconsin[4]					
Leonard Wood[2]	4,505	15.0	James M. Cox (Ohio)[2]	76	2.2
Hoover[2]	3,910	13.0	Others	3,391	97.8
Johnson[2]	2,413	8.0			
Lowden[2]	921	3.1			
Others	18,350	60.9			
April 13 Illinois					
Lowden	236,802	51.1	Edwards[2]	6,933	32.3
Leonard Wood	156,719	33.8	McAdoo[2]	3,838	17.9
Johnson	64,201	13.8	Cox[2]	266	1.2
Hoover[2]	3,401	.7	Others	10,418	48.6
Others	2,674	.6			
April 20 Nebraska					
Johnson	63,161	46.2	Gilbert M. Hitchcock (Neb.)	37,452	67.3
Leonard Wood	42,385	31.0	Others	18,230	32.7
John J. Pershing (Mo.)	27,669	20.3			
Others	3,432	2.5			
April 23 Montana					
Johnson	21,034	52.4	Others[2]	2,994	100.0
Leonard Wood	6,804	17.0			
Lowden	6,503	16.2			
Hoover	5,076	12.6			
Warren G. Harding (Ohio)	723	1.8			
April 27 Massachusetts					
Unpledged delegates	93,356	100.0	Unpledged delegates	21,226	100.0

Republican

Democratic

	Votes	%		Votes	%

April 27   New Jersey

	Votes	%		Votes	%
Leonard Wood	52,909	50.2	Edwards	4,163	91.4
Johnson	51,685	49.0	McAdoo[2]	180	4.0
Hoover	900	.9	Others	213	4.7

April 27   Ohio

	Votes	%		Votes	%
Harding	123,257	47.6	Cox	85,838	97.8
Leonard Wood	108,565	41.9	McAdoo[2]	292	.3
Johnson[2]	16,783	6.5	Others	1,647	1.9
Hoover[2]	10,467	4.0			

May 3   Maryland

	Votes	%			
Leonard Wood	15,900	66.4	[5]		
Johnson	8,059	33.6			

May 4   California

	Votes	%		Votes	%
Johnson	369,853	63.9	Unpledged delegates	23,831	100.0
Hoover	209,009	36.1			

May 4   Indiana

	Votes	%			
Leonard Wood	85,708	37.9	[5]		
Johnson	79,840	35.3			
Lowden	39,627	17.5			
Harding	20,782	9.2			

May 18   Pennsylvania

	Votes	%		Votes	%
Edward R. Wood (Pa.)	257,841	92.3	Palmer[6]	80,356	73.7
Johnson[2]	10,869	3.8	McAdoo	26,875	24.6
Leonard Wood[2]	3,878	1.4	Edwards[2]	674	.6
Hoover[2]	2,825	1.0	Others	1,132	1.0
Others[2]	4,059	1.5			

May 18   Vermont

	Votes	%		Votes	%
Leonard Wood	3,451	66.1	McAdoo[2]	137	31.4
Hoover[2]	564	10.8	Edwards[2]	58	13.3
Johnson[2]	402	7.7	Cox[2]	14	3.2
Lowden[2]	29	.5	Others	227	52.1
Others	777	14.9			

May 21   Oregon

	Votes	%		Votes	%
Johnson	46,163	38.4	McAdoo	24,951	98.6
Leonard Wood	43,770	36.5	Others	361	1.4
Lowden	15,581	13.0			
Hoover	14,557	12.1			

May 25   West Virginia

	Votes	%			
Leonard Wood	27,255	44.6	[5]		
Others	33,849 [7]	55.4			

Republican				**Democratic**		
	Votes	%			Votes	%

June 5   North Carolina

	Votes	%				
Johnson	15,375	73.3	[5]			
Leonard Wood	5,603	26.7				

TOTALS

	Votes	%			Votes	%
Johnson	965,651	30.3	Unpledged delegates	165,460	28.9
Leonard Wood	710,863	22.3	Palmer	91,543	16.0
Lowden	389,127	12.2	Cox	86,194	15.0
Hoover	303,212	9.5	McAdoo	74,987	13.1
Unpledged delegates	298,109	9.4	Hitchcock	37,452	6.6
Edward R. Wood	257,841	8.1	Edwards	28,470	5.0
Harding	144,762	4.5	Others[9]	87,565	15.3
Pershing	27,669	.9			
Others[8]	89,014	2.8		571,671	
	3,186,248				

1. Source: Louise Overacker, The Presidential Primaries (1926), p. 238-39. There was no preference vote. In the Republican primary, figures given were for delegates at large favoring Wood and Johnson. In the Democratic primary, although delegates were unpledged, the organization (Robert Charles Murchie) group was understood to be for Hoover. The highest Democratic Hoover delegate received 3,714 votes.

2. Write-in.

3. Source: Overacker, op. cit., p. 238.

4. No names entered for presidential preference in the Republican primary. The real contest lay between two lists of delegates, one headed by Robert M. La Follette and the other by Emanuel L. Philipp.

5. No names entered and no preference vote recorded.

6. Source for name of "favorite son" candidate: The New York Times.

7. Most of these votes were received by Sen. Howard Sutherland (R W.Va.). The figure is unofficial.

8. In addition to scattered votes, "others" includes Robert G. Ross who received 1,698 votes in the Nebraska primary.

9. In addition to scattered votes, "others" includes Robert G. Ross who received 13,179 in the Nebraska primary.

1924 Primaries

Republican	Votes	%	Democratic	Votes	%
March 11 New Hampshire					
Calvin Coolidge (Mass.)	17,170	100.0	Unpledged delegates	6,687	100.0
March 18 North Dakota					
Coolidge	52,815	42.1	William G. McAdoo (Calif.)	11,273	100.0
Robert M. LaFollette (Wis.)	40,252	32.1			
Hiram Johnson (Calif.)	32,363	25.8			
March 25 South Dakota					
Johnson	40,935	50.7	McAdoo[1]	6,983	77.4
Coolidge	39,791	49.3	Unpledged delegates[1]	2,040	22.6
April 1 Wisconsin [2]					
LaFollette[3]	40,738	62.5	McAdoo	54,922	68.2
Coolidge[3]	23,324	35.8	Alfred E. Smith (N.Y.)[3]	5,774	7.2
Johnson[3]	411	.6	Others	19,827	24.6
Others	688	1.1			
April 7 Michigan					
Coolidge	236,191	67.2	Henry Ford (Mich.)[4]	48,567	53.4
Johnson	103,739	29.5	Woodbridge N. Ferris (Mich.)[4]	42,028	46.2
Others	11,312	3.2	Others	435	.5
April 8 Illinois					
Coolidge	533,193	58.0	McAdoo	180,544	98.9
Johnson	385,590	42.0	Smith[3]	235	.1
LaFollette[3]	278	—	Others	1,724	.9
Others	21	—			
April 8 Nebraska					
Coolidge	79,676	63.6	McAdoo[3]	9,342	57.3
Johnson	45,032	35.9	Smith[3]	700	4.3
Others	627	.5	Others[3]	6,268	38.4
April 22 New Jersey					
Coolidge	111,739	89.1	George S. Silzer (N.J.)[5]	35,601	97.7
Johnson	13,626	10.9	Smith[3]	721	2.0
			McAdoo[3]	69	.2
			Others	38	.1
April 22 Pennsylvania					
Coolidge[3]	117,262	87.9	McAdoo[3]	10,376	43.7
Johnson[3]	4,345	3.3	Smith[3]	9,029	38.0
LaFollette[3]	1,224	.9	Others[3]	4,341	18.3
Others	10,523	7.9			
April 29 Massachusetts					
Coolidge	84,840	100.0	Unpledged delegates at large[6]	30,341	100.0
April 29 Ohio					
Coolidge	173,613	86.3	James M. Cox (Ohio)[5]	74,183	71.7
Johnson	27,578	13.7	McAdoo	29,267	28.3

Republican

Democratic

	Votes	%		Votes	%
May 5 Maryland					
Coolidge	19,657	93.7	[7]		
Unpledged delegates	1,326	6.3			
Johnson[3]	3	—			
May 6 California					
Coolidge	310,618	54.3	McAdoo	110,235	85.6
Johnson	261,566	45.7	Unpledged delegates	18,586	14.4
May 6 Indiana					
Coolidge	330,045	84.1	[7]		
Johnson	62,603	15.9			
May 16 Oregon					
Coolidge	99,187	76.8	McAdoo	33,664	100.0
Johnson	30,042	23.2			
May 27 West Virginia					
Coolidge	162,042	100.0	[7]		
May 28 Montana					
Coolidge	19,200	100.0	McAdoo	10,058	100.0
TOTALS					
Coolidge	2,410,363	68.4	McAdoo	456,733	59.8
Johnson	1,007,833	28.6	Cox	74,183	9.7
LaFollette	82,492	2.3	Unpledged delegates	57,654	7.5
Unpledged delegates	1,326	—	Ford	48,567	6.4
Others	23,171	.7	Ferris	42,028	5.5
			Silzer	35,601	4.7
	3,525,185		Smith	16,459	2.2
			Others	32,633	4.3
				763,858	

1. No presidential preference vote, as McAdoo's was the only name entered, but a contest developed between "McAdoo" and "anti-McAdoo" lists of delegates. Figures are average votes cast for these lists.

2. In Wisconsin the real contest in the Republican primary was between two lists of delegates, one led by La Follette and one by Emanuel L. Philipp. In the Democratic primary, the real contest was between two lists of delegates, one favoring Smith and one favoring McAdoo.

3. Write-in.

4. Source for names of "favorite son" candidates: Michigan Manual, 1925.

5. Source for names of "favorite son" candidates: The New York Times.

6. No presidential preference vote provided for. There were nine candidates for the eight places as delegates at large, one of whom announced his preference for Smith during the campaign and received the second highest number of votes.

7. No names entered and no presidential preference vote taken.

1928 Primaries

Republican			Democratic		
	Votes	%		Votes	%

March 13   New Hampshire

Unpledged delegates at large[1]	25,603	100.0	Unpledged delegates at large[1]	9,716	100.0

March 20   North Dakota

Frank O. Lowden (Ill.)	95,857	100.0	Alfred E. Smith (N.Y.)	10,822	100.0

April 2   Michigan

Herbert C. Hoover (Calif.)	282,809	97.6	Smith	77,276	98.3
Lowden	5,349	1.8	Thomas Walsh (Mont.)	1,034	1.3
Calvin Coolidge (Mass.)	1,666	.6	James A. Reed (Mo.)	324	.4

April 3   Wisconsin

George W. Norris (Neb.)	162,822	87.1	Reed	61,097	75.0
Hoover	17,659	9.4	Smith	19,781	24.3
Lowden	3,302	1.8	Walsh	541	.7
Coolidge	680	.4			
Charles G. Dawes (Ill.)	505	.3			
Others	1,894	1.0			

April 10   Illinois

Lowden	1,172,278	99.3	Smith	44,212	91.7
Hoover	4,368	.4	Reed	3,786	7.9
Coolidge	2,420	.2	William G. McAdoo (Calif.)	213	.4
Dawes	756	.1			
Others	946	.1			

April 10   Nebraska

Norris	96,726	91.8	Gilbert M. Hitchcock (Neb.)	51,019	91.5
Hoover	6,815	6.5	Smith	4,755	8.5
Lowden	711	.7			
Dawes	679	.7			
Coolidge	452	.4			

April 24   Ohio

Hoover	217,430	68.1	Smith	42,365	65.9
Frank B. Willis (Ohio)	84,461	26.5	Atlee Pomerene (Ohio)	13,957	21.7
Dawes	4,311	1.4	Victor Donahey (Ohio)	7,935	12.3
Lowden	3,676	1.2			
Others	9,190	2.9			

April 24   Pennsylvania

[2]			[2]		

April 28   Massachusetts

Hoover[3]	100,279	85.2	Smith	38,081	98.1
Coolidge[3]	7,767	6.6	Walsh	254	.7
Alvan Fuller (Mass.)	1,686	1.4	Others	478	1.2
Lowden[3]	1,040	.9			
Others	6,950	5.9			

May 1   California

Hoover	567,219	100.0	Smith	134,471	54.1
			Reed	60,004	24.1
			Walsh	46,770	18.8
			Others	7,263	2.9

Republican   Democratic

	Votes	%		Votes	%
May 7 Indiana					
James E. Watson (Ind.)	228,795	53.0	Evans Woollen (Ind.)	146,934	100.0
Hoover	203,279	47.0			
May 7 Maryland[4]					
Hoover	27,128	83.3	[5]		
Unpledged delegates	5,426	16.7			
May 8 Alabama					
[5]			Unpledged delegates at large[6]	138,957	100.0
May 15 New Jersey					
Hoover	382,907	100.0	Smith[3]	28,506	100.0
May 18 Oregon					
Hoover	101,129	98.7	Smith	17,444	48.5
Lowden	1,322	1.3	Walsh	11,272	31.3
			Reed	6,360	17.7
			Others	881	2.5
May 22 South Dakota					
Unpledged delegates at large[7]	34,264	100.0	Unpledged delegates at large[7]	6,221	100.0
May 29 West Virginia					
Guy D. Goff (W.Va.)	128,429	54.0	Smith	81,739	50.0
Hoover	109,303	46.0	Reed	75,796	46.4
			Others	5,789	3.5
June 5 Florida					
[5]			Unpledged delegates at large[8]	108,167	100.00

TOTALS					
Hoover	2,020,325	49.2	Smith	499,452	39.5
Lowden	1,283,535	31.2	Unpledged delegates	263,061	20.8
Norris	259,548	6.3	Reed	207,367	16.4
Watson	228,795	5.6	Woollen	146,934	11.6
Goff	128,429	3.1	Walsh	59,871	4.7
Willis	84,461	2.1	Hitchcock	51,019	4.0
Unpledged delegates	65,293	1.6	Pomerene	13,957	1.1
Coolidge	12,985	.3	Donahey	7,935	.6
Dawes	6,251	.2	McAdoo	213	—
Fuller	1,686	—	Others[10]	14,411	1.1
Others[9]	18,980	.5			
				1,264,220	
	4,110,288				

1. Winning Republican delegates were unofficially pledged to Hoover and winning Democratic delegates were unofficially pledged to Smith, according to Walter Kravitz, "Presidential Preferential Primaries: Results 1928-1956" (1960). p. 4.

2. No figures available.

3. Write-in.

4. Source: Kravitz, op. cit., p. 5.

5. No primary.

6. The Montgomery Advertiser of May 3. 1928, described the delegates as independent and anti-Smith.

7. Winning Republican delegates favored Lowden and winning Democratic delegates favored Smith, according to Kravitz, op. cit., p. 5.

8. The Miami Herald of June 6, 1928, described the delegates as unpledged and anti-Smith.

9. In addition to scattered votes, "others" includes Robert G. Ross who received 8.280 votes in the Ohio primary.

10. In addition to scattered votes, "others" includes Poling who received 7.263 votes in the California primary; and Workman who received 881 in the Oregon primary and 5.-789 in the West Virginia primary.

1932 Primaries

Republican			Democratic		
	Votes	%		Votes	%
March 8 New Hampshire					
Unpledged delegates at large[1]	22,903	100.0	Unpledged delegates at large[1]	15,401	100.0
March 15 North Dakota					
Joseph I. France (Md.)	36,000[2]	59.0	Franklin D. Roosevelt (N.Y.)	52,000[2]	61.9
Jacob S. Coxey (Ohio)	25,000[2]	41.0	William H. Murray (Okla.)	32,000[2]	38.1
March 23 Georgia					
[3]			Roosevelt	51,498	90.3
			Others	5,541	9.7
April 5 Wisconsin					
George W. Norris (Neb.)	139,514	95.5	Roosevelt	241,742	98.6
Herbert C. Hoover (Calif.)	6,588	4.5	Alfred E. Smith (N.Y.) [4]	3,502	1.4
April 12 Nebraska					
France	40,481	74.4	Roosevelt	91,393	63.5
Hoover	13,934	25.6	John N. Garner (Texas)	27,359	19.0
			Murray	25,214	17.5
April 13 Illinois					
France	345,498	98.7	James H. Lewis (Ill.)	590,130	99.8
Hoover	4,368	1.2	Roosevelt	1,084	.2
Charles G. Dawes (Ill.)	129	—	Smith	266	—
			Others[4]	72	—
April 26 Massachusetts					
Unpledged delegates at large[5]	57,534	100.0	Smith[5]	153,465	73.1
			Roosevelt[5]	56,454	26.9
April 26 Pennsylvania					
France	352,092	92.9	Roosevelt	133,002	56.6
Hoover	20,662	5.5	Smith	101,227	43.1
Others	6,126	1.6	Others	563	.2
May 2 Maryland					
Hoover	27,324	60.0	[6]		
France	17,008	37.3			
Unpledged delegates	1,236	2.7			
May 3 Alabama					
[3]			Unpledged delegates [7]	134,781	100.0
May 3 California					
Hoover	657,420	100.0	Garner	222,385	41.3
			Roosevelt	175,008	32.5
			Smith	141,517	26.3
May 3 South Dakota					
Johnson[8]	64,464	64.7	Roosevelt	35,370	100.0
Others	35,133	35.3			

Republican

Democratic

	Votes	%		Votes	%

May 10 Ohio

Coxey	75,844	58.9	Murray	112,512	96.4
France	44,853	34.8	Roosevelt[4]	1,999	1.7
Hoover	8,154	6.3	Smith[4]	951	.8
			George White (Ohio)	834	.7
			Newton D. Baker (Ohio)	289	.2
			Garner[4]	72	—

May 10 West Virginia

France	88,005	100.0	Roosevelt	219,671	90.3
			Murray	19,826	8.2
			Others	3,727	1.5

May 17 New Jersey

| France | 141,330 | 93.3 | Smith | 5,234 | 61.9 |
| Hoover | 10,116 | 6.7 | Roosevelt | 3,219 | 38.1 |

May 20 Oregon

France	72,681	69.0	Roosevelt	48,554	78.6
Hoover	32,599	31.0	Murray	11,993	19.4
			Others	1,214	2.0

June 7 Florida

[3]			Roosevelt	203,372	87.7
			Murray	24,847	10.7
			Others	3,645	1.6

TOTALS

France	1,137,948	48.5	Roosevelt	1,314,366	44.5
Hoover	781,165	33.3	Lewis	590,130	20.0
Norris	139,514	5.9	Smith	406,162	13.8
Coxey	100,844	4.3	Garner	249,816	8.5
Unpledged delegates	81,673	3.5	Murray	226,392	7.7
Johnson	64,464	2.7	Unpledged delegates	150,182	5.1
Dawes	129	—	White	834	—
Others[9]	41,259	1.8	Baker	289	—
			Others[10]	14,762	.5
	2,346,996			2,952,933	

1. Hoover delegates won the Republican primary and Roosevelt delegates won the Democratic primary, according to Kravitz, op. cit., p. 6.

2. Unofficial figures.

3. No primary.

4. Write-in.

5. Delegate-at-large vote in Republican and Democratic primaries. Hoover delegates won the Republican primary, according to Kravitz, op. cit., p. 6. The New York Times of April 28, 1932, also reported that the Republican delegates were pledged to Hoover.

6. No names entered, according to the Maryland Record of Election Returns.

7. These were unpledged delegates who favored Roosevelt, according to Kravitz, op. cit., p. 6.

8. The winning Republican delegation supported Hoover, according to Kravitz, op. cit., p. 7.

9. In addition to scattered votes, "others" includes Bogue who received 35,133 in the South Dakota primary.

10. In addition to scattered votes, "others" includes Leo J. Chassee who received 3,645 in the Florida primary and 3,727 in the West Virginia primary; and Howard who received 5,541 votes in the Georgia primary.

1936 Primaries

Republican   ## Democratic

March 10   New Hampshire

Unpledged delegates at large[1]	32,992	*100.0*	Unpledged delegates at large[1]	15,752	*100.0*

April 7   Wisconsin

William E. Borah (Idaho)	187,334	*98.2*	Franklin D. Roosevelt (N.Y.)	401,773	*100.0*
Alfred M. Landon (Kan.)	3,360	*1.8*	John N. Garner (Texas)	108	—
			Alfred E. Smith (N.Y.)	46	—

April 14   Illinois

Frank Knox (Ill.)	491,575	*53.7*	Roosevelt	1,416,411	*100.0*
Borah	419,220	*45.8*	Others[2]	411	—
Landon	3,775	*.4*			
Others[2]	205	—			

April 14   Nebraska

Borah	70,240	*74.5*	Roosevelt	139,743	*100.0*
Landon	23,117	*24.5*			
Others	973	*1.0*			

April 28   Massachusetts

Landon[2]	76,862	*80.6*	Roosevelt[2]	51,924	*85.9*
Herbert C. Hoover (Calif.)[2]	7,276	*7.6*	Smith[2]	2,928	*4.8*
Borah[2]	4,259	*4.5*	Charles E. Coughlin (Mich.)[2]	2,854	*4.7*
Knox[2]	1,987	*2.1*	Others[2]	2,774	*4.6*
Others[2]	5,032	*5.3*			

April 28   Pennsylvania

Borah	459,982	*100.0*	Roosevelt	720,309	*95.3*
			Henry Breckinridge (N.Y.)	35,351	*4.7*

May 4   Maryland

[3]			Roosevelt	100,269	*83.4*
			Breckinridge	18,150	*15.1*
			Unpledged delegates	1,739	*1.4*

May 5   California

Earl Warren (Calif.)	350,917	*57.4*	Roosevelt	790,235	*82.5*
Landon	260,170	*42.6*	Upton Sinclair (Calif.)	106,068	*11.1*
			John S. McGroarty (Calif.)	61,391	*6.4*

May 5   South Dakota

Warren E. Green[4]	44,518	*50.1*	Roosevelt	48,262	*100.0*
Borah	44,261	*49.9*			

May 12   Ohio

Stephen A. Day (Ohio)	155,732	*93.4*	Roosevelt	514,366	*94.0*
Landon	11,015	*6.6*	Breckinridge	32,950	*6.0*

May 12   West Virginia

Borah	105,855	*84.8*	Roosevelt	288,799	*97.3*
Others	18,986	*15.2*	Others	8,162	*2.7*

Republican   # Democratic

	Votes	%		Votes	%
May 15 Oregon					
Borah	91,949	90.2	Roosevelt	88,305	99.8
Landon	4,467	4.4	Others	208	.2
Others	5,557	5.4			
May 19 New Jersey					
Landon	347,142	79.2	Breckinridge	49,956	81.1
Borah	91,052	20.8	Roosevelt[2]	11,676	18.9
June 6 Florida					
[3]			Roosevelt	242,906	89.7
			Others	27,982	10.3
TOTALS					
Borah	1,474,152	44.4	Roosevelt	4,814,978	92.9
Landon	729,908	22.0	Breckinridge	136,407	2.6
Knox	493,562	14.9	Sinclair	106,068	2.0
Warren	350,917	10.6	McGroarty	61,391	1.2
Day	155,732	4.7	Unpledged delegates	17,491	.3
Green	44,518	1.3	Smith	2,974	.1
Unpledged delegates	32,992	1.0	Coughlin	2,854	.1
Hoover	7,276	.2	Garner	108	—
Others[5]	30,753	.9	Others[6]	39,537	.8
	3,319,810			5,181,808	

1. Delegates favorable to Knox won the Republican primary and Roosevelt delegates won the Democratic primary, according to Kravitz, op. cit., p. 8.

2. Write-in.

3. No preferential primary held.

4. These delegates were unpledged but favored Landon, according to Kravitz, op. cit., p. 9.

5. In addition to scattered votes, "others" includes Leo J. Chassee who received 18,986 votes in the West Virginia primary.

6. In addition to scattered votes, "others" includes Joseph A. Coutremarsh who received 27,982 votes in the Florida primary and 8.162 votes in the West Virginia primary.

1940 Primaries

	Republican			Democratic		
		Votes	%		Votes	%
March 12 New Hampshire						
Unpledged delegates at large		34,616	100.0	Unpledged delegates at large[1]	10,501	100.0
April 2 Wisconsin						
Thomas E. Dewey (N.Y.)		70,168	72.6	Franklin D. Roosevelt (N.Y.)	322,991	75.4
Arthur Vandenberg (Mich.)		26,182	27.1	John N. Garner (Texas)	105,662	24.6
Robert A. Taft (Ohio)		341	.4			
April 9 Illinois						
Dewey		977,225	99.9	Roosevelt	1,176,531	86.0
Others[2]		552	.1	Garner	190,801	14.0
				Others[2]	35	—
April 9 Nebraska						
Dewey		102,915	58.9	Roosevelt	111,902	100.0
Vandenberg		71,798	41.1			
April 23 Pennsylvania						
Dewey		52,661	66.7	Roosevelt	724,657	100.0
Franklin D. Roosevelt (N.Y.)		8,294	10.5			
Arthur H. James (Pa.)		8,172	10.3			
Taft		5,213	6.6			
Vandenberg		2,384	3.0			
Herbert C. Hoover (Calif.)		1,082	1.4			
Wendell Willkie (N.Y.)		707	.9			
Others		463	.6			
April 30 Massachusetts						
Unpledged delegates at large[3]		98,975	100.0	Unpledged delegates at large[3]	76,919	100.0
May 5 South Dakota						
Unpledged delegates		52,566	100.0	Unpledged delegates	27,636	100.0
May 6 Maryland						
Dewey		54,802	100.0	[4]		
May 7 Alabama						
[4]				Unpledged delegates at large[5]	196,508	100.0
May 7 California						
Jerrold L. Seawell[6]		538,112	100.0	Roosevelt	723,782	74.0
				Garner	114,594	11.7
				Unpledged delegates[6]	139,055	14.2
May 14 Ohio						
Taft		510,025	99.5	Unpledged delegates at large[7]	283,952	100.0
Dewey[2]		2,059	.4			
John W. Bricker (Ohio)		188	—			
Vandenberg[2]		83	—			
Willkie		53	—			
Others		69	—			

Republican   # Democratic

May 14 **West Virginia**

R. N. Davis (W.Va.)	106,123	*100.0*	H. C. Allen (W.Va.)	102,729	*100.0*

May 17 **Oregon**

Charles L. McNary (Ore.)	133,488	*95.9*	Roosevelt	109,913	*87.2*
Dewey	5,190	*3.7*	Garner	15,584	*12.4*
Taft	254	*.2*	Others	601	*.5*
Willkie	237	*.2*			
Vandenberg	36	—			

May 21 **New Jersey**

Dewey	340,734	*93.9*	Roosevelt [2]	34,278	*100.0*
Willkie [2]	20,143	*5.6*			
Roosevelt [2]	1,202	*.3*			
Taft [2]	595	*.2*			
Vandenberg [2]	168	—			

TOTALS

Dewey	1,605,754	*49.7*	Roosevelt	3,240,054	*71.7*
Seawell	538,112	*16.7*	Unpledged delegates	734,571	*16.4*
Taft	516,428	*16.0*	Garner	426,641	*9.5*
Unpledged delegates	186,157	*5.8*	Allen	102,729	*2.3*
McNary	133,488	*4.1*	Others	636	—
Davis	106,123	*3.3*			
Vandenberg	100,651	*3.1*		4,468,631	
Willkie	21,140	*.7*			
Roosevelt	9,496	*.3*			
James	8,172	*.3*			
Hoover	1,082	—			
Bricker	188	—			
Others	1,084	—			
	3,227,875				

---

1. *Roosevelt delegates won, according to Kravitz, op. cit., p. 10.*
2. *Write-in.*
3. *An unpledged Republican slate defeated a slate of delegates pledged to Dewey, according to Kravitz, op. cit., p. 10. Sixty-nine James A. Farley delegates and three unpledged delegates won in the Democratic primary, according to Kravitz, ibid. The New York Times of May 1, 1940, also reported that most Democratic delegates favored Farley.*
4. *No primary.*
5. *Winning delegates were pledged to "favorite son" candidate William B. Bankhead,*

then Speaker of the U.S. House of Representatives, according to Kravitz, op. cit., p. 10, and the Montgomery Advertiser *of May 8, 1940.*
6. *The Los Angeles Times of May 8, 1940, reported that the Republican delegation was unpledged. In the Democratic primary, according to Davis, p. 293, unpledged slates were headed by Willis Allen, head of the California "Ham and Eggs" pension ticket which received 90,718 votes; and by Lt. Gov. Ellis E. Patterson, whose slate, backed by Labor's Non-Partisan League, received 48,337 votes.*
7. *Democratic delegates were pledged to Charles Sawyer (Ohio), according to Ohio Election Statistics, 1940, and Kravitz, op. cit., p. 10.*

1944 Primaries

	Republican			Democratic	
	Votes	%		Votes	%
March 14 New Hampshire					
Unpledged delegates at large[1]	16,723	100.0	Unpledged delegates at large [1]	6,772	100.0
April 5 Wisconsin					
Douglas MacArthur (Wis.)	102,421	72.6	Franklin D. Roosevelt (N.Y.)	49,632	94.3
Thomas E. Dewey (N.Y.)	21,036	14.9	Others	3,014	5.7
Harold E. Stassen (Minn.)	7,928	5.6			
Wendell Willkie (N.Y.)	6,439	4.6			
Others	3,307	2.3			
April 11 Illinois					
MacArthur	550,354	92.0	Roosevelt	47,561	99.3
Dewey	9,192	1.5	Others	343	.7
Everett M. Dirksen (Ill.)	581	.1			
John W. Bricker (Ohio)	148	—			
Stassen	111	—			
Willkie	107	—			
Others	37,575	6.3			
April 11 Nebraska					
Stassen	51,800	65.7	Roosevelt	37,405	99.2
Dewey	18,418	23.3	Others	319	.8
Willkie	8,249	10.5			
Others	432	.5			
April 25 Massachusetts					
Unpledged delegates at large	53,511	100.0	Unpledged delegates at large	57,299	100.0
April 25 Pennsylvania					
Dewey[2]	146,706	83.8	Roosevelt	322,469	99.7
MacArthur[2]	9,032	5.2	Others	961	.3
Franklin D. Roosevelt (N.Y.)	8,815	5.0			
Willkie[2]	3,650	2.1			
Bricker[2]	2,936	1.7			
Edward Martin (Pa.)	2,406	1.4			
Stassen[2]	1,502	.9			
May 1 Maryland					
Unpledged delegates	17,600	78.9	[3]		
Willkie	4,701	21.1			
May 2 Alabama					
[3]			Unpledged delegates at large[4]	116,922	100.0
May 2 Florida					
[3]			Unpledged delegates at large[5]	118,518	100.0
May 2 South Dakota					
Charles A. Christopherson [6]	33,497	60.2	Fred Hildebrandt (S.D.)[6]	7,414	52.4
Others [6]	22,135	39.8	Others [6]	6,727	47.6

Republican			**Democratic**		
	Votes	%		Votes	%
May 9 Ohio					
Unpledged delegates at large [7]	360,139	*100.0*	Unpledged delegates at large [7]	164,915	*100.0*
May 9 West Virginia					
Unpledged delegates at large	91,602	*100.0*	Claude R. Linger (W.Va.)	59,282	*100.0*
May 16 California					
Earl Warren (Calif.)	594,439	*100.0*	Roosevelt	770,222	*100.0*
May 16 New Jersey					
Dewey	17,393	*86.2*	Roosevelt	16,884	*99.6*
Roosevelt [2]	1,720	*8.5*	Thomas E. Dewey (N.Y.)	60	*.4*
Willkie	618	*3.1*			
Bricker	203	*1.0*			
MacArthur	129	*.6*			
Stassen	106	*.5*			
May 19 Oregon					
Dewey [2]	50,001	*78.2*	Roosevelt	79,833	*98.7*
Stassen [2]	6,061	*9.5*	Others	1,057	*1.3*
Willkie [2]	3,333	*5.2*			
Bricker [2]	3,018	*4.7*			
MacArthur [2]	191	*.3*			
Others	1,340	*2.1*			
TOTALS					
MacArthur	662,127	*29.1*	Roosevelt	1,324,006	*70.9*
Warren	594,439	*26.2*	Unpledged delegates	464,426	*24.9*
Unpledged delegates	539,575	*23.8*	Linger	59,282	*3.2*
Dewey	262,746	*11.6*	Hildebrandt	7,414	*.4*
Stassen	67,508	*3.0*	Dewey	60	*—*
Christopherson	33,497	*1.5*	Others [9]	12,421	*.7*
Willkie	27,097	*1.2*			
Roosevelt	10,535	*.5*		1,867,609	
Bricker	6,305	*.3*			
Martin	2,406	*.1*			
Dirksen	581	*—*			
Others [8]	64,789	*2.9*			
	2,271,605				

1. *Nine unpledged and two Dewey delegates won the Republican primary, and Roosevelt delegates won the Democratic primary, according to Kravitz, op. cit., p. 12.*
2. *Write-in.*
3. *No primary.*
4. *The Montgomery Advertiser of May 3, 1944, reported that these delegates were pro-Roosevelt but uninstructed.*
5. *The New York Times of May 3, 1944, reported that a contest for delegates took place between supporters of Roosevelt and supporters of Sen. Harry F. Byrd (D Va.). A vote breakdown showing Roosevelt and Byrd strength is unavailable.*

6. *The winning Republican slate was pledged to Stassen, the losing Republican slate to Dewey and the two Democratic slates to Roosevelt, according to the office of the South Dakota secretary of state and Kravitz, op. cit., p. 12.*
7. *Bricker delegates won the Republican primary and Joseph T. Ferguson delegates won the Democratic primary, according to Kravitz, op. cit., p. 13.*
8. *In addition to scattered votes, "others" includes Riley A. Bender who received 37,575 votes in the Illinois primary and Joe H. Bottum who received 22,135 in the South Dakota primary.*
9. *In addition to scattered votes, "others" includes Powell who received 6,727 votes in the South Dakota primary.*

1948 Primaries

Republican			Democratic		
	Votes	%		Votes	%

March 9   New Hampshire

Unpledged delegates at large[1]	28,854	100.0	Unpledged delegates at large[1]	4,409	100.0

April 6   Wisconsin

Harold E. Stassen (Minn.)	64,076	39.4	Harry S Truman (Mo.)	25,415	83.8
Douglas MacArthur (Wis.)	55,302	34.0	Others	4,906	16.2
Thomas E. Dewey (N.Y.)	40,943	25.2			
Others	2,429	1.5			

April 13   Illinois

Riley A. Bender (Ill.)	324,029	96.9	Truman	16,299	81.7
MacArthur	6,672	2.0	Dwight D. Eisenhower (N.Y.)	1,709	8.6
Stassen	1,572	.5	Scott Lucas (Ill.)	427	2.1
Dewey	953	.3	Others[2]	1,513	7.6
Robert A. Taft (Ohio)	705	.2			
Others[2]	475	.1			

April 13   Nebraska

Stassen	80,979	43.5	Truman	67,672	98.7
Dewey	64,242	34.5	Others	894	1.3
Taft	21,608	11.6			
Arthur Vandenberg (Mich.)	9,590	5.2			
MacArthur	6,893	3.7			
Earl Warren (Calif.)	1,761	.9			
Joseph W. Martin (Mass.)	910	.5			
Others	24	—			

April 20   New Jersey[3]

Dewey	3,714	41.4	Truman	1,100	92.5
Stassen	3,123	34.8	Henry A. Wallace (Iowa)	87	7.3
MacArthur	718	8.0	Others	2	.2
Vandenberg	516	5.8			
Taft	495	5.5			
Dwight D. Eisenhower (N.Y.)	288	3.2			
Joseph W. Martin	64	.7			
Alfred E. Driscoll (N.J.)	44	—			
Warren	14	.2			

April 27   Massachusetts

Unpledged delegates at large[4]	72,191	100.0	Unpledged delegates at large[4]	51,207	100.0

April 27   Pennsylvania

Stassen[2]	81,242	31.5	Truman	328,891	96.0
Dewey[2]	76,988	29.8	Eisenhower	4,502	1.3
Edward Martin (Pa.)	45,072	17.5	Wallace	4,329	1.3
MacArthur[2]	18,254	7.1	Harold E. Stassen (Minn.)	1,301	.4
Taft[2]	15,166	5.9	Douglas MacArthur (Wis.)	1,220	.4
Vandenberg	8,818	3.4	Others	2,409	.7
Harry S Truman (Mo.)	4,907	1.9			
Eisenhower	4,726	1.8			
Henry A. Wallace (Iowa)	1,452	.6			
Others	1,537	.6			

May 4   Alabama

[5]			Unpledged delegates at large[6]	161,629	100.0

Republican   # Democratic

	Votes	%		Votes	%
May 4 Florida					
[5]			Others [7]	92,169	100.0
May 4 Ohio					
Unpledged delegates at large [8]	426,767	100.0	Unpledged delegates at large [8]	271,146	100.0
May 11 West Virginia					
Stassen	110,775	83.2	Unpledged delegates at large	157,102	100.0
Others	22,410	16.8			
May 21 Oregon					
Dewey	117,554	51.8	Truman	112,962	93.8
Stassen	107,946	47.6	Others	7,436	6.2
Others	1,474	.6			
June 1 California					
Warren	769,520	100.0	Truman	811,920	100.0
June 1 South Dakota					
Hitchcock [9]	45,463	100.0	Truman [9]	11,193	58.3
			Unpledged Delegates [9]	8,016	41.7

TOTALS					
Warren	771,295	29.1	Truman	1,375,452	63.9
Unpledged delegates	527,812	19.9	Unpledged delegates	653,509	30.4
Stassen	449,713	16.9	Eisenhower	6,211	.3
Bender	324,029	12.2	Wallace	4,416	.2
Dewey	304,394	11.5	Stassen	1,301	.1
MacArthur	87,839	3.3	MacArthur	1,220	.1
Hitchcock	45,463	1.7	Lucas	427	—
Edward Martin	45,072	1.7	Others	109,329	5.1
Taft	37,974	1.4			
Vandenberg	18,924	.7		2,151,865	
Eisenhower	5,014	.2			
Truman	4,907	.2			
Wallace	1,452	.1			
Joseph W. Martin	974	—			
Driscoll	44	—			
Others [10]	28,349	1.1			
	2,653,255				

1. *Six unpledged and two Dewey delegates won in the Republican primary, and Truman delegates won in the Democratic primary, according to Kravitz, op. cit., p. 14.*
2. *Write-in.*
3. *Source: Kravitz, op. cit., p. 14.*
4. *The Boston Globe of April 28, 1948, reported that the Republican delegation was "generally unpledged" but was expected to support the "favorite son" candidacy of Sen. Leverett Saltonstall (R Mass.) on the first convention ballot. The* Globe *reported that Democratic delegates were presumed to favor Truman's nomination.*
5. *No primary.*

6. *Unpledged, anti-Truman slate, according to Kravitz, op. cit., p. 15.*
7. *Unpledged slate, according to Kravitz, ibid.*
8. *Taft won 44 delegates and Stassen nine in the Republican primary, and W.A. Julian won 55 delegates and Bixler one in the Democratic primary, according to Kravitz., ibid.*
9. *Republican delegates were unpledged, according to Kravitz. op. cit., p. 15. In the Democratic primary, according to Davis. p. 297. the slate led by South Dakota Democratic Party Chairman Lynn Fellows endorsed Truman and the slate headed by former Rep. Fred Hildebrandt (D S.D.) ran uninstructed.*
10. *In addition to scattered votes. "others" includes Byer who received 15.675 votes and Vander Pyl who received 6.735 votes in the West Virginia primary.*

1952 Primaries

	Republican			Democratic		
	Votes	%		Votes	%

March 11   New Hampshire

Republican	Votes	%	Democratic	Votes	%
Dwight D. Eisenhower (N.Y.)	46,661	50.4	Estes Kefauver (Tenn.)	19,800	55.0
Robert A. Taft (Ohio)	35,838	38.7	Harry S Truman (Mo.)	15,927	44.2
Harold E. Stassen (Minn.)	6,574	7.1	Douglas MacArthur (Wis.)	151	.4
Douglas MacArthur (Wis.)[1]	3,227	3.5	James A. Farley (N.Y.)	77	.2
Others	230	.3	Adlai E. Stevenson (Ill.)	40	.1

March 18   Minnesota

Republican	Votes	%	Democratic	Votes	%
Stassen	129,706	44.4	Hubert H. Humphrey (Minn.)	102,527	80.0
Eisenhower[1]	108,692	37.2	Kefauver[1]	20,182	15.8
Taft[1]	24,093	8.2	Truman[1]	3,634	2.8
Earl Warren (Calif.)[1]	5,365	1.8	Dwight D. Eisenhower (N.Y.)	1,753	1.4
MacArthur[1]	1,369	.5			
Estes Kefauver (Tenn.)	386	.1			
Others	22,712	7.8			

April 1   Nebraska

Republican	Votes	%	Democratic	Votes	%
Taft[1]	79,357	36.2	Kefauver	64,531	60.3
Eisenhower[1]	66,078	30.1	Robert S. Kerr (Okla.)	42,467	39.7
Stassen	53,238	24.3			
MacArthur[1]	7,478	3.4			
Warren[1]	1,872	.9			
Others	11,178	5.1			

April 1   Wisconsin

Republican	Votes	%	Democratic	Votes	%
Taft	315,541	40.6	Kefauver	207,520	85.9
Warren	262,271	33.8	Others	34,005	14.1
Stassen	169,679	21.8			
Others	29,133	3.8			

April 8   Illinois

Republican	Votes	%	Democratic	Votes	%
Taft	935,867	73.6	Kefauver	526,301	87.7
Stassen	155,041	12.2	Stevenson	54,336	9.1
Eisenhower[1]	147,518	11.6	Truman	9,024	1.5
MacArthur[1]	7,504	.6	Eisenhower	6,655	1.1
Warren	2,841	.2	Others[1]	3,798	.6
Others	23,550	1.9			

April 15   New Jersey

Republican	Votes	%	Democratic	Votes	%
Eisenhower	390,591	60.7	Kefauver	154,964	100.0
Taft	228,916	35.6			
Stassen	23,559	3.7			

April 22   Pennsylvania

Republican	Votes	%	Democratic	Votes	%
Eisenhower	863,785	73.6	Kefauver[1]	93,160	53.3
Taft[1]	178,629	15.2	Eisenhower[1]	28,660	16.4
Stassen	120,305	10.3	Truman[1]	26,504	15.2
MacArthur[1]	6,028	.5	Robert A. Taft (Ohio)	8,311	4.8
Warren	3,158	.3	Averell Harriman (N.Y.)[1]	3,745	2.1
Harry S Truman (Mo.)	267	—	Stevenson[1]	3,678	2.1
Others	1,121	.1	Richard B. Russell (Ga.)[1]	1,691	1.0
			Others	9,026	5.2

April 29   Massachusetts

Republican	Votes	%	Democratic	Votes	%
Eisenhower[1]	254,898	69.8	Kefauver	29,287	55.7
Taft[1]	110,188	30.2	Eisenhower	16,007	30.5
			Truman	7,256	13.8

Republican

Democratic

	Votes	%		Votes	%

May 5 Maryland[2]

| [3] | | | Kefauver | 137,885 | 74.8 |
| | | | Unpledged delegates | 46,361 | 25.2 |

May 6 Florida

[3]			Russell	367,980	54.5
			Kefauver	285,358	42.3
			Others	21,296	3.2

May 6 Ohio

| Taft[4] | 663,791 | 78.8 | Kefauver[4] | 305,992 | 62.3 |
| Stassen[4] | 178,739 | 21.2 | Robert J. Bulkley (Ohio)[4] | 184,880 | 37.7 |

May 13 West Virginia

| Taft | 139,812 | 78.5 | Unpledged delegates at large | 191,471 | 100.0 |
| Stassen | 38,251 | 21.5 | | | |

May 16 Oregon

Eisenhower	172,486	64.6	Kefauver	142,440	72.3
Warren	44,034	16.5	William O. Douglas (Wash.)	29,532	15.0
MacArthur	18,603	7.0	Stevenson	20,353	10.3
Taft[1]	18,009	6.7	Eisenhower[1]	4,690	2.4
Wayne L. Morse (Ore.)	7,105	2.7			
Stassen	6,610	2.5			
Others	350	.1			

June 3 California

| Warren | 1,029,495 | 66.4 | Kefauver | 1,155,839 | 70.4 |
| Thomas H. Werdel (Calif.) | 521,110 | 33.6 | Edmund G. Brown (Calif.) | 485,578 | 29.6 |

June 3 South Dakota

| Taft | 64,695 | 50.3 | Kefauver | 22,812 | 66.0 |
| Eisenhower | 63,879 | 49.7 | Others[5] | 11,741 | 34.0 |

June 17 District of Columbia[6]

[3]			Harriman	14,075	
			Kefauver	3,377	
			Stevenson[1]	176	
			Others[1]	1,153	

TOTALS

Taft	2,794,736	35.8	Kefauver	3,169,448	64.3
Eisenhower	2,114,588	27.1	Brown	485,578	9.9
Warren	1,349,036	17.3	Russell	369,671	7.5
Stassen	881,702	11.3	Unpledged delegates	237,832	4.8
Werdel	521,110	6.7	Bulkley	184,880	3.8
MacArthur	44,209	.6	Humphrey	102,527	2.1
Morse	7,105	.1	Stevenson	78,583	1.6
Kefauver	386	—	Truman	62,345	1.3
Truman	267	—	Eisenhower	57,765	1.2
Others[7]	88,274	1.1	Kerr	42,467	.9
	———		Douglas	29,532	.6
	7,801,413		Harriman	17,820	.4
			Taft	8,311	.2
			MacArthur	151	—
			Farley	77	—
			Others[8]	81,019	1.6
				———	
				4,928,006	

1. Write-in.
2. Source: Kravitz, op. cit., p. 18, and the office of the Maryland secretary of state.
3. No primary.
4. Delegate-at-large vote.
5. These delegates ran on an uninstructed slate, according to Kravitz, op. cit., p. 19.
6. Source: David, Moos, and Goldman, Nominating Politics in 1952, Vol. 2, p. 331-332.
7. In addition to scattered votes, "others" includes Schneider who received 230 votes in the New Hampshire primary and 350 in the Oregon primary; Kenny who received 10,411 in the Nebraska primary; Ritter who received 26,208 and Stearns who received 2,925 in the Wisconsin primary; Slettendahl who received 22,712 in the Minnesota primary and Riley Bender who received 22,321 votes in the Illinois primary.
8. In addition to scattered votes, "others" includes Fox who received 18,322 votes and Charles Broughton who received 15,683 votes in the Wisconsin primary; Compton who received 11,331 and Shaw who received 9,965 in the Florida primary.

1956 Primaries

Republican			Democratic		
	Votes	%		Votes	%

March 13 New Hampshire

Dwight D. Eisenhower (Pa.)	56,464	98.9	Estes Kefauver (Tenn.)	21,701	84.6
Others	600	1.1	Others	3,945	15.4

March 20 Minnesota

Eisenhower	198,111	98.4	Kefauver	245,885	56.8
William F. Knowland (Calif.)	3,209	1.6	Adlai E. Stevenson (Ill.)	186,723	43.2
Others	51	—	Others	48	—

April 3 Wisconsin

Eisenhower	437,089	95.9	Kefauver	330,665[1]	100.0
Others	18,743	4.1			

April 10 Illinois

Eisenhower	781,710	94.9	Stevenson	717,742	95.3
Knowland	33,534	4.1	Kefauver[2]	34,092	4.5
Others	8,455	1.0	Others	1,640	.2

April 17 New Jersey

Eisenhower	357,066	100.0	Kefauver	117,056	95.7
Others	23	—	Others	5,230	4.3

April 24 Alaska (Territory)

Eisenhower	8,291	94.4	Stevenson	7,123	61.1
Knowland	488	5.6	Kefauver	4,536	38.9

April 24 Massachusetts

Eisenhower[2]	51,951	95.1	John W. McCormack (Mass.)[2]	26,128	47.9
Adlai E. Stevenson (Ill.)[2]	604	1.1	Stevenson[2]	19,024	34.9
Christian A. Herter (Mass.)[2]	550	1.0	Kefauver[2]	4,547	8.3
Richard M. Nixon (N.Y.)[2]	316	.6	Dwight D. Eisenhower (Pa.)[2]	1,850	3.4
John W. McCormack (Mass.)[2]	268	.5	John F. Kennedy (Mass.)[2]	949	1.7
Knowland[2]	250	.5	Averell Harriman (N.Y.)[2]	394	.7
Others[2]	700	1.3	Frank J. Lausche (Ohio)[2]	253	.5
			Others[2]	1,379	2.5

April 24 Pennsylvania

Eisenhower	951,932	95.5	Stevenson	642,172	93.6
Knowland	43,508	4.4	Kefauver[2]	36,552	5.3
Others	976	.1	Others	7,482	1.1

May 1 District of Columbia[3]

Eisenhower	18,101	100.0	Stevenson	17,306	66.2
			Kefauver	8,837	33.8

May 7 Maryland

Eisenhower	66,904	95.5	Kefauver	112,768	65.9
Unpledged delegates	3,131	4.5	Unpledged delegates	58,366	34.1

May 8 Indiana

Eisenhower	351,903	96.4	Kefauver	242,842[1]	100.0
Others	13,320	3.6			

Republican

Democratic

	Votes	%		Votes	%
May 8 Ohio					
John W. Bricker (Ohio)	478,453[1]	100.0	Lausche	276,670[1]	100.0
May 8 West Virginia					
Unpledged delegates at large	111,883[1]	100.0	Unpledged delegates at large	112,832[1]	100.0
May 15 Nebraska					
Eisenhower	102,576	99.8	Kefauver	55,265	94.0
Others	230	.2	Others	3,556	6.0
May 18 Oregon					
Eisenhower	231,418[1]	100.0	Stevenson[2]	98,131	60.2
			Kefauver[2]	62,987	38.6
			Harriman[2]	1,887	1.2
May 29 Florida					
Eisenhower	39,690	92.0	Stevenson	230,285	51.5
Knowland	3,457	8.0	Kefauver	216,549	48.5
June 5 California					
Eisenhower	1,354,764[1]	100.0	Stevenson	1,139,964	62.6
			Kefauver	680,722	37.4
June 5 Montana					
S.C. Arnold[4]	32,732	85.7	Kefauver	77,228[1]	100.0
Others	5,447	14.3			
June 5 South Dakota					
Unpledged delegates[5]	59,374[1]	100.0	Kefauver	30,940[1]	100.0

TOTALS					
Eisenhower	5,007,970	85.9	Stevenson	3,051,347	52.3
Bricker	478,453	8.2	Kefauver	2,278,636	39.1
Unpledged delegates	174,388	3.0	Lausche	276,923	4.7
Knowland	84,446	1.4	Unpledged delegates	171,198	2.9
S.C. Arnold	32,732	.6	McCormack	26,128	.4
Stevenson	604	—	Harriman	2,281	—
Herter	550	—	Eisenhower	1,850	—
Nixon	316	—	Kennedy	949	—
McCormack	268	—	Others	23,280	.4
Others[6]	48,545	.8			
	5,828,272			5,832,592	

1. Figures obtained from Scammon's office. In America Votes, Scammon did not record vote totals if a candidate was unopposed or if the primary was strictly for delegate selection.

2. Write-in.

3. Source: Davis, op. cit., pp. 300-301.

4. Voters cast their ballots for S. C. Arnold, "stand-in" candidate for Eisenhower.

5. Slate unofficially pledged to Eisenhower but appeared on the ballot as "No preference."

6. In addition to scattered votes, "others" includes Lar Daly who received 8,364 votes in the Illinois primary, 13,320 votes in the Indiana primary and 5,447 votes in the Montana primary; and John Bowman Chapple who received 18,743 votes in the Wisconsin primary.

1960 Primaries

	Republican				Democratic		
	Votes	%			Votes	%

March 8   New Hampshire

Republican	Votes	%	Democratic	Votes	%
Richard M. Nixon (N.Y.)	65,204	89.3	John F. Kennedy (Mass.)	43,372	85.2
Nelson A. Rockefeller (N.Y.)[1]	2,745	3.8	Others	7,527	14.8
John F. Kennedy (Mass.)[1]	2,196	3.0			
Others	2,886	4.0			

April 5   Wisconsin

Republican	Votes	%	Democratic	Votes	%
Nixon	339,383[2]	100.0	Kennedy	476,024	56.5
			Hubert H. Humphrey (Minn.)	366,753	43.5

April 12   Illinois

Republican	Votes	%	Democratic	Votes	%
Nixon	782,849[2]	99.9	Kennedy[1]	34,332	64.6
Others[1]	442[2]	.1	Adlai E. Stevenson (Ill.)[1]	8,029	15.1
			Stuart Symington (Mo.)[1]	5,744	10.8
			Humphrey[1]	4,283	8.1
			Lyndon B. Johnson (Texas)[1]	442	.8
			Others[1]	337	.6

April 19   New Jersey

Republican	Votes	%	Democratic	Votes	%
Unpledged delegates at large	304,766[2]	100.0	Unpledged delegates at large	217,608[2]	100.0

April 26   Massachusetts

Republican	Votes	%	Democratic	Votes	%
Nixon[1]	53,164	86.0	Kennedy[1]	91,607	92.4
Rockefeller[1]	4,068	6.6	Stevenson[1]	4,684	4.7
Kennedy[1]	2,989	4.8	Humphrey[1]	794	.8
Henry Cabot Lodge (Mass.)[1]	373	.6	Richard M. Nixon (Calif.)[1]	646	.7
Adlai E. Stevenson (Ill.)[1]	266	.4	Symington[1]	443	.4
Barry Goldwater (Ariz.)[1]	221	.4	Johnson[1]	268	.3
Dwight D. Eisenhower (Pa.)[1]	172	.3	Others[1]	721	.7
Others[1]	592	1.0			

April 26   Pennsylvania

Republican	Votes	%	Democratic	Votes	%
Nixon	968,538	98.1	Kennedy[1]	183,073	71.3
Rockefeller[1]	12,491	1.3	Stevenson[1]	29,660	11.5
Kennedy[1]	3,886	.4	Nixon[1]	15,136	5.9
Stevenson[1]	428	—	Humphrey[1]	13,860	5.4
Goldwater[1]	286	—	Symington[1]	6,791	2.6
Others[1]	1,202	.1	Johnson[1]	2,918	1.1
			Rockefeller[1]	1,078	.4
			Others[1]	4,297	1.7

May 3   District of Columbia[3]

Republican	Votes	%	Democratic	Votes	%
Unpledged delegates	9,468	100.0	Humphrey	8,239	57.4
			Wayne L. Morse (Ore.)	6,127	42.6

May 3   Indiana

Republican	Votes	%	Democratic	Votes	%
Nixon	408,408	95.4	Kennedy	353,832	81.0
Others	19,677	4.6	Others	82,937	19.0

May 3   Ohio

Republican	Votes	%	Democratic	Votes	%
Nixon	504,072[2]	100.0	Michael V. DiSalle (Ohio)	315,312[2]	100.0

Republican   # Democratic

	Votes	%		Votes	%
May 10 Nebraska					
Nixon[1]	74,356	93.8	Kennedy	80,408	88.7
Rockefeller[1]	2,028	2.6	Symington[1]	4,083	4.5
Goldwater[1]	1,068	1.3	Humphrey[1]	3,202	3.5
Others[1]	1,805	2.3	Stevenson[1]	1,368	1.5
			Johnson[1]	962	1.1
			Others[1]	669	.7
May 10 West Virginia					
Unpledged delegates at large	123,756[2]	100.0	Kennedy	236,510	60.8
			Humphrey	152,187	39.2
May 17 Maryland					
[4]			Kennedy	201,769	70.3
			Morse	49,420	17.2
			Unpledged delegates	24,350	8.5
			Others	11,417	4.0
May 20 Oregon					
Nixon	211,276	93.1	Kennedy	146,332	51.0
Rockefeller[1]	9,307	4.1	Morse	91,715	31.9
Kennedy[1]	2,864	1.3	Humphrey	16,319	5.7
Goldwater[1]	1,571	.7	Symington	12,496	4.4
Others[1]	2,015	.9	Johnson	11,101	3.9
			Stevenson[1]	7,924	2.8
			Others[1]	1,210	.4
May 24 Florida					
Nixon	51,036[2]	100.0	George A. Smathers (Fla.)	322,235[2]	100.0
June 7 California					
Nixon	1,517,652[2]	100.0	Edmund G. Brown (Calif.)	1,354,031	67.7
			George H. McLain (Calif.)	646,387	32.3
June 7 South Dakota					
Unpledged delegates	48,461[2]	100.0	Humphrey	24,773[2]	100.0
TOTALS					
Nixon	4,975,938	89.9	Kennedy	1,847,259	32.5
Unpledged delegates	486,451	8.8	Brown	1,354,031	23.8
Rockefeller	30,639	.6	McLain	646,387	11.4
Kennedy	11,935	.2	Humphrey	590,410	10.4
Goldwater	3,146	.1	Smathers	322,235	5.7
Stevenson	694	—	DiSalle	315,312	5.5
Lodge	373	—	Unpledged delegates	241,958	4.3
Eisenhower	172	—	Morse	147,262	2.6
Others[5]	28,619	.5	Stevenson	51,665	.9
			Symington	29,557	.5
	5,537,967		Nixon	15,782	.3
			Johnson	15,691	.3
			Others[6]	109,115	1.9
				5,686,664	

1. Write-in.
2. Figures obtained from Scammon's office. In America Votes, Scammon did not record vote totals if a candidate was unopposed or if the primary was strictly for delegate selection.
3. Source: District of Columbia Board of Elections.
4. No primary.
5. In addition to scattered votes, "others" includes Paul C. Fisher who received 2,388 votes in the New Hampshire primary and Frank R. Beckwith who received 19,677 in the Indiana primary.
6. In addition to scattered votes, "others" includes Lar Daly who received 40,853 votes in the Indiana primary and 7,536 in the Maryland primary; Paul C. Fisher who received 6,853 votes in the New Hampshire primary; John H. Latham who received 42,084 in the Indiana primary and Andrew J. Easter who received 3,881 votes in the Maryland primary.

1964 Primaries

	Republican			Democratic		
	Votes	%		Votes	%

March 10   New Hampshire

Henry Cabot Lodge (Mass.)[1]	33,007	*35.5*	Lyndon B. Johnson (Texas)[1]	29,317	*95.3*
Barry M. Goldwater (Ariz.)	20,692	*22.3*	Robert F. Kennedy (N.Y.)[1]	487	*1.6*
Nelson A. Rockefeller (N.Y.)	19,504	*21.0*	Henry Cabot Lodge (Mass.)[1]	280	*.9*
Richard M. Nixon (Calif.)[1]	15,587	*16.8*	Richard M. Nixon (Calif.)[1]	232	*.8*
Margaret Chase Smith (Maine)	2,120	*2.3*	Barry M. Goldwater (Ariz.)[1]	193	*.6*
Harold E. Stassen (Pa.)	1,373	*1.5*	Nelson A. Rockefeller (N.Y.)[1]	109	*.4*
William W. Scranton (Pa.)[1]	105	*.1*	Others[1]	159	*.5*
Others	465	*.5*			

April 7   Wisconsin

John W. Byrnes (Wis.)	299,612	*99.7*	John W. Reynolds (Wis.)	522,405	*66.2*
Unpledged delegate	816	*.3*	George C. Wallace (Ala.)	266,136	*33.8*

April 14   Illinois

Goldwater	512,840	*62.0*	Johnson[1]	82,027	*91.6*
Smith	209,521	*25.3*	Wallace[1]	3,761	*4.2*
Henry Cabot Lodge[1]	68,122	*8.2*	Robert F. Kennedy[1]	2,894	*3.2*
Nixon[1]	30,313	*3.7*	Others[1]	841	*.9*
George C. Wallace (Ala.)[1]	2,203	*.3*			
Rockefeller[1]	2,048	*.2*			
Scranton[1]	1,842	*.2*			
George W. Romney (Mich.)[1]	465	*.1*			
Others[1]	437	*.1*			

April 21   New Jersey

Henry Cabot Lodge[1]	7,896	*41.7*	Johnson[1]	4,863	*82.3*
Goldwater[1]	5,309	*28.0*	Wallace[1]	491	*8.3*
Nixon[1]	4,179	*22.1*	Robert F. Kennedy[1]	431	*7.3*
Scranton[1]	633	*3.3*	Others[1]	124	*2.1*
Rockefeller[1]	612	*3.2*			
Others[1]	304	*1.6*			

April 28   Massachusetts

Henry Cabot Lodge[1]	70,809	*76.9*	Johnson[1]	61,035	*73.4*
Goldwater[1]	9,338	*10.1*	Robert F. Kennedy[1]	15,870	*19.1*
Nixon[1]	5,460	*5.9*	Lodge[1]	2,269	*2.7*
Rockefeller[1]	2,454	*2.7*	Edward M. Kennedy (Mass.)[1]	1,259	*1.5*
Scranton[1]	1,709	*1.9*	Wallace[1]	565	*.7*
Lyndon B. Johnson (Texas)[1]	600	*.7*	Adlai E. Stevenson (Ill.)[1]	452	*.5*
Smith[1]	426	*.5*	Hubert H. Humphrey (Minn.)[1]	323	*.4*
George C. Lodge (Mass.)[1]	365	*.4*	Others[1]	1,436	*1.7*
Romney[1]	262	*.3*			
Others[1]	711	*.8*			

April 28   Pennsylvania

Scranton[1]	235,222	*51.9*	Johnson[1]	209,606	*82.8*
Henry Cabot Lodge[1]	92,712	*20.5*	Wallace[1]	12,104	*4.8*
Nixon[1]	44,396	*9.8*	Robert F. Kennedy[1]	12,029	*4.8*
Goldwater[1]	38,669	*8.5*	William W. Scranton (Pa.)[1]	8,156	*3.2*
Johnson[1]	22,372	*4.9*	Lodge[1]	4,895	*1.9*
Rockefeller[1]	9,123	*2.0*	Others[1]	6,438	*2.5*
Wallace[1]	5,105	*1.1*			
Others[1]	5,269	*1.2*			

May 2   Texas

Goldwater	104,137	*74.7*	[2]		
Henry Cabot Lodge[1]	12,324	*8.8*			
Rockefeller	6,207	*4.5*			
Nixon[1]	5,390	*3.9*			
Stassen	5,273	*3.8*			
Smith	4,816	*3.5*			
Scranton[1]	803	*.6*			
Others[1]	373	*.3*			

Republican   # Democratic

	Votes	%		Votes	%
May 5 District of Columbia[3]					
[3]			Unpledged delegates	41,095	100.0
May 5 Indiana					
Goldwater	267,935	67.0	Matthew E. Welsh (Ind.)	376,023	64.9
Stassen	107,157	26.8	Wallace	172,646	29.8
Others	24,588	6.2	Others	30,367	5.2
May 5 Ohio					
James A. Rhodes (Ohio)	615,754[4]	100.0	Albert S. Porter (Ohio)	493,619[4]	100.0
May 12 Nebraska					
Goldwater	68,050	49.1	Johnson[1]	54,713	89.3
Nixon[1]	43,613	31.5	Robert F. Kennedy[1]	2,099	3.4
Henry Cabot Lodge[1]	22,622	16.3	Wallace[1]	1,067	1.7
Rockefeller[1]	2,333	1.7	Lodge[1]	1,051	1.7
Scranton[1]	578	.4	Nixon[1]	833	1.4
Johnson[1]	316	.2	Goldwater[1]	603	1.0
Others[1]	1,010	.7	Others[1]	904	1.5
May 12 West Virginia					
Rockefeller	115,680[4]	100.0	Unpledged delegates at large	131,432[4]	100.0
May 15 Oregon					
Rockefeller	94,190	33.0	Johnson	272,099[4]	99.5
Henry Cabot Lodge	79,169	27.7	Wallace[1]	1,365[4]	.5
Goldwater	50,105	17.6			
Nixon	48,274	16.9			
Smith	8,087	2.8			
Scranton	4,509	1.6			
Others	1,152	.4			
May 19 Maryland					
Unpledged delegates	57,004	58.2	Daniel B. Brewster (Md.)	267,106	53.1
Others	40,994	41.8	Wallace	214,849	42.7
			Unpledged delegates	12,377	2.5
			Others	8,275	1.6
May 26 Florida					
Unpledged delegates	58,179	57.8	Johnson	393,339[4]	100.0
Goldwater	42,525	42.2			
June 2 California					
Goldwater	1,120,403	51.6	Unpledged delegates[5]	1,693,813	68.0
Rockefeller	1,052,053	48.4	Unpledged delegates[5]	798,431	32.0
June 2 South Dakota					
Unpledged delegates	57,653	68.0	Unpledged delegates	28,142[4]	100.0
Goldwater	27,076	32.0			

Republican

	Votes	%
TOTALS		
Goldwater	2,267,079	38.2
Rockefeller	1,304,204	22.0
Rhodes	615,754	10.4
Henry Cabot Lodge	386,661	6.5
Byrnes	299,612	5.0
Scranton	245,401	4.1
Smith	224,970	3.8
Nixon	197,212	3.3
Unpledged delegates	173,652	2.9
Stassen	113,803	1.9
Johnson	23,288	.4
Wallace	7,308	.1
Romney	727	—
George C. Lodge	365	—
Others[6]	75,303	1.3
	5,935,339	

Democratic

	Votes	%
Unpledged delegates	2,705,290	43.3
Johnson	1,106,999	17.7
Wallace	672,984	10.8
Reynolds	522,405	8.4
Porter	493,619	7.9
Welsh	376,023	6.0
Brewster	267,106	4.3
Robert F. Kennedy	33,810	.5
Henry Cabot Lodge	8,495	.1
Scranton	8,156	.1
Edward M. Kennedy	1,259	—
Nixon	1,065	—
Goldwater	796	—
Stevenson	452	—
Humphrey	323	—
Rockefeller	109	—
Others[7]	48,544	.8
	6,247,435	

1. *Write-in.*

2. *No primary authorized.*

3. *Source: District of Columbia Board of Elections. No figures available for vote for delegates to Republican convention.*

4. *Figures obtained from Scammon's office. In* America Votes, *Scammon did not record vote totals if a candidate was unopposed or if the primary was strictly for delegate selection.*

5. *Gov. Edmund G. Brown (D Calif.) headed the winning slate of delegates and Mayor Sam Yorty of Los Angeles headed the losing slate.*

6. *In addition to scattered votes, "others" includes Norman LePage who received 82 votes in the New Hampshire primary; Frank R. Beckwith who received 17,884 votes and Joseph G. Ettl who received 6,704 votes in the Indiana primary; John W. Steffey who received 22,135 votes and Robert E. Ennis who received 18,859 votes in the Maryland primary.*

7. *In addition to scattered votes, "others" includes Lar Daly who received 15,160 votes, John H. Latham who received 8,067 votes and Fay T. Carpenter Swain who received 7,140 votes in the Indiana primary; and Andrew J. Easter who received 8,275 votes in the Maryland primary.*

1968 Primaries*

<table>
<tr><th align="center" colspan="3">Republican</th><th align="center" colspan="3">Democratic</th></tr>
</table>

March 12   New Hampshire

Richard M. Nixon (N.Y.)	80,666	77.6	Lyndon B. Johnson (Texas)[1]	27,520	49.6
Nelson A. Rockefeller (N.Y.)[1]	11,241	10.8	Eugene J. McCarthy (Minn.)	23,263	41.9
Eugene J. McCarthy (Minn.)[1]	5,511	5.3	Richard M. Nixon (N.Y.)[1]	2,532	4.6
Lyndon B. Johnson (Texas)[1]	1,778	1.7	Others	2,149	3.9
George W. Romney (Mich.)	1,743	1.7			
Harold E. Stassen (Pa.)	429	.4			
Others	2,570	2.5			

April 2   Wisconsin

Nixon	390,368	79.7	McCarthy	412,160	56.2
Ronald Reagan (Calif.)	50,727	10.4	Johnson	253,696	34.6
Stassen	28,531	5.8	Robert F. Kennedy (N.Y.)[1]	46,507	6.3
Rockefeller[1]	7,995	1.6	Unpledged delegates	11,861	1.6
Unpledged delegates	6,763	1.4	George C. Wallace (Ala.)[1]	4,031	.5
Romney[1]	2,087	.4	Hubert H. Humphrey (Minn.)[1]	3,605	.5
Others	3,382	.7	Others	1,142	.2

April 23   Pennsylvania

Nixon[1]	171,815	59.7	McCarthy	428,259	71.7
Rockefeller[1]	52,915	18.4	Robert F. Kennedy[1]	65,430	11.0
McCarthy[1]	18,800	6.5	Humphrey[1]	51,998	8.7
George C. Wallace (Ala.)[1]	13,290	4.6	Wallace[1]	24,147	4.0
Robert F. Kennedy (N.Y.)[1]	10,431	3.6	Johnson[1]	21,265	3.6
Reagan[1]	7,934	2.8	Nixon[1]	3,434	.6
Hubert H. Humphrey (Minn.)[1]	4,651	1.6	Others[1]	2,556	.4
Johnson[1]	3,027	1.1			
Raymond P. Shafer (Pa.)[1]	1,223	.4			
Others[1]	3,487	1.2			

April 30   Massachusetts

Rockefeller[1]	31,964	30.0	McCarthy	122,697	49.3
John A. Volpe (Mass.)	31,465	29.5	Robert F. Kennedy[1]	68,604	27.6
Nixon[1]	27,447	25.8	Humphrey[1]	44,156	17.7
McCarthy[1]	9,758	9.2	Johnson[1]	6,890	2.8
Reagan[1]	1,770	1.7	Nelson A. Rockefeller (N.Y.)[1]	2,275	1.0
Kennedy[1]	1,184	1.1	Wallace[1]	1,688	.7
Others[1]	2,933	2.8	Others[1]	2,593	1.0

May 7   District of Columbia

Nixon-Rockefeller[2]	12,102	90.1	Robert F. Kennedy[3]	57,555	62.5
Unpledged delegates[2]	1,328	9.9	Humphrey[3]	32,309	35.1
			Humphrey[3]	2,250	2.4

May 7   Indiana

Nixon	508,362[4]	100.0	Robert F. Kennedy	328,118	42.3
			Roger D. Branigin (Ind.)	238,700	30.7
			McCarthy	209,695	27.0

May 7   Ohio

James A. Rhodes (Ohio)	614,492[4]	100.0	Stephen M. Young (Ohio)	549,140[4]	100.0

Republican   # Democratic

	Votes	%		Votes	%

May 14   **Nebraska**[5]

	Votes	%		Votes	%
Nixon	140,336	70.0	Robert F. Kennedy	84,102	51.7
Reagan	42,703	21.3	McCarthy	50,655	31.2
Rockefeller[1]	10,225	5.1	Humphrey[1]	12,087	7.4
Stassen	2,638	1.3	Johnson	9,187	5.6
McCarthy[1]	1,544	.8	Nixon[1]	2,731	1.7
Others	3,030	1.5	Ronald Reagan (Calif.)[1]	1,905	1.2
			Wallace[1]	1,298	.8
			Others	646	.4

May 14   **West Virginia**

	Votes	%		Votes	%
Unpledged delegates at large	81,039[4]	100.0	Unpledged delegates at large	149,282[4]	100.0

May 28   **Florida**

	Votes	%		Votes	%
Unpledged delegates	51,509[4]	100.0	George A. Smathers (Fla.)	236,242	46.1
			McCarthy	147,216	28.7
			Unpledged delegates	128,899	25.2

May 28   **Oregon**

	Votes	%		Votes	%
Nixon	203,037	65.0	McCarthy	163,990	44.0
Reagan	63,707	20.4	Robert F. Kennedy	141,631	38.0
Rockefeller[1]	36,305	11.6	Johnson	45,174	12.1
McCarthy[1]	7,387	2.4	Humphrey[1]	12,421	3.3
Kennedy[1]	1,723	.6	Reagan[1]	3,082	.8
			Nixon[1]	2,974	.8
			Rockefeller[1]	2,841	.8
			Wallace[1]	957	.3

June 4   **California**

	Votes	%		Votes	%
Reagan	1,525,091[4]	100.0	Robert F. Kennedy	1,472,166	46.3
			McCarthy	1,329,301	41.8
			Unpledged delegates	380,286	12.0

June 4   **New Jersey**

	Votes	%		Votes	%
Nixon[1]	71,809	81.1	McCarthy[1]	9,906	36.1
Rockefeller[1]	11,530	13.0	Robert F. Kennedy[1]	8,603	31.3
Reagan[1]	2,737	3.1	Humphrey[1]	5,578	20.3
McCarthy[1]	1,358	1.5	Wallace[1]	1,399	5.1
Others[1]	1,158	1.3	Nixon[1]	1,364	5.0
			Others[1]	596	2.2

June 4   **South Dakota**

	Votes	%		Votes	%
Nixon	68,113[4]	100.0	Robert F. Kennedy	31,826	49.5
			Johnson	19,316	30.0
			McCarthy	13,145	20.4

June 11   **Illinois**

	Votes	%		Votes	%
Nixon[1]	17,490	78.1	McCarthy[1]	4,646	38.6
Rockefeller[1]	2,165	9.7	Edward M. Kennedy (Mass.)[1]	4,052	33.7
Reagan[1]	1,601	7.1	Humphrey[1]	2,059	17.1
Others[1]	1,147	5.1	Others[1]	1,281	10.6

Republican

Reagan	1,696,270	37.9
Nixon	1,679,443	37.5
Rhodes	614,492	13.7
Rockefeller	164,340	3.7
Unpledged delegates	140,639	3.1
McCarthy	44,358	1.0
Stassen	31,598	.7
Volpe	31,465	.7
Robert F. Kennedy	13,338	.3
Wallace	13,290	.3
Nixon-Rockefeller[2]	12,102	.3
Johnson	4,805	.1
Humphrey	4,651	.1
Romney	3,830	.1
Shafer	1,223	—
Others[6]	17,707	.4
	4,473,551	

Democratic

McCarthy	2,914,933	38.7
Robert F. Kennedy	2,304,542	30.6
Unpledged delegates	670,328	8.9
Young	549,140	7.3
Johnson	383,048	5.1
Branigin	238,700	3.2
Smathers	236,242	3.1
Humphrey	166,463	2.2
Wallace	33,520	.4
Nixon	13,035	.2
Rockefeller	5,116	.1
Reagan	4,987	.1
Edward M. Kennedy	4,052	.1
Others[7]	10,963	.1
	7,535,069	

*Delegate selection primaries were held in Alabama and New York. In America Votes, Scammon did not record vote totals if the primary was strictly for delegate selection and there was no presidential preference voting.

1. Write-in.

2. Prior to the primary, the District Republican organization agreed to divide the nine delegate votes, with six going to Nixon and three going to Rockefeller, according to the 1968 Congressional Quarterly Almanac, Vol. XXIV. Figures obtained from Scammon's office.

3. Figures obtained from Scammon's office. Two slates favored Humphrey; a member of an "independent" Humphrey slate received 2,250 votes.

4. Figures obtained from Scammon's office. In America Votes, Scammon did not record vote totals if a candidate was unopposed or if the primary was strictly for delegate selection.

5. In the American Party presidential primary, Wallace received 493 of the 504 votes cast, or 97.8% of the vote, according to the office of the Nebraska secretary of state.

6. In addition to scattered votes, "others" includes Willis E. Stone who received 527 votes, Herbert F. Hoover who received 247 votes, David Watumull who received 161 votes, William W. Evans who received 151 votes, Elmer W. Coy who received 73 votes and Don DuMont who received 39 votes in the New Hampshire primary; and Americus Liberator who received 1,302 votes in the Nebraska primary.

7. In addition to scattered votes, "others" includes John G. Crommelin who received 186 votes, Richard E. Lee who received 170 votes and Jacob J. Gordon who received 77 votes in the New Hampshire primary.

1972 Primaries*

Republican			**Democratic**		
	Votes	%		Votes	%

March 7   New Hampshire

	Votes	%		Votes	%
Richard M. Nixon (Calif.)	79,239	67.6	Edmund S. Muskie (Maine)	41,235	46.4
Paul N. McCloskey (Calif.)	23,190	19.8	George S. McGovern (S.D.)	33,007	37.1
John M. Ashbrook (Ohio)	11,362	9.7	Sam Yorty (Calif.)	5,401	6.1
Others	3,417	2.9	Wilbur D. Mills (Ark.)[1]	3,563	4.0
			Vance Hartke (Ind.)	2,417	2.7
			Edward M. Kennedy (Mass.)[1]	954	1.1
			Hubert H. Humphrey (Minn.)[1]	348	.4
			Henry M. Jackson (Wash.)[1]	197	.2
			George C. Wallace (Ala.)[1]	175	.2
			Others	1,557	1.8

March 14   Florida

	Votes	%		Votes	%
Nixon	360,278	87.0	Wallace	526,651	41.6
Ashbrook	36,617	8.8	Humphrey	234,658	18.6
McCloskey	17,312	4.2	Jackson	170,156	13.5
			Muskie	112,523	8.9
			John V. Lindsay (N.Y.)	82,386	6.5
			McGovern	78,232	6.2
			Shirley Chisholm (N.Y.)	43,989	3.5
			Eugene J. McCarthy (Minn.)	5,847	.5
			Mills	4,539	.4
			Hartke	3,009	.2
			Yorty	2,564	.2

March 21   Illinois

	Votes	%		Votes	%
Nixon[1]	32,550	97.0	Muskie	766,914	62.6
Ashbrook[1]	170	.5	McCarthy	444,260	36.3
McCloskey[1]	47	.1	Wallace[1]	7,017	.6
Others[1]	802	2.4	McGovern[1]	3,687	.3
			Humphrey[1]	1,476	.1
			Chisholm[1]	777	.1
			Jackson[1]	442	—
			Kennedy[1]	242	—
			Lindsay[1]	118	—
			Others	211	—

April 4   Wisconsin

	Votes	%		Votes	%
Nixon	277,601	96.9	McGovern	333,528	29.6
McCloskey	3,651	1.3	Wallace	248,676	22.0
Ashbrook	2,604	.9	Humphrey	233,748	20.7
None of the names shown	2,315	.8	Muskie	115,811	10.3
Others	273	.1	Jackson	88,068	7.8
			Lindsay	75,579	6.7
			McCarthy	15,543	1.4
			Chisholm	9,198	.8
			None of the names shown	2,450	.2
			Yorty	2,349	.2
			Patsy T. Mink (Hawaii)	1,213	.1
			Mills	913	.1
			Hartke	766	.1
			Kennedy[1]	183	—
			Others	559	—

Republican   # Democratic

April 25   **Massachusetts**

Nixon	99,150	81.2	McGovern	325,673	52.7
McCloskey	16,435	13.5	Muskie	131,709	21.3
Ashbrook	4,864	4.0	Humphrey	48,929	7.9
Others	1,690	1.4	Wallace	45,807	7.4
			Chisholm	22,398	3.6
			Mills	19,441	3.1
			McCarthy	8,736	1.4
			Jackson	8,499	1.4
			Kennedy[1]	2,348	.4
			Lindsay	2,107	.3
			Hartke	874	.1
			Yorty	646	.1
			Others	1,349	.2

April 25   **Pennsylvania**

Nixon[1]	153,886	83.3	Humphrey	481,900	35.1
George C. Wallace (Ala.)[1]	20,472	11.1	Wallace	292,437	21.3
Others[1]	10,443	5.7	McGovern	280,861	20.4
			Muskie	279,983	20.4
			Jackson	38,767	2.8
			Chisholm[1]	306	—
			Others	585	—

May 2   **District of Columbia**

[2]

			Walter E. Fauntroy (D.C.)	21,217	71.8
			Unpledged delegates	8,343	28.2

May 2   **Indiana**

Nixon	417,069	100.0	Humphrey	354,244	47.1
			Wallace	309,495	41.2
			Muskie	87,719	11.7

May 2   **Ohio**

Nixon	692,828	100.0	Humphrey	499,680	41.2
			McGovern	480,320	39.6
			Muskie	107,806	8.9
			Jackson	98,498	8.1
			McCarthy	26,026	2.1

May 4   **Tennessee**

Nixon	109,696	95.8	Wallace	335,858	68.2
Ashbrook	2,419	2.1	Humphrey	78,350	15.9
McCloskey	2,370	2.1	McGovern	35,551	7.2
Others	4	—	Chisholm	18,809	3.8
			Muskie	9,634	2.0
			Jackson	5,896	1.2
			Mills	2,543	.5
			McCarthy	2,267	.5
			Hartke	1,621	.3
			Lindsay	1,476	.3
			Yorty	692	.1
			Others	24	—

	Republican			**Democratic**	
	Votes	%		Votes	%

May 6 North Carolina

	Votes	%		Votes	%
Nixon	159,167	94.8	Wallace	413,518	50.3
McCloskey	8,732	5.2	Terry Sanford (N.C.)	306,014	37.3
			Chisholm	61,723	7.5
			Muskie	30,739	3.7
			Jackson	9,416	1.1

May 9 Nebraska

	Votes	%		Votes	%
Nixon	179,464	92.4	McGovern	79,309	41.3
McCloskey	9,011	4.6	Humphrey	65,968	34.3
Ashbrook	4,996	2.6	Wallace	23,912	12.4
Others	801	.4	Muskie	6,886	3.6
			Jackson	5,276	2.7
			Yorty	3,459	1.8
			McCarthy	3,194	1.7
			Chisholm	1,763	.9
			Lindsay	1,244	.6
			Mills	377	.2
			Kennedy[1]	293	.2
			Hartke	249	.1
			Others	207	.1

May 9 West Virginia

	Votes	%		Votes	%
Unpledged delegates at large	95,813[3]	100.0	Humphrey	246,596	66.9
			Wallace	121,888	33.1

May 16 Maryland

	Votes	%		Votes	%
Nixon	99,308	86.2	Wallace	219,687	38.7
McCloskey	9,223	8.0	Humphrey	151,981	26.8
Ashbrook	6,718	5.8	McGovern	126,978	22.4
			Jackson	17,728	3.1
			Yorty	13,584	2.4
			Muskie	13,363	2.4
			Chisholm	12,602	2.2
			Mills	4,776	.8
			McCarthy	4,691	.8
			Lindsay	2,168	.4
			Mink	573	.1

May 16 Michigan

	Votes	%		Votes	%
Nixon	321,652	95.5	Wallace	809,239	51.0
McCloskey	9,691	2.9	McGovern	425,694	26.8
Unpledged delegates	5,370	1.6	Humphrey	249,798	15.7
Others	30	—	Chisholm	44,090	2.8
			Muskie	38,701	2.4
			Unpledged delegates	10,700	.7
			Jackson	6,938	.4
			Hartke	2,862	.2
			Others	51	—

May 23 Oregon

	Votes	%		Votes	%
Nixon	231,151	82.0	McGovern	205,328	50.2
McCloskey	29,365	10.4	Wallace	81,868	20.0
Ashbrook	16,696	5.9	Humphrey	51,163	12.5
Others	4,798	1.7	Jackson	22,042	5.4
			Kennedy	12,673	3.1
			Muskie	10,244	2.5
			McCarthy	8,943	2.2
			Mink	6,500	1.6
			Lindsay	5,082	1.2
			Chisholm	2,975	.7
			Mills	1,208	.3
			Others	618	.2

Republican   # Democratic

May 23 **Rhode Island**	Votes	%		Votes	%
Nixon	4,953	88.3	McGovern	15,603	41.2
McCloskey	337	6.0	Muskie	7,838	20.7
Ashbrook	175	3.1	Humphrey	7,701	20.3
Unpledged delegates	146	2.6	Wallace	5,802	15.3
			Unpledged delegates	490	1.3
			McCarthy	245	.6
			Jackson	138	.4
			Mills	41	.1
			Yorty	6	—
June 6 **California**					
Nixon	2,058,825	90.1	McGovern	1,550,652	43.5
Ashbrook	224,922	9.8	Humphrey	1,375,064	38.6
Others	175	—	Wallace[1]	268,551	7.5
			Chisholm	157,435	4.4
			Muskie	72,701	2.0
			Yorty	50,745	1.4
			McCarthy	34,203	1.0
			Jackson	28,901	.8
			Lindsay	26,246	.7
			Others	20	—
June 6 **New Jersey**					
Unpledged delegates at large	215,719[3]	100.0	Chisholm	51,433	66.9
			Sanford	25,401	33.1
June 6 **New Mexico**					
Nixon	49,067	88.5	McGovern	51,011	33.3
McCloskey	3,367	6.1	Wallace	44,843	29.3
None of the names shown	3,035	5.5	Humphrey	39,768	25.9
			Muskie	6,411	4.2
			Jackson	4,236	2.8
			None of the names shown	3,819	2.5
			Chisholm	3,205	2.1
June 6 **South Dakota**					
Nixon	52,820	100.0	McGovern	28,017	100.0
TOTALS					
Nixon	5,378,704	86.9	Humphrey	4,121,372	25.8
Unpledged delegates	317,048	5.1	McGovern	4,053,451	25.3
Ashbrook	311,543	5.0	Wallace	3,755,424	23.5
McCloskey	132,731	2.1	Muskie	1,840,217	11.5
Wallace	20,472	.3	McCarthy	553,955	3.5
None of the names shown	5,350	.1	Jackson	505,198	3.2
Others[4]	22,433	.4	Chisholm	430,703	2.7
			Sanford	331,415	2.1
	6,188,281		Lindsay	196,406	1.2
			Yorty	79,446	.5
			Mills	37,401	.2
			Fauntroy	21,217	.1
			Unpledged delegates	19,533	.1
			Kennedy	16,693	.1
			Hartke	11,798	.1
			Mink	8,286	.1
			None of the names shown	6,269	—
			Others[5]	5,181	—
				15,993,965	

* Delegate selection primaries were held in Alabama and New York. In America Votes, Scammon did not record vote totals if the primary was strictly for delegate selection and there was no presidential preference voting.

1. Write-in.
2. No Republican primary in 1972.

3. Figures obtained from Scammon's office. In America Votes, Scammon did not record vote totals if the primary was strictly for delegate selection.
4. In addition to scattered votes, "others" includes Patrick Paulsen, who received 1,211 votes in the New Hampshire primary.
5. In addition to scattered votes, "others" includes Edward T. Coll, who received 280 votes in the New Hampshire primary and 589 votes in the Massachusetts primary.

1976 Primaries*

Republican			Democratic		
	Votes	%		Votes	%
February 24 New Hampshire					
Gerald R. Ford (Mich.)	55,156	49.4	Jimmy Carter (Ga.)	23,373	28.4
Ronald Reagan (Calif.)	53,569	48.0	Morris K. Udall (Ariz.)	18,710	22.7
Others[1]	2,949	2.6	Birch Bayh (Ind.)	12,510	15.2
			Fred R. Harris (Okla.)	8,863	10.8
			Sargent Shriver (Md.)	6,743	8.2
			Hubert H. Humphrey (Minn.)	4,596	5.6
			Henry M. Jackson (Wash.)	1,857	2.3
			George C. Wallace (Ala.)	1,061	1.3
			Ellen McCormack(N.Y.)	1,007	1.2
			Others	3,661	4.8
March 2 Massachusetts					
Ford	115,375	61.2	Jackson	164,393	22.3
Reagan	63,555	33.7	Udall	130,440	17.7
None of the names shown	6,000	3.2	Wallace	123,112	16.7
Others[1]	3,519	1.8	Carter	101,948	13.9
			Harris	55,701	7.6
			Shriver	53,252	7.2
			Bayh	34,963	4.8
			McCormack	25,772	3.5
			Milton J. Shapp (Pa.)	21,693	2.9
			None of the names shown	9,804	1.3
			Humphrey[1]	7,851	1.1
			Edward M. Kennedy (Mass.)[1]	1,623	0.2
			Lloyd Bentsen (Texas)	364	—
			Others	4,905	0.7
March 2 Vermont					
Ford	27,014	84.0	Carter	16,335	42.2
Reagan[1]	4,892	15.2	Shriver	10,699	27.6
Others[1]	251	—	Harris	4,893	12.6
			McCormack	3,324	8.6
			Others	3,463	9.0
March 9 Florida					
Ford	321,982	52.8	Carter	448,844	34.5
Reagan	287,837	47.2	Wallace	396,820	30.5
			Jackson	310,944	23.9
			None of the names shown	37,626	2.9
			Shapp	32,198	2.5
			Udall	27,235	2.1
			Bayh	8,750	.7
			McCormack	7,595	.6
			Shriver	7,084	.5
			Harris	5,397	.4
			Robert C. Byrd (W.Va.)	5,042	.4
			Frank Church (Idaho)	4,906	.4
			Others	7,889	.6
March 16 Illinois					
Ford	456,750	58.9	Carter	630,915	48.1
Reagan	311,295	40.1	Wallace	361,798	27.6
Lar Daly (Ill.)	7,582	1.0	Shriver	214,024	16.3
Others[1]	266	—	Harris	98,862	7.5
			Others[1]	6,315	.5

Republican   # Democratic

	Votes	%		Votes	%
March 23 North Carolina					
Reagan	101,468	52.4	Carter	324,437	53.6
Ford	88,897	45.9	Wallace	210,166	34.7
None of the names shown	3,362	1.7	Jackson	25,749	4.3
			None of the names shown	22,850	3.8
			Udall	14,032	2.3
			Harris	5,923	1.0
			Bentsen	1,675	.3
April 6 Wisconsin					
Ford	326,869	55.2	Carter	271,220	36.6
Reagan	262,126	44.3	Udall	263,771	35.6
None of the names shown	2,234	.3	Wallace	92,460	12.5
Others[1]	583	—	Jackson	47,605	6.4
			McCormack	26,982	3.6
			Harris	8,185	1.1
			None of the names shown	7,154	1.0
			Shriver	5,097	.7
			Bentsen	1,730	.2
			Bayh	1,255	.2
			Shapp	596	.1
			Others[1]	14,473	2.0
April 27 Pennsylvania					
Ford	733,472	92.1	Carter	511,905	37.0
Reagan[1]	40,510	5.1	Jackson	340,340	24.6
Others[1]	22,678	2.8	Udall	259,166	18.7
			Wallace	155,902	11.3
			McCormack	38,800	2.8
			Shapp	32,947	2.4
			Bayh	15,320	1.1
			Harris	13,067	.9
			Humphrey[1]	12,563	.9
			Others	5,032	.3
May 4 District of Columbia					
[2]			Carter	10,521	31.6
			Walter E. Fauntroy (unpledged delegates)	10,149	30.5
			Udall	6,999	21.0
			Walter E. Washington (unpledged delegates)	5,161	15.5
			Harris	461	1.4
May 4 Georgia					
Reagan	128,671	68.3	Carter	419,272	83.4
Ford	59,801	31.7	Wallace	57,594	11.5
			Udall	9,755	1.9
			Byrd	3,628	.7
			Jackson	3,358	.7
			Church	2,477	.5
			Shriver	1,378	.3
			Bayh	824	.2
			Harris	699	.1
			McCormack	635	.1
			Bentsen	277	.1
			Shapp	181	—
			Others	2,393	.5

Republican   # Democratic

May 4 **Indiana**	Votes	%		Votes	%
Reagan	323,779	51.3	Carter	417,480	68.0
Ford	307,513	48.7	Wallace	93,121	15.2
			Jackson	72,080	11.7
			McCormack	31,708	5.2

May 11 **Nebraska**					
Reagan	113,493	54.5	Church	67,297	38.5
Ford	94,542	45.4	Carter	65,833	37.6
Others	379	.1	Humphrey	12,685	7.2
			Kennedy	7,199	4.1
			McCormack	6,033	3.4
			Wallace	5,567	3.2
			Udall	4,688	2.7
			Jackson	2,642	1.5
			Harris	811	.5
			Bayh	407	.2
			Shriver	384	.2
			Others[1]	1,467	.8

May 11 **West Virginia**					
Ford	88,386	56.8	Byrd	331,639	89.0
Reagan	67,306	43.2	Wallace	40,938	11.0

May 18 **Maryland**					
Ford	96,291	58.0	Edmund G. Brown Jr. (Calif.)	286,672	48.4
Reagan	69,680	42.0	Carter	219,404	37.1
			Udall	32,790	5.5
			Wallace	24,176	4.1
			Jackson	13,956	2.4
			McCormack	7,907	1.3
			Harris	6,841	1.2

May 18 **Michigan**					
Ford	690,180	64.9	Carter	307,559	43.4
Reagan	364,052	34.3	Udall	305,134	43.1
Unpledged delegates	8,473	.8	Wallace	49,204	6.9
Others[1]	109	—	Unpledged delegates	15,853	2.2
			Jackson	10,332	1.5
			McCormack	7,623	1.1
			Shriver	5,738	.8
			Harris	4,081	.6
			Others[1]	3,142	.4

May 25 **Arkansas**					
Reagan	20,628	63.4	Carter	314,306	62.6
Ford	11,430	35.1	Wallace	83,005	16.5
Unpledged delegates	483	1.5	Unpledged delegates	57,152	11.4
			Udall	37,783	7.5
			Jackson	9,554	1.9

May 25 **Idaho**					
Reagan	66,743	74.3	Church	58,570	78.7
Ford	22,323	24.9	Carter	8,818	11.9
Unpledged delegates	727	.8	Humphrey	1,700	2.3
			Brown[1]	1,453	2.0
			Wallace	1,115	1.5
			Udall	981	1.3
			Unpledged delegates	964	1.3
			Jackson	485	.7
			Harris	319	.4

Republican   # Democratic

	Votes	%		Votes	%
May 25 Kentucky					
Ford	67,976	50.9	Carter	181,690	59.4
Reagan	62,683	46.9	Wallace	51,540	16.8
Unpledged delegates	1,781	1.3	Udall	33,262	10.9
Others	1,088	.8	McCormack	17,061	5.6
			Unpledged delegates	11,962	3.9
			Jackson	8,186	2.7
			Others	2,305	.8
May 25 Nevada					
Reagan	31,637	66.3	Brown	39,671	52.7
Ford	13,747	28.8	Carter	17,567	23.3
None of the names shown	2,365	5.0	Church	6,778	9.0
			None of the names shown	4,603	6.1
			Wallace	2,490	3.3
			Udall	2,237	3.0
			Jackson	1,896	2.5
May 25 Oregon					
Ford	150,181	50.3	Church	145,394	33.6
Reagan	136,691	45.8	Carter	115,310	26.7
Others[1]	11,663	3.9	Brown[1]	106,812	24.7
			Humphrey	22,488	5.2
			Udall	11,747	2.7
			Kennedy	10,983	2.5
			Wallace	5,797	1.3
			Jackson	5,298	1.2
			McCormack	3,753	.9
			Harris	1,344	.3
			Bayh	743	.2
			Others[1]	2,963	.7
May 25 Tennessee					
Ford	120,685	49.8	Carter	259,243	77.6
Reagan	118,997	49.1	Wallace	36,495	10.9
Unpledged delegates	2,756	1.1	Udall	12,420	3.7
Others[1]	97	—	Church	8,026	2.4
			Unpledged delegates	6,148	1.8
			Jackson	5,672	1.7
			McCormack	1,782	.5
			Harris	1,628	.5
			Brown[1]	1,556	.5
			Shapp	507	.2
			Humphrey[1]	109	—
			Others[1]	492	.1
June 1 Montana					
Reagan	56,683	63.1	Church	63,448	59.4
Ford	31,100	34.6	Carter	26,329	24.6
None of the names shown	1,996	2.2	Udall	6,708	6.3
			None of the names shown	3,820	3.6
			Wallace	3,680	3.4
			Jackson	2,856	2.7
June 1 Rhode Island					
Ford	9,365	65.3	Unpledged delegates	19,035	31.5
Reagan	4,480	31.2	Carter	18,237	30.2
Unpledged delegates	507	3.5	Church	16,423	27.2
			Udall	2,543	4.2
			McCormack	2,468	4.1
			Jackson	756	1.3
			Wallace	507	.8
			Bayh	247	.4
			Shapp	132	.2

Republican

Democratic

	Votes	%		Votes	%
June 1 South Dakota					
Reagan	43,068	51.2	Carter	24,186	41.2
Ford	36,976	44.0	Udall	19,510	33.3
None of the names shown	4,033	4.8	None of the names shown	7,871	13.4
			McCormack	4,561	7.8
			Wallace	1,412	2.4
			Harris	573	1.0
June 8 California			Jackson	558	1.0
Reagan	1,604,836	65.5	Brown	2,013,210	59.0
Ford	845,655	34.5	Carter	697,092	20.4
Others[1]	20	—	Church	250,581	7.3
			Udall	171,501	5.0
			Wallace	102,292	3.0
			Unpledged delegates	78,595	2.3
			Jackson	38,634	1.1
			McCormack	29,242	.9
			Harris	16,920	.5
			Bayh	11,419	.3
			Others[1]	215	—
June 8 New Jersey					
Ford	242,122	100.00	Carter	210,655	58.4
			Church	49,034	13.6
			Jackson	31,820	8.8
			Wallace	31,183	8.6
			McCormack	21,774	6.0
			Others	16,373	4.5
June 8 Ohio					
Ford	516,111	55.2	Carter	593,130	52.3
Reagan	419,646	44.8	Udall	240,342	21.2
			Church	157,884	13.9
			Wallace	63,953	5.6
			Gertrude W. Donahey (unpledged delegates)	43,661	3.9
			Jackson	35,404	3.1

TOTALS

	Votes	%		Votes	%
Ford	5,529,899	53.3	Carter	6,235,609	38.8
Reagan	4,758,325	45.9	Brown	2,449,374	15.3
None of the names shown	19,990	0.2	Wallace	1,995,388	12.4
Unpledged delegates	14,727	0.1	Udall	1,611,754	10.0
Daly	7,582	0.1	Jackson	1,134,375	7.1
Others[3]	43,602	0.4	Church	830,818	5.2
			Byrd	340,309	2.1
	10,374,125		Shriver	304,399	1.9
			Unpledged delegates	248,680	1.5
			McCormack	238,027	1.5
			Harris	234,568	1.5
			None of the names shown	93,728	0.6
			Shapp	88,254	0.5
			Bayh	86,438	0.5
			Humphrey	61,992	0.4
			Kennedy	19,805	0.1
			Bentsen	4,046	—
			Others[4]	75,088	0.5
				16,052,652	

Delegate selection primaries were held in Alabama, New York and Texas. In America Votes, Scammon did not record vote totals if the primary was strictly for delegate selection and there was no presidential preference voting.

1. Write-in.

2. Ford unopposed. No primary held.

3. In addition to scattered write-in votes, "others" include Tommy Klein, who received 1,088 votes in Kentucky.

4. In addition to scattered write-in votes, "others" include Frank Ahern who received 1,487 votes in Georgia; Stanley Arnold, 371 votes in New Hampshire; Arthur O. Blessitt, 828 votes in New Hampshire and 7,889 in Georgia; Frank Bona, 135 votes in New Hampshire and 263 in Georgia; Billy Joe Clegg, 174 votes in New Hampshire; Abram Eisenman, 351 votes in Georgia; John S. Gonas, 2,288 votes in New Jersey; Jesse Gray, 3,574 votes in New Jersey; Robert L. Kelleher, 87 votes in New Hampshire, 1,603 in Massachusetts and 139 in Georgia; Rick Loewenherz, 49 votes in New Hampshire; Frank Lomento, 3,555 votes in New Jersey, Floyd L. Lunger, 3,935 votes in New Jersey; H. R. H. "Fifi" Rockefeller, 2,305 votes in Kentucky; George Roden, 153 votes in Georgia; Ray Rollinson, 3,021 votes in New Jersey; Terry Sanford, 53 votes in New Hampshire and 351 votes in Massachusetts; Bernard B. Schechter, 173 votes in New Hampshire.

1980 Primaries [1]

Republican			Democratic		
	Votes	%		Votes	%

February 17 **Puerto Rico**

March 16

	Votes	%		Votes	%
George Bush (Texas) [2]	111,940	60.1	Jimmy Carter (Ga.)	449,681	51.7
Howard H. Baker Jr. (Tenn.) [3]	68,934	37.0	Edward M. Kennedy (Mass.)	418,068	48.0
Benjamin Fernandez (Calif.)	2,097	1.1	Edmund G. Brown Jr. (Calif.) [5]	1,660	0.2
John B. Connally (Texas) [4]	1,964	1.1	Others	826	0.1
Harold Stassen (N.Y.)	672	0.4			
Robert Dole (Kan.)	483	0.3			
Others	281	0.1			

February 26 **New Hampshire**

	Votes	%		Votes	%
Ronald Reagan (Calif.)	72,983	49.6	Carter	52,692	47.1
Bush	33,443	22.7	Kennedy	41,745	37.3
Baker	18,943	12.1	Brown	10,743	9.6
John B. Anderson (Ill.) [6]	14,458	9.8	Lyndon LaRouche (N.Y.)	2,326	2.1
Philip M. Crane (Ill.)	2,618	1.8	Richard Kay (Ohio)	566	0.5
Connally	2,239	1.5	Others*	3,858	3.4
Others*	1,876	1.3			

March 4 **Massachusetts**

	Votes	%		Votes	%
Bush	124,365	31.0	Kennedy	590,393	65.1
Anderson	122,987	30.7	Carter	260,401	28.7
Reagan	115,334	28.8	Brown	31,498	3.5
Baker	19,366	4.8	Others*	5,368	0.6
Connally	4,714	1.2	No preference	19,663	2.2
Crane	4,669	1.2			
Gerald R. Ford (Mich.) *	3,398	0.8			
Fernandez	374	0.1			
Stassen	218	0.1			
Others*	2,581	0.6			
No preference	2,243	0.6			

March 4 **Vermont**

	Votes	%		Votes	%
Reagan	19,720	30.1	Carter	29,015	73.1
Anderson	19,030	29.0	Kennedy	10,135	25.5
Bush	14,226	21.7	Brown*	358	0.9
Baker	8,055	12.3	LaRouche*	6	
Ford*	2,300	3.5	Others	189	0.5
Crane	1,238	1.9			
Connally	884	1.3			
Stassen	105	0.2			
Others*	53				

March 8 **South Carolina**

	Votes	%
Reagan	79,549	54.7
Connally	43,113	29.6
Bush	21,569	14.8
Baker	773	0.5
Fernandez	171	0.1
Stassen	150	0.1
Dole	117	0.1
Others*	59	

Republican

	Votes	%

Democratic

	Votes	%

March 11 **Alabama**

Republican	Votes	%	Democratic	Votes	%
Reagan	147,352	69.7	Carter	193,734	81.6
Bush	54,730	25.9	Kennedy	31,382	13.2
Crane	5,099	2.4	Brown	9,529	4.0
Baker	1,963	0.9	Others	1,149	0.5
Connally	1,077	0.5	Unpledged delegates	1,670	0.7
Stassen	544	0.3			
Dole	447	0.2			
Others	141				

March 11 **Florida**

Republican	Votes	%	Democratic	Votes	%
Reagan	345,699	56.2	Carter	666,321	60.7
Bush	185,996	30.2	Kennedy	254,727	23.2
Anderson	56,636	9.2	Brown	53,474	4.9
Crane	12,000	2.0	Kay	19,160	1.7
Baker	6,345	1.0	No preference	104,321	9.5
Connally	4,958	0.8			
Stassen	1,377	0.2			
Dole	1,086	0.2			
Fernandez	898	0.1			

March 11 **Georgia**

Republican	Votes	%	Democratic	Votes	%
Reagan	146,500	73.2	Carter	338,772	88.0
Bush	25,293	12.6	Kennedy	32,315	8.4
Anderson	16,853	8.4	Brown	7,255	1.9
Crane	6,308	3.2	Cliff Finch (Miss.)	1,378	0.4
Connally	2,388	1.2	Kay	840	0.2
Baker	1,571	0.8	LaRouche	513	0.1
Fernandez	809	0.4	Unpledged delegates	3,707	1.0
Dole	249	0.1			
Stassen	200	0.1			

March 18 **Illinois**

Republican	Votes	%	Democratic	Votes	%
Reagan	547,355	48.4	Carter	780,787	65.0
Anderson	415,193	36.7	Kennedy	359,875	30.0
Bush	124,057	11.0	Brown	39,168	3.3
Crane	24,865	2.2	LaRouche	19,192	1.6
Baker	7,051	0.6	Anderson*	1,643	0.1
Connally	4,548	0.4	Others*	402	
Dole	1,843	0.2			
Ford*	1,106	0.3			
Others	4,063	0.1			

March 25 **Connecticut**

Republican	Votes	%	Democratic	Votes	%
Bush	70,367	38.6	Kennedy	98,662	46.9
Reagan	61,735	33.9	Carter	87,207	41.5
Anderson	40,354	22.1	LaRouche	5,617	2.7
Baker	2,446	1.3	Brown	5,386	2.6
Crane	1,887	1.0	Unpledged delegates	13,403	6.4
Connally	598	0.3			
Dole	333	0.2			
Fernandez	308	0.2			
Unpledged delegates	4,256	2.3			

Republican	Votes	%	**Democratic**	Votes	%

March 25 New York

			Kennedy	582,757	58.9
			Carter	406,305	41.1

April 1 Kansas

Reagan	179,739	63.0	Carter	109,807	56.6
Anderson	51,924	18.2	Kennedy	61,318	31.6
Bush	35,838	12.6	Brown	9,434	4.9
Baker	3,603	1.3	Finch	629	0.3
Connally	2,067	0.7	Others	1,567	0.8
Fernandez	1,650	0.6	None of the names shown	11,163	5.8
Crane	1,367	0.5			
Stassen	383	0.1			
Others	2,101	0.4			
None of the names shown	6,726	2.4			

April 1 Wisconsin

Reagan	364,898	40.2	Carter	353,662	56.2
Bush	276,164	30.4	Kennedy	189,520	30.1
Anderson	248,623	27.4	Brown	74,496	11.8
Baker	3,298	0.4	LaRouche	6,896	1.1
Crane	2,951	0.3	Finch	1,842	0.3
Connally	2,312	0.3	Others*	509	0.1
Fernandez	1,051	0.1	None of the names shown	2,694	0.4
Stassen	1,010	0.1			
Others*	4,951	0.5			
None of the names shown	2,595	0.3			

April 5 Louisiana

Reagan	31,212	74.9	Carter	199,956	55.7
Bush	7,818	18.8	Kennedy	80,797	22.5
Stassen	126	0.3	Brown	16,774	4.7
Fernandez	84	0.2	Finch	11,153	3.1
Others	222	0.5	Kay	3,362	0.9
None of the names shown	2,221	5.3	Others	5,085	1.4
			Unpledged delegates	41,614	11.6

April 22 Pennsylvania

Bush	626,759	50.5	Kennedy	736,854	45.7
Reagan	527,916	42.5	Carter	732,332	45.4
Baker	30,846	2.5	Brown	37,669	2.3
Anderson	26,890	2.1	Anderson*	9,182	0.6
Connally	10,656	0.9	Bush*	2,074	0.1
Stassen	6,767	0.5	Reagan*	1,097	0.1
Fernandez	2,521	0.2	Ford*	150	
Others	9,056	0.8	No preference	93,865	5.8

May 3 Texas

Reagan	268,798	51.0	Carter	770,390	55.9
Bush	249,819	47.4	Kennedy	314,129	22.8
Unpledged delegates	8,152	1.5	Brown	35,585	2.6
			Unpledged delegates	257,250	18.7

Republican

Democratic

	Votes	%		Votes	%

May 6 District of Columbia

Bush	4,973	66.1	Kennedy	39,561	61.7
Anderson	2,025	26.9	Carter	23,697	36.9
Crane	270	3.6	LaRouche	892	1.4
Stassen	201	2.7			
Fernandez	60	0.8			

May 6 Indiana

Reagan	419,016	73.7	Carter	398,949	67.7
Bush	92,955	16.4	Kennedy	190,492	32.3
Anderson	56,342	9.9			

May 6 North Carolina

Reagan	113,854	67.6	Carter	516,778	70.1
Bush	36,631	21.8	Kennedy	130,684	17.7
Anderson	8,542	5.1	Brown	21,420	2.9
Baker	2,543	1.5	No preference	68,380	9.3
Connally	1,107	0.7			
Dole	629	0.4			
Crane	547	0.3			
No preference	4,538	2.7			

May 6 Tennessee

Reagan	144,625	74.1	Carter	221,658	75.2
Bush	35,274	18.1	Kennedy	53,258	18.1
Anderson	8,722	4.5	Brown	5,612	1.9
Crane	1,574	0.8	Finch	1,663	0.6
Baker*	16		LaRouche	925	0.3
Ford*	14		Others*	49	
Connally*	1		Unpledged delegates	11,515	3.9
Others*	8				
Unpledged delegates	4,976	2.5			

May 13 Maryland

Reagan	80,557	48.2	Carter	226,528	47.5
Bush	68,389	40.9	Kennedy	181,091	38.0
Anderson	16,244	9.7	Brown	14,313	3.0
Crane	2,113	1.3	Finch	4,891	1.0
			LaRouche	4,388	0.9
			Unpledged delegates	45,879	9.6

May 13 Nebraska

Reagan	155,995	76.0	Carter	72,120	46.9
Bush	31,380	15.3	Kennedy	57,826	37.6
Anderson	11,879	5.8	Brown	5,478	3.6
Dole	1,420	0.7	LaRouche	1,169	0.8
Crane	1,062	0.5	Others*	1,247	0.8
Stassen	799	0.4	Unpledged delegates	16,041	10.4
Fernandez	400	0.2			
Others*	2,268	1.1			

	Republican				Democratic		
		Votes	%			Votes	%

May 20 Michigan

Republican	Votes	%	Democratic	Votes	%
Bush	341,998	57.5	Brown	23,043	29.4
Reagan	189,184	31.8	LaRouche	8,948	11.4
Anderson	48,947	8.2	Others*	10,048	12.8
Fernandez	2,248	0.4	Unpledged delegates	36,385	46.4
Stassen	1,938	0.3			
Others*	596	0.1			
Unpledged delegates	10,265	1.7			

May 20 Oregon

Republican	Votes	%	Democratic	Votes	%
Reagan	170,449	54.0	Carter	208,693	56.7
Bush	109,210	34.6	Kennedy	114,651	31.1
Anderson	32,118	10.2	Brown	34,409	9.3
Crane	2,324	0.7	Anderson*	5,407	1.5
Others*	1,265	0.4	Reagan*	2,206	0.6
			Bush*	1,838	0.5

May 27 Arkansas

Republican	Votes	%	Democratic	Votes	%
			Carter	269,375	60.1
			Kennedy	78,542	17.5
			Finch	19,469	4.3
			Unpledged delegates	80,904	18.0

May 27 Idaho

Republican	Votes	%	Democratic	Votes	%
Reagan	111,868	82.9	Carter	31,383	62.2
Anderson	13,130	9.7	Kennedy	11,087	22.0
Bush	5,416	4.0	Brown	2,078	4.1
Crane	1,024	0.8	Unpledged delegates	5,934	11.8
Unpledged delegates	3,441	2.6			

May 27 Kentucky

Republican	Votes	%	Democratic	Votes	%
Reagan	78,072	82.4	Carter	160,819	66.9
Bush	6,861	7.2	Kennedy	55,167	23.0
Anderson	4,791	5.1	Kay	2,609	1.1
Stassen	1,223	1.3	Finch	2,517	1.0
Fernandez	764	0.8	Unpledged delegates	19,219	8.0
Unpledged delegates	3,084	3.3			

May 27 Nevada

Republican	Votes	%	Democratic	Votes	%
Reagan	39,352	83.0	Carter	25,159	37.6
Bush	3,078	6.5	Kennedy	19,296	28.8
None of the names shown	4,965	10.5	None of the names shown	22,493	33.6

June 3 California

Republican	Votes	%	Democratic	Votes	%
Reagan	2,057,923	80.3	Kennedy slate	1,507,142	44.8
Anderson	349,315	13.6	Carter slate	1,266,276	37.6
Bush	125,113	4.9	Brown slate	135,962	4.0
Crane	21,465	0.8	LaRouche slate	71,779	2.1
Fernandez	10,242	0.4	Others*	51	
Others*	14		Unpledged slate	382,759	11.4

Republican

Democratic

	Votes	%		Votes	%

June 3 **New Mexico**

	Votes	%		Votes	%
Reagan	37,982	63.8	Kennedy	73,721	46.3
Anderson	7,171	12.0	Carter	66,621	41.8
Bush	5,892	9.9	LaRouche	4,798	3.0
Crane	4,412	7.4	Finch	4,490	2.8
Fernandez	1,795	3.0	Unpledged delegates	9,734	6.1
Stassen	947	1.6			
Unpledged delegates	1,347	2.3			

June 3 **New Jersey**

	Votes	%		Votes	%
Reagan	225,959	81.3	Kennedy	315,109	56.2
Bush	47,447	17.1	Carter	212,387	37.9
Stassen	4,571	1.6	LaRouche	13,913	2.5
			Unpledged delegates	19,499	3.5

June 3 **Montana**

	Votes	%		Votes	%
Reagan	68,744	86.6	Carter	66,922	51.5
Bush	7,665	9.7	Kennedy	47,671	36.7
No preference	3,014	3.8	No preference	15,466	11.9

June 3 **Ohio**

	Votes	%		Votes	%
Reagan	692,288	80.8	Carter	605,744	51.1
Bush	164,485	19.2	Kennedy	523,874	44.2
			LaRouche	35,268	3.0
			Kay	21,524	1.8

June 3 **Rhode Island**

	Votes	%		Votes	%
Reagan	3,839	72.0	Kennedy	26,179	68.3
Bush	993	18.6	Carter	9,907	25.8
Stassen	107	2.0	LaRouche	1,160	3.0
Fernandez	48	0.9	Brown	310	0.8
Unpledged delegates	348	6.5	Unpledged delegates	771	2.0

June 3 **South Dakota**

	Votes	%		Votes	%
Reagan slate	72,861	82.2	Kennedy slate	33,418	48.6
Bush slate	3,691	4.2	Carter slate	31,251	45.4
Stassen slate	987	1.1	Uncommitted slate	4,094	6.0
No preference slate	5,366	6.1			

June 3 **West Virginia**

	Votes	%		Votes	%
Reagan	115,407	83.6	Carter	197,687	62.2
Bush	19,509	14.1	Kennedy	120,247	37.8
Stassen	3,100	2.2			

June 3 **Mississippi**

	Votes	%
Reagan slate	23,028	89.4
Bush slate	2,105	8.2
Unslated	618	2.4

Republican

TOTALS [7]	Votes	%
Reagan	7,709,793	60.8
Bush	2,958,093	23.3
Anderson	1,572,174	12.4
Baker	112,219	0.9
Crane	97,793	0.8
Connally	80,661	0.6
Stassen	24,753	0.2
Fernandez	23,423	0.2
Dole	7,298	0.1
Unpledged delegates	38,708	0.3
No preference	15,161	0.1
None of the names shown	14,286	0.1
Others [8]	36,089	0.3
	12,690,451	

Democratic

	Votes	%
Carter	9,593,335	51.2
Kennedy	6,963,625	37.1
Brown	573,636	3.1
LaRouche	177,784	1.0
Kay	48,061	0.3
Finch	48,032	0.3
Unpledged delegates	950,378	5.1
No preference	301,695	1.6
None of the names shown	36,350	0.1
Others [9]	54,929	0.3
	18,747,825	

* Write-in vote.

1. In 1980 35 states, the District of Columbia and Puerto Rico held presidential primaries. California Democrats and South Dakota Republicans and Democrats held state-type preference primaries. In New York, Democrats had a presidential preference, but Republicans held primaries for the selection of delegates only, without indication of presidential preference. In Mississippi, Republicans elected delegates by congressional districts pledged to candidates and the vote indicated is for the highest of each slate's candidates in each congressional district. In Arkansas, the Republicans did not hold a primary although Democrats did. In South Carolina, the Democrats did not hold a primary but Republicans did. The vote in Ohio is for delegates at-large pledged to specific candidates and elected as a group. The Republican and Democratic primaries in Puerto Rico were held on two different dates: February 17 and March 16, respectively.

2. Bush withdrew May 26.
3. Baker withdrew March 5.
4. Connally withdrew March 9.
5. Brown withdrew April 1.
6. Anderson withdrew April 24.
7. Totals exclude Puerto Rico, where citizens are unable to vote in the general election.
8. Other vote includes: 4,357 for Alvin J. Jacobsen; 3,757 for V. A. Kelley; 1,063 for R. W. Yeager; 483 for Alvin G. Carris; 355 for Nick Belluso; 311 for William E. Carlson; 244 for Donald Badgley; 67 for C. Leon Pickett; and 25,452 scattered.
9. Other vote includes: 4,022 for Bob Maddox; 609 for William L. Nuckols; 571 for Frank Ahern; 364 for Ray Rollinson, and 47,128 scattered.

Nominating Conventions

Although the presidential nominating convention has been a target of criticism throughout its existence, it has survived to become a traditional fixture of American politics. The longevity and general acceptance of the convention is in large part due to its multiplicity of functions — functions that the convention uniquely combines.

The convention is a nominating body, used by the Democrats, Republicans and most of the principal third parties over the past 150 years. The convention writes a platform, presenting the positions of the party on issues of the campaign. The convention serves as the supreme governing body of the political party, making major decisions on party affairs that in the interim between the conventions are made by the national committee with the guidance of the party chairman. The convention also serves as the ultimate campaign rally, gathering together thousands of party leaders and rank and file members from across the country in an atmosphere that varies widely, sometimes encouraging sober discussion but often resembling a carnival. And the convention serves as a forum for compromise among the diverse elements within a party, allowing the discussion and often the satisfactory solution of differing points of view. There have been many critics of the convention process, but because it successfully combines a multiplicity of functions, the convention has endured.

The convention is an outgrowth of the American political experience. Nowhere is it mentioned in the Constitution, nor has the authority of the convention ever been a subject of congressional legislation. Rather, the convention is the evolutionary result of the American presidential selection process. The convention has been the accepted nominating method of the major political parties since the election of 1832, but internal changes within the convention system have been massive since the early, formative years.

Convention Sites

In the pre-Civil-War period, conventions were frequently held in small buildings, even churches, and attracted only several hundred delegates and a minimum of spectators. Transportation and communications were slow, so most conventions were held in the late spring in a city centrally located geographically. Baltimore, Md., was the most popular convention city in the pre-Civil-War period, hosting the first six Democratic conventions (1832 through 1852), two Whig conventions, one National Republican

convention, and the 1831 Anti-Masonic gathering — America's first national nominating convention.

With the nation's westward expansion, Chicago, Ill., in the heartland of America, emerged as the most frequent convention center. Since hosting its first convention in 1860, Chicago has been the site of 24 major party conventions (14 Republican, 10 Democratic). But in recent years, other factors have emerged to be considered along with geographic centrality in the choice of a convention city. The pledge of a financial contribution by the convention city to the party is a major consideration in site selection. The contribution, made in cash and goods and services, in recent years has often been in the vicinity of $1 million and is used to help defray expenses of the party in running the convention. Adequate hotel and convention hall facilities are also of prime importance, as modern-day conventions attract thousands of delegates, party officials, spectators and media representatives. In the last decade convention security has become an increasingly important factor in site selection. A reason given for the choice of Miami Beach, Florida, by the Republicans in 1968 and by both major parties in 1972 was the city's island location, believed to be a strategic advantage in the control of any disruptive protest demonstrations. For the party that controls the White House, often the overriding factor in any site selection decision is the personal preference of the incumbent president. His choice often carries great weight in the final selection of a convention city.

The choice of the convention site is made by the national committees of the two parties about one year before the convention is to take place and is the first major step in the quadrennial convention process. It is followed several months later by announcement of the convention call, the establishment of the major convention committees — credentials, rules, and platform (resolutions), the appointment of convention officers and finally the holding of the convention itself. While these basic steps in the quadrennial process have undergone little change over the past 150 years, there have been major alterations within the nominating convention system.

The call to the convention sets the date and site of the meeting, and is issued early in each election year, if not before. The call to the first Democratic convention, held in 1832, was issued by the New Hampshire Legislature. Early Whig conventions were called by party members in Congress. With the establishment of national committees later in the 19th century, the function of issuing the convention

Democratic Conventions, 1832–1980

Year	City	Dates	Presidential Nominee	Vice Presidential Nominee	No. of Pres. Ballots
1832	Baltimore	May 21-23	Andrew Jackson	Martin Van Buren	1
1835	Baltimore	May 20-22	Martin Van Buren	Richard M. Johnson	1
1840	Baltimore	May 5-6	Martin Van Buren	—[1]	1
1844	Baltimore	May 27-29	James K. Polk	George M. Dallas	9
1848	Baltimore	May 22-25	Lewis Cass	William O. Butler	4
1852	Baltimore	June 1-5	Franklin Pierce	William R. King	49
1856	Cincinnati	June 2-6	James Buchanan	John C. Breckinridge	17
1860	Charleston	April 23-May 3	Deadlocked		57
	Baltimore	June 18-23	Stephen A. Douglas	Benjamin Fitzpatrick Herschel V. Johnson[2]	2
1864	Chicago	August 29-31	George B. McClellan	George H. Pendleton	1
1868	New York	July 4-9	Horatio Seymour	Francis P. Blair	22
1872	Baltimore	July 9-10	Horace Greeley	Benjamin G. Brown	1
1876	St. Louis	June 27-29	Samuel J. Tilden	Thomas A. Hendricks	2
1880	Cincinnati	June 22-24	Winfield S. Hancock	William H. English	2
1884	Chicago	July 8-11	Grover Cleveland	Thomas A. Hendricks	2
1888	St. Louis	June 5-7	Grover Cleveland	Allen G. Thurman	1
1892	Chicago	June 21-23	Grover Cleveland	Adlai E. Stevenson	1
1896	Chicago	July 7-11	William J. Bryan	Arthur Sewall	5
1900	Kansas City	July 4-6	William J. Bryan	Adlai E. Stevenson	1
1904	St. Louis	July 6-9	Alton S. Parker	Henry G. Davis	1
1908	Denver	July 7-10	William J. Bryan	John W. Kern	1
1912	Baltimore	June 25-July 2	Woodrow Wilson	Thomas R. Marshall	46
1916	St. Louis	June 14-16	Woodrow Wilson	Thomas R. Marshall	1
1920	San Francisco	June 28-July 6	James M. Cox	Franklin D. Roosevelt	43
1924	New York	June 24-July 9	John W. Davis	Charles W. Bryan	103
1928	Houston	June 26-29	Alfred E. Smith	Joseph T. Robinson	1
1932	Chicago	June 27-July 2	Franklin D. Roosevelt	John N. Garner	4
1936	Philadelphia	June 23-27	Franklin D. Roosevelt	John N. Garner	Acclamation
1940	Chicago	July 15-18	Franklin D. Roosevelt	Henry A. Wallace	1
1944	Chicago	July 19-21	Franklin D. Roosevelt	Harry S Truman	1
1948	Philadelphia	July 12-14	Harry S Truman	Alben W. Barkley	1
1952	Chicago	July 21-26	Adlai E. Stevenson	John J. Sparkman	3
1956	Chicago	Aug. 13-17	Adlai E. Stevenson	Estes Kefauver	1
1960	Los Angeles	July 11-15	John F. Kennedy	Lyndon B. Johnson	1
1964	Atlantic City	Aug. 24-27	Lyndon B. Johnson	Hubert H. Humphrey	Acclamation
1968	Chicago	Aug. 26-29	Hubert H. Humphrey	Edmund S. Muskie	1
1972	Miami Beach	July 10-13	George McGovern	Thomas F. Eagleton R. Sargent Shriver[3]	1
1976	New York	July 12-15	Jimmy Carter	Walter F. Mondale	1
1980	New York	Aug. 11-14	Jimmy Carter	Walter F. Mondale	1

1. The 1840 Democratic convention did not nominate a candidate for vice president.

2. The 1860 Democratic convention nominated Benjamin Fitzpatrick, who declined the nomination shortly after the convention adjourned. On June 25 the Democratic National Committee selected Herschel V. Johnson as the party's candidate for vice president.

3. The 1972 Democratic convention nominated Thomas F. Eagleton, who withdrew from the ticket on July 31. On Aug. 8 the Democratic National Committee selected R. Sargent Shriver as the party's candidate for vice president.

call fell to these new party organizations. Each national committee presently has the responsibility for allocating delegates to each state.

Delegate Selection

The method of allocating delegates to the individual states and territories has been modified by both parties in the 20th century. Throughout the existence of the convention system in the 19th century, both the Democrats and Republicans distributed votes to the states based on their Electoral College strength. The first deviation from this procedure was made by the Republicans after their divisive 1912 convention, in which President William Howard Taft won renomination over former President Theodore Roosevelt, due largely to nearly solid support from the South — a region vastly over-represented in relation to its number of

Republican Conventions, 1856-1980

Year	City	Dates	Presidential Nominee	Vice Presidential Nominee	No. of Pres. Ballots
1856	Philadelphia	June 17-19	John C. Fremont	William L. Dayton	2
1860	Chicago	May 16-18	Abraham Lincoln	Hannibal Hamlin	3
1864	Baltimore	June 7-8	Abraham Lincoln	Andrew Johnson	1
1868	Chicago	May 20-21	Ulysses S. Grant	Schuyler Colfax	1
1872	Philadelphia	June 5-6	Ulysses S. Grant	Henry Wilson	1
1876	Cincinnati	June 14-16	Rutherford B. Hayes	William A. Wheeler	7
1880	Chicago	June 2-8	James A. Garfield	Chester A. Arthur	36
1884	Chicago	June 3-6	James G. Blaine	John A. Logan	4
1888	Chicago	June 19-25	Benjamin Harrison	Levi P. Morton	8
1892	Minneapolis	June 7-10	Benjamin Harrison	Whitelaw Reid	1
1896	St. Louis	June 16-18	William McKinley	Garret A. Hobart	1
1900	Philadelphia	June 19-21	William McKinley	Theodore Roosevelt	1
1904	Chicago	June 21-23	Theodore Roosevelt	Charles W. Fairbanks	1
1908	Chicago	June 16-19	William H. Taft	James S. Sherman	1
1912	Chicago	June 18-22	William H. Taft	James S. Sherman Nicholas Murray Butler[1]	1
1916	Chicago	June 7-10	Charles E. Hughes	Charles W. Fairbanks	3
1920	Chicago	June 8-12	Warren G. Harding	Calvin Coolidge	10
1924	Cleveland	June 10-12	Calvin Coolidge	Charles G. Dawes	1
1928	Kansas City	June 12-15	Herbert Hoover	Charles Curtis	1
1932	Chicago	June 14-16	Herbert Hoover	Charles Curtis	1
1936	Cleveland	June 9-12	Alfred M. Landon	Frank Knox	1
1940	Philadelphia	June 24-28	Wendell L. Willkie	Charles L. McNary	6
1944	Chicago	June 26-28	Thomas E. Dewey	John W. Bricker	1
1948	Philadelphia	June 21-25	Thomas E. Dewey	Earl Warren	3
1952	Chicago	July 7-11	Dwight D. Eisenhower	Richard M. Nixon	1
1956	San Francisco	Aug. 20-23	Dwight D. Eisenhower	Richard M. Nixon	1
1960	Chicago	July 25-28	Richard M. Nixon	Henry Cabot Lodge	1
1964	San Francisco	July 13-16	Barry Goldwater	William E. Miller	1
1968	Miami Beach	Aug. 5-8	Richard M. Nixon	Spiro T. Agnew	1
1972	Miami Beach	Aug. 21-23	Richard M. Nixon	Spiro T. Agnew	1
1976	Kansas City	Aug. 16-19	Gerald R. Ford	Robert Dole	1
1980	Detroit	July 14-17	Ronald Reagan	George Bush	1

1. The 1912 Republican convention nominated James S. Sherman, who died on Oct. 30. The Republican National Committee subsequently selected Nicholas Murray Butler to receive the Republican electoral votes for vice president.

Source for Data on Conventions: Bain, Richard C. and Parris, Judith H. *Convention Decisions and Voting Records*, Brookings Institution, Washington, D.C. 1973.

Republican voters. Before their 1916 convention the Republicans reduced the allocation of votes to the Southern states, marking the first major move by either party in modifying its delegate allocation method. At their 1924 convention the Republicans applied the first bonus system, by which states were awarded extra votes for supporting the Republican presidential candidate in the previous election. The concept of bonus votes, applied as a reward to the states for supporting the party ticket, has been used and expanded by both parties since that time.

The Democrats first used a bonus system in 1944, completing a compromise arrangement with Southern states for abolishing the party's controversial two-thirds nominating rule. Since then, both parties have used various delegate allocation formulas. At their 1972 convention the Republicans revised the method used in allocating delegates and added more than 900 new delegate slots. The Ripon Society, an organization of liberal Republicans, sued to have the new rules overturned. They argued that, be-

cause of the extra delegates awarded to states that voted Republican in the previous presidential election, small Southern and Western states were favored at the expense of the more populous but less Republican Eastern states. The challenge failed when the Supreme Court in February 1976 refused to hear the case and thus let stand a U.S. Court of Appeals decision upholding the rules.

Only 116 delegates from 13 states attended the initial national nominating convention held by the Anti-Masons in 1831, but with the addition of more states and the adoption of increasingly complex voting allocation formulas by the major parties, the size of conventions spiraled. The 1976 Republican convention had 2,259 delegates, while the Democrats in the same year had 3,075 delegates (casting 3,008 votes). The expanded size in part reflected the democratization of the conventions, with less command by a few party leaders and the dramatic growth of youth, women and minority delegates. Increased representation by such groups was one of the major reasons given by the

Republicans for the 60 percent increase in delegate strength authorized by the 1972 convention (and effective for the 1976 gathering). The Democrats adopted new rules in June 1978 expanding the number of delegates by 10 percent to provide extra representation for state and local officials. The new rules also required that women account for at least 50 percent of the delegates to the 1980 convention.

With the increased size of conventions has come a formalization in the method of delegate selection. In the formative years of the convention system, delegate selection was often haphazard and informal. At the Democratic convention in 1835, the state of Maryland had 188 delegates to cast the state's 10 votes. On the other hand, the 15 votes for the state of Tennessee were cast by a traveling businessman, who inadvertently happened to be in the convention city at the time of the convention. While the number of delegates and the number of votes allocated tended to be equal or nearly so later in the 19th century, domination of national conventions was frequently exercised by a few party bosses.

Two basic methods of delegate selection were employed in the 19th century and continued to be used into the 20th: the caucus method, by which delegates were chosen by meetings at the local or state level; and the appointment method, by which delegates were appointed by the governor or a powerful state leader.

Presidential Primaries

A revolutionary new mechanism for delegate selection emerged during the early 1900s: the presidential primary election in which delegates were elected directly by the voters. Initially popular during the progressive era, interest in the primary system waned and was not revived until after World War II. The system flourished in the 1970s, and by 1980 presidential primaries reached the record number of 37.

In October 1975 the Democratic National Committee (DNC) established a commission, headed by Michigan State Chairman Morley Winograd, to study the effect of the growing number of presidential primaries. The following year it was given the additional job of reviewing the delegate selection rules.

The Winograd Commission, as it came to be known, was composed of 58 members from the diverse elements of the Democratic Party. Its final recommendations were made in January 1978 and adopted, after some modifications, by the DNC at a June 1978 meeting.

Party activists criticized the commission's revisions, charging that it was chipping away some of the rules adopted in the previous 10 years that ensured openness and grass-roots participation, while substituting a set of revisions that was a thinly disguised effort to facilitate President Carter's renomination in 1980.

Winograd claimed that his commission, rather than making drastic revisions, had merely "fine tuned" previously adopted rules. He argued that the basic objective of earlier rules commissions to stimulate grass-roots participation had been accomplished. Winograd added that while some activists might have desired sweeping reform, there was little sentiment in the party as a whole for major rules changes.

Among the commission's revisions were rules to shorten the period when the delegate selection season could be started in every state from six to three months (stretching from the second Tuesday in March to the second Tuesday in June), to require primary states to set candidate filing deadlines 30 to 90 days before the election, to increase the size of state delegations by 10 percent to accommodate state party and elected officials and to limit participation in the delegate selection process to Democrats only. Banned by this last rule were crossover primaries where voters could participate in the Democratic election without designating their party affiliation.

No exemption was to be permitted for crossovers in 1980 (as had been allowed in 1976) but states in violation of the other rules could apply for exemptions if they were unable to change state laws to comply with the new rules.

Credentials Disputes

Before the opening of a convention, the national committee compiles a temporary roll of delegates. The roll is referred to the convention's credentials committee, which holds hearings on the challenges and makes recommendations to the convention, the final arbiter of all disputes.

Some of the most bitter convention battles have concerned the seating of contested delegations. In the 20th century most of the heated credentials fights have concerned delegations from the South. In the Republican Party the challenges focused on the power of the Republican state organizations to dictate the selection of delegates. The issue was hottest in 1912 and 1952, when the party throughout most of the South was a skeletal structure whose power was largely restricted to selection of convention delegates. Within the Democratic Party the question of Southern credentials emerged after World War II on the volatile issues of civil rights and party loyalty. Important credentials challenges on these issues occurred at the 1948, 1952, 1964 and 1968 Democratic conventions.

There were numerous credentials challenges at the 1972 Democratic convention, but unlike its immediate predecessors the challenges involved delegations from across the nation and focused on violations of the party's newly adopted guidelines.

After their 1952 credentials battle, the Republicans established a contest committee within the national committee to review credentials challenges before the convention. After their divisive 1968 convention the Democrats also created a formal credentials procedure within the national committee to review all challenges before the opening of the convention.

Equally important to the settlement of credentials challenges are the rules under which the convention operates. The Republican Party adopts a completely new set of rules at every convention. Although large portions of the existing rules are enacted each time, general revision is always possible.

After its 1968 convention the Democratic Party set out to reform itself and the convention system. The Commission on Rules and the Commission on Party Structure and Delegate Selection, both created by the 1968 convention, proposed many changes that were accepted by the national committee. As a result, a formal set of rules was adopted for the first time at the party's 1972 convention.

Two-Thirds and Unit Rules

Although not having a formal set of rules before 1972, the Democratic Party throughout the bulk of its history operated with two critical and controversial rules never used by the Republicans: the unit rule and the two-thirds nominating rule. The unit rule enabled the majority of a delegation, if authorized by its state party, to cast the entire vote of the delegation for one candidate or position. In use since the earliest Democratic conventions, the unit rule was abolished by the 1968 convention.

From its first convention in 1832 until its elimination over a century later at the 1936 convention, the Democrats employed the two-thirds nominating rule, which required any candidate for president or vice president to win not just a simple majority but a two-thirds majority. Viewed as a boon to the South since it allowed that region a virtual veto power over any possible nominee, the rule was abolished with the stipulation that the South would receive an increased vote allocation at later conventions.

In its century of use the two-thirds rule frequently produced protracted, multi-ballot conventions, often giving the Democrats a degree of turbulence the Republicans, requiring only a simple majority, did not have. Between 1832 and 1932, seven Democratic conventions took more than 10 ballots to select a presidential candidate. In contrast, in their entire convention history (1856 through 1976), the Republicans have had just one convention that required more than 10 ballots to select a presidential candidate.

One controversy that surfaced during the 1980 Democratic Party convention concerned a convention rule that bound delegates to vote on the first ballot for the candidates under whose banner they had been elected. Supporters of Sen. Edward M. Kennedy, D-Mass., had devoted their initial energies to prying the nomination from incumbent President Jimmy Carter by trying unsuccessfully to open the convention by defeating that rule. The final tally on the rule showed 1,936.42 delegates favoring the binding rule and 1,390.580 opposing it. Passage of the binding rule assured Carter's renomination, and shortly after the vote, Kennedy ended his nine-month challenge to the president by announcing that his name would not be placed in nomination Aug. 13.

Convention Officers

Credentials, rules and platform are the major convention committees, but each party has additional committees including one in charge of convention arrangements. Within the Republican Party the arrangements committee recommends a slate of convention officers to the national committee, which in turn refers the names to the committee on permanent organization for confirmation. The people the committee chooses are subject to the approval of the convention. In the Democratic Party, this function is performed by the rules committee.

Both in the Democratic and Republican parties, the presiding officer during the bulk of the convention is the permanent chairman. Over the past quarter century the position has usually gone to the party's leader in the House of Representatives. However, this loose precedent was broken in the Democratic Party by a rule adopted at the 1972 convention requiring that the position alternate every four years between the sexes.

Party Platforms

The adoption of a party platform is one of the principal functions of a convention. The platform committee is charged with the responsibility of writing a party platform to be presented to the convention for its approval.

The main problem of a platform committee is to write a platform all party candidates can use in their campaigns. For this reason, platforms often fit the description given them by the late Wendell L. Willkie, Republican presidential candidate in 1940: "fusions of ambiguity."

Despite the best efforts of platform-builders to compromise their differences in the comparative privacy of the committee room, they sometimes encounter so controversial a subject that it cannot be compromised. Under these conditions, dissident committee members often submit a minority report to the convention floor. Open floor fights are not unusual and like credentials battles, often serve as an indicator of the strength of the various candidates.

When the party has an incumbent president, the platform is often drafted in the White House, or at least approved by the president. Rarely is a platform adopted by a party that criticizes its incumbent president.

The first platform was adopted by the Democrats in 1840. It was a short document less than 1,000 words long. Since then the platforms with few exceptions have grown longer and longer, covering more issues and making an appeal to more interest groups. The platform adopted by the Republicans in 1976 was nearly 20,000 words long. The Democrats, however, bucked the trend toward longer platforms by adopting one in 1976 that was about half the length of their 25,000-word 1972 document. However, the Democrats' 1980 platform contained a record 40,000 words, and the Republicans' was almost as long.

The Republicans' 1980 platform mirrored the convention's emphasis on party unity and generally followed front-runner Ronald Reagan's wishes, in contrast to 1976, when platform deliberations had been marked by discord between the Reagan faction and incumbent President Gerald R. Ford. The 1980 platform was more a blueprint for victory in November than a definitive statement of party views. Rather than slug it out over specifics, the party's moderate and conservative wings agreed to blur their differences in order to appear united, to broaden the party's appeal and to smooth the way to the White House for their nominee. On a few issues, platform writers veered from traditional Republican positions. On others, they went out of their way to embrace policies that meshed with Reagan's views more than their own. But for the most part, they managed to fashion a policy statement that pleased no party faction entirely but with which all could live reasonably.

In contrast to the Republicans' harmony, the 1980 Democratic convention was marked by bitter contests over the party platform that was adopted Aug. 13 after two days of prolonged and sometimes raucus debate that pitted Carter against Kennedy and a coalition of special interest groups. The final document was filled with so many concessions to the Kennedy forces that it won only a halfhearted endorsement from the president.

In many key areas the platform bore little resemblance to the document that Carter operatives took to the first platform drafting meeting June 17. During that session numerous minor changes proposed by Kennedy backers were accepted. Then, two weeks before the convention, Carter began to yield on more substantive issues. By the time the platform debate started, Carter had accepted eight of Kennedy's minority reports. During the debate, six other minority planks were adopted either with Carter's acquiescence or in spite of his opposition.

Selection By Caucus Method

Although about three-fourths of the delegates to the 1980 nominating conventions were chosen in presidential primaries, party caucuses also had a share of the limelight. In 1980 15 states used the caucus method to select delegates to the nominating conventions, while 27 states used the primary method and 8 states employed a hybrid method of primaries and caucuses. Indeed, the Jan. 21, 1980, Iowa precinct caucuses assumed an importance that rivaled the traditionally important New Hampshire primary. In the process, the Iowa caucuses raised public consciousness of a delegate selection method that had been on the decline throughout the last decade.

The impact of caucuses in the 1970s decreased as the number of primaries grew dramatically. During the 1960s, a candidate sought to run well in primary states mainly to have a bargaining chip with which to deal with powerful leaders in the caucus states. Republicans Barry Goldwater in 1964 and Richard Nixon in 1968 and Democrat Hubert H. Humphrey in 1968 all built up solid majorities among caucus state delegates that carried them to their parties' nominations. Humphrey did not even enter a primary in 1968.

But since 1968 candidates have placed their principal emphasis on primary campaigning. First George McGovern, D-S.D. — and then incumbent Republican President Gerald R. Ford and Democratic challenger Jimmy Carter in 1976 — all won their parties' nominations by winning a large majority of the primary state delegates. Neither McGovern nor Ford won a majority of the caucus state delegates. Carter was able to win a majority only after his opponents' campaigns collapsed.

Complex Method

Compared to a primary, the caucus system is relatively complex. Instead of focusing on a single primary election ballot, the caucus presents a multi-tiered system that involves meetings scheduled over several weeks, sometimes even months. While there is mass participation at the first level only, meetings at this step often last several hours and attract only the most enthusiastic and dedicated party members.

The operation of the caucus varies from state to state, and each party has its own set of rules. But most use a process that begins with precinct caucuses or some other type of local mass meeting open to all party voters. Participants, often publicly declaring their votes, elect delegates to the next stage in the process.

In smaller states such as Delaware and Hawaii, delegates are elected directly to a state convention, where the national convention delegates are chosen.

In larger states like Iowa, there is at least one more step. Most frequently, delegates are elected at the precinct caucuses to county conventions, where the national convention delegates are chosen. In Iowa, Democrats hold their district conventions in April and their state convention in mid-June. Iowa Republicans hold district caucuses during the state convention in early June.

Participation, even at the first level of the caucus process, is usually much lower than in primary states. In few states did caucus turnout exceed 10 percent of those eligible to participate in 1976. Caucus participants usually are local party leaders and activists, not newcomers to the process. Many rank-and-file voters find a caucus complex and confusing; others find it intimidating.

In a caucus state the focus is on one-on-one campaigning. Time, not money, is the most valuable resource. Because organization and personal campaigning are so important, an early start is far more crucial in a caucus state than a primary. And because only a small segment of the electorate is targeted in most caucus states, candidates usually use media advertising sparingly. On the average, candidates in 1976 spent about $5 in every primary state for every $1 they spent in a caucus state.

Although the basic steps in the caucus process are the same for both parties, the rules that govern them are vastly different. Democratic rules have been revamped substantially since 1968, establishing national standards for grass-roots participation. Republican rules have remained largely unchanged with the states given wide latitude in drawing up their delegate selection plans. Democratic caucuses are open to Democrats only. Republicans allow crossovers where state law permits, creating a wide range of variations. The first step of the Democratic caucus process must be open, well-publicized mass meetings. In most states Republicans do the same. Generally, voters may only participate in the election of local party officials, who meet to begin the caucus process.

Caucus Revival

The most tangible evidence of a revival of the caucus process is found in the percentage of delegates elected from caucus states. For both parties this figure was on a sharp decline throughout the 1970s. But Democrats broke the downward trend and actually elected more delegates by the caucus process in 1980 than in 1976. The principal reason for the upward swing was that two of the largest delegations — Texas and Michigan — switched from primaries to caucuses to choose delegates. Those two switches more than offset the moves of the Democratic parties in Connecticut, Kansas, Louisiana, New Mexico and Puerto Rico from caucuses to primaries.

Throughout the 1970s, Republicans elected a larger proportion of their delegates from caucus states than did the Democrats. But that changed in 1980, with only 24 percent of the GOP convention coming from caucus states (compared to 31 percent in 1976 and 53 percent in 1968).

During the 1980 presidential campaign both Carter and Reagan reaped the harvest of early organization and grass-roots strength by garnering substantial leads in the caucus states. Carter won 64 percent of Democratic delegates in caucus states compared to 58 percent in primary states, while Reagan won 83 percent of caucus-selected delegates and 78 percent of the delegates elected in primaries.

Third Party Platforms

Throughout American history, many daring and controversial political platforms adopted by third parties have been rejected as too radical in their own time by the major parties. Yet these proposals have later won popular acceptance, made their way into the major party platforms — and into law.

Ideas such as the graduated income tax, popular election of senators, women's suffrage, minimum wages, social security, day-care centers and the 18-year-old vote were advocated by Populists, Progressives and other independents long before they were finally accepted by the nation as a whole.

The radical third parties and their platforms have been anathema to the established wisdom of the day, denounced as impractical, dangerous, destructive of moral virtues and even traitorous. They have been anti-establishment and more far-reaching in their proposed solutions to problems than the major parties have dared to be.

In contrast to the third parties, Democrats and Republicans traditionally have been much more chary of adopting radical platform planks. Trying to appeal to a broad range of voters, the two major parties have tended to compromise differences or to turn down controversial planks.

The Democratic Party has been more ready than the Republicans to adopt once-radical ideas, but there is usually a considerable time lag between their origin in third parties and their eventual adoption in Democratic platforms. For example, while the Democrats by 1912 had adopted many of the Populist planks of the 1890s, the Bull Moose Progressives of that year were already way ahead of them in proposals for social legislation. Not until 1932 were many of the 1912 Progressive planks adopted by the Democrats. Similarly, not until the 1960s did Democratic platforms incorporate many of the more far-reaching proposals put forward by the 1948 Progressives.

Communications and the Media

Major changes in the national nominating convention have resulted from the massive advances in transportation and communication particularly evident in the 20th century.

A major impact of the revolution in transportation has affected the scheduling of conventions. In the 19th century, conventions were sometimes held a year or more before the election and at the latest were completed by late spring of the election year. With the ability of people to assemble quickly, conventions in recent years have been held later in the election year, usually in July or August. Advances in transportation have also affected site location. Geographic centrality is no longer the primary consideration in the selection of a convention city. Increasingly, coastal cities have been chosen as convention hosts.

The invention of new means of communication, particularly television, have had a further impact on the convention system. The changes spurred by the media have primarily been cosmetic ones, designed to give the convention a look of efficiency that was not so necessary in earlier days. As the conduct of the convention has undergone closer scrutiny by the American electorate, both parties have made major efforts to cut back the frivolity and hoopla, and to accentuate the more sober aspects of the convention process.

Radio coverage of conventions began in 1924; television coverage was initiated 16 years later. One of the first changes inspired by the media age was the termination of the custom that a presidential candidate not appear at the convention, but accept his nomination in a ceremony several weeks later. Franklin D. Roosevelt was the first major party candidate to break this tradition, when, in 1932, he delivered his acceptance speech in person before the Democratic convention. Thomas E. Dewey 12 years later became the first Republican nominee to give his acceptance speech to the convention. Since then the final activity of both the Democratic and Republican conventions has been the delivery of the acceptance speeches by the vice presidential and presidential nominees.

In addition to curbing the circus-like aspects of the convention, party leaders in recent years have streamlined the schedule, with the assumption that the interest level of most of the viewing public for politics is limited. The result has been shorter speeches and generally fewer roll calls than at those conventions in the pre-television era.

Showmanship

Party leaders desire to put on a good show for the viewing public with the hope of winning votes for their party in November. The convention is a showcase, designed to show the party as both a model of democracy and an efficient, harmonious body. The schedule of convention activities is drawn up with an eye on the peak evening television viewing hours. There is an attempt to put the party's major selling points — the highly partisan keynote speech, the nominating ballots, and the candidates' acceptance speeches — on in prime time. As well, with an equal awareness of the television audience, party leaders often try to keep evidence of bitter party factionalism — such as explosive credentials and platform battles — out of the peak viewing period.

In the media age, the appearance of fairness is important, and in a sense, this need to look fair and open has assisted the movement in recent years for party reform. Some influential party leaders, skeptical of reform of the convention, have found resistance difficult in the glare of television.

Before the revolution in the means of transportation and communication, conventions met in relative anonymity. Today, the convention is held in all the privacy of a fishbowl, with every action and every rumor closely scrutinized. It has become a media event, and as such has become a target for political demonstrations that can be not only an embarrassment to the party but a security problem as well.

But in spite of its difficulties, the convention system has survived. As the nation has grown over the past century and a half, the convention has evolved as well, changing its form but retaining its variety of functions which accounts for the remarkable longevity of the convention system. Criticism has been leveled at the convention, but no substitute has yet been offered that would nominate a presidential ticket, adopt a party platform, act as the supreme governing body of the party and serve as a massive campaign rally and propaganda forum. In addition to these functions, a convention is a place where compromise can take place — compromise often mandatory in a major political party that combines viewpoints that stretch across the political spectrum.

Political Party Nominees, 1831-1980

The following pages contain a comprehensive list of major and minor party nominees for president and vice president since 1831 when the first nominating convention was held by the Anti-Masonic Party.

In many cases, minor parties made only token efforts at a presidential campaign. Often, third party candidates declined to run after being nominated by the convention, or their names appeared on the ballots of only a few states. In some cases the names of minor candidates did not appear on any state ballots and they received only a scattering of write-in votes, if any. As a result, some of these candidates do not appear in the presidential elections returns. *(pp. 83-130)*

The basic source used to compile the list was Joseph Nathan Kane's *Facts About the Presidents,* 3rd edition, The H. W. Wilson Co., New York, 1974. To verify the names appearing in Kane, Congressional Quarterly consulted the following additional sources: Richard M. Scammon's *America at the Polls,* University of Pittsburgh Press, 1965; *America Votes 8* (1968), Congressional Quarterly, 1969; *America Votes 10* (1972), Congressional Quarterly, 1973; *Encyclopedia of American History,* edited by Richard B. Morris, Harper and Row, New York, 1965; *Dictionary of American Biography,* Charles Scribner's Sons, 1928-1936; *Facts on File,* Facts on File Inc., New York 1945-75; *History of U.S. Political Parties,* Vols. I-IV, edited by Arthur M. Schlesinger, Bowker, New York, 1973; *History of American Presidential Elections, 1789-1968,* edited by Arthur M. Schlesinger, McGraw Hill, New York, 1971; and *Who Was Who in America,* Vol. I-V (1607-1968), Marquis Who's Who, Chicago. The source for the 1976 and 1980 candidates was Richard M. Scammon's *America Votes 12* (1976), and *America Votes 14* (1981).

When these sources contained information in conflict with Kane, the conflicting information is included in a footnote. Where a candidate appears in Kane, *but could not be verified in another source,* an asterisk appears beside the candidate's name on the list. *(Footnotes, p. 78)*

Election of 1832

Democratic Party
President: Andrew Jackson, Tennessee
Vice President: Martin Van Buren, New York
National Republican Party
President: Henry Clay, Kentucky
Vice President: John Sergeant, Pennsylvania
Independent Party
President: John Floyd, Virginia
Vice President: Henry Lee, Massachusetts
Anti-Masonic Party
President: William Wirt, Maryland
Vice President: Amos Ellmaker, Pennsylvania

Election of 1836

Democratic Party
President: Martin Van Buren, New York
Vice President: Richard Mentor Johnson, Kentucky
Whig Party
President: William Henry Harrison, Hugh Lawson White, Daniel Webster
Vice President: Francis Granger, John Tyler.
The Whigs nominated regional candidates in 1836 hoping that each candidate would carry his region and deny Democrat Van Buren an electoral vote majority. Webster was the Whig candidate in Massachusetts; Harrison in the rest of New England, the middle Atlantic states and the West; and White in the South.
Granger was the running mate of Harrison and Webster. Tyler was White's running mate.

Election of 1840

Whig Party
President: William Henry Harrison, Ohio
Vice President: John Tyler, Virginia
Democratic Party
President: Martin Van Buren, New York

The Democratic convention adopted a resolution which left the choice of vice presidential candidates to the states. Democratic electors divided their vice presidential votes among incumbent Richard M. Johnson (48 votes), Littleton W. Tazewell (11 votes) and James K. Polk (1 vote).
Liberty Party
President: James Gillespie Birney, New York
Vice President: Thomas Earle, Pennsylvania

Election of 1844

Democratic Party
President: James Knox Polk, Tennessee
Vice President: George Mifflin Dallas, Pennsylvania
Whig Party
President: Henry Clay, Kentucky
Vice President: Theodore Frelinghuysen, New Jersey
Liberty Party
President: James Gillespie Birney, New York
Vice President: Thomas Morris, Ohio
National Democratic
President: John Tyler, Virginia
Vice President: None
Tyler withdrew from the race in favor of the Democrat, Polk.

Election of 1848

Whig Party
President: Zachary Taylor, Louisiana
Vice President: Millard Fillmore, New York
Democratic Party
President: Lewis Cass, Michigan
Vice President: William Orlando Butler, Kentucky
Free Soil Party
President: Martin Van Buren, New York
Vice President: Charles Francis Adams, Massachusetts
Free Soil (Barnburners—Liberty Party)
President: John Parker Hale, New Hampshire
Vice President: Leicester King, Ohio
Later John Parker Hale relinquished the nomination.

National Liberty Party
President: Gerrit Smith, New York
Vice President: Charles C. Foote, Michigan

Election of 1852

Democratic Party
President: Franklin Pierce, New Hampshire
Vice President: William Rufus De Vane King, Alabama
Whig Party
President: Winfield Scott, New Jersey
Vice President: William Alexander Graham, North Carolina
Free Soil
President: John Parker Hale, New Hampshire
Vice President: George Washington Julian, Indiana

Election of 1856

Democratic Party
President: James Buchanan, Pennsylvania
Vice President: John Cabell Breckinridge, Kentucky
Republican Party
President: John Charles Fremont, California
Vice President: William Lewis Dayton, New Jersey
American (Know-Nothing) Party
President: Millard Fillmore, New York
Vice President: Andrew Jackson Donelson, Tennessee
Whig Party (the "Silver Grays")
President: Millard Fillmore, New York
Vice President: Andrew Jackson Donelson, Tennessee
North American Party
President: Nathaniel Prentice Banks, Massachusetts
Vice President: William Freame Johnson, Pennsylvania
    Banks and Johnson declined the nominations and gave their support to the Republicans.

Election of 1860

Republican Party
President: Abraham Lincoln, Illinois
Vice President: Hannibal Hamlin, Maine
Democratic Party
President: Stephen Arnold Douglas, Illinois
Vice President: Herschel Vespasian Johnson, Georgia
Southern Democratic Party
President: John Cabell Breckinridge, Kentucky
Vice President: Joseph Lane, Oregon
Constitutional Union Party
President: John Bell, Tennessee
Vice President: Edward Everett, Massacusetts

Election of 1864

Republican Party
President: Abraham Lincoln, Illinois
Vice President: Andrew Johnson, Tennessee
Democratic Party
President: George Brinton McClellan, New York
Vice President: George Hunt Pendleton, Ohio
Independent Republican Party
President: John Charles Fremont, California
Vice President: John Cochrane, New York
    Fremont and Cochrane declined and gave their support to the Republican Party nominees

Election of 1868

Republican Party
President: Ulysses Simpson Grant, Illinois
Vice President: Schuyler Colfax, Indiana
Democratic Party
President: Horatio Seymour, New York
Vice President: Francis Preston Blair, Jr., Missouri

Election of 1872

Republican Party
President: Ulysses Simpson Grant, Illinois
Vice President: Henry Wilson, Massachusetts

Liberal Republican Party
President: Horace Greeley, New York
Vice President: Benjamin Gratz Brown, Missouri
Independent Liberal Republican Party (Opposition Party)
President: William Slocum Groesbeck, Ohio
Vice President: Frederick Law Olmsted, New York
Democratic Party
President: Horace Greeley, New York
Vice President: Benjamin Gratz Brown, Missouri
Straight-out Democratic Party
President: Charles O'Conor, New York
Vice President: John Quincy Adams, Massachusetts
Prohibition Party
President: James Black, Pennsylvania
Vice President: John Russell, Michigan
People's Party (Equal Rights Party)
President: Victoria Claflin Woodhull, New York
Vice President: Frederick Douglass
Labor Reform Party
President: David Davis, Illinois
Vice President: Joel Parker, New Jersey
Liberal Republican Party of Colored Men
President: Horace Greeley, New York
Vice President: Benjamin Gratz Brown, Missouri
National Working Men's Party
President: Ulysses Simpson Grant, Illinois
Vice President: Henry Wilson, Massachusetts

Election of 1876

Republican Party
President: Rutherford Birchard Hayes, Ohio
Vice President: William Almon Wheeler, New York
Democratic Party
President: Samuel Jones Tilden, New York
Vice President: Thomas Andrews Hendricks, Indiana
Greenback Party
President: Peter Cooper, New York
Vice President: Samuel Fenton Cary, Ohio
Prohibition Party
President: Green Clay Smith, Kentucky
Vice President: Gideon Tabor Stewart, Ohio
American National Party
President: James B. Walker, Illinois
Vice President: Donald Kirkpatrick, New York*

Election of 1880

Republican Party
President: James Abram Garfield, Ohio
Vice President: Chester Alan Arthur, New York
Democratic Party
President: Winfield Scott Hancock, Pennsylvania
Vice President: William Hayden English, Indiana
Greenback Labor Party
President: James Baird Weaver, Iowa
Vice President: Benjamin J. Chambers, Texas
Prohibition Party
President: Neal Dow, Maine
Vice President: Henry Adams Thompson, Ohio
American Party
President: John Wolcott Phelps, Vermont
Vice President: Samuel Clarke Pomeroy, Kansas*

Election of 1884

Democratic Party
President: Grover Cleveland, New York
Vice President: Thomas Andrews Hendricks, Indiana
Republican Party
President: James Gillespie Blaine, Maine
Vice President: John Alexander Logan, Illinois
Anti-Monopoly Party
President: Benjamin Franklin Butler, Massachusetts
Vice President: Absolom Madden West, Mississippi
Greenback Party
President: Benjamin Franklin Butler, Massachusetts
Vice President: Absolom Madden West, Mississippi

Prohibition Party
President: John Pierce St. John, Kansas
Vice President: William Daniel, Maryland
American Prohibition Party
President: Samuel Clarke Pomeroy, Kansas
Vice President: John A. Conant, Connecticut
Equal Rights Party
President: Belva Ann Bennett Lockwood, District of Columbia
Vice President: Marietta Lizzie Bell Stow, California

Election of 1888

Republican Party
President: Benjamin Harrison, Indiana
Vice President: Levi Parsons Morton, New York
Democratic Party
President: Grover Cleveland, New York
Vice President: Allen Granberry Thurman, Ohio
Prohibition Party
President: Clinton Bowen Fisk, New Jersey
Vice President: John Anderson Brooks, Missouri*
Union Labor Party
President: Alson Jenness Streeter, Illinois
Vice President: Charles E. Cunningham, Arkansas*
United Labor Party
President: Robert Hall Cowdrey, Illinois
Vice President: William H. T. Wakefield, Kansas*
American Party
President: James Langdon Curtis, New York
Vice President: Peter Dinwiddie Wigginton, California*
Equal Rights Party
President: Belva Ann Bennett Lockwood, District of Columbia
Vice President: Alfred Henry Love, Pennsylvania*
Industrial Reform Party
President: Albert E. Redstone, California*
Vice President: John Colvin, Kansas*

Election of 1892

Democratic Party
President; Grover Cleveland, New York
Vice President: Adlai Ewing Stevenson, Illinois
Republican Party
President: Benjamin Harrison, Indiana
Vice President: Whitelaw Reid, New York
People's Party of America
President: James Baird Weaver, Iowa
Vice President: James Gaven Field, Virginia
Prohibition Party
President: John Bidwell, California
Vice President: James Britton Cranfill, Texas
Socialist Labor Party
President: Simon Wing, Massachusetts
Vice President: Charles Horatio Matchett, New York*

Election of 1896

Republican Party
President: William McKinley, Ohio
Vice President: Garret Augustus Hobart, New Jersey
Democratic Party
President: William Jennings Bryan, Nebraska
Vice President: Arthur Sewall, Maine
People's Party (Populist)
President: William Jennings Bryan, Nebraska
Vice President: Thomas Edward Watson, Georgia
National Democratic Party
President: John McAuley Palmer, Illinois
Vice President: Simon Bolivar Buckner, Kentucky
Prohibition Party
President: Joshua Levering, Maryland
Vice President: Hale Johnson, Illinois*
Socialist Labor Party
President: Charles Horatio Matchett, New York
Vice President: Matthew Maguire, New Jersey
National Party
President: Charles Eugene Bentley, Nebraska
Vice President: James Haywood Southgate, North Carolina*

National Silver Party (Bi-Metallic League)
President: William Jennings Bryan, Nebraska
Vice President: Arthur Sewall, Maine

Election of 1900

Republican Party
President: William McKinley, Ohio
Vice President: Theodore Roosevelt, New York
Democratic Party
President: William Jennings Bryan, Nebraska
Vice President: Adlai Ewing Stevenson, Illinois
Prohibition Party
President: John Granville Woolley, Illinois
Vice President: Henry Brewer Metcalf, Rhode Island
Social-Democratic Party
President: Eugene Victor Debs, Indiana
Vice President: Job Harriman, California
People's Party (Populist—Anti-Fusionist faction)
President: Wharton Barker, Pennsylvania
Vice President: Ignatius Donnelly, Minnesota
Socialist Labor Party
President: Joseph Francis Malloney, Massachusetts
Vice President: Valentine Remmel, Pennsylvania
Union Reform Party
President: Seth Hockett Ellis, Ohio
Vice President: Samuel T. Nicholson, Pennsylvania
United Christian Party
President: Jonah Fitz Randolph Leonard, Iowa
Vice President: David H. Martin, Pennsylvania
People's Party (Populist—Fusionist faction)
President: William Jennings Bryan, Nebraska
Vice President: Adlai Ewing Stevenson, Illinois
Silver Republican Party
President: William Jennings Bryan, Nebraska
Vice President: Adlai Ewing Stevenson, Illinois
National Party
President: Donelson Caffery, Louisiana
Vice President: Archibald Murray Howe, Massachusetts*

Election of 1904

Republican Party
President: Theodore Roosevelt, New York
Vice President: Charles Warren Fairbanks, Indiana
Democratic Party
President: Alton Brooks Parker, New York
Vice President: Henry Gassaway Davis, West Virginia
Socialist Party
President: Eugene Victor Debs, Indiana
Vice President: Benjamin Hanford, New York
Prohibition Party
President: Silas Comfort Swallow, Pennsylvania
Vice President: George W. Carroll, Texas
People's Party (Populists)
President: Thomas Edward Watson, Georgia
Vice President: Thomas Henry Tibbles, Nebraska
Socialist Labor Party
President: Charles Hunter Corregan, New York
Vice President: William Wesley Cox, Illinois
Continental Party
President: Austin Holcomb
Vice President: A. King, Missouri

Election of 1908

Republican Party
President: William Howard Taft, Ohio
Vice President: James Schoolcraft Sherman, New York
Democratic Party
President: William Jennings Bryan, Nebraska
Vice President: John Worth Kern, Indiana
Socialist Party
President: Eugene Victor Debs
Vice President: Benjamin Hanford
Prohibition Party
President: Eugene Wilder Chafin, Illinois
Vice President: Aaron Sherman Watkins, Ohio

Independence Party
President: Thomas Louis Hisgen, Massachusetts
Vice President: John Temple Graves, Georgia
People's Party (Populist)
President: Thomas Edward Watson, Georgia
Vice President: Samuel Williams, Indiana
Socialist Labor Party
President: August Gillhaus, New York
Vice President: Donald L. Munro, Virginia
United Christian Party
President: Daniel Braxton Turney, Illinois
Vice President: Lorenzo S. Coffin, Iowa

Election of 1912

Democratic Party
President: Woodrow Wilson, New Jersey
Vice President: Thomas Riley Marshall, Indiana
Progressive Party ("Bull Moose" Party)
President: Theodore Roosevelt, New York
Vice President: Hiram Warren Johnson, California
Republican Party
President: William Howard Taft, Ohio
Vice President: James Schoolcraft Sherman, New York
Sherman died Oct. 30; replaced by Nicholas Murray
Butler, New York
Socialist Party
President: Eugene Victor Debs, Indiana
Vice President: Emil Seidel, Wisconsin
Prohibition Party
President: Eugene Wilder Chafin, Illinois
Vice President: Aaron Sherman Watkins, Ohio
Socialist Labor Party
President: Arthur Elmer Reimer, Massachusetts
Vice President: August Gillhaus, New York[1]

Election of 1916

Democratic Party
President: Woodrow Wilson, New Jersey
Vice President: Thomas Riley Marshall, Indiana
Republican Party
President: Charles Evans Hughes, New York
Vice President: Charles Warren Fairbanks, Indiana
Socialist Party
President: Allan Louis Benson, New York
Vice President: George Ross Kirkpatrick, New Jersey
Prohibition Party
President: James Franklin Hanly, Indiana
Vice President: Ira Landrith, Tennessee
Socialist Labor Party
President: Arthur Elmer Reimer, Massachusetts*
Vice President: Caleb Harrison, Illinois*
Progressive Party
President: Theodore Roosevelt, New York
Vice President: John Milliken Parker, Louisiana

Election of 1920

Republican Party
President: Warren Gamaliel Harding, Ohio
Vice President: Calvin Coolidge, Massachusetts
Democratic Party
President: James Middleton Cox, Ohio
Vice President: Franklin Delano Roosevelt, New York
Socialist Party
President: Eugene Victor Debs, Indiana
Vice President: Seymour Stedman, Illinois
Farmer Labor Party
President: Parley Parker Christensen, Utah
Vice President: Maximilian Sebastian Hayes, Ohio
Prohibition Party
President: Aaron Sherman Watkins, Ohio
Vice President: David Leigh Colvin, New York
Socialist Labor Party
President: William Wesley Cox, Missouri
Vice President: August Gillhaus, New York
Single Tax Party
President: Robert Colvin Macauley, Pennsylvania
Vice President: R. G. Barnum, Ohio

American Party
President: James Edward Ferguson, Texas
Vice President: William J. Hough

Election of 1924

Republican Party
President: Calvin Coolidge, Massachusetts
Vice President: Charles Gates Dawes, Illinois
Democratic Party
President: John William Davis, West Virginia
Vice President: Charles Wayland Bryan, Nebraska
Progressive Party
President: Robert La Follette, Wisconsin
Vice President: Burton Kendall Wheeler, Montana
Prohibition Party
President: Herman Preston Faris, Missouri
Vice President: Marie Caroline Brehm, California
Socialist Labor Party
President: Frank T. Johns, Oregon
Vice President: Verne L. Reynolds, New York
Socialist Party
President: Robert La Follette, New York
Vice President: Burton Kendall Wheeler, Montana
Workers Party (Communist Party)
President: William Zebulon Foster, Illinois
Vice President: Benjamin Gitlow, New York
American Party
President: Gilbert Owen Nations, District of Columbia
Vice President: Charles Hiram Randall, California[2]
Commonwealth Land Party
President: William J. Wallace, New Jersey
Vice President: John Cromwell Lincoln, Ohio
Farmer Labor Party
President: Duncan McDonald, Illinois*
Vice President: William Bouck, Washington*
Greenback Party
President: John Zahnd, Indiana*
Vice President: Roy M. Harrop, Nebraska*

Election of 1928

Republican Party
President: Herbert Clark Hoover, California
Vice President: Charles Curtis, Kansas
Democratic Party
President: Alfred Emanuel Smith, New York
Vice President: Joseph Taylor Robinson, Arkansas
Socialist Party
President: Norman Mattoon Thomas, New York
Vice President: James Hudson Maurer, Pennsylvania
Workers Party (Communist Party)
President: William Zebulon Foster, Illinois
Vice President: Benjamin Gitlow, New York
Socialist Labor Party
President: Verne L. Reynolds, Michigan
Vice President: Jeremiah D. Crowley, New York
Prohibition Party
President: William Frederick Varney, New York
Vice President: James Arthur Edgerton, Virginia
Farmer Labor Party
President: Frank Elbridge Webb, California
Vice President: Will Vereen, Georgia[3]
Greenback Party
President: John Zahnd, Indiana*
Vice President: Wesley Henry Bennington, Ohio*

Election of 1932

Democratic Party
President: Franklin Delano Roosevelt, New York
Vice President: John Nance Garner, Texas
Republican Party
President: Herbert Clark Hoover, California
Vice President: Charles Curtis, Kansas
Socialist Party
President: Norman Mattoon Thomas, New York
Vice President: James Hudson Maurer, Pennsylvania

Communist Party
President: William Zebulon Foster, Illinois
Vice President: James William Ford, New York
Prohibition Party
President: William David Upshaw, Georgia
Vice President: Frank Stewart Regan, Illinois
Liberty Party
President: William Hope Harvey, Arkansas
Vice President: Frank B. Hemenway, Washington
Socialist Labor Party
President: Verne L. Reynolds, New York
Vice President: John W. Aiken, Massachusetts
Farmer Labor Party
President: Jacob Sechler Coxey, Ohio
Vice President: Julius J. Reiter, Minnesota
Jobless Party
President: James Renshaw Cox, Pennsylvania
Vice President: V. C. Tisdal, Oklahoma
National Party
President: Seymour E. Allen, Massachusetts

Election of 1936

Democratic Party
President: Franklin Delano Roosevelt, New York
Vice President: John Nance Garner, Texas
Republican Party
President: Alfred Mossman Landon, Kansas
Vice President: Frank Knox, Illinois
Union Party
President: William Lemke, North Dakota
Vice President: Thomas Charles O'Brien, Massachusetts
Socialist Party
President: Norman Mattoon Thomas, New York
Vice President: George A. Nelson, Wisconsin
Communist Party
President: Earl Russell Browder, Kansas
Vice President: James William Ford, New York
Prohibition Party
President: David Leigh Colvin, New York
Vice President: Alvin York, Tennessee
Socialist Labor Party
President: John W. Aikin, Massachusetts
Vice President: Emil F. Teichert, New York
National Greenback Party
President: John Zahnd, Indiana*
Vice President: Florence Garvin, Rhode Island*

Election of 1940

Democratic Party
President: Franklin Delano Roosevelt, New York
Vice President: Henry Agard Wallace, Iowa
Republican Party
President: Wendell Lewis Willkie, New York
Vice President: Charles Linza McNary, Oregon
Socialist Party
President: Norman Mattoon Thomas, New York
Vice President: Maynard C. Krueger, Illinois
Prohibition Party
President: Roger Ward Babson, Massachusetts
Vice President: Edgar V. Moorman, Illinois
Communist Party (Workers Party)
President: Earl Russell Browder, Kansas
Vice President: James William Ford, New York
Socialist Labor Party
President: John W. Aiken, Massachusetts
Vice President: Aaron M. Orange, New York
Greenback Party
President: John Zahnd, Indiana*
Vice President: James Elmer Yates, Arizona*

Election of 1944

Democratic Party
President: Franklin Delano Roosevelt, New York
Vice President: Harry S Truman, Missouri
Republican Party
President: Thomas Edmund Dewey, New York

Vice President: John William Bricker, Ohio
Socialist Party
President: Norman Mattoon Thomas, New York
Vice President: Darlington Hoopes, Pennsylvania
Prohibition Party
President: Claude A. Watson, California
Vice President: Andrew Johnson, Kentucky
Socialist Labor Party
President: Edward A. Teichert, Pennsylvania
Vice President: Arla A. Albaugh, Ohio
America First Party
President: Gerald Lyman Kenneth Smith, Michigan
Vice President: Henry A. Romer, Ohio

Election of 1948

Democratic Party
President: Harry S Truman, Missouri
Vice President: Alben William Barkley, Kentucky
Republican Party
President: Thomas Edmund Dewey, New York
Vice President: Earl Warren, California
States' Rights Democratic Party
President: James Strom Thurmond, South Carolina
Vice President: Fielding Lewis Wright, Mississippi
Progressive Party
President: Henry Agard Wallace, Iowa
Vice President: Glen Hearst Taylor, Idaho
Socialist Party
President: Norman Mattoon Thomas, New York
Vice President: Tucker Powell Smith, Michigan
Prohibition Party
President: Claude A. Watson, California
Vice President: Dale Learn, Pennsylvania
Socialist Labor Party
President: Edward A. Teichert, Pennsylvania
Vice President: Stephen Emery, New York
Socialist Workers Party
President: Farrell Dobbs, New York
Vice President: Grace Carlson, Minnesota
Christian Nationalist Party
President: Gerald Lyman Kenneth Smith, Missouri
Vice President: Henry A. Romer, Ohio
Greenback Party
President: John G. Scott, New York
Vice President: Granville B. Leeke, Indiana*
Vegetarian Party
President: John Maxwell, Illinois
Vice President: Symon Gould, New York*

Election of 1952

Republican Party
President: Dwight David Eisenhower, New York
Vice President: Richard Milhous Nixon, California
Democratic Party
President: Adlai Ewing Stevenson, Illinois
Vice President: John Jackson Sparkman, Alabama
Progressive Party
President: Vincent William Hallinan, California
Vice President: Charlotta A. Bass, New York
Prohibition Party
President: Stuart Hamblen, California
Vice President: Enoch Arden Holtwick, Illinois
Socialist Labor Party
President: Eric Hass, New York
Vice President: Stephen Emery, New York
Socialist Party
President: Darlington Hoopes, Pennsylvania
Vice President: Samuel Herman Friedman, New York
Socialist Workers Party
President: Farrell Dobbs, New York
Vice President: Myra Tanner Weiss, New York
America First Party
President: Douglas MacArthur, Wisconsin
Vice President: Harry Flood Byrd, Virginia

American Labor Party
President: Vincent William Hallinan, California
Vice President: Charlotta A. Bass, New York

American Vegetarian Party
President: Daniel J. Murphy, California
Vice President: Symon Gould, New York*

Church of God Party
President: Homer Aubrey Tomlinson, New York
Vice President: Willie Isaac Bass, North Carolina*

Constitution Party
President: Douglas MacArthur, Wisconsin
Vice President: Harry Flood Byrd, Virginia

Greenback Party
President: Frederick C. Proehl, Washington
Vice President: Edward J. Bedell, Indiana

Poor Man's Party
President: Henry B. Krajewski, New Jersey
Vice President: Frank Jenkins, New Jersey

Election of 1956

Republican Party
President: Dwight David Eisenhower, Pennsylvania
Vice President: Richard Milhous Nixon, California

Democratic Party
President: Adlai Ewing Stevenson, Illinois
Vice President: Estes Kefauver, Tennessee

States' Rights Party
President: Thomas Coleman Andrews, Virginia
Vice President: Thomas Harold Werdel, California
Ticket also favored by Constitution Party.

Prohibition Party
President: Enoch Arden Holtwick, Illinois
Vice President: Edward M. Cooper, California

Socialist Labor Party
President: Eric Hass, New York
Vice President: Georgia Cozzini, Wisconsin

Texas Constitution Party
President: William Ezra Jenner, Indiana*
Vice President: Joseph Bracken Lee, Utah*

Socialist Workers Party
President: Farrell Dobbs, New York
Vice President: Myra Tanner Weiss, New York

American Third Party
President: Henry Krajewski, New Jersey
Vice President: Ann Marie Yezo, New Jersey

Socialist Party
President: Darlington Hoopes, Pennsylvania
Vice President: Samuel Herman Friedman, New York

Pioneer Party
President: William Langer, North Dakota*
Vice President: Burr McCloskey, Illinois*

American Vegetarian Party
President: Herbert M. Shelton, California*
Vice President: Symon Gould, New York*

Greenback Party
President: Frederick C. Proehl, Washington
Vice President: Edward Kirby Meador, Massachusetts*

States' Rights Party of Kentucky
President: Harry Flood Byrd, Virginia
Vice President: William Ezra Jenner, Indiana

South Carolinians for Independent Electors
President: Harry Flood Byrd, Virginia

Christian National Party
President: Gerald Lyman Kenneth Smith
Vice President: Charles I. Robertson

Election of 1960

Democratic Party
President: John Fitzgerald Kennedy, Massachusetts
Vice President: Lyndon Baines Johnson, Texas

Republican Party
President: Richard Milhous Nixon, California
Vice President: Henry Cabot Lodge, Massachusetts

National States' Rights Party
President: Orval Eugene Faubus, Arkansas
Vice President: John Geraerdt Crommelin, Alabama

Socialist Labor Party
President: Eric Hass, New York
Vice President: Georgia Cozzini, Wisconsin

Prohibition Party
President: Rutherford Losey Decker, Missouri
Vice President: Earle Harold Munn, Michigan

Socialist Workers Party
President: Farrell Dobbs, New York
Vice President: Myra Tanner Weiss, New York

Conservative Party of New Jersey
President: Joseph Bracken Lee, Utah
Vice President: Kent H. Courtney, Louisiana

Conservative Party of Virginia
President: C. Benton Coiner, Virginia
Vice President: Edward M. Silverman, Virginia

Constitution Party (Texas)
President: Charles Loten Sullivan, Mississippi
Vice President: Merritt B. Curtis, District of Columbia

Constitution Party (Washington)
President: Merritt B. Curtis, District of Columbia
Vice President: B. N. Miller

Greenback Party
President: Whitney Hart Slocomb, California*
Vice President: Edward Kirby Meador, Massachusetts*

Independent Afro-American Party
President: Clennon King, Georgia
Vice President: Reginald Carter

Tax Cut Party (America First Party; American Party)
President: Lar Daly, Illinois
Vice President: Merritt Barton Curtis, District of Columbia

Theocratic Party
President: Homer Aubrey Tomlinson, New York
Vice President: Raymond L. Teague, Alaska*

Vegetarian Party
President: Symon Gould, New York
Vice President: Christopher Gian-Cursio, Florida

Election of 1964

Democratic Party
President: Lyndon Baines Johnson, Texas
Vice President: Hubert Horatio Humphrey, Minnesota

Republican Party
President: Barry Morris Goldwater, Arizona
Vice President: William Edward Miller, New York

Socialist Labor Party
President: Eric Hass, New York
Vice President: Henning A. Blomen, Massachusetts

Prohibition Party
President: Earle Harold Munn, Michigan
Vice President: Mark Shaw, Massachusetts

Socialist Workers Party
President: Clifton DeBerry, New York
Vice President: Edward Shaw, New York

National States' Rights Party
President: John Kasper, Tennessee
Vice President: J. B. Stoner, Georgia

Constitution Party
President: Joseph B. Lightburn, West Virginia
Vice President: Theodore C. Billings, Colorado

Independent States' Rights Party
President: Thomas Coleman Andrews, Virginia
Vice President: Thomas H. Werdel, California*

Theocratic Party
President: Homer Aubrey Tomlinson, New York
Vice President: William R. Rogers, Missouri*

Universal Party
President: Kirby James Hensley, California
Vice President: John O. Hopkins, Iowa

Election of 1968

Republican Party
President: Richard Milhous Nixon, New York
Vice President: Spiro Theodore Agnew, Maryland
Democratic Party
President: Hubert Horatio Humphrey, Minnesota
Vice President: Edmund Sixtus Muskie, Maine
American Independent Party
President: George Corley Wallace, Alabama
Vice President: Curtis Emerson LeMay, Ohio
LeMay replaced S. Marvin Griffin, who originally had been
selected.
Peace and Freedom Party
President: Eldridge Cleaver
Vice President: Judith Mage, New York
Socialist Labor Party
President: Henning A. Blomen, Massachusetts
Vice President: George Sam Taylor, Pennsylvania
Socialist Workers Party
President: Fred Halstead, New York
Vice President: Paul Boutelle, New Jersey
Prohibition Party
President: Earle Harold Munn, Sr., Michigan
Vice President: Rolland E. Fisher, Kansas
Communist Party
President: Charlene Mitchell, California
Vice President: Michael Zagarell, New York
Constitution Party
President: Richard K. Troxell, Texas
Vice President: Merle Thayer, Iowa
Freedom and Peace Party
President: Dick Gregory (Richard Claxton Gregory), Illinois
Patriotic Party
President: George Corley Wallace, Alabama
Vice President: William Penn Patrick, California*
Theocratic Party
President: William R. Rogers, Missouri
Universal Party
President: Kirby James Hensley, California
Vice President: Rcscoe B. MacKenna

Election of 1972

Republican Party
President: Richard Milhous Nixon, California
Vice President: Spiro Theodore Agnew, Maryland
Democratic Party
President: George Stanley McGovern, South Dakota
Vice President: Thomas Francis Eagleton, Missouri
Eagleton resigned and was replaced on August 8, 1972, by
Robert Sargent Shriver, Maryland, selected by the Democratic
National Committee.
American Independent Party
President: John George Schmitz, California
Vice President: Thomas Jefferson Anderson, Tennessee
Socialist Workers Party
President: Louis Fisher, Illinois
Vice President: Genevieve Gunderson, Minnesota
Socialist Labor Party
President: Linda Jenness, Georgia
Vice President: Andrew Pulley, Illinois
Communist Party
President: Gus Hall, New York
Vice President: Jarvis Tyner
Prohibition Party
President: Earle Harold Munn, Sr., Michigan
Vice President: Marshall Uncapher
Libertarian Party
President: John Hospers, California
Vice President: Theodora Nathan, Oregon

People's Party
President: Benjamin McLane Spock
Vice President: Julius Hobson, District of Columbia
America First Party
President: John V. Mahalchik
Vice President: Irving Homer
Universal Party
President: Gabriel Green
Vice President: Daniel Fry

Election of 1976

Democratic Party
President: Jimmy Carter, Georgia
Vice President: Walter F. Mondale, Minnesota
Republican Party
President: Gerald R. Ford, Michigan
Vice President: Robert Dole, Kansas
Independent Candidate
President: Eugene J. McCarthy, Minnesota
Vice President: none [4]
Libertarian Party
President: Roger MacBride, Virginia
Vice President: David P. Bergland, California
American Independent Party
President: Lester Maddox, Georgia
Vice President: William Dyke, Wisconsin
American Party
President: Thomas J. Anderson, Tennessee
Vice President: Rufus Shackleford, Florida
Socialist Workers Party
President: Peter Camejo, California
Vice President: Willie Mae Reid, California
Communist Party
President: Gus Hall, New York
Vice President: Jarvis Tyner, New York
People's Party
President: Margaret Wright, California
Vice President: Benjamin Spock, New York
U.S. Labor Party
President: Lyndon H. LaRouche, New York
Vice President: R.W. Evans, Michigan
Prohibition Party
President: Benjamin C. Bubar, Maine
Vice President: Earl F. Dodge, Colorado
Socialist Labor Party
President: Jules Levin, New Jersey
Vice President: Constance Blomen, Massachusetts
Socialist Party
President: Frank P. Zeidler, Wisconsin
Vice President: J. Quinn Brisben, Illinois
Restoration Party
President: Ernest L. Miller
Vice President: Roy N. Eddy
United American Party
President: Frank Taylor
Vice President: Henry Swan

Election of 1980 [5]

Republican Party
President: Ronald Reagan, California
Vice President: George Bush, Texas

Democratic Party
President: Jimmy Carter, Georgia
Vice President: Walter F. Mondale, Minnesota

Independent Candidate
President: John B. Anderson, Illinois
Vice President: Patrick J. Lucey, Wisconsin

Libertarian Party
  President: Edward E. Clark, California
  Vice President: David Koch, New York

Citizens Party
  President: Barry Commoner, New York
  Vice President: LaDonna Harris, New Mexico

Communist Party
  President: Gus Hall, New York
  Vice President: Angela Davis, California

American Independent Party
  President: John R. Rarick, Louisiana
  Vice President: Matilde Zimmerman

Socialist Workers
  President: Andrew Pulley, Illinois
  Vice President: Frank L. Varnum, Calif.

  President: Clifton DeBerry, California
  Vice President: Matilde Zimmermann

  President: Richard Congress, Ohio
  Vice President: Matilde Zimmerman

Right to Life
  President: Ellen McCormack, New York
  Vice President: Carroll Driscoll, New Jersey

Peace and Freedom
  President: Maureen Smith, California
  Vice President: Elizabeth Barron

Workers World
  President: Dierdre Griswold, New Jersey
  Vice President: Larry Holmes, New York

Statesman
  President: Benjamin C. Bubar, Maine
  Vice President: Earl F. Dodge, Colorado

Socialist
  President: David McReynolds, New York
  Vice President: Diane Drufenbrock, Wisconsin

American
  President: Percy L. Greaves, New York
  Vice President: Frank L. Varnum, California

  President: Frank W. Shelton, Utah
  Vice President: George E. Jackson

Middle Class
  President: Kurt Lynen, New Jersey
  Vice President: Harry Kieve, New Jersey

Down With Lawyers
  President: Bill Gahres, New Jersey
  Vice President: J. F. Loghlin, New Jersey

Independent
  President: Martin E. Wendelken
  (no vice presidential candidate)

Natural Peoples
  President: Harley McLain, North Dakota
  Vice President: Jewelie Goeller, North Dakota

1. *1912: Schlesinger's* History of Presidential Elections *lists the Socialist Labor Party vice presidential candidates as Francis. No first name is given for Francis.*

2. *1924: Scammon's* America at the Polls *lists the American Party vice presidential candidate as Leander L. Pickett.*

3. *1928:* America at the Polls *lists the Farmer Labor Party vice presidential candidate as L. R. Tillman.*

4. *1976: McCarthy, who ran as an independent with no party designation, had no national running mate, favoring the elimination of the office. But as various state laws required a running mate, he had different ones in different states, amounting to nearly two dozen, all political unknowns.*

* *Candidates appeared in Kane's* Facts About the Presidents *but could not be verified in another source: see text p. 71.*

5. *1980: In several cases vice presidential nominees were different from those listed for most states, and the Socialist Workers and American party nominees for president varied from state to state. For example, because Pulley, the major standard bearer for the Socialist Workers Party was only 29 years old, his name was not allowed on the ballot on some states (the Constitution requires presidential candidates to be at least 35 years old). Hence, the party ran other candidates in those states. In a number of states candidates appeared on the ballot with variants of the party designations listed, without any party designation, or with entirely different party names.*

The Popular Vote

Few elements of the American political system have changed so markedly over the years as has the electorate. Since the early days of the nation, when the voting privilege was limited to the upper economic classes, one voting barrier after another has fallen to pressures for wider suffrage. First nonproperty-holding males, then women, then black Americans and finally young people pushed for the franchise. By the early 1970s, almost every restriction on voting had been removed, and virtually every adult citizen 18 years of age and older had won the right to vote.

Actions to expand the electorate have taken place at both the state and federal levels. Voting qualifications have varied widely in the states because of a provision of the federal Constitution (Article I, Section 2) permitting the states to set their own voting standards. Early in the nation's history, the states dropped their property qualifications for voting but some retained literacy tests as late as 1970.

On the federal level, the Constitution has been amended five times to circumvent state qualifications denying the franchise to certain categories of persons. The 14th Amendment, ratified in 1868, directed Congress to reduce the number of representatives from any state that disfranchised adult male citizens for any reason other than commission of a crime. However, no such reduction was ever made. The 15th Amendment, ratified in 1870, prohibited denial of the right to vote "on account of race, color or previous condition of servitude," while the 19th Amendment in 1920 prohibited denial of that right "on account of sex." The 24th Amendment, which came into effect in 1964, barred denial of the right to vote in any federal election "by reason of failure to pay any poll tax or other tax." Finally, in 1971, the 26th Amendment lowered the voting age to 18 in federal, state and local elections.

Congress in the 1950s and 1960s enacted a series of statutes to enforce the 15th Amendment's guaranty against racial discrimination in voting. A law passed in 1970 nullified state residence requirements of longer than 30 days for voting in presidential elections, suspended literacy tests for a five-year period (the suspension was made permanent in 1975) and lowered the minimum voting age from 21 years, the requirement then in effect in most states, to 18. Subsequently, a Supreme Court ruling upheld the voting-age change for federal elections but invalidated it for state and local elections. In the same decision (*Oregon v. Mitchell*, 400 U.S. 112, 1970) the court upheld the provision on residence requirements and sustained the suspension of literacy tests with respect to both state and local elections. The 26th Amendment was ratified six months after the court's decision.

The right to vote in presidential elections was extended to citizens of the District of Columbia by the 23rd Amendment, ratified in 1961. District residents had been disfranchised from national elections except for a brief period in the 1870s when they elected a nonvoting delegate to the House of Representatives. In 1970 Congress took another step toward full suffrage for District residents by again authorizing the election of a non-voting delegate to the House, beginning in 1971.

Voting Trends

Statistics show that each major liberalization of election laws has resulted in a sharp increase in the number of persons voting. From 1824 to 1856, a period in which states gradually relaxed their property and taxpaying qualifications for voting, voter participation in presidential elections increased from 3.8 percent to 16.7 percent of the total population. In 1920, when the 19th Amendment giving women the franchise went into effect, voter participation increased to 25.1 percent of the population.

Between 1932 and 1976 both the number of voters in presidential elections and the voting-age population almost doubled. Except for the 1948 presidential election, when barely more than half the voting-age population was estimated to have gone to the polls, the turnout in the postwar years through 1968 was approximately 60 percent, according to Census Bureau surveys. This relatively high percentage was due largely to passage of new civil rights laws encouraging blacks to vote.

Despite a steady increase in the numbers of persons voting in the 1970s, voter turnout actually declined as a percentage of eligible voters who voted. Voter participation reached a modern peak of 63.1 percent in the 1960 presidential election. It declined steadily over the next decade, falling to 61.8 percent in 1964, 60.7 percent in 1968 and 55.4 percent in 1972. Voting in the off-year congressional elections, always lower than in presidential years, also declined during this period.

According to the Census Bureau, 54.4 percent of the voting-age population went to the polls in 1976. In 1980 voting declined further, with only an estimated 53 percent of the 162.8 million Americans of voting age bothering to vote. This was the fifth consecutive presidential election in which the voter turnout decreased. (Census Bureau surveys, it should be pointed out, are based on polls of eligible voters rather than on actual counts of the voting-age population or of registered voters. The bureau defines "eligible" voters as all adult civilians of voting age — 18 and older and registered or not — except persons in penal or other institutions. The number of registered voters nationwide at any given time is impossible to calculate. States have different registration deadlines before an election; persons who move may be registered in more than one state at the same time or temporarily may not be recorded in any state; and some states do not require pre-registration before voting, while others do not require towns and municipalities to keep registration records. Thus in a few states without registration requirements, the Census Bureau considers all eligible voters as registered voters as well.)

Changes in the age distribution of the electorate figured prominently in the 1970s decline. Due to the surge in the birth rate beginning in 1947, the youth population has been the most rapidly growing group. However, young adults have tended to vote in much smaller proportions than the rest of the voting-age population. When approximately 11 million young voters entered the electorate in 1972 when the voting age was lowered to 18, the percentage of eligible Americans who voted dropped sharply even though the total number of voters who cast ballots for president rose to 77,625,000, 4.4 million more than in 1968.

In addition to changes in the composition of the electorate, political scientists have attributed the decline in the percentage of Americans voting to several factors: long periods of political stability; the predictable outcome of many races; and the lack of appeal of some candidates.

Studies by the Census Bureau have shown a marked difference in participation among various classes of voters. In general, the studies have found higher participation rates among whites, persons 45 to 65 years of age, non-Southerners, persons with higher family incomes and white-collar employees and professionals. Private studies have shown repeatedly that higher voter turnout in an election generally favors Democrats while lower ones favor Republicans. Far more voters are registered as Democrats.

As the voting population grew, political parties became increasingly important in the electoral process in the 19th century. As the power of the individual's vote became more and more diluted, voters found parties a convenient mechanism for defining political issues and mobilizing the strength to push a particular policy through to enactment and execution. After the rise and fall of numerous different political parties during the first half of the 19th century, most voting strength became and remained polarized in two major parties — the Republican and the Democratic. This changed somewhat in the 20th century. The Progressive movement won a sizable following in the early years of the century, and Americans who refused to register in either of the major parties — the independent voters — increased appreciably in the post-World War II years.

Broadening the Franchise

During the first few decades of the Republic, all 13 of the original states limited the franchise to property holders and taxpayers. Seven of the states required ownership of land or a life estate as opposed to a leased estate as a qualification for voting, while the other six permitted persons to substitute either evidence of ownership of certain amounts of personal property or payment of taxes as a prerequisite to vote.

The framers of the Constitution apparently were content to have the states limit the right to vote to adult males who had a real stake in good government. This meant, in most cases, persons in the upper economic levels. Not wishing to discriminate against any particular type of property owner (uniform federal voting standards inevitably would have conflicted with some of the state standards), the Constitutional Convention adopted without dissent the recommendation of its Committee of Detail providing that qualifications for the electors of the House of Representatives "shall be the same . . . as those of the electors in the several states of the most numerous branch of their own legislatures."

Under this provision fewer than one-half of the adult white men in the United States were eligible to vote at the outset in federal elections. Because no state made women eligible (although states were not forbidden to do so), only one white adult in four qualified to go to the polls. Slaves, both blacks and Indians, were ineligible, and they comprised almost one-fifth of the American population as enumerated in the census of 1790. Also ineligible were white indentured servants, whose status was little better than that of the slaves.

Actually, these early state practices represented a liberalization of restrictions on voting that had prevailed at one time in the colonial period. Roman Catholics had been disfranchised in almost every colony, Jews in most colonies, Quakers and Baptists in some. In Rhode Island, Jews remained legally ineligible to vote until 1842.

For half a century before the Civil War there was a steady broadening of the electorate. The new western settlements supplied a stimulus to the principle of universal manhood suffrage, and Jacksonian democracy encouraged its acceptance. Gradually, the seven states making property ownership a condition for voting substituted a taxpaying requirement: Delaware in 1792; Maryland in 1810; Connecticut in 1818; Massachusetts in 1821; New York in 1821; Rhode Island in 1842, and Virginia in 1850. By the mid-19th century, most states had removed even the taxpaying qualifications although some jurisdictions persisted in this practice into the 20th century.

The trend toward a broadened franchise continued in the 20th century with women obtaining the vote and racial barriers to black voting slowly eliminated. Once Congress acted, the Supreme Court steadily backed its power to ensure the right to vote. In general, by the 200th anniversary of the nation the only remaining restrictions prevented voting by the insane, convicted felons and otherwise eligible voters who were unable to meet short residence requirements for voting.

Voting Behavior

A precise breakdown that shows which groups of voters (blacks, women, etc.) have higher turnout rates has never been possible. It would require an elaborate questionnaire for every eligible voter asking whether the person had participated in the election, and an honest answer from the voter.

In place of a complete survey, the Census Bureau has attempted to measure voting behavior by taking a random sample of the electorate in every election year since 1964. The Survey Research Center-Center for Political Studies at the University of Michigan also analyzes voting behavior. Again, these surveys cannot be precise because they are based on people's responses. Estimates made from the survey differ from the actual ballot count because people frequently report that they or members of their families voted when in fact they did not.

The Census Bureau reported that its preliminary survey following the 1980 election showed that the proportion of the voting-age population who said they were registered to vote in 1980 (67 percent) was the same as in 1976. This was a decrease from 1968 when 74 percent of the voting-age population reported being registered. Sixty-one percent of the white population of voting age reported they voted in 1980 compared with only 51 percent of the black population and 30 percent of the Spanish-origin population. However, the report noted that the differences in voter turnout were almost entirely the result of differences in the proportion of the population who were registered — ranging from a high of 68 percent of the white population to 60 percent of the black population and only 36 percent of the Spanish-origin population.

There was little difference in voter participation for men and women. In 1964 the reported voting rate for men (72 percent) was about 5 percent higher than for women.

The largest decline in voter turnout in the elections since 1964 occurred in the North and West where voter participation declined by 12 percentage points for whites and 19 percentage points for blacks. In the South there were relatively smaller changes in voter turnout between 1964 and 1980. Although there was an increase in the voter turnout rate for blacks from 44 percent in 1964 to 48 percent in 1980, there was a decrease for whites from 60 percent to 57 percent.

There were a number of reasons for the low voter turnout in 1980. Various surveys pointed to a growing sense of powerlessness among the electorate, a feeling that one person's vote was not important and a belief that it made no difference which party won.

Another reason for declining turnouts was that even in 1980 voting could be a time-consuming process. Citizens first must register. Though requirements have been eased, only five states — Maine, Minnesota, North Dakota, Oregon and Wisconsin — permit election day registration.

Voter turnout varies according to region. Fewer voters go to the polls in one-party regions, especially in the South. And, as mentioned earlier, the actual turnout always is lower than the numbers obtained from surveys since people are reluctant to admit they did not vote.

Ironically, in 1912, 1924, 1948 and 1980 — when there have been major third party candidates — turnout has been lower than in the previous election.

Party Affiliation

According to a Gallup Poll released in April 1981, 28 percent of American voters considered themselves Republicans and 41 percent considered themselves Democrats, a decline of 4 percentage points for the Democratic Party since 1975. The number of independent voters dropped from 33 percent in 1975 to 31 percent in 1981. The 28 percent Republican figure was the highest in nine years.

The breakdown of political affiliation emerging from a Gallup Poll conducted in late 1980 indicated that blacks continued to consider themselves Democrats. Persons with a college education identified with Republicans or independents more often than with Democrats. Regionally, independents were strongest in the Midwest and weakest in the South and West, and Republicans were strongest in the West and relatively weak in the South. The Democratic Party was relatively weak in the Midwest.

Sources for Popular Returns

The popular election returns presented in this section (pages 83-130) were obtained, except for 1976 and 1980 or where indicated by a footnote, from the Historical Archive of the Inter-University Consortium for Political Research (ICPR) at the University of Michigan. The 1976 and 1980 returns and party designations were taken from Richard M. Scammon's *America Votes 12* (Washington: Congressional Quarterly, 1977) and *America Votes 14* (Washington: Elections Research Center, 1981). The returns cover the period from 1824 through the 1980 presidential election. The starting date for the ICPR collection was based on consideration of such factors as the pronounced trend by 1824 for the election of presidential electors by popular vote, as well as the availability, accessibility and quality of the returns. The bulk of the ICPR election data collection consists of returns at the county level in computer readable form.

The collection of ICPR presidential returns — part of a larger project involving gubernatorial, House and Senate returns — began in 1962 under grants from the Social Science Research Council and the National Science Foundation. Scholars searched state and local archives, newspaper files and other sources for the data. In as many cases as possible, multiple sources were consulted. Although general preference was given to official sources, these scholars were charged with evaluating all available sources in terms of their quality and completeness.

While the complete source annotations for the collection are too extensive to publish here, information on the sources for returns from specific elections can be obtained through the ICPR.

For each presidential election from 1824 to 1980, the following information is provided in the tables for the popular returns:

● The total nationwide popular vote and the plurality of the candidate who received the greatest number of votes.

● Names and party affiliations of major candidates.

● State-by-state breakdown of the popular vote and the percentage of the vote received by each candidate.

● The plurality received by the candidate who carried each state.

● The total national popular vote and percentage of the vote received by each candidate.

● The aggregate vote and percentage of the total vote received in each state by minor party candidates, minor parties running unpledged electors or unidentified votes. These figures appear in the column designated "Other." A complete breakdown of the votes included in the "Other" column appears on pages 121-130. The general index contains entries for all candidates.

Party Designation

In the ICPR data, the distinct — and in many cases, *multiple* — party designations appearing in the original sources are preserved. Thus, in the ICPR returns for 1968, George C. Wallace ran for president under a variety of party designations in different states — "Democratic," "American," "American Independent," "Independent," "George Wallace Party," "Conservative," "American Party of Missouri," "Independent American," "Courage" and "George Wallace and Independent."

In order to provide a single party designation for presidential candidates, Congressional Quarterly has aggregated under a *single party designation* the votes of candidates who are listed in the ICPR data as receiving votes under more than one party designation. Two sources were used for assigning party designation. For the elections 1824 through 1964, the source for party designation is Svend Petersen's *A Statistical History of the American Presidential Elections* (Frederick Ungar, New York, 1968).

For the 1968, 1972, 1976 and 1980 elections, the source for party designation is Scammon's *America Votes 8* (Washington: Congressional Quarterly, 1970), *America Votes 10* (1973), *America Votes 12* (1977) and *America Votes 14* (1981). For 1968, Scammon lists Wallace as an "American Independent," and Congressional Quarterly follows this usage.

Vote Totals and Percentages

The total popular vote for each candidate in a given election was determined by adding the votes received by that candidate in each state (including write-in votes where available), even though the vote totals for some states may have come from sources other than ICPR.

The percentage of the vote received in each state by any candidate or party has been calculated to two decimal places and rounded to one place; thus, 0.05 percent is listed as 0.1 percent. The percentage of the nationwide vote was calculated to three decimal places and rounded to two; thus, 0.005 percent is listed as 0.01 percent. Due to rounding, state percentages and national percentages do not always equal 100 percent.

Pluralities

The plurality column represents the difference between the vote received by the first and second place finishers in each state. In a few cases, votes included in the "Other" column were needed to calculate the plurality. In these cases, a footnote provides an explanation. *(See, for example, Georgia in the 1916 election, p. 103)*

1824 Presidential Election

Total Popular Votes: 365,833
Jackson's Plurality: 38,149

STATE	JOHN Q. ADAMS (Democratic-Republican)		ANDREW JACKSON (Democratic-Republican)		HENRY CLAY (Democratic-Republican)		WILLIAM H. CRAWFORD (Democratic-Republican)		OTHER[1]		PLURALITY
	Votes	%	Votes	%	Votes	%	Votes	%	Votes	%	
Alabama	2,422	17.8	9,429	69.3	96	.2	1,656	12.2			7,007
Connecticut	7,494	70.4					1,965	18.5	1,188	11.2	5,529
Illinois	1,516	32.5	1,272	27.2	1,036	22.2	847	18.1			244
Indiana	3,071	19.4	7,444	47.0	5,316	33.6			7		2,128
Kentucky			6,356	27.2	16,982	72.8					10,626
Maine[2]	10,289	81.5					2,336	18.5			7,953
Maryland[2]	14,632	44.1	14,523	43.7	695	2.1	3,364	10.1			109
Massachusetts	30,687	73.0							11,369	27.0	24,071[3]
Mississippi	1,654	33.8	3,121	63.8			119	2.4			1,467
Missouri	159	4.6	1,166	34.0	2,042	59.5	32	.9	33	1.0	876
New Hampshire[2]	9,389	93.6					643	6.4			8,746
New Jersey	8,309	41.9	10,332	52.1			1,196	6.0			2,023
North Carolina			20,231	56.0			15,622	43.3	256	.7	4,609
Ohio[2]	12,280	24.5	18,489	37.0	19,255	38.5					766
Pennsylvania	5,441	11.6	35,736	75.9	1,690	3.6	4,206	8.9			30,295
Rhode Island	2,144	91.5							200	8.5	1,944
Tennessee[2]	216	1.0	20,197	97.5			312	1.5			19,885
Virginia	3,419	22.2	2,975	19.4	419	2.7	8,558	55.7			5,139
Totals	**113,122**	*30.92*	**151,271**	*41.34*	**47,531**	*12.99*	**40,856**	*11.17*	**13,053**	*3.57*	

1828 Presidential Election

Total Popular Votes: 1,148,018
Jackson's Plurality: 141,656

STATE	ANDREW JACKSON (Democratic-Republican)		JOHN Q. ADAMS (National-Republican)		OTHER[1]		PLURALITY
	Votes	%	Votes	%	Votes	%	
Alabama	16,736	89.9	1,878	10.1	4		14,858
Connecticut	4,448	23.0	13,829	71.4	1,101	5.7	9,381
Georgia[2]	19,362	96.8	642	3.2			18,720
Illinois	9,560	67.2	4,662	32.8			4,898
Indiana	22,201	56.6	17,009	43.4			5,192
Kentucky	39,308	55.5	31,468	44.5			7,840
Louisiana	4,605	53.0	4,082	47.0			523
Maine	13,927	40.0	20,773	59.7	89	.3	6,846
Maryland	22,782	49.8	23,014	50.3			232
Massachusetts	6,012	15.4	29,836	76.4	3,226	8.3	23,824
Mississippi	6,763	81.1	1,581	19.0			5,182
Missouri	8,232	70.6	3,422	29.4			4,810
New Hampshire	20,212	45.9	23,823	54.1			3,611
New Jersey	21,809	47.9	23,753	52.1	8		1,944
New York	139,412	51.5	131,563	48.6			7,849
North Carolina	37,814	73.1	13,918	26.9	15		23,896
Ohio	67,596	51.6	63,453	48.4			4,143
Pennsylvania	101,457	66.7	50,763	33.4			50,694
Rhode Island	820	22.9	2,755	77.0	5	.1	1,935
Tennessee[4]	44,293	95.2	2,240	4.8			42,053
Vermont	8,350	25.4	24,363	74.2	120	.4	16,013
Virginia	26,854	69.0	12,070	31.0			14,784
Totals	**642,553**	*55.97*	**500,897**	*43.63*	**4,568**	*.40*	

1. *For breakdown of "Other" vote, see minor candidate vote totals, p. 121.*
2. *Figures from Svend Petersen, A Statistical History of the American Presidential Elections, (New York, 1968), p. 18.*
3. *Plurality of 24,071 votes is calculated on the basis of 6,616 for unpledged electors.*
4. *Figures from Petersen, op cit., p. 20.*

1832 Presidential Election

Total Popular Votes: 1,293,973
Jackson's Plurality: 217,575

STATE	ANDREW JACKSON (Democrat)		HENRY CLAY (National-Republican)		WILLIAM WIRT (Anti-Masonic)		OTHER[1]		PLURALITY
	Votes	%	Votes	%	Votes	%	Votes	%	
Alabama	14,286	99.9	5	.1					14,281
Connecticut	11,269	34.3	18,155	55.3	3,409	10.4			6,886
Delaware	4,110	49.0	4,276	51.0					166
Georgia[2]	20,750	100.0							20,750
Illinois	14,609	68.0	6,745	31.4	97	.5	30	.1	7,864
Indiana	31,652	55.4	25,473	44.6	27	.1			6,179
Kentucky	36,292	45.5	43,449	54.5					7,157
Louisiana	3,908	61.7	2,429	38.3					1,479
Maine	33,978	54.7	27,331	44.0	844	1.4			6,647
Maryland	19,156	50.0	19,160	50.0					4
Massachusetts	13,933	20.6	31,963	47.3	14,692	21.7	7,031	10.4	17,271
Mississippi	5,750	100.0							5,750
Missouri[2]	5,192	100.0							5,192
New Hampshire	24,855	56.8	18,938	43.2					5,917
New Jersey	23,826	49.9	23,466	49.1	468	1.0			360
New York	168,497	52.1	154,896	47.9					13,601
North Carolina	25,261	84.8	4,538	15.2					20,723
Ohio	81,246	51.3	76,566	48.4	538	.3			4,680
Pennsylvania	90,973	57.7			66,706	42.3			24,267
Rhode Island	2,051	35.7	2,871	50.0	819	14.3	6	.1	820
Tennessee	28,078	95.4	1,347	4.6					26,731
Vermont	7,865	24.3	11,161	34.5	13,112	40.5	206	.6	1,951
Virginia	34,243	75.0	11,436	25.0	3				22,807
Totals	**701,780**	**54.23**	**484,205**	**37.42**	**100,715**	**7.78**	**7,273**	**.56**	

1836 Presidential Election

Total Popular Votes: 1,503,534
Van Buren's Plurality: 213,360

STATE	MARTIN VAN BUREN (Democrat)		WILLIAM H. HARRISON (Whig)		HUGH L. WHITE (Whig)		DANIEL WEBSTER (Whig)		OTHER[1]		PLURALITY
	Votes	%	Votes	%	Votes	%	Votes	%	Votes	%	
Alabama	20,638	55.3			16,658	44.7					3,980
Arkansas	2,380	64.1			1,334	35.9					1,046
Connecticut	19,294	50.7	18,799	49.4							495
Delaware	4,154	46.7	4,736	53.2					5	.1	582
Georgia	22,778	48.2			24,481	51.8					1,703
Illinois	18,369	54.7	15,220	45.3							3,149
Indiana	33,084	44.5	41,339	55.6							8,255
Kentucky	33,229	47.4	36,861	52.6							3,632
Louisiana	3,842	51.7			3,583	48.3					259
Maine	22,825	58.9	14,803	38.2					1,112	2.9	8,022
Maryland	22,267	46.3	25,852	53.7							3,585
Massachusetts	33,486	44.8					41,201	55.1	45	.1	7,715
Michigan	6,507	54.0	5,545	46.0							962
Mississippi	10,297	51.3			9,782	48.7					515
Missouri[3]	10,995	60.0			7,337	40.0					3,658
New Hampshire	18,697	75.0	6,228	25.0							12,469
New Jersey	25,592	49.5	26,137	50.5							545
New York	166,795	54.6	138,548	45.4							28,247
North Carolina	26,631	53.1			23,521	46.9			1		3,110
Ohio	97,122	47.9	105,809	52.1							8,687
Pennsylvania	91,466	51.2	87,235	48.8							4,231
Rhode Island	2,962	52.2	2,710	47.8					1		252
Tennessee	26,170	42.1			36,027	57.9					9,857
Vermont	14,040	40.0	20,994	59.8					65	.2	6,954
Virginia	30,556	56.6			23,384	43.4			5		7,172
Totals	**764,176**	**50.83**	**550,816**	**36.63**	**146,107**	**9.72**	**41,201**	**2.74**	**1,234**	**.08**	

1. For breakdown of "Other" vote, see minor candidate vote totals, p. 121.
2. Figures from Petersen, op. cit., p. 21.
3. Figures from Petersen, op. cit., p. 22.

1840 Presidential Election

Total Popular Votes: 2,411,808
Harrison's Plurality: 146,536

STATE	WILLIAM H. HARRISON (Whig)		MARTIN VAN BUREN (Democrat)		JAMES G. BIRNEY (Liberty)		OTHER[1]		PLURALITY
	Votes	%	Votes	%	Votes	%	Votes	%	
Alabama	28,515	45.6	33,996	54.4					5,481
Arkansas	5,160	43.6	6,679	56.4					1,519
Connecticut	31,598	55.6	25,281	44.5					6,317
Delaware	5,967	55.0	4,872	44.9			13	.1	1,095
Georgia	40,339	55.8	31,983	44.2					8,356
Illinois	45,574	48.9	47,441	50.9	160	.2			1,867
Indiana	65,280	55.5	51,696	44.0	30		599	.5	13,584
Kentucky	58,488	64.2	32,616	35.8					25,872
Louisiana	11,296	59.7	7,616	40.3					3,680
Maine	46,612	50.2	46,190	49.8					422
Maryland	33,528	53.8	28,752	46.2					4,776
Massachusetts	72,852	57.4	52,355	41.3	1,618	1.3			20,497
Michigan	22,933	52.1	21,096	47.9					1,837
Mississippi	19,515	53.4	17,010	46.6					2,505
Missouri	22,954	43.4	29,969	56.6					7,015
New Hampshire	26,310	43.9	32,774	54.7	872	1.5			6,464
New Jersey	33,351	51.7	31,034	48.2	69	.1			2,317
New York	226,001	51.2	212,733	48.2	2,809	.6			13,268
North Carolina	46,567	57.7	34,168	42.3					12,399
Ohio	148,043	54.3	123,944	45.4	903	.3			24,099
Pennsylvania	144,023	50.1	143,672	49.9					351
Rhode Island	5,213	60.4	3,263	37.8	19	.2	136	1.6	1,950
Tennessee	60,194	55.7	47,951	44.3					12,243
Vermont	32,440	63.9	18,006	35.5	317	.6	19		14,434
Virginia	42,637	49.4	43,757	50.7					1,120
Totals	**1,275,390**	**52.88**	**1,128,854**	**46.81**	**6,797**	**.28**	**767**	**.03**	

1844 Presidential Election

Total Popular Votes: 2,703,659
Polk's Plurality: 39,490

STATE	JAMES K. POLK (Democrat)		HENRY CLAY (Whig)		JAMES G. BIRNEY (Liberty)		OTHER[1]		PLURALITY
	Votes	%	Votes	%	Votes	%	Votes	%	
Alabama	37,401	59.0	26,002	41.0					11,399
Arkansas	9,546	63.0	5,604	37.0					3,942
Connecticut	29,841	46.2	32,832	50.8	1,943	3.0			2,991
Delaware	5,970	48.8	6,271	51.2			6	.1	301
Georgia	44,147	51.2	42,100	48.8					2,047
Illinois	58,795	53.9	45,854	42.1	3,469	3.2	939	.9	12,941
Indiana	70,183	50.1	67,866	48.4	2,108	1.5			2,317
Kentucky	51,988	45.9	61,249	54.1					9,261
Louisiana	13,782	51.3	13,083	48.7					699
Maine	45,719	53.8	34,378	40.5	4,836	5.7			11,341
Maryland	32,706	47.6	35,984	52.4					3,278
Massachusetts	53,039	40.2	67,062	50.8	10,830	8.2	1,106	.8	14,023
Michigan	27,737	49.9	24,185	43.5	3,638	6.6			3,552
Mississippi	25,846	57.4	19,158	42.6					6,688
Missouri	41,322	57.0	31,200	43.0					10,122
New Hampshire	27,160	55.2	17,866	36.3	4,161	8.5			9,294
New Jersey	37,495	49.4	38,318	50.5	131	.2			823
New York	237,588	48.9	232,482	47.9	15,812	3.3			5,106
North Carolina	39,287	47.6	43,232	52.4			2		3,945
Ohio	149,127	47.8	155,091	49.7	8,082	2.6			5,964
Pennsylvania	167,311	50.5	161,195	48.6	3,139	1.0			6,116
Rhode Island	4,867	39.9	7,322	60.1			5		2,455
Tennessee	59,917	50.0	60,040	50.1					123
Vermont	18,041	37.0	26,770	54.9	3,954	8.1			8,729
Virginia	50,679	53.1	44,860	47.0					5,819
Totals	**1,339,494**	**49.54**	**1,300,004**	**48.08**	**62,103**	**2.30**	**2,058**	**.08**	

1. For breakdown of "Other" vote, see minor candidate vote totals, p. 121.

1848 Presidential Election

Total Popular Votes: 2,879,184
Taylor's Plurality: 137,933

STATE	ZACHARY TAYLOR (Whig)		LEWIS CASS (Democrat)		MARTIN VAN BUREN (Free Soil)		OTHER [1]		PLURALITY
	Votes	%	Votes	%	Votes	%	Votes	%	
Alabama	30,482	49.4	31,173	50.6			4		691
Arkansas	7,587	44.9	9,301	55.1					1,714
Connecticut	30,318	48.6	27,051	43.4	5,005	8.0	24		3,267
Delaware	6,440	51.8	5,910	47.5	82	.7			530
Florida	4,120	57.2	3,083	42.8					1,037
Georgia	47,532	51.5	44,785	48.5					2,747
Illinois	52,853	42.4	55,952	44.9	15,702	12.6	89	.1	3,099
Indiana	69,668	45.7	74,695	49.0	8,031	5.3			5,027
Iowa	9,930	44.6	11,238	50.5	1,103	5.0			1,308
Kentucky	67,145	57.5	49,720	42.5					17,425
Louisiana	18,487	54.6	15,379	45.4					3,108
Maine	35,273	40.3	40,195	45.9	12,157	13.9			4,922
Maryland	37,702	52.1	34,528	47.7	129	.2			3,174
Massachusetts	61,072	45.3	35,281	26.2	38,333	28.5	62	.1	22,739
Michigan	23,947	36.8	30,742	47.2	10,393	16.0			6,795
Mississippi	25,911	49.4	26,545	50.6					634
Missouri	32,671	44.9	40,077	55.1					7,406
New Hampshire	14,781	29.5	27,763	55.4	7,560	15.1			12,982
New Jersey	40,015	51.5	36,901	47.5	829	1.1			3,114
New York	218,583	47.9	114,319	25.1	120,497	26.4	2,545	.6	98,086
North Carolina	44,054	55.2	35,772	44.8					8,282
Ohio	138,656	42.2	154,782	47.1	35,523	10.8	26		16,126
Pennsylvania	185,730	50.3	172,186	46.7	11,176	3.0			13,544
Rhode Island	6,705	60.7	3,613	32.7	726	6.6	5	.1	3,092
Tennessee	64,321	52.5	58,142	47.5					6,179
Texas	5,281	31.1	11,644	68.5			75	.4	6,363
Vermont	23,117	48.3	10,943	22.9	13,837	28.9			9,280
Virginia	45,265	49.2	46,739	50.8					1,474
Wisconsin	13,747	35.1	15,001	38.3	10,418	26.6			1,254
Totals	1,361,393	47.28	1,223,460	42.49	291,501	10.12	2,830	.10	

1. For breakdown of "Other" vote, see minor candidate vote totals, p. 121.

1852 Presidential Election

Total Popular Votes: 3,161,830
Pierce's Plurality: 220,568

STATE	FRANKLIN PIERCE (Democrat)		WINFIELD SCOTT (Whig)		JOHN P. HALE (Free Soil)		OTHER[1]		PLURALITY
	Votes	%	Votes	%	Votes	%	Votes	%	
Alabama	26,881	60.9	15,061	34.1			2,205	5.0	11,820
Arkansas	12,173	62.2	7,404	37.8					4,769
California	40,721	53.0	35,972	46.8	61	.1	56	.1	4,749
Connecticut	33,249	49.8	30,359	45.5	3,161	4.7	12		2,890
Delaware	6,318	49.9	6,293	49.7	62	.5			25
Florida	4,318	60.0	2,875	40.0					1,443
Georgia[2]	40,516	64.7	16,660	26.6			5,450	8.7	23,856
Illinois	80,378	51.9	64,733	41.8	9,863	6.4			15,645
Indiana	95,340	52.1	80,907	44.2	6,929	3.8			14,433
Iowa	17,763	50.2	15,856	44.8	1,606	4.5	139	.4	1,907
Kentucky	53,949	48.3	57,428	51.4	266	.2			3,479
Louisiana	18,647	51.9	17,255	48.1					1,392
Maine	41,609	50.6	32,543	39.6	8,030	9.8			9,066
Maryland	40,022	53.3	35,077	46.7	21				4,945
Massachusetts	44,569	35.1	52,683	41.5	28,023	22.1	1,828	1.4	8,114
Michigan	41,842	50.5	33,860	40.8	7,237	8.7			7,982
Mississippi	26,896	60.5	17,558	39.5					9,338
Missouri	38,817	56.4	29,984	43.6					8,833
New Hampshire	28,503	56.4	15,486	30.6	6,546	13.0			13,017
New Jersey	44,301	52.8	38,551	45.9	336	.4	738	.9	5,750
New York	262,083	50.2	234,882	45.0	25,329	4.9			27,201
North Carolina	39,788	50.4	39,043	49.5			60	.1	745
Ohio	169,193	47.9	152,577	43.2	31,133	8.8			16,616
Pennsylvania	198,568	51.2	179,182	46.2	8,500	2.2	1,670	.4	19,386
Rhode Island	8,735	51.4	7,626	44.9	644	3.8			1,109
Tennessee	56,900	49.3	58,586	50.7					1,686
Texas	14,857	73.5	5,356	26.5			10	.1	9,501
Vermont	13,044	29.8	22,173	50.6	8,621	19.7			9,129
	73,872	55.7	58,732	44.3					15,140
	33,658	52.0	22,240	34.4	8,842	13.7			11,418
Totals	**1,607,510**	**50.84**	**1,386,942**	**43.87**	**155,210**	**4.91**	**12,168**	**.38**	

1. For breakdown of "Other" vote, see minor candidate vote totals, p. 121.
2. Figures from Petersen, op. cit., p. 31.

1856 Presidential Election

Total Popular Votes: 4,054,647
Buchanan's Plurality: 493,727

STATE	JAMES BUCHANAN (Democrat)		JOHN C. FREMONT (Republican)		MILLARD FILLMORE (Whig-American)		OTHER[1]		PLURALITY
	Votes	%	Votes	%	Votes	%	Votes	%	
Alabama	46,739	62.1			28,552	37.9			18,187
Arkansas	21,910	67.1			10,732	32.9			11,178
California	53,342	48.4	20,704	18.8	36,195	32.8	14		17,147
Connecticut	35,028	43.6	42,717	53.2	2,615	3.3			7,689
Delaware	8,004	54.8	310	2.1	6,275	43.0	9	.1	1,729
Florida	6,358	56.8			4,833	43.2			1,525
Georgia	56,581	57.1			42,439	42.9			14,142
Illinois	105,528	44.1	96,275	40.2	37,531	15.7			9,253
Indiana	118,670	50.4	94,375	40.1	22,356	9.5			24,295
Iowa	37,568	40.7	45,073	48.8	9,669	10.5			7,505
Kentucky	74,642	52.5			67,416	47.5			7,226
Louisiana	22,164	51.7			20,709	48.3			1,455
Maine	39,140	35.7	67,279	61.3	3,270	3.0			28,139
Maryland	39,123	45.0	285	.3	47,452	54.6			8,329
Massachusetts	39,244	23.1	108,172	63.6	19,626	11.5	3,006	1.8	68,928
Michigan	52,136	41.5	71,762	57.2	1,660	1.3			19,626
Mississippi	35,456	59.4			24,191	40.6			11,265
Missouri	57,964	54.4			48,522	45.6			9,442
New Hampshire	31,891	45.7	37,473	53.7	410	.6			5,582
New Jersey	46,943	47.2	28,338	28.5	24,115	24.3			18,605
New York	195,878	32.8	276,004	46.3	124,604	20.9			80,126
North Carolina	48,243	56.8			36,720	43.2			11,523
Ohio	170,874	44.2	187,497	48.5	28,121	7.3	148		16,623
Pennsylvania	230,772	50.1	147,963	32.1	82,202	17.8			82,809
Rhode Island	6,680	33.7	11,467	57.9	1,675	8.5			4,787
Tennessee	69,704	52.2			63,878	47.8			5,826
Texas	31,995	66.7			16,010	33.4			15,985
Vermont	10,569	20.9	39,561	78.1	545	1.1			28,992
Virginia	90,083	60.0			60,150	40.0			29,933
Wisconsin	52,843	43.9	67,090	55.7	580	.5			14,247
Totals	1,836,072	45.28	1,342,345	33.11	873,053	21.53	3,177	.08	

1. For breakdown of "Other" vote, see minor candidate vote totals, p. 121.

1860 Presidential Election

Total Popular Vote: 4,685,561
Lincoln's Plurality: 485,706

STATE	ABRAHAM LINCOLN (Republican)		STEPHEN A. DOUGLAS (Democrat)		JOHN C. BRECKINRIDGE (Southern Democrat)		JOHN BELL (Constitutional Union)		OTHER[1]		PLURALITY
	Votes	%	Votes	%	Votes	%	Votes	%	Votes	%	
Alabama			13,618	15.1	48,669	54.0	27,835	30.9			20,834
Arkansas			5,357	9.9	28,732	53.1	20,063	37.1			8,669
California	38,733	32.3	37,999	31.7	33,969	28.4	9,111	7.6	15		734
Connecticut	43,488	58.1	15,431	20.6	14,372	19.2	1,528	2.0			28,057
Delaware	3,822	23.7	1,066	6.6	7,339	45.5	3,888	24.1			3,451
Florida			223	1.7	8,277	62.2	4,801	36.1			3,476
Georgia			11,581	10.9	52,176	48.9	42,960	40.3			9,216
Illinois	172,171	50.7	160,215	47.2	2,331	.7	4,914	1.5	35		11,956
Indiana	139,033	51.1	115,509	42.4	12,295	4.5	5,306	2.0			23,524
Iowa	70,302	54.6	55,639	43.2	1,035	.8	1,763	1.4			14,663
Kentucky[2]	1,364	.9	25,651	17.5	53,143	36.3	66,058	45.2			12,915
Louisiana			7,625	15.1	22,681	44.9	20,204	40.0			2,477
Maine	62,811	62.2	29,693	29.4	6,368	6.3	2,046	2.0			33,118
Maryland	2,294	2.5	5,966	6.5	42,482	45.9	41,760	45.1			722
Massachusetts	106,684	62.8	34,370	20.2	6,163	3.6	22,331	13.2	328	.2	72,314
Michigan	88,481	57.2	65,057	42.0	805	.5	415	.3			23,424
Minnesota	22,069	63.4	11,920	34.3	748	2.2	50	.1	17	.1	10,149
Mississippi			3,282	4.8	40,768	59.0	25,045	36.4			15,723
Missouri	17,028	10.3	58,801	35.5	31,362	18.9	58,372	35.3			429
New Hampshire	37,519	56.9	25,887	39.3	2,125	3.2	412	.6			11,632
New Jersey[2]	58,346	48.1	62,869	51.9							4,523
New York	362,646	53.7	312,510	46.3							50,136
North Carolina			2,737	2.8	48,846	50.5	45,129	46.7			3,717
Ohio	231,709	52.3	187,421	42.3	11,406	2.6	12,194	2.8	136		44,288
Oregon	5,329	36.1	4,136	28.0	5,075	34.4	218	1.5			254
Pennsylvania	268,030	56.3	16,765	3.5	178,871	37.5	12,776	2.7			89,159
Rhode Island	12,244	61.4	7,707	38.6							4,537
Tennessee			11,281	7.7	65,097	44.6	69,728	47.7			4,631
Texas			18		47,454	75.5	15,383	24.5			32,071
Vermont	33,808	75.7	8,649	19.4	218	.5	1,969	4.4			25,159
Virginia	1,887	1.1	16,198	9.7	74,325	44.5	74,481	44.6			156
Wisconsin	86,110	56.6	65,021	42.7	887	.6	161	.1			21,089
Totals	**1,865,908**	**39.82**	**1,380,202**	**29.46**	**848,019**	**18.09**	**590,901**	**12.61**	**531**	**.01**	

1. For breakdown of "Other" vote, see minor candidate vote totals, p. 121.
2. Figures from Petersen, op. cit., p. 37.

1864 Presidential Election

Total Popular Votes: 4,031,887
Lincoln's Plurality: 405,581

STATE[2]	ABRAHAM LINCOLN (Republican)		GEORGE B. MCCLELLAN (Democrat)		OTHER[1]		PLURALITY
	Votes	%	Votes	%	Votes	%	
California	62,053	58.6	43,837	41.4			18,216
Connecticut	44,673	51.4	42,285	48.6			2,388
Delaware	8,155	48.2	8,767	51.8			612
Illinois	189,512	54.4	158,724	45.6			30,788
Indiana	149,887	53.5	130,230	46.5			19,657
Iowa	83,858	63.1	49,089	36.9			34,769
Kansas	17,089	79.2	3,836	17.8	655	3.0	13,253
Kentucky	27,787	30.2	64,301	69.8			36,514
Maine	67,805	59.1	46,992	40.9			20,813
Maryland	40,153	55.1	32,739	44.9			7,414
Massachusetts	126,742	72.2	48,745	27.8	6		77,997
Michigan	91,133	55.1	74,146	44.9			16,987
Minnesota	25,031	59.0	17,376	41.0	26	.1	7,655
Missouri	72,750	69.7	31,596	30.3			41,154
Nevada	9,826	59.8	6,594	40.2			3,232
New Hampshire	36,596	52.6	33,034	47.4			3,562
New Jersey	60,724	47.2	68,020	52.8			7,296
New York	368,735	50.5	361,986	49.5			6,749
Ohio	265,674	56.4	205,609	43.6			60,065
Oregon	9,888	53.9	8,457	46.1	5		1,431
Pennsylvania	296,292	51.6	277,443	48.4			18,849
Rhode Island	14,349	62.2	8,718	37.8			5,631
Vermont	42,419	76.1	13,321	23.9			29,098
West Virginia	23,799	68.2	11,078	31.8			12,721
Wisconsin	83,458	55.9	65,884	44.1			17,574
Totals	**2,218,388**	**55.02**	**1,812,807**	**44.96**	**692**	**.02**	

1. *For breakdown of "Other" vote, see minor candidate vote totals, p. 121.*
2. *Eleven Confederate states did not participate in election because of the Civil War.*

1868 Presidential Election

Total Popular Votes: 5,722,440
Grant's Plurality: 304,906

STATE[2]	ULYSSES S. GRANT (Republican)		HORATIO SEYMOUR (Democrat)		OTHER[1]		PLURALITY
	Votes	%	Votes	%	Votes	%	
Alabama	76,667	51.3	72,921	48.8	6		3,746
Arkansas	22,112	53.7	19,078	46.3			3,034
California	54,588	50.2	54,068	49.8			520
Connecticut	50,789	51.5	47,781	48.5			3,008
Delaware	7,614	41.0	10,957	59.0			3,343
Georgia	57,109	35.7	102,707	64.3			45,598
Illinois	250,304	55.7	199,116	44.3			51,188
Indiana	176,548	51.4	166,980	48.6			9,568
Iowa	120,399	61.9	74,040	38.1			46,359
Kansas	30,027	68.8	13,600	31.2	3		16,427
Kentucky	39,566	25.5	115,889	74.6			76,323
Louisiana	33,263	29.3	80,225	70.7			46,962
Maine	70,502	62.4	42,460	37.6			28,042
Maryland	30,438	32.8	62,357	67.2			31,919
Massachusetts	136,379	69.8	59,103	30.2	26		77,276
Michigan	128,563	57.0	97,069	43.0			31,494
Minnesota	43,545	60.8	28,075	39.2			15,470
Missouri	86,860	57.0	65,628	43.0			21,232
Nebraska	9,772	63.9	5,519	36.1			4,253
Nevada	6,474	55.4	5,215	44.6			1,259
New Hampshire	37,718	55.2	30,575	44.8	11		7,143
New Jersey	80,132	49.1	83,001	50.9			2,869
New York	419,888	49.4	429,883	50.6			9,995
North Carolina	96,939	53.4	84,559	46.6			12,380
Ohio	280,159	54.0	238,506	46.0			41,653
Oregon	10,961	49.6	11,125	50.4			164
Pennsylvania	342,280	52.2	313,382	47.8			28,898
Rhode Island	13,017	66.7	6,494	33.3			6,523
South Carolina	62,301	57.9	45,237	42.1			17,064
Tennessee	56,628	68.4	26,129	31.6			30,499
Vermont	44,173	78.6	12,051	21.4			32,122
West Virginia	29,015	58.8	20,306	41.2			8,709
Wisconsin	108,920	56.3	84,708	43.8			24,212
Totals	3,013,650	52.66	2,708,744	47.34	46		

1. For breakdown of "Other" vote, see minor candidate vote totals, p. 122.
2. Mississippi, Texas and Virginia did not participate in the election due to Reconstruction. In Florida the state legislature cast the electoral vote.

1872 Presidential Election

Total Popular Votes: 6,467,679
Grant's Plurality: 763,474

STATE	ULYSSES S. GRANT (Republican)		HORACE GREELEY (Democrat, Liberal Republican)		CHARLES O'CONOR (Straight Out Democrat)		OTHER[1]		PLURALITY
	Votes	%	Votes	%	Votes	%	Votes	%	
Alabama	90,272	53.2	79,444	46.8					10,828
Arkansas	41,373	52.2	37,927	47.8					3,446
California	54,007	56.4	40,717	42.5	1,061	1.1			13,290
Connecticut	50,307	52.4	45,685	47.6					4,622
Delaware	11,129	51.0	10,205	46.8	488	2.2			924
Florida	17,763	53.5	15,427	46.5					2,336
Georgia	62,550	45.0	76,356	55.0					13,806
Illinois	241,936	56.3	184,884	43.0	3,151	.7			57,052
Indiana	186,147	53.2	163,632	46.8					22,515
Iowa	131,566	60.8	71,189	32.9	2,221	1.0	11,389	5.2	60,377
Kansas	66,805	66.5	32,970	32.8	156	.2	581	.5	33,835
Kentucky	88,766	46.4	99,995	52.3	2,374	1.2			11,229
Louisiana	71,663	55.7	57,029	44.3					14,634
Maine	61,426	67.9	29,097	32.1					32,329
Maryland	66,760	49.7	67,687	50.3					927
Massachusetts	133,455	69.3	59,195	30.7					74,260
Michigan	138,768	62.6	78,651	35.5	2,879	1.3	1,271	.6	60,117
Minnesota	56,040	61.4	35,131	38.5			168	.2	20,909
Mississippi	82,175	63.5	47,282	36.5					34,893
Missouri	119,196	43.7	151,434	55.5	2,429	.9			32,238
Nebraska	18,329	70.7	7,603	29.3					10,726
Nevada	8,413	57.4	6,236	42.6					2,177
New Hampshire	37,168	53.9	31,425	45.6			313	.5	5,743
New Jersey	91,656	54.5	76,456	45.5					15,200
New York	440,738	53.2	387,282	46.8					53,456
North Carolina	94,772	57.4	70,130	42.5	261	.2			24,642
Ohio	281,852	53.2	244,320	46.2	1,163	.2	2,100	.4	37,532
Oregon	11,818	58.8	7,742	38.5	547	2.7			4,076
Pennsylvania	349,589	62.3	212,040	37.8					137,549
Rhode Island	13,665	71.9	5,329	28.1					8,336
South Carolina	72,290	75.7	22,699	23.8	204	.2	259	.3	49,591
Tennessee	85,655	47.8	93,391	52.2					7,736
Texas	47,910	41.4	67,675	58.5	115	.1			19,765
Vermont	41,481	79.2	10,927	20.9					30,554
Virginia	93,463	50.5	91,647	49.5	85	.1			1,816
West Virginia	32,320	51.7	29,532	47.3	615	1.0			2,788
Wisconsin	105,012	54.6	86,390	44.9	853	.4			18,622
Totals	3,598,235	55.63	2,834,761	43.83	18,602	.29	16,081	.25	

1. *For breakdown of "Other" vote, see minor candidate vote totals, p. 122.*

1876 Presidential Election[2]

Total Popular Votes: 8,413,101
Tilden's Plurality: 254,235

STATE	RUTHERFORD B. HAYES[2] (Republican)		SAMUEL J. TILDEN[2] (Democrat)		PETER COOPER (Greenback)		OTHER[1]		PLURALITY
	Votes	%	Votes	%	Votes	%	Votes	%	
Alabama	68,708	40.0	102,989	60.0			2		34,281
Arkansas	38,649	39.9	58,086	59.9	211	.2			19,437
California	79,258	50.9	76,460	49.1	47		19		2,798
Connecticut	59,033	48.3	61,927	50.7	774	.6	400	.3	2,894
Delaware	10,752	44.6	13,381	55.5					2,629
Florida	23,849	51.0	22,927	49.0					922
Georgia	50,533	28.0	130,157	72.0					79,624
Illinois	278,232	50.2	258,611	46.7	17,207	3.1	318	.1	19,621
Indiana	208,011	48.3	213,529	49.5	9,533	2.2			5,518
Iowa	171,326	58.4	112,121	38.2	9,431	3.2	520	.2	59,205
Kansas	78,324	63.1	37,902	30.5	7,770	6.3	138	.1	40,422
Kentucky	97,568	37.4	160,060	61.4			2,998	1.2	62,492
Louisiana	75,315	51.7	70,508	48.4					4,807
Maine	66,300	56.6	49,917	42.7			828	.7	16,383
Maryland	71,980	44.0	91,779	56.1					19,799
Massachusetts	150,063	57.8	108,777	41.9			779	.3	41,286
Michigan	166,901	52.4	141,665	44.5	9,023	2.8	837	.3	25,236
Minnesota	72,962	58.8	48,799	39.3	2,399	1.9			24,163
Mississippi	52,603	31.9	112,173	68.1					59,570
Missouri	145,027	41.4	202,086	57.6	3,497	1.0			57,059
Nebraska	31,915	64.8	17,343	35.2					14,572
Nevada	10,383	52.7	9,308	47.3					1,075
New Hampshire	41,540	51.8	38,510	48.1			93	.1	3,030
New Jersey	103,517	47.0	115,962	52.7	714	.3			12,445
New York	489,207	48.2	521,949	51.4	1,978	.2	2,369	.2	32,742
North Carolina	108,484	46.4	125,427	53.6					16,943
Ohio	330,698	50.2	323,182	49.1	3,058	.5	1,712	.3	7,516
Oregon	15,207	50.9	14,157	47.4	509	1.7			1,050
Pennsylvania	384,157	50.6	366,204	48.3	7,209	1.0	1,403	.2	17,953
Rhode Island	15,787	59.6	10,712	40.4					5,075
South Carolina	91,786	50.2	90,897	49.8					889
Tennessee	89,566	40.2	133,177	59.8					43,611
Texas	45,013	29.7	106,372	70.2			46		61,359
Vermont	44,092	68.4	20,254	31.4			114	.2	23,838
Virginia	95,518	40.4	140,770	59.6					45,252
West Virginia	41,997	42.2	56,546	56.8	1,104	1.1			14,549
Wisconsin	130,050	50.6	123,922	48.2	1,509	.6	1,695	.7	6,128
Totals	4,034,311	47.95	4,288,546	50.97	75,973	.90	14,271	.17	

1. For breakdown of "Other" vote, see minor candidate vote totals, p. 122.
2. For resolution of disputed 1876 election, see p. 138.

1880 Presidential Election

Total Popular Votes: 9,210,420
Garfield's Plurality: 1,898

STATE	JAMES A. GARFIELD (Republican)		WINFIELD S. HANCOCK (Democrat)		JAMES B. WEAVER (Greenback)		OTHER[1]		PLURALITY
	Votes	%	Votes	%	Votes	%	Votes	%	
Alabama	56,350	37.1	91,130	60.0	4,422	2.9			34,780
Arkansas	41,661	38.7	60,489	56.1	4,079	3.8	1,543	1.4	18,828
California	80,282	48.9	80,426	49.0	3,381	2.1	129	.1	144
Colorado	27,450	51.3	24,647	46.0	1,435	2.7	14		2,803
Connecticut	67,071	50.5	64,411	48.5	868	.7	448	.3	2,660
Delaware	14,148	48.0	15,181	51.5	129	.4			1,033
Florida	23,654	45.8	27,964	54.2					4,310
Georgia	54,470	34.6	102,981	65.4					48,511
Illinois	318,036	51.1	277,321	44.6	26,358	4.2	590	.1	40,715
Indiana	232,169	49.3	225,523	47.9	13,066	2.8			6,646
Iowa	183,904	56.9	105,845	32.8	32,327	10.0	1,064	.3	78,059
Kansas	121,520	60.4	59,789	29.7	19,710	9.8	35		61,731
Kentucky	106,490	39.9	148,875	55.7	11,506	4.3	233	.1	42,385
Louisiana	38,978	37.3	65,047	62.3	437	.4			26,069
Maine	74,052	51.5	65,211	45.3	4,409	3.1	231	.2	8,841
Maryland	78,515	45.6	93,706	54.4					15,191
Massachusetts	165,198	58.5	111,960	39.6	4,548	1.6	799	.3	53,238
Michigan	185,335	52.5	131,596	37.3	34,895	9.9	1,250	.4	53,739
Minnesota	93,939	62.3	53,314	35.4	3,267	2.2	286	.2	40,625
Mississippi	34,844	29.8	75,750	64.7	5,797	5.0	677	.6	40,906
Missouri	153,647	38.7	208,600	52.5	35,042	8.8			54,953
Nebraska	54,979	62.9	28,523	32.7	3,853	4.4			26,456
Nevada	8,732	47.6	9,611	52.4					879
New Hampshire	44,856	51.9	40,797	47.2	528	.6	180	.2	4,059
New Jersey	120,555	49.0	122,565	49.8	2,617	1.1	191	.1	2,010
New York	555,544	50.3	534,511	48.4	12,373	1.1	1,517	.1	21,033
North Carolina	115,616	48.0	124,204	51.6	1,126	.5			8,588
Ohio	375,048	51.7	340,867	47.0	6,456	.9	2,613	.4	34,181
Oregon	20,619	50.5	19,955	48.9	267	.7			664
Pennsylvania	444,704	50.8	407,428	46.6	20,667	2.4	1,984	.2	37,276
Rhode Island	18,195	62.2	10,779	36.9	236	.8	25	.1	7,416
South Carolina	57,954	34.1	111,236	65.5	567	.3	36		53,282
Tennessee	107,677	44.3	129,569	53.3	6,017	2.5			21,892
Texas	50,217	21.5	156,010	66.8	27,405	11.7			105,793
Vermont	45,567	70.0	18,316	28.1	1,215	1.9			27,251
Virginia	83,533	39.5	128,083	60.5					44,550
West Virginia	46,243	41.1	57,390	51.0	9,008	8.0			11,147
Wisconsin	144,406	54.0	114,650	42.9	7,986	3.0	160	.1	29,756
Totals	4,446,158	48.27	4,444,260	48.25	305,997	3.32	14,005	.15	

1. For breakdown of "Other" vote, see minor candidate vote totals, p. 122.

1884 Presidential Election

Total Popular Votes: 10,049,754
Cleveland's Plurality: 25,685

STATE	GROVER CLEVELAND (Democrat)		JAMES G. BLAINE (Republican)		BENJAMIN F. BUTLER (Greenback)		JOHN P. ST. JOHN (Prohibition)		OTHER[1]		PLURALITY
	Votes	%	Votes	%	Votes	%	Votes	%	Votes	%	
Alabama	92,736	60.4	59,444	38.7	762	.5	610	.4	72	.1	33,292
Arkansas	72,734	57.8	51,198	40.7	1,847	1.5					21,536
California	89,288	45.3	102,369	52.0	2,037	1.0	2,965	1.5	329	.2	13,081
Colorado	27,723	41.7	36,084	54.3	1,956	2.9	756	1.1			8,361
Connecticut	67,167	49.0	65,879	48.0	1,682	1.2	2,493	1.8			1,288
Delaware	16,957	56.6	12,953	43.2	10		64	.2			4,004
Florida	31,769	53.0	28,031	46.7			72	.1	118	.2	3,738
Georgia	94,667	65.9	48,603	33.8	145	.1	195	.1			46,064
Illinois	312,351	46.4	337,469	50.2	10,776	1.6	12,074	1.8			25,118
Indiana	244,989	49.8	238,466	48.5	8,194	1.7					6,523
Iowa	177,316	47.0	197,089	52.3			1,499	.4	1,297	.3	19,773
Kansas	90,111	33.9	154,410	58.1	16,341	6.2	4,311	1.6	468	.2	64,299
Kentucky	152,961	55.3	118,690	42.9	1,691	.6	3,139	1.1			34,271
Louisiana	62,594	57.2	46,347	42.4	120	.1	338	.3			16,247
Maine	52,153	40.0	72,217	55.3	3,955	3.0	2,160	1.7	6		20,064
Maryland	96,866	52.1	85,748	46.1	578	.3	2,827	1.5			11,118
Massachusetts	122,352	40.3	146,724	48.4	24,382	8.0	9,923	3.3	2		24,372
Michigan	149,835	37.2	192,669	47.8	42,252	10.5	18,403	4.6			42,834
Minnesota	70,065	36.9	111,685	58.8	3,583	1.9	4,684	2.5			41,620
Mississippi	77,653	64.3	43,035	35.7							34,618
Missouri	236,023	53.5	203,081	46.0			2,164	.5			32,942
Nebraska	54,391	40.5	76,912	57.3			2,899	2.2			22,521
Nevada	5,577	43.6	7,176	56.2	26	.2					1,599
New Hampshire	39,198	46.3	43,254	51.1	554	.7	1,580	1.9			4,056
New Jersey	127,747	49.0	123,436	47.3	3,486	1.3	6,156	2.4	28		4,311
New York	563,048	48.3	562,001	48.2	16,955	1.5	24,999	2.1			1,047
North Carolina	142,905	53.3	125,021	46.6			430	.2			17,884
Ohio	368,280	46.9	400,092	51.0	5,179	.7	11,069	1.4			31,812
Oregon	24,598	46.7	26,845	51.0	726	1.4	479	.9	35	.1	2,247
Pennsylvania	394,772	43.9	472,792	52.6	16,992	1.9	15,154	1.7			78,020
Rhode Island	12,391	37.8	19,030	58.1	422	1.3	928	2.8			6,639
South Carolina	69,845	75.3	21,730	23.4					1,237	1.3	48,115
Tennessee	133,770	51.5	124,101	47.7	957	.4	1,150	.4			9,669
Texas	223,209	69.5	91,234	28.4	3,310	1.0	3,489	1.1			131,975
Vermont	17,331	29.2	39,514	66.5	785	1.3	1,752	3.0	27	.1	22,183
Virginia	145,491	51.1	139,356	48.9			130	.1			6,135
West Virginia	67,311	50.9	63,096	47.8	799	.6	939	.7			4,215
Wisconsin	146,447	45.8	161,155	50.4	4,594	1.4	7,651	2.4			14,708
Totals	**4,874,621**	**48.50**	**4,848,936**	**48.25**	**175,096**	**1.74**	**147,482**	**1.47**	**3,619**	**.04**	

1. For breakdown of "Other" vote, see minor candidate vote totals, p. 122.

1888 Presidential Election

Total Popular Votes: 11,383,320
Cleveland's Plurality: 90,596 [2]

STATE	BENJAMIN HARRISON (Republican)		GROVER CLEVELAND (Democrat)		CLINTON B. FISK (Prohibition)		ALSON J. STREETER (Union Labor)		OTHER [1]		PLURALITY
	Votes	%	Votes	%	Votes	%	Votes	%	Votes	%	
Alabama	57,177	32.7	117,314	67.0	594	.3					60,137
Arkansas	59,752	38.0	86,062	54.8	614	.4	10,630	6.8			26,310
California	124,816	49.7	117,729	46.8	5,761	2.3			3,033	1.2	7,087
Colorado	50,772	55.2	37,549	40.8	2,182	2.4	1,266	1.4	177	.2	13,223
Connecticut	74,584	48.4	74,920	48.7	4,234	2.8	240	.2			336
Delaware	12,950	43.5	16,414	55.2	399	1.3			1		3,464
Florida	26,529	39.9	39,557	59.5	414	.6					13,028
Georgia	40,499	28.3	100,493	70.3	1,808	1.3	136	.1			59,994
Illinois	370,475	49.5	348,351	46.6	21,703	2.9	7,134	1.0	150		22,124
Indiana	263,366	49.1	260,990	48.6	9,939	1.9	2,693	.5			2,376
Iowa	211,607	52.3	179,876	44.5	3,550	.9	9,105	2.3	556	.1	31,731
Kansas	182,845	55.2	102,739	31.0	6,774	2.1	37,838	11.4	937	.3	80,106
Kentucky	155,138	45.0	183,830	53.3	5,223	1.5	677	.2			28,692
Louisiana	30,660	26.5	85,032	73.4	160	.1	39				54,372
Maine	73,730	57.5	50,472	39.4	2,691	2.1	1,344	1.1	16		23,258
Maryland	99,986	47.4	106,188	50.3	4,767	2.3					6,202
Massachusetts	183,892	53.4	151,590	44.0	8,701	2.5			60		32,302
Michigan	236,387	49.7	213,469	44.9	20,945	4.4	4,555	1.0			22,918
Minnesota	142,492	54.2	104,372	39.7	15,201	5.8	1,097	.4			38,120
Mississippi	30,095	26.0	85,451	73.8	240	.2					55,356
Missouri	236,252	45.3	261,943	50.2	4,539	.9	18,625	3.6			25,691
Nebraska	108,417	53.5	80,552	39.8	9,435	4.7	4,226	2.1			27,865
Nevada	7,229	57.5	5,303	42.2	41	.3					1,926
New Hampshire	45,734	50.4	43,382	47.8	1,596	1.8			58	.1	2,352
New Jersey	144,347	47.5	151,493	49.9	7,794	2.6					7,146
New York	650,338	49.3	635,965	48.2	30,231	2.3	627	.1	2,587	.2	14,373
North Carolina	134,784	47.2	147,902	51.8	2,840	1.0			37		13,118
Ohio	416,054	49.6	395,456	47.1	24,356	2.9	3,491	.4			20,598
Oregon	33,291	53.8	26,518	42.9	1,676	2.7			404	.7	6,773
Pennsylvania	526,091	52.7	446,633	44.8	20,947	2.1	3,873	.4	24		79,458
Rhode Island	21,969	53.9	17,530	43.0	1,251	3.1	18		7		4,439
South Carolina	13,736	17.2	65,824	82.3					437	.6	52,088
Tennessee	138,978	45.8	158,699	52.3	5,969	2.0	48				19,721
Texas	88,604	25.0	232,189	65.5	4,739	1.3	28,880	8.2			143,585
Vermont	45,193	71.2	16,788	26.5	1,460	2.3			35	.1	28,405
Virginia	150,399	49.5	152,004	50.0	1,684	.6					1,605
West Virginia	78,171	49.0	78,677	49.4	1,084	.7	1,508	1.0			506
Wisconsin	176,553	49.8	155,232	43.8	14,277	4.0	8,552	2.4			21,321
Totals	5,443,892	47.82	5,534,488	48.62	249,813	2.19	146,602	1.29	8,519	.07	

1. For breakdown of "Other" vote, see minor candidate vote totals, p. 122.
2. Harrison won the election. See p. 134.

1892 Presidential Election

Total Popular Votes: 12,056,097
Cleveland's Plurality: 372,639

STATE	GROVER CLEVELAND (Democrat) Votes	%	BENJAMIN HARRISON (Republican) Votes	%	JAMES B. WEAVER (Populist) Votes	%	JOHN BIDWELL (Prohibition) Votes	%	OTHER[1] Votes	%	PLURALITY
Alabama	138,135	59.4	9,184	4.0	84,984	36.6	240	.1			53,151
Arkansas	87,834	59.3	47,072	31.8	11,831	8.0	113	.1	1,267	.9	40,762
California	118,151	43.8	118,027	43.8	25,311	9.4	8,096	3.0			124
Colorado			38,620	41.1	53,584	57.1	1,677	1.8			14,964
Connecticut	82,395	50.1	77,030	46.8	809	.5	4,026	2.5	333	.2	5,365
Delaware	18,581	49.9	18,077	48.6			564	1.5	13		504
Florida	30,153	85.0			4,843	13.7	475	1.3			25,310
Georgia	129,446	58.0	48,408	21.7	41,939	18.8	988	.4	2,345	1.1	81,038
Idaho			8,599	44.3	10,520	54.2	288	1.5			1,921
Illinois	426,281	48.8	399,308	45.7	22,207	2.5	25,871	3.0			26,973
Indiana	262,740	47.5	255,615	46.2	22,208	4.0	13,050	2.4			7,125
Iowa	196,367	44.3	219,795	49.6	20,595	4.7	6,402	1.4			23,428
Kansas			156,134	48.3	162,888	50.3	4,569	1.4			6,754
Kentucky	175,461	51.5	135,462	39.7	23,500	6.9	6,441	1.9			39,999
Louisiana	87,926	76.5	26,963	23.5							60,963
Maine	48,049	41.3	62,936	54.1	2,396	2.1	3,066	2.6	4		14,887
Maryland	113,866	53.4	92,736	43.5	796	.4	5,877	2.8			21,130
Massachusetts	176,813	45.2	202,814	51.9	3,210	.8	7,539	1.9	652	.2	26,001
Michigan	202,396	43.4	222,708	47.7	20,031	4.3	20,857	4.5	925	.2	20,312
Minnesota	100,589	37.6	122,736	45.8	30,399	11.3	14,117	5.3			22,147
Mississippi	40,030	76.2	1,398	2.7	10,118	19.3	973	1.9			29,912
Missouri	268,400	49.6	227,646	42.0	41,204	7.6	4,333	.8			40,754
Montana	17,690	39.8	18,871	42.4	7,338	16.5	562	1.3			1,181
Nebraska	24,956	12.5	87,213	43.6	83,134	41.5	4,902	2.5			4,079
Nevada	703	6.5	2,811	26.0	7,226	66.8	86	.8			4,415
New Hampshire	42,081	47.1	45,658	51.1	292	.3	1,297	1.5			3,577
New Jersey	170,987	50.7	156,059	46.2	969	.3	8,133	2.4	1,337	.4	14,928
New York	654,868	49.0	609,350	45.6	16,429	1.2	38,190	2.9	17,956	1.3	45,518
North Carolina	132,951	47.4	100,346	35.8	44,336	15.8	2,637	.9			32,605
North Dakota[2]			17,519	48.5	17,700	49.0	899	2.5			181
Ohio	404,115	47.5	405,187	47.7	14,850	1.8	26,012	3.1			1,072
Oregon	14,243	18.2	35,002	44.7	26,875	34.3	2,258	2.9			8,127
Pennsylvania	452,264	45.1	516,011	51.5	8,714	.9	25,123	2.5	888	.1	63,747
Rhode Island	24,336	45.8	26,975	50.7	228	.4	1,654	3.1	3		2,639
South Carolina	54,680	77.6	13,345	18.9	2,407	3.4			72	.1	41,335
South Dakota	8,894	12.7	34,714	49.5	26,552	37.8					8,162
Tennessee	136,468	51.4	100,537	37.8	23,918	9.0	4,809	1.8			35,931
Texas	236,979	57.7	70,982	17.3	96,649	23.5	2,164	.5	4,086	1.0	140,330
Vermont	16,325	29.3	37,992	68.1	42	.1	1,424	2.6	10		21,667
Virginia	164,136	56.2	113,098	38.7	12,275	4.2	2,729	.9			51,038
Washington	29,802	33.9	36,459	41.5	19,165	21.8	2,542	2.9			6,657
West Virginia	84,467	49.4	80,292	46.9	4,167	2.4	2,153	1.3			4,175
Wisconsin	177,325	47.7	171,101	46.1	9,919	2.7	13,136	3.5			6,224
Wyoming			8,454	50.6	7,722	46.2	498	3.0	29	.2	732
Totals	5,551,883	46.05	5,179,244	42.96	1,024,280	8.50	270,770	2.25	29,920	.25	

1. For breakdown of "Other" vote, see minor candidate vote totals, p. 122.
2. Figures from Petersen, op. cit., p. 60.

1896 Presidential Election

Total Popular Votes: 13,935,738
McKinley's Plurality: 596,985

STATE	WILLIAM McKINLEY (Republican)		WILLIAM J. BRYAN (Democrat, Populist)		JOHN M. PALMER (National Democrat)		JOSHUA LEVERING (Prohibition)		OTHER[1]		PLURALITY
	Votes	%	Votes	%	Votes	%	Votes	%	Votes	%	
Alabama	55,673	28.6	130,298	67.0	6,375	3.3	2,234	1.2			74,625
Arkansas	37,512	25.1	110,103	73.7			889	.6	892	.6	72,591
California	146,756	49.2	144,877	48.5	1,730	.6	2,573	.9	2,662	.9	1,879
Colorado	26,271	13.9	161,005	84.9	1		1,717	.9	545	.3	134,734
Connecticut	110,285	63.2	56,740	32.5	4,336	2.5	1,806	1.0	1,227	.7	53,545
Delaware	20,450	53.2	16,574	43.1	966	2.5	466	1.2			3,876
Florida	11,298	24.3	32,756	70.4	1,778	3.8	656	1.4			21,458
Georgia	59,395	36.6	93,885	57.8	3,670	2.3	5,483	3.4	47		34,490
Idaho	6,324	21.3	23,135	78.1			172	.6			16,811
Illinois	607,130	55.7	465,593	42.7	6,307	.6	9,796	.9	1,940	.2	141,537
Indiana	323,754	50.8	305,538	48.0	2,145	.3	3,061	.5	2,591	.4	18,216
Iowa	289,293	55.5	223,744	42.9	4,516	.9	3,192	.6	805	.2	65,549
Kansas	159,484	47.5	173,049	51.5	1,209	.4	1,723	.5	620	.2	13,565
Kentucky	218,171	48.9	217,894	48.9	5,084	1.1	4,779	1.1			277
Louisiana	22,037	21.8	77,175	76.4	1,834	1.8					55,138
Maine	80,403	67.9	34,587	29.2	1,867	1.6	1,562	1.3			45,816
Maryland	136,959	54.7	104,150	41.6	2,499	1.0	5,918	2.4	723	.3	32,809
Massachusetts	278,976	69.5	105,414	26.3	11,749	2.9	2,998	.8	2,132	.5	173,562
Michigan	293,336	53.8	237,164	43.5	6,923	1.3	4,978	.9	3,182	.6	56,172
Minnesota	193,503	56.6	139,735	40.9	3,222	.9	4,348	1.3	954	.3	53,768
Mississippi	4,819	6.9	63,355	91.0	1,021	1.5	396	.6			58,536
Missouri	304,940	45.2	363,667	54.0	2,365	.4	2,169	.3	891	.1	58,727
Montana	10,509	19.7	42,628	79.9			193	.4			32,119
Nebraska	103,064	46.2	115,007	51.5	2,885	1.3	1,242	.6	983	.4	11,943
Nevada	1,938	18.8	8,348	81.2							6,410
New Hampshire	57,444	68.7	21,650	25.9	3,520	4.2	779	.9	277	.3	35,794
New Jersey	221,367	59.7	133,675	36.0	6,373	1.7			9,599	2.6	87,692
New York	819,838	57.6	551,369	38.7	18,950	1.3	16,052	1.1	17,667	1.2	268,469
North Carolina	155,122	46.8	174,408	52.6	578	.2	635	.2	594	.2	19,286
North Dakota	26,335	55.6	20,686	43.7			358	.8	12		5,649
Ohio	525,991	51.9	477,497	47.1	1,858	.2	5,068	.5	3,881	.4	48,494
Oregon	48,700	50.0	46,739	48.0	977	1.0	919	.9			1,961
Pennsylvania	728,300	61.0	433,228	36.3	11,000	.9	19,274	1.6	2,553	.2	295,072
Rhode Island	37,437	68.3	14,459	26.4	1,166	2.1	1,160	2.1	563	1.0	22,978
South Carolina	9,313	13.5	58,801	85.3	824	1.2					49,488
South Dakota	41,040	49.5	41,225	49.7			672	.8			185
Tennessee	148,683	46.3	167,168	52.1	1,953	.6	3,099	1.0			18,485
Texas	163,894	30.3	370,308	68.4	5,022	.9	1,794	.3			206,414
Utah	13,491	17.3	64,607	82.7							51,116
Vermont	51,127	80.1	10,367	16.7	1,341	2.1	733	1.2			40,490
Virginia	135,379	45.9	154,708	52.5	2,129	.7	2,350	.8	108		19,329
Washington	39,153	41.8	53,314	57.0			968	1.0	148	.2	14,361
West Virginia	105,379	52.2	94,480	46.8	678	.3	1,220	.6			10,899
Wisconsin	268,135	59.9	165,523	37.0	4,584	1.0	7,507	1.7	1.660	.4	102,612
Wyoming	10,072	47.8	10,862	51.6			133	.6			790
Totals	7,108,480	51.01	6,511,495	46.73	133,435	.96	125,072	.90	57,256	.41	

1. For breakdown of "Other" vote, see minor candidate vote totals, p. 122.

1900 Presidential Election

Total Popular Votes: 13,970,470
McKinley's Plurality: 859,694

STATE	WILLIAM McKINLEY (Republican)		WILLIAM J. BRYAN (Democrat)		JOHN C. WOOLLEY (Prohibition)		EUGENE V. DEBS (Socialist)		OTHER[1]		PLURALITY
	Votes	%	Votes	%	Votes	%	Votes	%	Votes	%	
Alabama	55,612	34.8	97,129	60.8	2,763	1.7			4,188	2.6	41,517
Arkansas	44,800	35.0	81,242	63.5	584	.5			1,340	1.1	36,442
California	164,755	54.5	124,985	41.3	5,024	1.7			7,554	2.5	39,770
Colorado	92,701	42.0	122,705	55.6	3,790	1.7	686	.3	1,013	.5	30,004
Connecticut	102,572	56.9	74,014	41.1	1,617	.9	1,029	.6	963	.5	28,558
Delaware	22,535	53.7	18,852	44.9	546	1.3	56	.1			3,683
Florida	7,355	18.6	28,273	71.3	2,244	5.7	634	1.6	1,143	2.9	20,918
Georgia	34,260	28.2	81,180	66.9	1,402	1.2			4,568	3.8	46,920
Idaho	27,198	46.9	29,484	50.9	857	1.5			445	.8	2,286
Illinois	597,985	52.8	503,061	44.4	17,626	1.6	9,687	.9	3,539	.3	94,924
Indiana	336,063	50.6	309,584	46.6	13,718	2.1	2,374	.4	2,355	.4	26,479
Iowa	307,799	58.0	209,261	39.5	9,502	1.8	2,743	.5	1,040	.2	98,538
Kansas[2]	185,955	52.6	162,601	46.0	3,605	1.0	1,605	.5			23,534
Kentucky	227,132	48.5	235,126	50.2	2,890	.6	766	.2	2,351	.5	7,994
Louisiana	14,234	21.0	53,668	79.0					4		39,434
Maine	65,412	61.9	36,822	34.8	2,581	2.4	878	.8			28,590
Maryland	136,151	51.5	122,237	46.2	4,574	1.7	900	.3	524	.2	13,914
Massachusetts	238,866	57.6	156,997	37.9	6,202	1.5	9,607	2.3	3,132	.8	81,869
Michigan	316,014	58.1	211,432	38.9	11,804	2.2	2,820	.5	1,719	.3	104,582
Minnesota	190,461	60.2	112,901	35.7	8,555	2.7	3,065	1.0	1,329	.4	77,560
Mississippi	5,707	9.7	51,706	87.6					1,642	2.8	45,999
Missouri	314,092	45.9	351,922	51.5	5,965	.9	6,139	.9	5,540	.8	37,830
Montana	25,409	39.8	37,311	58.4	306	.5	711	1.1	119	.2	11,902
Nebraska	121,835	50.5	114,013	47.2	3,655	1.5	823	.3	1,104	.5	7,822
Nevada	3,849	37.8	6,347	62.3							2,498
New Hampshire	54,799	59.3	35,489	38.4	1,270	1.4	790	.9	16		19,310
New Jersey	221,707	55.3	164,808	41.1	7,183	1.8	4,609	1.2	2,743	.7	56,899
New York	822,013	53.1	678,462	43.8	22,077	1.4	12,869	.8	12,622	.8	143,551
North Carolina	132,997	45.5	157,733	53.9	990	.3			798	.3	24,736
North Dakota	35,898	62.1	20,524	35.5	735	1.3	517	.9	109	.2	15,374
Ohio	543,918	52.3	474,882	45.7	10,203	1.0	4,847	.5	6,223	.6	69,036
Oregon	46,172	55.5	32,810	39.4	2,536	3.1	1,464	1.8	269	.3	13,362
Pennsylvania	712,665	60.7	424,232	36.2	27,908	2.4	4,831	.4	3,574	.3	288,433
Rhode Island	33,784	59.7	19,812	35.0	1,529	2.7			1,423	2.5	13,972
South Carolina	3,525	7.0	47,173	93.1							43,648
South Dakota	54,574	56.8	39,538	41.1	1,541	1.6	176	.2	340	.4	15,036
Tennessee	123,108	45.0	145,240	53.0	3,844	1.4	346	.1	1,322	.5	22,132
Texas	131,174	30.9	267,945	63.1	2,642	.6	1,846	.4	20,727	4.9	136,771
Utah	47,089	50.6	44,949	48.3	205	.2	717	.8	111	.1	2,140
Vermont	42,569	75.7	12,849	22.9	383	.7	39	.1	372	.7	29,720
Virginia	115,769	43.8	146,079	55.3	2,130	.8			230	.1	30,310
Washington	57,455	53.4	44,833	41.7	2,363	2.2	2,006	1.9	866	.8	12,622
West Virginia	119,829	54.3	98,807	44.8	1,628	.7	286	.1	246	.1	21,022
Wisconsin	265,760	60.1	159,163	36.0	10,027	2.3	7,048	1.6	503	.1	106,597
Wyoming	14,482	58.6	10,164	41.1			21	.1	41	.2	4,318
Totals	7,218,039	51.67	6,358,345	45.51	209,004	1.50	86,935	.62	98,147	.70	

1. For breakdown of "Other" vote, see minor candidate vote totals, p. 123.
2. Figures from Petersen, op. cit., p. 67.

1904 Presidential Election

Total Popular Votes: 13,518,964
Roosevelt's Plurality: 2,543,695

STATE	THEODORE ROOSEVELT (Republican)		ALTON PARKER (Democrat)		EUGENE V. DEBS (Socialist)		SILAS C. SWALLOW (Prohibition)		OTHER[1]		PLURALITY
	Votes	%	Votes	%	Votes	%	Votes	%	Votes	%	
Alabama	22,472	20.7	79,797	73.4	853	.8	612	.6	5,051	4.6	57,325
Arkansas	46,760	40.2	64,434	55.4	1,816	1.6	992	.9	2,326	2.0	17,674
California	205,226	61.9	89,294	26.9	29,535	8.9	7,380	2.2	333	.1	115,932
Colorado	134,661	55.3	100,105	41.1	4,304	1.8	3,438	1.4	1,159	.5	34,556
Connecticut	111,089	58.1	72,909	38.2	4,543	2.4	1,506	.8	1,089	.6	38,180
Delaware	23,705	54.1	19,347	44.1	146	.3	607	1.4	51	.1	4,358
Florida	8,314	21.5	26,449	68.3	2,337	6.0			1,605	4.2	18,135
Georgia	24,004	18.3	83,466	63.7	196	.2	685	.5	22,635	17.3	59,462
Idaho	47,783	65.8	18,480	25.5	4,949	6.8	1,013	1.4	352	.5	29,303
Illinois	632,645	58.8	327,606	30.4	69,225	6.4	34,770	3.2	12,249	1.1	305,039
Indiana	368,289	54.0	274,356	40.2	12,023	1.8	23,496	3.4	4,042	.6	93,933
Iowa	307,907	63.4	149,141	30.7	14,847	3.1	11,601	2.4	2,207	.5	158,766
Kansas	213,455	64.9	86,164	26.2	15,869	4.8	7,306	2.2	6,253	1.9	127,291
Kentucky	205,457	47.1	217,170	49.8	3,599	.8	6,603	1.5	3,117	.7	11,713
Louisiana	5,205	9.7	47,708	88.5	995	1.9					42,503
Maine	65,432	67.4	27,642	28.5	2,102	2.2	1,510	1.6	337	.4	37,790
Maryland	109,497	48.8	109,446	48.8	2,247	1.0	3,034	1.4	5		51
Massachusetts	257,813	57.9	165,746	37.2	13,604	3.1	4,279	1.0	3,658	.8	92,067
Michigan	361,863	69.5	134,163	25.8	8,942	1.7	13,312	2.6	2,163	.4	227,700
Minnesota	216,651	74.0	55,187	18.8	11,692	4.0	6,253	2.1	3,077	1.1	161,464
Mississippi	3,280	5.6	53,480	91.1	462	.8			1,499	2.6	50,200
Missouri	321,449	49.9	296,312	46.0	13,009	2.0	7,191	1.1	5,900	.9	25,137
Montana	33,994	53.5	21,816	34.3	5,675	8.9	339	.5	1,744	2.8	12,178
Nebraska	138,558	61.4	52,921	23.4	7,412	3.3	6,323	2.8	20,518	9.1	85,637
Nevada	6,864	56.7	3,982	32.9	925	7.6			344	2.8	2,882
New Hampshire	54,157	60.1	34,071	37.8	1,090	1.2	750	.8	83	.1	20,086
New Jersey	245,164	56.7	164,566	38.1	9,587	2.2	6,845	1.6	6,085	1.4	80,598
New York	859,533	53.1	683,981	42.3	36,883	2.3	20,787	1.3	16,581	1.0	175,552
North Carolina	82,442	39.7	124,091	59.7	124	.1	342	.2	819	.4	41,649
North Dakota	52,595	75.1	14,273	20.4	2,009	2.9	1,137	1.6			38,322
Ohio	600,095	59.8	344,674	34.3	36,260	3.6	19,339	1.9	4,027	.4	255,421
Oregon	60,309	67.3	17,327	19.3	7,479	8.3	3,795	4.2	746	.8	42,982
Pennsylvania	840,949	68.0	337,998	27.3	21,863	1.8	33,717	2.7	2,211	.2	502,951
Rhode Island	41,605	60.6	24,839	36.2	956	1.4	768	1.1	488	.7	16,766
South Carolina	2,570	4.6	53,320	95.4							50,750
South Dakota	72,083	71.1	21,969	21.7	3,138	3.1	2,965	2.9	1,240	1.2	50,114
Tennessee	105,363	43.4	131,653	54.2	1,354	.6	1,889	.8	2,491	1.0	26,290
Texas	51,307	22.0	167,088	71.5	2,788	1.2	3,933	1.7	8,493	3.6	115,781
Utah	62,446	61.5	33,413	32.9	5,767	5.7					29,033
Vermont	40,459	78.0	9,777	18.8	859	1.7	792	1.5	1		30,682
Virginia	48,180	37.0	80,649	61.8	202	.2	1,379	1.1			32,469
Washington	101,540	70.0	28,098	19.4	10,023	6.9	3,229	2.2	2,261	1.6	73,442
West Virginia	132,620	55.3	100,855	42.0	1,573	.7	4,599	1.9	339	.1	31,765
Wisconsin	280,314	63.2	124,205	28.0	28,240	6.4	9,872	2.2	809	.2	156,109
Wyoming	20,489	66.9	8,930	29.2	987	3.2	208	.7			11,559
Totals	7,626,593	56.41	5,082,898	37.60	402,489	2.98	258,596	1.91	148,388	1.10	

1. For breakdown of "Other" vote, see minor candidate vote totals, p. 123.

1908 Presidential Election

Total Popular Votes: 14,882,734
Taft's Plurality: 1,269,457

STATE	WILLIAM H. TAFT (Republican)		WILLIAM J. BRYAN (Democrat)		EUGENE V. DEBS (Socialist)		EUGENE W. CHAFIN (Prohibition)		OTHER[1]		PLURALITY
	Votes	%	Votes	%	Votes	%	Votes	%	Votes	%	
Alabama	25,561	24.3	74,391	70.8	1,450	1.4	690	.7	3,060	2.9	48,830
Arkansas	56,684	37.3	87,020	57.3	5,842	3.9	1,026	.7	1,273	.8	30,336
California	214,398	55.5	127,492	33.0	28,659	7.4	11,770	3.0	4,306	1.1	86,906
Colorado	123,693	46.9	126,644	48.0	7,960	3.0	5,559	2.1	2		2,951
Connecticut	112,815	59.4	68,255	35.9	5,113	2.7	2,380	1.3	1,340	.7	44,560
Delaware	25,014	52.1	22,055	45.9	239	.5	670	1.4	29		2,959
Florida	10,654	21.6	31,104	63.0	3,747	7.6	1,356	2.8	2,499	5.1	20,450
Georgia	41,355	31.2	72,350	54.6	584	.4	1,452	1.1	16,763	12.7	30,995
Idaho	52,621	54.1	36,162	37.2	6,400	6.6	1,986	2.0	124	.1	16,459
Illinois	629,932	54.5	450,810	39.0	34,711	3.0	29,364	2.5	10,437	.9	179,122
Indiana	348,993	48.4	338,262	46.9	13,476	1.9	18,036	2.5	2,350	.3	10,731
Iowa	275,210	55.6	200,771	40.6	8,287	1.7	9,837	2.0	665	.1	74,439
Kansas	197,316	52.5	161,209	42.9	12,420	3.3	5,030	1.3	68	.2	36,107
Kentucky	235,711	48.0	244,092	49.7	4,093	.8	5,885	1.2	938	.2	8,381
Louisiana	8,958	11.9	63,568	84.6	2,514	3.4			77	.1	54,610
Maine	66,987	63.0	35,403	33.3	1,758	1.7	1,487	1.4	700	.7	31,584
Maryland	116,513	48.9	115,908	48.6	2,323	1.0	3,302	1.4	485	.2	605
Massachusetts	265,966	58.2	155,533	34.0	10,778	2.4	4,373	1.0	20,255	4.4	110,433
Michigan	333,313	61.9	174,619	32.5	11,527	2.1	16,785	3.1	1,880	.4	158,694
Minnesota	195,843	59.3	109,401	33.1	14,472	4.4	10,114	3.1	424	.1	86,442
Mississippi	4,363	6.5	60,287	90.1	978	1.5			1,276	1.9	55,924
Missouri	347,203	48.5	346,574	48.4	15,431	2.2	4,209	.6	2,424	.3	629
Montana	32,471	46.9	29,511	42.6	5,920	8.6	838	1.2	493	.7	2,960
Nebraska	126,997	47.6	131,099	49.1	3,524	1.3	5,179	1.9			4,102
Nevada	10,775	43.9	11,212	45.7	2,103	8.6			436	1.8	437
New Hampshire	53,144	59.3	33,655	37.6	1,299	1.5	905	1.0	592	.7	19,489
New Jersey	265,298	56.8	182,522	39.1	10,249	2.2	4,930	1.1	4,112	.9	82,776
New York	870,070	53.1	667,468	40.7	38,451	2.4	22,667	1.4	39,694	2.4	202,602
North Carolina	114,887	45.5	136,928	54.2	372	.2	354	.1	13		22,041
North Dakota	57,680	61.0	32,884	34.8	2,421	2.6	1,496	1.6	43	.1	24,796
Ohio	572,312	51.0	502,721	44.8	33,795	3.0	11,402	1.0	1,322	.1	69,591
Oklahoma	110,473	43.5	122,362	48.1	21,425	8.4					11,889
Oregon	62,454	56.5	37,792	34.2	7,322	6.6	2,682	2.4	289	.3	24,662
Pennsylvania	745,779	58.8	448,782	35.4	33,914	2.7	36,694	2.9	2,281	.2	296,997
Rhode Island	43,942	60.8	24,706	34.2	1,365	1.9	1,016	1.4	1,288	1.8	19,236
South Carolina	3,945	5.9	62,288	93.8	100	.2			46	.1	58,343
South Dakota	67,536	58.8	40,266	35.1	2,846	2.5	4,039	3.5	88	.1	27,270
Tennessee	117,977	45.9	135,608	52.7	1,870	.7	301	.1	1,424	.6	17,631
Texas	65,605	22.4	216,662	74.0	7,779	2.7	1,626	.6	1,241	.4	151,057
Utah	61,165	56.2	42,610	39.2	4,890	4.5			92	.1	18,555
Vermont	39,552	75.1	11,496	21.8			799	1.5	833	1.6	28,056
Virginia	52,572	38.4	82,946	60.5	255	.2	1,111	.8	181	.1	30,374
Washington	106,062	57.8	58,383	31.8	14,177	7.7	4,700	2.6	248	.1	47,679
West Virginia	137,869	53.4	111,410	43.2	3,679	1.4	5,140	2.0		.1	26,459
Wisconsin	247,744	54.5	166,662	36.7	28,147	6.2	11,565	2.5	320	.1	81,082
Wyoming	20,846	55.4	14,918	39.7	1,715	4.6	66	.2	63	.2	5,928
Totals	7,676,258	51.58	6,406,801	43.05	420,380	2.82	252,821	1.70	126,474	.85	

1. For breakdown of "Other" vote, see minor candidate vote totals, p. 123.

1912 Presidential Election

Total Popular Votes: 15,040,963
Wilson's Plurality: 2,173,945

STATE	WOODROW WILSON (Democrat)		THEODORE ROOSEVELT (Progressive)		WILLIAM H. TAFT (Republican)		EUGENE V. DEBS (Socialist)		OTHER[1]		PLURALITY
	Votes	%	Votes	%	Votes	%	Votes	%	Votes	%	
Alabama	82,438	69.9	22,680	19.2	9,807	8.3	3,029	2.6	5		59,758
Arizona	10,324	43.6	6,949	29.3	2,986	12.6	3,163	13.4	265	1.1	3,375
Arkansas	68,814	55.0	21,644	17.3	25,585	20.5	8,153	6.5	908	.7	43,229
California	283,436	41.8	283,610	41.8	3,847	.6	79,201	11.7	27,783	4.1	174
Colorado	113,912	42.8	71,752	27.0	58,386	22.0	16,366	6.2	5,538	2.1	42,160
Connecticut	74,561	39.2	34,129	17.9	68,324	35.9	10,056	5.3	3,334	1.8	6,237
Delaware	22,631	46.5	8,886	18.3	15,997	32.9	556	1.1	620	1.3	6,634
Florida	35,343	69.5	4,555	9.0	4,279	8.4	4,806	9.5	1,854	3.7	30,537
Georgia	93,087	76.6	21,985	18.1	5,191	4.3	1,058	.9	149	.1	71,102
Idaho	33,921	32.1	25,527	24.1	32,810	31.0	11,960	11.3	1,536	1.5	1,111
Illinois	405,048	35.3	386,478	33.7	253,593	22.1	81,278	7.1	19,776	1.7	18,570
Indiana	281,890	43.1	162,007	24.8	151,267	23.1	36,931	5.6	22,379	3.4	119,883
Iowa	185,322	37.6	161,819	32.9	119,805	24.3	16,967	3.5	8,440	1.7	23,503
Kansas	143,663	39.3	120,210	32.9	74,845	20.5	26,779	7.3	63		23,453
Kentucky	219,484	48.5	101,766	22.5	115,510	25.5	11,646	2.6	4,308	1.0	103,974
Louisiana	60,871	76.8	9,283	11.7	3,833	4.8	5,261	6.6			51,588
Maine	51,113	39.4	48,495	37.4	26,545	20.5	2,541	2.0	947	.7	2,618
Maryland	112,674	48.6	57,789	24.9	54,956	23.7	3,996	1.7	2,566	1.1	54,885
Massachusetts	173,408	35.5	142,228	29.1	155,948	32.0	12,616	2.6	3,856	.8	17,460
Michigan	150,201	27.4	213,243	38.9	151,434	27.6	23,060	4.2	10,033	1.8	61,809
Minnesota	106,426	31.8	125,856	37.7	64,334	19.3	27,505	8.2	10,098	3.0	19,430
Mississippi	57,324	88.9	3,549	5.5	1,560	2.4	2,050	3.2			53,775
Missouri	330,746	47.4	124,375	17.8	207,821	29.8	28,466	4.1	7,158	1.0	122,925
Montana	28,129	35.1	22,709	28.3	18,575	23.1	10,811	13.5	32		5,420
Nebraska	109,008	43.7	72,681	29.1	54,226	21.7	10,185	4.1	3,383	1.4	36,327
Nevada	7,986	39.7	5,620	27.9	3,196	15.9	3,313	16.5			2,366
New Hampshire	34,724	39.5	17,794	20.2	32,927	37.4	1,981	2.3	535	.6	1,797
New Jersey	178,638	41.2	145,679	33.6	89,066	20.5	15,948	3.7	4,332	1.0	32,959
New Mexico	20,437	41.9	8,347	17.1	17,164	35.2	2,859	5.9			3,273
New York	655,573	41.3	390,093	24.6	455,487	28.7	63,434	4.0	23,728	1.5	200,086
North Carolina	144,407	59.2	69,135	28.4	29,129	12.0	987	.4	118	.1	75,272
North Dakota	29,549	34.2	25,726	29.8	22,990	26.6	6,966	8.1	1,243	1.4	3,823
Ohio	424,834	41.0	229,807	22.2	278,168	26.8	90,164	8.7	14,141	1.4	146,666
Oklahoma	119,143	47.0			90,726	35.8	41,630	16.4	2,195	.9	28,417
Oregon	47,064	34.3	37,600	27.4	34,673	25.3	13,343	9.7	4,360	3.2	9,464
Pennsylvania	395,637	32.5	444,894	36.5	273,360	22.5	83,614	6.9	20,231	1.7	49,257
Rhode Island	30,412	39.0	16,878	21.7	27,703	35.6	2,049	2.6	852	1.1	2,709
South Carolina	48,355	95.9	1,293	2.6	536	1.1	164	.3	55	.1	47,062
South Dakota	48,942	42.1	58,811	50.6			4,664	4.0	3,910	3.4	9,869
Tennessee	133,021	52.8	54,041	21.5	60,475	24.0	3,564	1.4	832	.3	72,546
Texas	218,921	72.7	26,715	8.9	28,310	9.4	24,884	8.3	2,131	.7	190,611
Utah	36,576	32.6	24,174	21.5	42,013	37.4	8,999	8.0	510	.5	5,437
Vermont	15,350	24.4	22,129	35.2	23,303	37.1	928	1.5	1,094	1.7	1,174
Virginia	90,332	66.0	21,776	15.9	23,288	17.0	820	.6	759	.6	67,044
Washington	86,840	26.9	113,698	35.2	70,445	21.8	40,134	12.4	11,682	3.6	26,858
West Virginia	113,097	42.1	79,112	29.4	56,754	21.1	15,248	5.7	4,517	1.7	33,985
Wisconsin	164,230	41.1	62,448	15.6	130,596	32.7	33,476	8.4	9,225	2.3	33,634
Wyoming	15,310	36.2	9,232	21.8	14,560	34.4	2,760	6.5	421	1.0	750
Totals	6,293,152	41.84	4,119,207	27.39	3,486,333	23.18	900,369	5.99	241,902	1.61	

1. For breakdown of "Other" vote, see minor candidate vote totals, p. 124.

1916 Presidential Election

Total Popular Votes: 18,535,022
Wilson's Plurality: 579,511

STATE	WOODROW WILSON (Democrat)		CHARLES E. HUGHES (Republican)		ALLAN L. BENSON (Socialist)		J. FRANK HANLY (Prohibition)		OTHER[1]		PLURALITY
	Votes	%	Votes	%	Votes	%	Votes	%	Votes	%	
Alabama	99,116	76.0	28,662	22.0	1,916	1.5	741	.6			70,454
Arizona	33,170	57.2	20,522	35.4	3,174	5.5	1,153	2.0			12,648
Arkansas	112,211	66.0	48,879	28.7	6,999	4.1	2,015	1.2			63,332
California	465,936	46.6	462,516	46.3	42,898	4.3	27,713	2.8	187		3,420
Colorado	177,496	60.8	101,388	34.7	9,951	3.4	2,793	1.0	409	.1	76,108
Connecticut	99,786	46.7	106,514	49.8	5,179	2.4	1,789	.8	606	.3	6,728
Delaware	24,753	47.8	26,011	50.2	480	.9	566	1.1			1,258
Florida	55,984	69.3	14,611	18.1	5,353	6.6	4,786	5.9			41,373
Georgia	127,754	79.5	11,294	7.0	941	.6			20,692	12.9	107,062[2]
Idaho	70,054	52.0	55,368	41.1	8,066	6.0	1,127	.8			14,686
Illinois	950,229	43.3	1,152,549	52.6	61,394	2.8	26,047	1.2	2,488	.1	202,320
Indiana	334,063	46.5	341,005	47.4	21,860	3.0	16,368	2.3	5,557	.8	6,942
Iowa	221,699	42.9	280,439	54.3	10,976	2.1	3,371	.7	2,253	.1	58,740
Kansas	314,588	50.0	277,658	44.1	24,685	3.9	12,882	2.1			36,930
Kentucky	269,990	51.9	241,854	46.5	4,734	.9	3,039	.6	461	.1	28,136
Louisiana	79,875	85.9	6,466	7.0	284	.3			6,349	6.8	73,409
Maine	64,033	47.0	69,508	51.0	2,177	1.6	596	.4			5,475
Maryland	138,359	52.8	117,347	44.8	2,674	1.0	2,903	1.1	756	.3	21,012
Massachusetts	247,885	46.6	268,784	50.5	11,058	2.1	2,993	.6	1,102	.2	20,899
Michigan	283,993	43.9	337,952	52.2	16,012	2.5	8,085	1.3	831	.1	53,959
Minnesota	179,155	46.3	179,544	46.4	20,117	5.2	7,793	2.0	758	.2	389
Mississippi	80,422	93.3	4,253	4.9	1,484	1.7			520		76,169
Missouri	398,032	50.6	369,339	46.9	14,612	1.9	3,887	.5	903	.1	28,693
Montana	101,104	56.8	66,933	37.6	9,634	5.4			338	.2	34,171
Nebraska	158,827	55.3	117,771	41.0	7,141	2.5	2,952	1.0	624	.2	41,056
Nevada	17,776	53.4	12,127	36.4	3,065	9.2	346	1.0			5,649
New Hampshire	43,781	49.1	43,725	49.1	1,318	1.5	303	.3			56
New Jersey	211,018	42.7	268,982	54.4	10,405	2.1	3,182	.6	855	.2	57,964
New Mexico	33,693	50.4	31,097	46.5	1,977	3.0	112	.2			2,596
New York	759,426	44.5	879,238	57.5	45,944	2.7	19,031	1.1	2,666	.2	119,812
North Carolina	168,383	58.1	120,890	41.7	509	.2	55				47,493
North Dakota	55,206	47.8	53,471	46.3	5,716	5.0	997	.9			1,735
Ohio	604,161	51.9	514,753	44.2	38,092	3.3	8,085	.7			89,408
Oklahoma	148,123	50.7	97,233	33.3	45,091	15.4	1,646	.6	234	.1	50,890
Oregon	120,087	45.9	126,813	48.5	9,711	3.7	4,729	1.8	310	.1	6,726
Pennsylvania	521,784	40.2	703,823	54.3	42,638	3.3	28,525	2.2	419		182,039
Rhode Island	40,394	46.0	44,858	51.1	1,914	2.2	470	.5	180	.2	4,464
South Carolina	61,845	96.7	1,550	2.4	135	.2			420	.7	60,295
South Dakota	59,191	45.9	64,217	49.8	3,760	2.9	1,774	1.4			5,026
Tennessee	153,280	56.3	116,223	42.7	2,542	.9	145	.1			37,057
Texas	287,415	77.0	64,999	17.4	18,960	5.1	1,936	.5			222,416
Utah	84,145	58.8	54,137	37.8	4,460	3.1	149	.1	254	.2	30,008
Vermont	22,708	35.2	40,250	62.4	798	1.2	709	1.1	10		17,542
Virginia	101,840	67.0	48,384	31.8	1,056	.7	678	.5	67		53,456
Washington	183,388	48.1	167,208	43.9	22,800	6.0	6,868	1.8	730	.2	16,180
West Virginia	140,403	48.5	143,124	49.4	6,144	2.1					2,721
Wisconsin	191,363	42.8	220,822	49.4	27,631	6.2	7,318	1.6			29,459
Wyoming	28,376	54.7	21,698	41.8	1,459	2.8	373	.7			6,678
Totals	**9,126,300**	**49.24**	**8,546,789**	**46.11**	**589,924**	**3.18**	**221,030**	**1.19**	**50,979**	**.28**	

1. For breakdown of "Other" vote, see minor candidate vote totals, p. 124.
2. Plurality of 107,062 votes is calculated on the basis of 20,692 votes cast for the Progressive Party.

1920 Presidential Election

Total Popular Votes: 26,753,786
Harding's Plurality: 6,992,430

STATE	WARREN G. HARDING (Republican)		JAMES M. COX (Democrat)		EUGENE V. DEBS (Socialist)		PARLEY P. CHRISTENSEN (Farmer-Labor)		OTHER[1]		PLURALITY
	Votes	%	Votes	%	Votes	%	Votes	%	Votes	%	
Alabama	74,719	31.9	156,064	66.7	2,402	1.0			766	.3	81,345
Arizona	37,016	55.6	29,546	44.4							7,470
Arkansas	71,107	38.7	107,406	58.5	5,108	2.8					36,299
California	624,992	66.2	229,191	24.3	64,076	6.8			25,672	2.7	395,801
Colorado	171,709	59.4	103,721	35.9	7,860	2.7	2,898	1.0	2,807	1.0	67,988
Connecticut	229,238	62.7	120,721	33.0	10,350	2.8	1,947	.5	3,262	.9	108,517
Delaware	52,858	55.7	39,911	42.1	988	1.0	82	.1	1,025	1.1	12,947
Florida[2]	44,853	30.8	90,515	62.0	5,189	3.6			5,124	3.5	45,662
Georgia	42,981	28.7	106,112	70.9	558	.4					63,131
Idaho	88,975	65.6	46,579	34.3	38				32		42,396
Illinois	1,420,480	67.8	534,395	25.5	74,747	3.6	49,632	2.4	15,461	.8	886,085
Indiana	696,370	55.1	511,364	40.5	24,713	2.0	16,499	1.3	14,028	1.1	185,006
Iowa	634,674	70.9	227,924	25.5	16,981	1.9	10,321	1.2	5,185	.6	406,750
Kansas	369,268	64.8	185,464	32.5	15,511	2.7			75		183,804
Kentucky	451,480	49.2	457,203	49.8	6,409	.7			3,250	.4	5,723
Louisiana	38,539	30.5	87,355	69.2					342	.3	48,816
Maine	136,355	65.5	69,306	33.3	2,210	1.1			310	.2	67,049
Maryland	236,117	55.1	180,626	42.2	8,876	2.1	1,645	.4	1,186	.3	55,491
Massachusetts	681,153	68.6	276,691	27.8	32,265	3.3			3,607	.4	404,462
Michigan	755,941	72.8	231,046	22.3	28,446	2.7	10,163	1.0	12,385	1.2	524,895
Minnesota	519,421	70.6	142,994	19.4	56,106	7.6			17,317	2.4	376,427
Mississippi	11,527	14.0	69,252	84.0	1,639	2.0					57,725
Missouri	727,252	54.6	574,799	43.2	20,342	1.5	3,108	.2	6,739	.5	152,453
Montana	109,680	61.0	57,746	32.1			12,283	6.8			51,934
Nebraska	247,498	64.7	119,608	31.3	9,600	2.5			6,037	1.6	127,890
Nevada	15,479	56.9	9,851	36.2	1,864	6.9					5,628
New Hampshire	95,196	59.8	62,662	39.4	1,234	.8					32,534
New Jersey	611,541	67.7	256,887	28.4	27,141	3.0	2,200	.2	6,114	.7	354,654
New Mexico	57,634	54.7	46,668	44.3			1,097	1.0			10,966
New York	1,871,167	64.6	781,238	27.0	203,201	7.0	18,413	.6	24,494	.9	1,089,929
North Carolina	232,819	43.2	305,367	56.7	446	.1			17		72,548
North Dakota	158,997	77.7	37,409	18.3	8,273	4.0					121,588
Ohio	1,182,022	58.5	780,037	38.6	57,147	2.8			2,447	.1	401,985
Oklahoma	243,465	50.2	215,798	44.5	25,698	5.3					27,667
Oregon	143,592	60.2	80,019	33.6	9,801	4.1			5,110	2.2	63,573
Pennsylvania	1,218,216	65.8	503,843	27.2	70,571	3.8	15,705	.9	44,282	2.4	714,373
Rhode Island	107,463	64.0	55,062	32.8	4,351	2.6			1,105	.7	52,401
South Carolina	2,244	3.4	64,170	96.1	28				366	.6	61,926
South Dakota	109,874	60.7	35,938	19.8			34,406	19.0	900	.5	73,936
Tennessee	219,229	51.2	206,558	48.3	2,249	.5					12,671
Texas	114,384	23.5	288,933	59.4	8,122	1.7			75,010	15.4	174,549
Utah	81,555	55.9	56,639	38.8	3,159	2.2	4,475	3.1			24,916
Vermont	67,964	75.8	20,884	23.3					818	.9	47,080
Virginia	87,456	37.9	141,670	61.3	808	.4	240	.1	826	.4	54,214
Washington	223,137	56.0	84,298	21.1	8,913	2.2	77,246	19.4	5,111	1.3	138,839
West Virginia	282,010	55.3	220,789	43.3	5,609	1.1			1,526	.3	61,221
Wisconsin	498,576	71.1	113,196	16.2	80,635	11.5			8,648	1.2	385,380
Wyoming	35,091	64.2	17,429	31.9			2,180	4.0			17,662
Totals	16,133,314	60.30	9,140,884	34.17	913,664	3.42	264,540	.99	301,384	1.13	

1. For breakdown of "Other" vote, see minor candidate vote totals, p. 124.
2. Figures from Petersen, op. cit., p. 83.

1924 Presidential Election

Total Popular Votes: 29,075,959
Coolidge's Plurality: 7,331,384

STATE	CALVIN COOLIDGE (Republican)		JOHN W. DAVIS (Democrat)		ROBERT M. LAFOLLETTE (Progressive)		HERMAN P. FARIS (Prohibition)		OTHER[1]		PLURALITY
	Votes	%	Votes	%	Votes	%	Votes	%	Votes	%	
Alabama	40,615	25.0	113,138	69.7	8,040	5.0	562	.4			72,523
Arizona	30,516	41.3	26,235	35.5	17,210	23.3					4,281
Arkansas	40,518	29.3	84,759	61.2	13,146	9.5			10		44,241
California	733,196	57.2	105,514	8.2	424,649	33.1	18,436	1.4	122		308,547
Colorado	193,956	59.4	75,238	23.0	57,368	17.6					118,718
Connecticut	246,322	61.5	110,184	27.5	42,416	10.6			1,373	.3	136,138
Delaware	52,441	57.7	33,445	36.8	4,979	5.5			16		18,996
Florida	30,633	28.1	62,083	56.9	8,625	7.9	5,498	5.0	2,315	2.1	31,450
Georgia	30,300	18.2	123,260	74.1	12,687	7.6					92,960
Idaho	72,084	48.1	24,217	16.2	53,664	35.8					18,420
Illinois	1,453,321	58.8	576,975	23.4	432,027	17.5	2,367	.1	5,377	.2	876,346
Indiana	703,042	55.3	492,245	38.7	71,700	5.6	4,416	.4	987	.1	210,797
Iowa	537,458	55.0	160,382	16.4	274,448	28.1			4,482	.5	263,010
Kansas	407,671	61.5	156,320	23.6	98,462	14.9			3		251,351
Kentucky	396,758	48.8	375,543	46.1	38,465	4.7			3,093	.4	21,215
Louisiana	24,670	20.2	93,218	76.4					4,063	3.3	68,548
Maine	138,440	72.0	41,964	21.8	11,382	5.9			406	.2	96,476
Maryland	162,414	45.3	148,072	41.3	47,157	13.2			987	.3	14,342
Massachusetts	703,476	62.3	280,817	24.9	141,225	12.5			4,304	.4	422,659
Michigan	874,631	75.4	152,359	13.1	122,014	10.5	6,085	.5	5,330	.5	722,272
Minnesota	420,759	51.2	55,913	6.8	339,192	41.3			6,282	.8	81,567
Mississippi	8,384	7.5	100,057	89.4	3,448	3.1					91,673
Missouri	648,486	49.6	572,962	43.8	83,996	6.4	1,418	.1	1,231	.1	75,524
Montana	74,246	42.5	33,867	19.4	65,985	37.8			370	.2	8,261
Nebraska	218,985	47.2	137,299	29.6	105,681	22.8	1,594	.3			81,686
Nevada	11,243	41.8	5,909	22.0	9,769	36.3					1,474
New Hampshire	98,575	59.8	57,201	34.7	8,993	5.5					41,374
New Jersey	675,162	62.2	297,743	27.4	108,901	10.0	1,337	.1	2,936	.3	377,419
New Mexico	54,745	48.5	48,542	43.0	9,543	8.5					6,203
New York	1,820,058	55.8	950,796	29.1	474,913	14.6			18,172	.6	869,262
North Carolina	190,754	39.6	284,190	59.0	6,651	1.4	13				93,436
North Dakota	94,931	47.7	13,858	7.0	89,922	45.2			370	.2	5,009
Ohio	1,176,130	58.3	477,888	23.7	358,008	17.8			4,271	.2	698,242
Oklahoma	225,756	42.8	255,798	48.5	41,142	7.8			5,134	1.0	30,042
Oregon	142,579	51.0	67,589	24.2	68,403	24.5			908	.3	74,176
Pennsylvania	1,401,481	65.4	409,192	19.1	307,567	14.3	9,779	.5	16,700	.8	992,289
Rhode Island	125,286	59.6	76,606	36.5	7,628	3.6			595	.3	48,680
South Carolina	1,123	2.2	49,008	96.6	623	1.2			1		47,885
South Dakota	101,299	49.7	27,214	13.4	75,200	36.9					26,099
Tennessee	130,831	43.5	159,339	52.9	10,666	3.5	94		100		28,508
Texas	130,794	19.8	485,443	73.7	42,879	6.5					354,649
Utah	77,327	49.3	46,908	29.9	32,662	20.8					30,419
Vermont	80,498	78.2	16,124	15.7	5,943	5.8	316	.3	5		64,374
Virginia	73,328	32.8	139,717	62.5	10,369	4.6			189	.1	66,389
Washington	220,224	52.3	42,842	10.2	150,727	35.8			7,709	1.8	69,497
West Virginia	288,635	49.5	257,232	44.1	36,723	6.3			1,072	.2	31,403
Wisconsin	311,614	37.1	68,096	8.1	453,678	54.0	2,918	.4	4,441	.5	142,064
Wyoming	41,858	52.4	12,868	16.1	25,174	31.5					16,684
Totals	15,717,553	54.06	8,386,169	28.84	4,814,050	16.56	54,833	.19	103,354	.36	

1. For breakdown of "Other" vote, see minor candidate vote totals, p. 124.

1928 Presidential Election

Total Popular Votes: 36,790,364
Hoover's Plurality: 6,411,806

STATE	HERBERT C. HOOVER (Republican)		ALFRED E. SMITH (Democrat)		NORMAN M. THOMAS (Socialist)		WILLIAM Z. FOSTER (Communist)		OTHER[1]		PLURALITY
	Votes	%	Votes	%	Votes	%	Votes	%	Votes	%	
Alabama	120,725	48.5	127,796	51.3	460	.2					7,071
Arizona	52,533	57.6	38,537	42.2			184	.2			13,996
Arkansas	77,785	39.3	119,195	60.3	434	.2	317	.2			41,410
California	1,147,929	63.9	614,365	34.2	19,595	1.1	112		14,655	.8	533,564
Colorado	252,924	64.8	132,747	34.0	2,630	.7	675	.2	1,092	.3	120,177
Connecticut	296,614	53.6	252,040	45.6	3,019	.6	730	.1	622	.1	44,574
Delaware	68,860	65.8	35,354	33.8	329	.3	58	.1			33,506
Florida	144,168	57.1	100,721	39.9	4,036	1.6	3,704	1.5			43,447
Georgia	99,368	43.4	129,602	56.6	124	.1	64				30,234
Idaho	97,322	64.2	52,926	34.9	1,293	.9					44,396
Illinois	1,770,723	57.0	1,312,235	42.2	19,138	.6	3,581	.1	1,812	.1	458,488
Indiana	848,290	59.7	562,691	39.6	3,871	.3	321		6,141	.4	285,599
Iowa	623,570	61.8	379,011	37.6	2,960	.3	328		3,320	.3	244,559
Kansas	513,672	72.0	193,003	27.1	6,205	.9	319				320,669
Kentucky	558,064	59.3	381,060	40.5	846	.1	307		354		177,004
Louisiana	51,160	23.7	164,655	76.3							113,495
Maine	179,923	68.6	81,179	31.0	1,065	.4					98,744
Maryland	301,479	57.1	223,626	42.3	1,701	.3	636	.1	906	.2	77,853
Massachusetts	775,566	49.2	792,758	50.2	6,262	.4	2,461	.2	776	.1	17,192
Michigan	965,396	70.4	396,762	28.9	3,516	.3	2,881	.2	3,527	.3	568,634
Minnesota	560,977	57.8	396,451	40.8	6,774	.7	4,853	.5	1,921	.2	164,526
Mississippi	26,202	17.3	124,445	82.2					788	.5	98,243
Missouri	834,080	55.6	662,684	44.2	3,739	.3			342		171,396
Montana	113,472	58.4	78,638	40.5	1,690	.9	577	.3			34,834
Nebraska	345,745	63.2	197,950	36.2	3,433	.6					147,795
Nevada	18,327	56.5	14,090	43.5							4,237
New Hampshire	115,404	58.7	80,715	41.0	465	.2	173	.1			34,689
New Jersey	925,285	59.8	616,162	39.8	4,866	.3	1,240	.1	642		309,123
New Mexico	69,708	59.0	48,211	40.8			158	.1			21,497
New York	2,193,344	49.8	2,089,863	47.4	107,332	2.4	10,876	.3	4,211	.1	103,481
North Carolina	348,923	54.9	286,227	45.1							62,696
North Dakota	131,419	54.8	106,648	44.5	842	.4	936	.4			24,771
Ohio	1,627,546	64.9	864,210	34.5	8,683	.4	2,836	.1	5,071	.2	763,336
Oklahoma	394,046	63.7	219,174	35.4	3,924	.6			1,283	.2	174,872
Oregon	205,341	64.2	109,223	34.1	2,720	.9	1,094	.3	1,564	.5	96,118
Pennsylvania	2,055,382	65.2	1,067,586	33.9	18,647	.6	4,726	.2	4,271	.1	987,796
Rhode Island	117,522	49.6	118,973	50.2			283	.1	416	.2	1,451
South Carolina	5,858	8.5	62,700	91.4	47	.1					56,842
South Dakota	157,603	60.2	102,660	39.2	443	.2	224	.1	927	.4	54,943
Tennessee	195,195	55.5	156,169	44.4	590	.2	70				39,026
Texas	367,036	51.7	341,458	48.1	641	.1	209				25,578
Utah	94,485	53.5	80,985	45.9	954	.5	46				13,500
Vermont	90,404	66.9	44,440	32.9					347	.3	45,964
Virginia	164,609	53.9	140,146	45.9	250	.1	179	.1	180	.1	24,463
Washington	335,503	67.1	156,772	31.4	2,615	.5	1,083	.2	4,068	.8	178,731
West Virginia	375,551	58.4	263,784	41.0	1,313	.2	401	.1	1,703	.3	111,767
Wisconsin	544,205	53.5	450,259	44.3	18,213	1.8	1,528	.2	2,626	.3	93,946
Wyoming	52,748	63.7	29,299	35.4	788	1.0					23,449
Totals	21,411,991	58.20	15,000,185	40.77	266,453	.72	48,170	.13	63,565	.17	

1. For breakdown of "Other" vote, see minor candidate vote totals, p. 125.

1932 Presidential Election

Total Popular Votes: 39,749,382
Roosevelt's Plurality: 7,066,619

STATE	FRANKLIN D. ROOSEVELT (Democrat)		HERBERT C. HOOVER (Republican)		NORMAN M. THOMAS (Socialist)		WILLIAM Z. FOSTER (Communist)		OTHER[1]		PLURALITY
	Votes	%	Votes	%	Votes	%	Votes	%	Votes	%	
Alabama	207,732	84.7	34,647	14.1	2,060	.8	676	.3	13		173,085
Arizona	79,264	67.0	36,104	30.5	2,618	2.2	256	.2	9		43,160
Arkansas	186,829	86.3	27,465	12.7	1,166	.5	157	.1	952	.4	159,364
California	1,324,157	58.4	847,902	37.4	63,299	2.8			30,464	1.3	476,255
Colorado	250,151	54.9	188,364	41.3	13,591	3.0	758	.2	2,824	.6	61,787
Connecticut	281,632	47.4	288,420	48.5	20,480	3.5	1,364	.2	2,287	.4	6,788
Delaware	54,319	48.1	57,073	50.6	1,376	1.2	133	.1			2,754
Florida	206,307	74.9	69,170	25.1							137,137
Georgia	234,118	91.6	19,863	7.8	461	.2	23		1,125	.4	214,255
Idaho	109,479	58.7	71,312	38.2	526	.3	491	.3	4,660	2.5	38,167
Illinois	1,882,304	55.2	1,432,756	42.0	67,258	2.0	15,582	.5	10,026	.3	449,548
Indiana	862,054	54.7	677,184	42.9	21,388	1.4	2,187	.1	14,084	.9	184,870
Iowa	598,019	57.7	414,433	40.0	20,467	2.0	559	.1	3,209	.3	183,586
Kansas	424,204	53.6	349,498	44.1	18,276	2.3					74,706
Kentucky	580,574	59.1	394,716	40.2	3,858	.4	275		3,663	.4	185,858
Louisiana	249,418	92.8	18,853	7.0					533	.2	230,565
Maine	128,907	43.2	166,631	55.8	2,489	.8	162	.1	255	.1	37,724
Maryland	314,314	61.5	184,184	36.0	10,489	2.1	1,031	.2	1,036	.2	130,130
Massachusetts	800,148	50.6	736,959	46.6	34,305	2.2	4,821	.3	3,881	.2	63,189
Michigan	871,700	52.4	739,894	44.4	39,205	2.4	9,318	.6	4,648	.3	131,806
Minnesota	600,806	59.9	363,959	36.3	25,476	2.5	6,101	.6	6,501	.7	236,847
Mississippi	140,168	96.0	5,170	3.5	675	.5					134,998
Missouri	1,025,406	63.7	564,713	35.1	16,374	1.0	568		2,833	.2	460,693
Montana	127,476	58.8	78,134	36.0	7,902	3.7	1,801	.8	1,461	.7	49,342
Nebraska	359,082	63.0	201,177	35.3	9,876	1.7					157,905
Nevada	28,756	69.5	12,622	30.5							16,134
New Hampshire	100,680	49.0	103,629	50.4	947	.5	264	.1			2,949
New Jersey	806,394	49.5	775,406	47.6	42,981	2.6	2,908	.2	1,811	.1	30,988
New Mexico	95,089	62.8	54,146	35.7	1,771	1.2	133	.1	389	.3	40,943
New York	2,534,959	54.1	1,937,963	41.3	177,397	3.8	27,956	.6	10,339	.2	596,996
North Carolina	497,566	69.9	208,344	29.3	5,585	.8					289,222
North Dakota	178,350	69.6	71,772	28.0	3,521	1.4	830	.3	1,817	.7	106,578
Ohio	1,301,695	49.9	1,227,319	47.0	64,094	2.5	7,231	.3	9,389	.4	74,376
Oklahoma	516,468	73.3	188,165	26.7							328,303
Oregon	213,871	58.0	136,019	36.9	15,450	4.2	1,681	.5	1,730	.5	77,852
Pennsylvania	1,295,948	45.3	1,453,540	50.8	91,223	3.2	5,659	.2	12,807	.5	157,592
Rhode Island	146,604	55.1	115,266	43.3	3,138	1.2	546	.2	616	.2	31,338
South Carolina	102,347	98.0	1,978	1.9	82	.1			4		100,369
South Dakota	183,515	63.6	99,212	34.4	1,551	.5	364	.1	3,796	1.3	84,303
Tennessee	259,463	66.5	126,752	32.5	1,796	.5	254	.1	1,998	.5	132,711
Texas	767,585	88.2	97,852	11.2	4,416	.5	204		387	.1	669,733
Utah	116,749	56.6	84,513	41.0	4,087	2.0	946	.5			32,236
Vermont	56,266	41.1	78,984	57.7	1,533	1.1	195	.1	2		22,718
Virginia	203,979	68.5	89,634	30.1	2,382	.8	86		1,858	.6	114,345
Washington	353,260	57.5	208,645	33.9	17,080	2.8	2,972	.5	32,844	5.3	144,615
West Virginia	405,124	54.5	330,731	44.5	5,133	.7	444	.1	2,342	.3	74,393
Wisconsin	707,410	63.5	347,741	31.2	53,379	4.8	3,105	.3	3,165	.3	359,669
Wyoming	54,370	56.1	39,583	40.8	2,829	2.9	180	.2			14,787
Totals	22,825,016	57.42	15,758,397	39.64	883,990	2.22	102,221	.26	179,758	.45	

1. For breakdown of "Other" vote, see minor candidate vote totals, p. 125.

1936 Presidential Election

Total Popular Votes: 45,642,303
Roosevelt's Plurality: 11,068,093

STATE	FRANKLIN D. ROOSEVELT (Democrat)		ALFRED M. LANDON (Republican)		WILLIAM LEMKE (Union)		NORMAN M. THOMAS (Socialist)		OTHER[1]		PLURALITY
	Votes	%	Votes	%	Votes	%	Votes	%	Votes	%	
Alabama	238,131	86.4	35,358	12.8	543	.2	242	.1	1,397	.5	202,773
Arizona	86,722	69.9	33,433	26.9	3,307	2.7	317	.3	384	.3	53,289
Arkansas	146,756	81.8	32,049	17.9			446	.3	167	.1	114,707
California	1,766,836	67.0	836,431	31.7			11,325	.4	23,794	.9	930,405
Colorado	294,599	60.3	181,267	37.1	9,962	2.0	1,594	.3	824	.2	113,332
Connecticut	382,129	55.3	278,685	40.4	21,805	3.2	5,683	.8	2,421	.4	103,444
Delaware	69,702	54.6	54,014	42.3	442	.4	172	.1	3,273	2.5	15,688
Florida	249,117	76.1	78,248	23.9							170,869
Georgia	255,364	87.1	36,943	12.6	136	.1	68		660	.2	218,421
Idaho	125,683	63.0	66,232	33.2	7,677	3.9					59,451
Illinois	2,282,999	57.7	1,570,393	39.7	89,430	2.3	7,530	.2	5,362	.1	712,606
Indiana	934,974	56.6	691,570	41.9	19,407	1.2	3,856	.2	1,090	.1	243,404
Iowa	621,756	54.4	487,977	42.7	29,887	2.6	1,373	.1	1,944	.2	133,779
Kansas	464,520	53.7	397,727	46.0	497	.1	2,770	.3			66,793
Kentucky	541,944	58.5	369,702	39.9	12,532	1.4	649	.1	1,472	.2	172,242
Louisiana	292,802	88.8	36,697	11.1					93		256,105
Maine[2]	126,333	41.6	168,823	55.6	7,581	2.5	783	.3	720	.2	42,490
Maryland	389,612	62.4	231,435	37.0			1,629	.3	2,220	.4	158,177
Massachusetts	942,716	51.2	768,613	41.8	118,639	6.5	5,111	.3	5,278	.3	174,103
Michigan	1,016,794	56.3	699,733	38.8	75,795	4.2	8,208	.5	4,568	.3	317,061
Minnesota	698,811	61.8	350,461	31.0	74,296	6.6	2,872	.3	3,535	.3	348,350
Mississippi	157,333	97.0	4,467	2.8			342	.2			152,866
Missouri	1,111,043	60.8	697,891	38.2	14,630	.8	3,454	.2	1,617	.1	413,152
Montana	159,690	69.3	63,598	27.6	5,539	2.4	1,066	.5	609	.3	96,092
Nebraska	347,445	57.1	247,731	40.7	12,847	2.1					99,714
Nevada	31,925	72.8	11,923	27.2							20,002
New Hampshire	108,460	49.7	104,642	48.0	4,819	2.2			193	.1	3,818
New Jersey	1,083,549	59.6	719,421	39.6	9,405	.5	3,892	.2	2,860	.2	364,128
New Mexico	105,848	62.7	61,727	36.5	924	.6	343	.2	104	.1	44,121
New York	3,293,222	58.8	2,180,670	39.0			86,897	1.6	35,609	.6	1,112,552
North Carolina	616,141	73.4	223,294	26.6							392,847
North Dakota	163,148	59.6	72,751	26.6	36,708	13.4	552	.2	557	.2	90,397
Ohio	1,747,140	58.0	1,127,855	37.4	132,212	4.4			5,251	.2	619,285
Oklahoma	501,069	66.8	245,122	32.7			2,211	.3	1,328	.2	255,947
Oregon	266,733	64.4	122,706	29.6	21,831	5.3	2,143	.5	608	:2	144,027
Pennsylvania	2,353,987	56.9	1,690,200	40.8	67,478	1.6	14,599	.4	12,172	.3	663,787
Rhode Island	164,338	53.0	125,031	40.3	19,569	6.3			1,340	.4	39,307
South Carolina	113,791	98.6	1,646	1.4							112,145
South Dakota	160,137	54.0	125,977	42.5	10,338	3.5					34,160
Tennessee	328,083	68.9	146,520	30.8	296	.1	692	.2	960	.2	181,563
Texas	730,843	86.9	104,728	12.5	3,193	.4	1,067	.1	772	.1	626,115
Utah	150,248	69.3	64,555	29.8	1,121	.5	432	.2	323	.2	85,693
Vermont	62,124	43.2	81,023	56.4					542	.4	18,899
Virginia	234,980	70.2	98,336	29.4	233	.1	313	.1	728	.2	136,644
Washington	459,579	66.4	206,885	29.9	17,463	2.5	3,496	.5	4,908	.7	252,694
West Virginia	502,872	60.6	325,486	39.2			832	.1	1,173	.1	177,386
Wisconsin	802,984	63.8	380,828	30.3	60,297	4.8	10,626	.8	3,825	.3	422,156
Wyoming	62,624	60.6	38,739	37.5	1,653	1.6	200	.2	166	.2	23,885
Totals	27,747,636	60.79	16,679,543	36.54	892,492	1.96	187,785	.41	134,847	.30	

1. For breakdown of "Other" vote, see minor candidate vote totals, p. 125.
2. Figures from Petersen, op. cit., p. 94.

1940 Presidential Election

Total Popular Votes: 49,840,443
Roosevelt's Plurality: 4,927,188

STATE	FRANKLIN D. ROOSEVELT (Democrat)		WENDELL WILLKIE (Republican)		NORMAN M. THOMAS (Socialist)		ROGER W. BABSON (Prohibition)		OTHER[1]		PLURALITY
	Votes	%	Votes	%	Votes	%	Votes	%	Votes	%	
Alabama	250,723	85.2	42,167	14.3	100		698	.2	509	.2	208,556
Arizona	95,267	63.5	54,030	36.0			742	.5			41,237
Arkansas	157,258	78.4	42,122	21.0	301	.2	793	.4			115,136
California	1,877,618	57.4	1,351,419	41.3	16,506	.5	9,400	.3	13,848	.4	526,199
Colorado	265,364	48.4	279,022	50.9	1,899	.4	1,597	.3	378	.1	13,658
Connecticut	417,621	53.4	361,819	46.3					2,062	.3	55,802
Delaware	74,599	54.7	61,440	45.1	110	.1	187	.1			13,159
Florida	359,334	74.0	126,158	26.0							233,176
Georgia	265,194	84.8	46,495	14.9			983	.3	14		218,699
Idaho	127,842	54.4	106,509	45.3	484	.2			276	.1	21,333
Illinois	2,149,934	51.0	2,047,240	48.5	10,914	.3	9,190	.2			102,694
Indiana	874,063	49.0	899,466	50.5	2,075	.1	6,437	.4	706		25,403
Iowa	578,802	47.6	632,370	52.0			2,284	.2	1,976	.2	53,568
Kansas	364,725	42.4	489,169	56.9	2,347	.3	4,056	.5			124,444
Kentucky	557,312	57.4	410,384	42.3	1,062	.1	1,465	.2			146,928
Louisiana	319,751	85.9	52,446	14.1					108		267,305
Maine	156,478	48.8	163,951	51.1					411	.1	7,473
Maryland	384,552	58.3	269,534	40.8	4,093	.6	11		1,940	.3	115,018
Massachusetts	1,076,522	53.1	939,700	46.4	4,091	.2	1,370	.1	5,310	.3	136,822
Michigan	1,032,991	49.5	1,039,917	49.9	7,593	.4	1,795	.1	3,633	.2	6,926
Minnesota	644,196	51.5	596,274	47.7	5,454	.4			5,264	.4	47,922
Mississippi	168,267	95.7	7,363	4.2	193	.1					160,904
Missouri	958,476	52.3	871,009	47.5	2,226	.1	1,809	.1	209		87,467
Montana	145,698	58.8	99,579	40.2	1,443	.6	664	.3	489	.2	46,119
Nebraska	263,677	42.8	352,201	57.2							88,524
Nevada	31,945	60.1	21,229	39.9							10,716
New Hampshire	125,292	53.2	110,127	46.8							15,165
New Jersey	1,016,404	51.5	944,876	47.9	2,823	.1	852		9,260	.5	71,528
New Mexico	103,699	56.6	79,315	43.3	143	.1	100	.1			24,384
New York	3,251,918	51.6	3,027,478	48.0	18,950	.3	3,250	.1			224,440
North Carolina	609,015	74.0	213,633	26.0							395,382
North Dakota	124,036	44.2	154,590	55.1	1,279	.5	325	.1	545	.2	30,554
Ohio	1,733,139	52.2	1,586,773	47.8							146,366
Oklahoma	474,313	57.4	348,872	42.2			3,027	.4			125,441
Oregon	258,415	53.7	219,555	45.6	398	.1	154		2,678	.6	38,860
Pennsylvania	2,171,035	53.2	1,889,848	46.3	10,967	.3			6,864	.2	281,187
Rhode Island	182,182	56.7	138,653	43.2			74		239	.1	43,529
South Carolina	95,470	95.6	4,360	4.4							91,110
South Dakota	131,362	42.6	177,065	57.4							45,703
Tennessee	351,601	67.3	169,153	32.4	463	.1	1,606	.3			182,448
Texas	861,390	80.9	201,866	19.0	628	.1	928	.1	215		659,524
Utah	153,833	62.2	92,973	37.6	198	.1			191	.1	60,860
Vermont	64,269	44.9	78,371	54.8					422	.3	14,102
Virginia	235,961	68.1	109,363	31.6	282	.1	882	.3	120		126,598
Washington	462,145	58.2	322,123	40.6	4,586	.6	1,686	.2	3,293	.4	140,022
West Virginia	495,662	57.1	372,414	42.9							123,248
Wisconsin	704,811	50.2	679,206	48.3	15,071	1.1	2,148	.2	4,263	.3	25,605
Wyoming	59,287	52.8	52,633	46.9	148	.1	172	.2			6,654
Totals	27,263,448	54.70	22,336,260	44.82	116,827	.23	58,685	.12	65,223	.13	

1. For breakdown of "Other" vote, see minor candidate vote totals, p. 125.

1944 Presidential Election

Total Popular Votes: 47,974,819
Roosevelt's Plurality: 3,598,564

STATE	FRANKLIN D. ROOSEVELT (Democrat)		THOMAS E. DEWEY (Republican)		NORMAN M. THOMAS (Socialist)		CLAUDE A. WATSON (Prohibition)		OTHER[1]		PLURALITY
	Votes	%	Votes	%	Votes	%	Votes	%	Votes	%	
Alabama	198,904	81.3	44,478	18.2	189	.1	1,054	.4			154,426
Arizona	80,926	58.8	56,287	40.9			421	.3			24,639
Arkansas	148,965	70.0	63,556	29.8	438	.2					85,409
California	1,988,564	56.5	1,512,965	43.0	2,515	.1	14,770	.4	2,061	.1	475,599
Colorado[2]	234,331	46.4	268,731	53.2	1,977	.4					34,400
Connecticut	435,146	52.3	390,527	46.9	5,097	.6			1,220	.2	44,619
Delaware	68,166	54.4	56,747	45.3	154	.1	294	.2			11,419
Florida	339,377	70.3	143,215	29.7							196,162
Georgia	268,187	81.7	56,507	17.2	6		36		3,373	1.0	211,680
Idaho	107,399	51.6	100,137	48.1	282	.1	503	.2			7,262
Illinois	2,079,479	51.5	1,939,314	48.1	180		7,411	.2	9,677	.2	140,165
Indiana	781,403	46.7	875,891	52.4	2,223	.1	12,574	.8			94,488
Iowa	499,876	47.5	547,267	52.0	1,511	.1	3,752	.4	193		47,391
Kansas	287,458	39.2	442,096	60.3	1,613	.2	2,609	.4			154,638
Kentucky	472,589	54.5	392,448	45.2	535	.1	2,023	.2	317		80,141
Louisiana	281,564	80.6	67,750	19.4					69		213,814
Maine	140,631	47.5	155,434	52.4					335	.1	14,803
Maryland	315,983	52.0	292,150	48.0							23,833
Massachusetts	1,035,296	52.8	921,350	47.0			973	.1	3,046	.1	113,946
Michigan	1,106,899	50.2	1,084,423	49.2	4,598	.2	6,503	.3	2,800	.1	22,476
Minnesota	589,864	52.4	527,416	46.9	5,048	.5			3,176	.3	62,448
Mississippi[3]	168,621	93.6	11,613	6.4							157,008
Missouri	807,804	51.4	761,524	48.4	1,751	.1	1,195	.1	220		46,280
Montana	112,566	54.3	93,163	44.9	1,296	.6	340	.2			19,403
Nebraska	233,246	41.4	329,880	58.6							96,634
Nevada	29,623	54.6	24,611	45.4							5,012
New Hampshire	119,663	52.1	109,916	47.9	46						9,747
New Jersey	987,874	50.3	961,335	49.0	3,358	.2	4,255	.2	6,939	.4	26,539
New Mexico	81,338	53.5	70,559	46.4			147	.1			10,779
New York	3,304,238	52.3	2,987,647	47.3	10,553	.2			14,352	.2	316,591
North Carolina	527,408	66.7	263,155	33.3							264,253
North Dakota	100,144	45.5	118,535	53.8	954	.4	549	.3			18,391
Ohio	1,570,763	49.8	1,582,293	50.2							11,530
Oklahoma	401,549	55.6	319,424	44.2			1,663	.2			82,125
Oregon	248,635	51.8	225,365	46.9	3,785	.8	2,362	.5			23,270
Pennsylvania	1,940,481	51.1	1,835,054	48.4	11,721	.3	5,751	.2	1,789	.1	105,427
Rhode Island	175,356	58.6	123,487	41.3			433	.1			51,869
South Carolina	90,601	87.6	4,617	4.5			365	.4	7,799	7.5	82,802[4]
South Dakota	96,711	41.7	135,365	58.3							38,654
Tennessee	308,707	60.5	200,311	39.2	792	.2	882	.2			108,396
Texas	820,048	71.4	191,372	16.7	592	.1	1,013	.1	135,661	11.8	628,676
Utah	150,088	60.5	97,833	39.4	340	.1					52,255
Vermont	53,806	43.0	71,420	57.0					14		17,614
Virginia	242,276	62.4	145,243	37.4	417	.1	459	.1	90		97,033
Washington	486,774	56.8	361,689	42.2	3,824	.5	2,396	.3	1,645	.2	125,085
West Virginia	392,777	54.9	322,819	45.1							69,958
Wisconsin	650,413	48.6	674,532	50.4	13,205	1.0			1,002	.1	24,119
Wyoming	49,419	48.8	51,921	51.2							2,502
Totals	25,611,936	53.39	22,013,372	45.89	79,000	.16	74,733	.16	195,778	.41	

1. For breakdown of "Other" vote, see minor candidate vote totals, p. 126.
2. Figures from Richard M. Scammon, America at the Polls (Pittsburgh, 1965), p. 71.
3. Ibid., p. 250.
4. Plurality of 82,802 votes is calculated on the basis of 7,799 votes cast for Southern Democratic electors.

1948 Presidential Election

Total Popular Votes: 48,692,442
Truman's Plurality: 2,135,570

STATE	HARRY S TRUMAN (Democrat)		THOMAS E. DEWEY (Republican)		J. STROM THURMOND (States' Rights Democrat)		HENRY A. WALLACE (Progressive)		OTHER[1]		PLURALITY
	Votes	%	Votes	%	Votes	%	Votes	%	Votes	%	
Alabama			40,930	19.0	171,443	79.7	1,522	.7	1,026	.5	130,513
Arizona	95,251	53.8	77,597	43.8			3,310	1.9	907	.5	17,654
Arkansas	149,659	61.7	50,959	21.0	40,068	16.5	751	.3	1,038	.4	98,700
California	1,913,134	47.6	1,895,269	47.1	1,228		190,381	4.7	21,526	.5	17,865
Colorado	267,288	51.9	239,714	46.5			6,115	1.2	2,120	.4	27,574
Connecticut	423,297	47.9	437,754	49.6			13,713	1.6	8,754	1.0	14,457
Delaware	67,813	48.8	69,588	50.0			1,050	.8	622	.5	1,775
Florida	281,988	48.8	194,280	33.6	89,755	15.5	11,620	2.0			87,708
Georgia	254,646	60.8	76,691	18.3	85,135	20.3	1,636	.4	736	.2	169,511
Idaho	107,370	50.0	101,514	47.3			4,972	2.3	960	.4	5,856
Illinois	1,994,715	50.1	1,961,103	49.2					28,228	.7	33,612
Indiana	807,833	48.8	821,079	49.6			9,649	.6	17,653	1.1	13,246
Iowa	522,380	50.3	494,018	47.6			12,125	1.2	9,749	.9	28,362
Kansas	351,902	44.6	423,039	53.6			4,603	.6	9,275	1.2	71,137
Kentucky	466,756	56.7	341,210	41.5	10,411	1.3	1,567	.2	2,714	.3	125,546
Louisiana	136,344	32.8	72,657	17.5	204,290	49.1	3,035	.7	10		67,946
Maine	111,916	42.4	150,234	56.9			1,884	.7			38,318
Maryland	286,521	47.8	294,814	49.2	2,467	.4	9,983	1.7	5,235	.9	8,293
Massachusetts	1,151,788	54.7	909,370	43.2			38,157	1.8	7,832	.4	242,418
Michigan	1,003,448	47.6	1,038,595	49.2			46,515	2.2	21,051	1.0	35,147
Minnesota	692,966	57.2	483,617	39.9			27,866	2.3	7,777	.6	209,349
Mississippi	19,384	10.1	4,995	2.5	167,538	87.2	225	.1			148,154
Missouri	917,315	58.1	655,039	41.5	42		3,998	.3	2,234	.1	262,276
Montana	119,071	53.1	96,770	43.2			7,307	3.3	1,124	.5	22,301
Nebraska	224,165	45.9	264,774	54.2							40,609
Nevada	31,290	50.4	29,357	47.3			1,469	2.4			1,933
New Hampshire	107,995	46.7	121,299	52.4	7		1,970	.9	169	.1	13,304
New Jersey	895,455	45.9	981,124	50.3			42,683	2.2	30,293	1.6	85,669
New Mexico	105,240	56.3	80,303	43.0			1,037	.6	253	.1	24,937
New York	2,780,204	45.0	2,841,163	46.0			509,559	8.3	46,283	.7	60,959
North Carolina	459,070	58.0	258,572	32.7	69,652	8.8	3,915	.5			200,498
North Dakota	95,812	43.4	115,139	52.2	374	.2	8,391	3.8	1,000	.5	19,327
Ohio	1,452,791	49.5	1,445,684	49.2			37,487	1.3			7,107
Oklahoma	452,782	62.8	268,817	37.3							183,965
Oregon	243,147	46.4	260,904	49.8			14,978	2.9	5,051	1.0	17,757
Pennsylvania	1,752,426	46.9	1,902,197	50.9			55,161	1.5	25,564	.7	149,771
Rhode Island	188,736	57.6	135,787	41.4			2,619	.8	560	.2	52,949
South Carolina	34,423	24.1	5,386	3.8	102,607	72.0	154	.1	1		68,184
South Dakota	117,653	47.0	129,651	51.8			2,801	1.1			11,998
Tennessee	270,402	49.1	202,914	36.9	73,815	13.4	1,864	.3	1,288	.2	67,488
Texas	750,700	65.4	282,240	24.6	106,909	9.3	3,764	.3	3,632	.3	468,460
Utah	149,151	54.0	124,402	45.0			2,679	1.0	74		24,749
Vermont	45,557	36.9	75,926	61.5			1,279	1.0	619	.5	30,369
Virginia	200,786	47.9	172,070	41.0	43,393	10.4	2,047	.5	960	.2	28,716
Washington	476,165	52.6	386,315	42.7			31,692	3.5	10,887	1.2	89,850
West Virginia	429,188	57.3	316,251	42.2			3,311	.4			112,937
Wisconsin	647,310	50.7	590,959	46.3			25,282	2.0	13,249	1.0	56,351
Wyoming	52,354	51.6	47,947	47.3			931	.9	193	.2	4,407
Totals	24,105,587	49.51	21,970,017	45.12	1,169,134	2.40	1,157,057	2.38	290,647	.60	

1. For breakdown of "Other" vote, see minor candidate vote totals, p. 126.

1952 Presidential Election

Total Popular Votes: 61,551,118
Eisenhower's Plurality: 6,621,485

STATE	DWIGHT D. EISENHOWER (Republican) Votes	%	ADLAI E. STEVENSON (Democrat) Votes	%	VINCENT HALLINAN (Progressive) Votes	%	STUART HAMBLEN (Prohibition) Votes	%	OTHER[1] Votes	%	PLURALITY
Alabama	149,231	35.0	275,075	64.6			1,814	.4			125,844
Arizona	152,042	58.4	108,528	41.7							43,514
Arkansas	177,155	43.8	226,300	55.9			886	.2	459	.1	49,145
California	2,897,310	56.3	2,197,548	42.7	24,692	.5	16,117	.3	7,561	.2	699,762
Colorado	379,782	60.3	245,504	39.0	1,919	.3			2,898	.5	134,278
Connecticut	611,012	55.7	481,649	43.9	1,466	.1			2,779	.3	129,363
Delaware	90,059	51.8	83,315	47.9	155	.1	234	.1	262	.1	6,744
Florida	544,036	55.0	444,950	45.0							99,086
Georgia	198,961	30.3	456,823	69.7					1		257,862
Idaho	180,707	65.4	95,081	34.4	443	.2			23		85,626
Illinois	2,457,327	54.8	2,013,920	44.9					9,811	.2	443,407
Indiana	1,136,259	58.1	801,530	41.0	1,222	.1	15,335	.8	979	.1	334,729
Iowa	808,906	63.8	451,513	35.6	5,085	.4	2,882	.2	358		357,393
Kansas	616,302	68.8	273,296	30.5			6,038	.7	530	.1	343,006
Kentucky	495,029	49.8	495,729	49.9	336		1,161	.1	893	.1	700
Louisiana	306,925	47.1	345,027	52.9							38,102
Maine	232,353	66.2	118,806	33.8							113,547
Maryland	499,424	55.4	395,337	43.8	7,313	.8					104,087
Massachusetts	1,292,325	54.2	1,083,525	45.5	4,636	.2	886		2,026	.1	208,800
Michigan	1,551,529	55.4	1,230,657	44.0	3,922	.1	10,331	.4	2,153	.1	320,872
Minnesota	763,211	55.3	608,458	44.1	2,666	.2	2,147	.2	3,001	.2	154,753
Mississippi	112,966	39.6	172,553	60.4							59,587
Missouri	959,429	50.7	929,830	49.1	987	.1	885	.1	931	.1	29,599
Montana	157,394	59.4	106,213	40.1	723	.3	548	.2	159	.1	51,181
Nebraska	421,603	69.2	188,057	30.9							233,546
Nevada	50,502	61.5	31,688	38.6							18,814
New Hampshire	166,287	60.9	106,663	39.1							59,624
New Jersey	1,373,613	56.8	1,015,902	42.0	5,589	.2	989		22,461	.9	357,711
New Mexico	132,170	55.5	105,435	44.2	225	.1	297	.1	250	.1	26,735
New York	3,952,815	55.5	3,104,601	43.6	64,211	.9			6,614	.1	848,214
North Carolina	558,107	46.1	652,803	53.9							94,696
North Dakota	191,712	71.0	76,694	28.4	344	.1	302	.1	1,075	.4	115,018
Ohio	2,100,391	56.8	1,600,367	43.2							500,024
Oklahoma	518,045	54.6	430,939	45.4							87,106
Oregon	420,815	60.5	270,579	38.9	3,665	.5					150,236
Pennsylvania	2,415,789	52.7	2,146,269	46.9	4,222	.1	8,951	.2	5,738	.1	269,520
Rhode Island	210,935	50.9	203,293	49.1	187	.1			83		7,642
South Carolina	168,043	49.3	172,957	50.7			1				4,914
South Dakota	203,857	69.3	90,426	30.7							113,431
Tennessee	446,147	50.0	443,710	49.7	887	.1	1,432	.2	379		2,437
Texas	1,102,818	53.1	969,227	46.7	294		1,983	.1	1,563	.1	133,591
Utah	194,190	58.9	135,364	41.1							58,826
Vermont	109,717	71.5	43,299	28.2	282	.2			203	.1	66,418
Virginia	349,037	56.3	268,677	43.4	311	.1			1,664	.3	80,360
Washington	599,107	54.3	492,845	44.7	2,460	.2			8,296	.8	106,262
West Virginia	419,970	48.1	453,578	51.9							33,608
Wisconsin	979,744	61.0	622,175	38.7	2,174	.1			3,277	.2	357,569
Wyoming	81,049	62.7	47,934	37.1			194	.2	76	.1	33,115
Totals	33,936,137	55.13	27,314,649	44.38	140,416	.23	73,413	.12	86,503	.14	

1. For breakdown of "Other" vote, see minor candidate vote totals, p. 126.

1956 Presidential Election

Total Popular Votes: 62,025,372
Eisenhower's Plurality: 9,555,073

STATE	DWIGHT D. EISENHOWER (Republican)		ADLAI E. STEVENSON (Democrat)		T. COLEMAN ANDREWS (Constitution)		ERIC HASS (Socialist-Labor)		OTHER[1]		PLURALITY
	Votes	%	Votes	%	Votes	%	Votes	%	Votes	%	
Alabama	195,694	39.5	279,542	56.4					20,333	4.1	83,848
Arizona	176,990	61.0	112,880	38.9	303	.1					64,110
Arkansas	186,287	45.8	213,277	52.5	7,008	1.7					26,990
California	3,027,668	55.4	2,420,135	44.3	6,087	.1	300		12,168	.2	607,533
Colorado	394,479	59.5	263,997	39.8	759	.1	3,308	.5	531	.1	130,482
Connecticut	711,837	63.7	405,079	36.3							306,758
Delaware	98,057	55.1	79,421	44.6			110	.1	400	.2	18,636
Florida	643,849	57.2	480,371	42.7					1,542	.1	163,478
Georgia	222,778	33.3	444,688	66.4					2,189	.3	221,910
Idaho	166,979	61.2	105,868	38.8	126	.1			16		61,111
Illinois	2,623,327	59.5	1,775,682	40.3			8,342	.2	56		847,645
Indiana	1,182,811	59.9	783,908	39.7			1,334	.1	6,554	.3	398,903
Iowa	729,187	59.1	501,858	40.7	3,202	.3	125		192		227,329
Kansas	566,878	65.4	296,317	34.2					3,048	.4	270,561
Kentucky[2]	572,192	54.3	476,453	45.2			358		4,802	.5	95,739
Louisiana	329,047	53.3	243,977	39.5					44,520	7.2	85,070
Maine	249,238	70.9	102,468	29.1							146,770
Maryland	559,738	60.0	372,613	40.0							187,125
Massachusetts	1,393,197	59.3	948,190	40.4			5,573	.2	1,546	.1	445,007
Michigan	1,713,647	55.6	1,359,898	44.2					6,923	.2	353,749
Minnesota	719,302	53.7	617,525	46.1			2,080	.2	1,098	.1	101,777
Mississippi	60,683	24.5	144,453	58.2					42,961	17.3	83,770
Missouri	914,289	49.9	918,273	50.1							3,984
Montana	154,933	57.1	116,238	42.9							38,695
Nebraska	378,108	65.5	199,029	34.5							179,079
Nevada	56,049	58.0	40,640	42.0							15,409
New Hampshire	176,519	66.1	90,364	33.8	111						86,155
New Jersey	1,606,942	64.7	850,337	34.2	5,317	.2	6,736	.3	14,980	.6	756,605
New Mexico	146,788	57.8	106,098	41.8	364	.1	69		607	.2	40,690
New York	4,340,340	61.2	2,750,769	38.8							1,589,571
North Carolina	575,069	49.3	590,530	50.7							15,461
North Dakota	156,766	61.7	96,742	38.1	483	.2					60,024
Ohio	2,262,610	61.1	1,439,655	38.9							822,955
Oklahoma	473,769	55.1	385,581	44.9							88,188
Oregon	406,393	55.3	329,204	44.8							77,189
Pennsylvania	2,585,252	56.5	1,981,769	43.3			7,447	.2	2,035		603,483
Rhode Island	225,819	58.3	161,790	41.7							64,029
South Carolina	75,634	25.2	136,278	45.4	2				88,509	29.5	47,769[3]
South Dakota	171,569	58.4	122,288	41.6							49,281
Tennessee	462,288	49.2	456,507	48.6	19,820	2.1			789	.1	5,781
Texas	1,080,619	55.3	859,958	44.0	14,591	.8					220,661
Utah	215,631	64.6	118,364	35.4							97,267
Vermont	110,390	72.2	42,540	27.8					39		67,850
Virginia	386,459	55.4	267,760	38.4	42,964	6.2	351	.1	444	.1	118,699
Washington	620,430	53.9	523,002	45.4			7,457	.7			97,428
West Virginia	449,297	54.1	381,534	45.9							67,763
Wisconsin	954,844	61.6	586,768	37.8	6,918	.5	710	.1	1,318	.1	368,076
Wyoming	74,573	60.1	49,554	39.9							25,019
Totals	35,585,245	57.37	26,030,172	41.97	108,055	.17	44,300	.07	257,600	.42	

1. For breakdown of "Other" vote, see minor candidate vote totals, p. 127.
2. Figures from Petersen, op. cit., p. 109.
3. Plurality of 47,769 votes is calculated on the basis of Stevenson's vote and the 88,509 votes cast for unpledged electors.

1960 Presidential Election

Total Popular Votes: 68,828,960
Kennedy's Plurality: 114,673

STATE	JOHN F. KENNEDY (Democrat)		RICHARD M. NIXON (Republican)		ERIC HASS (Socialist-Labor)		UNPLEDGED		OTHER[1]		PLURALITY
	Votes	%	Votes	%	Votes	%	Votes	%	Votes	%	
Alabama	318,303	56.8	236,110	42.1					6,083	1.1	82,193
Alaska	29,809	49.1	30,953	50.9							1,144
Arizona	176,781	44.4	221,241	55.5	469	.1					44,460
Arkansas[2]	215,049	50.2	184,508	43.1					28.952	6.8	30,541
California	3,224,099	49.6	3,259,722	50.1	1,051				21,706	.3	35,623
Colorado	330,629	44.9	402,242	54.6	2,803	.4			563	.1	71,613
Connecticut	657,055	53.7	565,813	46.3							91,242
Delaware	99,590	50.6	96,373	49.0	82				638	.3	3,217
Florida	748,700	48.5	795,476	51.5							46,776
Georgia	458,638	62.5	274,472	37.4					245		184,166
Hawaii	92,410	50.0	92,295	50.0							115
Idaho	138,853	46.2	161,597	53.8							22,744
Illinois	2,377,846	50.0	2,368,988	49.8	10,560	.2			15		8,858
Indiana	952,358	44.6	1,175,120	55.0	1,136	.1			6,746	.3	222,762
Iowa	550,565	43.2	722,381	56.7	230				634	.1	171,816
Kansas	363,213	39.1	561,474	60.5					4,138	.5	198,261
Kentucky	521,855	46.4	602,607	53.6							80,752
Louisiana	407,339	50.4	230,980	28.6					169,572	21.0	176,359
Maine	181,159	43.0	240,608	57.1							59,449
Maryland	565,808	53.6	489,538	46.4					3		76,270
Massachusetts	1,487,174	5.2	976,750	39.6	3,892	.2			1,664	.1	510,424
Michigan	1,687,269	50.9	1,620,428	48.8	1,718	.1			8,682	.3	66,841
Minnesota	779,933	50.6	757,915	49.2	962	.1			3,077	.2	22,018
Mississippi	108,362	36.3	73,561	24.7			116,248[3]	39.0			7,886
Missouri	972,201	50.3	962,218	49.7							9,983
Montana	134,891	48.6	141,841	51.1					847	.3	6,950
Nebraska	232,542	37.9	380,553	62.1							148,011
Nevada	54,880	51.2	52,387	48.8							2,493
New Hampshire	137,772	46.6	157,989	53.4							20,217
New Jersey	1,385,415	50.0	1,363,324	49.2	4,262	.2			20.110	.7	22,091
New Mexico	156,027	50.2	153,733	49.4	570	.2			777	.3	2,294
New York	3,830,085	52.5	3,446,419	47.3					14.319	.2	383,666
North Carolina	713,136	52.1	655,420	47.9							57,716
North Dakota	123,963	44.5	154,310	55.4					158	.1	30,347
Ohio	1,944,248	46.7	2,217,611	53.3							273,363
Oklahoma	370,111	41.0	533,039	59.0					•		162,928
Oregon	367,402	47.3	408,065	52.6					959	.1	40,663
Pennsylvania	2,556,282	51.1	2,439,956	48.7	7,185	.1			3.118	.1	116,326
Rhode Island	258,032	63.6	147,502	36.4							110,530
South Carolina	198,121	51.2	188,558	48.8					1		9,563
South Dakota	128,070	41.8	178,417	58.2							50,347
Tennessee	481,453	45.8	556,577	52.9					13.746	1.3	75,124
Texas	1,167,935	50.5	1,121,693	48.5					22.213	1.0	46,242
Utah	169,248	45.2	205,361	54.8					100		36,113
Vermont	69,186	41.4	98,131	58.7					7		28,945
Virginia	362,327	47.0	404,521	52.4	397	.1			4,204	.5	42,194
Washington	599,298	48.3	629,273	50.7	10,895	.9			2.106	.2	29,975
West Virginia	441,786	52.7	395,995	47.3							45,791
Wisconsin	830,805	48.1	895,175	51.8	1,310	.1			1,792	.1	64,370
Wyoming	63,331	45.0	77,451	55.0							14,120
Totals	34,221,344	49.72	34,106,671	49.55	47,522	.07	116,248	.17	337,175	.48	

1. For breakdown of "Other" vote, see minor candidate vote totals, p. 127.
2. Figures from Petersen, op. cit., p. 113.
3. Votes for unpledged electors who cast electoral votes for Harry F. Byrd (D Va.), which carried the state.

1964 Presidential Election

Total Popular Votes: 70,641,104
Johnson's Plurality: 15,948,746

STATE	LYNDON B. JOHNSON (Democrat)		BARRY M. GOLDWATER (Republican)		ERIC HASS (Socialist-Labor)		CLIFTON DEBERRY (Socialist Workers)		OTHER[1]		PLURALITY
	Votes	%	Votes	%	Votes	%	Votes	%	Votes	%	
Alabama			479,085	69.5					210,733	30.6	268,353[3]
Alaska	44,329	65.9	22,930	34.1							21,399
Arizona	237,753	49.5	242,535	50.5	482	.1					4,782
Arkansas	314,197	56.1	243,264	43.4					2,965	.5	70,933
California	4,171,877	59.1	2,879,108	40.8	489		378		5,725	.1	1,292,769
Colorado	476,024	61.3	296,767	38.2	302		2,537	.3	1,355	.2	179,257
Connecticut	826,269	67.8	390,996	32.1					1,313	.1	435,273
Delaware	122,704	61.0	78,078	38.8	113	.1			425	.2	44,626
D.C.[2]	169,796	85.5	28,801	14.5							140,995
Florida	948,540	51.2	905,941	48.9							42,599
Georgia	522,163	45.9	616,584	54.1					195		94,421
Hawaii	163,249	78.8	44,022	21.2							119,227
Idaho	148,920	50.9	143,557	49.1							5,363
Illinois	2,796,833	59.5	1,905,946	40.5					62		890,887
Indiana	1,170,848	56.0	911,118	43.6	1,374	.1			8,266	.4	259,730
Iowa	733,030	61.9	449,148	37.9	182		159		2,020	.2	283,882
Kansas	464,028	54.1	386,579	45.1	1,901	.2			5,393	.6	77,449
Kentucky	669,659	64.0	372,977	35.7					3,469	.3	296,682
Louisiana	387,068	43.2	509,225	56.8							122,157
Maine	262,264	68.8	118,701	31.2							143,563
Maryland	730,912	65.5	385,495	34.5							345,417
Massachusetts	1,786,422	76.2	549,727	23.4	4,755	.2			3,894	.2	1,236,695
Michigan	2,136,615	66.7	1,060,152	33.1	1,704	.1	3,817	.1	814		1,076,463
Minnesota	991,117	63.8	559,624	36.0	2,544	.2	1,177	.1			431,493
Mississippi	52,616	12.9	356,512	87.1							303,896
Missouri	1,164,344	64.1	653,535	36.0							510,809
Montana	164,246	59.0	113,032	40.6			332	.1	1,018	.4	51,214
Nebraska	307,307	52.6	276,847	47.4							30,460
Nevada	79,339	58.6	56,094	41.4							23,245
New Hampshire	182,065	63.6	104,029	36.4							78,036
New Jersey	1,867,671	65.6	963,843	33.9	7,075	.3	8,181	.3			903,828
New Mexico	194,015	59.0	132,838	40.4	1,217	.4			543	.2	61,177
New York	4,913,156	68.6	2,243,559	31.3	6,086	.1	3,211		268		2,669,597
North Carolina	800,139	56.2	624,841	43.9							175,298
North Dakota	149,784	58.0	108,207	41.9			224	.1	174	.1	41,577
Ohio	2,498,331	62.9	1,470,865	37.1							1,027,466
Oklahoma	519,834	55.8	412,665	44.3							107,169
Oregon	501,017	63.7	282,779	36.0					2,509	.3	218,238
Pennsylvania	3,130,954	64.9	1,673,657	34.7	5,092	.1	10,456	.2	2,531	.1	1,457,297
Rhode Island	315,463	80.9	74,615	19.1							240,848
South Carolina	215,723	41.1	309,048	58.9					8		93,325
South Dakota	163,010	55.6	130,108	44.4							32,902
Tennessee	635,047	55.5	508,965	44.5					34		126,082
Texas	1,663,185	63.3	958,566	36.5					5,060	.2	704,619
Utah	219,628	54.7	181,785	45.3							37,843
Vermont	108,127	66.3	54,942	33.7					20		53,185
Virginia	558,038	53.5	481,334	46.2	2,895	.3					76,704
Washington	779,699	62.0	470,366	37.4	7,772	.6	537				309,333
West Virginia	538,087	67.9	253,953	32.1							284,134
Wisconsin	1,050,424	62.1	638,495	37.7	1,204	.1	1,692	.1			411,929
Wyoming	80,718	56.6	61,998	43.4							18,720
Totals	**43,126,584**	**61.05**	**27,177,838**	**38.47**	**45,187**	**.06**	**32,701**	**.05**	**258,794**	**.37**	

1. For breakdown of "Other" vote, see minor candidate vote totals, p. 127.
2. Figures from Richard M. Scammon, America at the Polls (Pittsburgh, 1965), p. 521.
3. Plurality of 268,353 votes is calculated on the basis of Goldwater's vote and the 210,732 votes cast for unpledged Democrats.

1968 Presidential Election

Total Popular Votes: 73,203,370
Nixon's Plurality: 510,645

STATE	RICHARD M. NIXON (Republican)		HUBERT H. HUMPHREY (Democrat)		GEORGE C. WALLACE (American Independent)		HENNING A. BLOMEN (Socialist Labor)		OTHER[1]		PLURALITY
	Votes	%	Votes	%	Votes	%	Votes	%	Votes	%	
Alabama	146,591	14.0	195,918	18.8	687,664	65.8			14,332	1.4	491,746
Alaska	37,600	45.3	35,411	42.7	10,024	12.1					2,189
Arizona	266,721	54.8	170,514	35.0	46,573	9.6	75		3,053	.6	96,207
Arkansas[2]	190,759	30.8	188,228	30.4	240,982	38.9					50,223
California	3,467,664	47.8	3,244,318	44.7	487,270	6.7	341		51,994	.7	223,346
Colorado	409,345	50.5	335,174	41.3	60,813	7.5	3,016	.4	2,851	.3	74,171
Connecticut	556,721	44.3	621,561	49.5	76,650	6.1			1,300	.1	64,840
Delaware	96,714	45.1	89,194	41.6	28,459	13.3					7,520
D.C.[3]	31,012	18.2	139,566	81.8							108,554
Florida	886,804	40.5	676,794	30.9	624,207	28.5					210,010
Georgia	380,111	30.4	334,440	26.8	535,550	42.8			173		155,439
Hawaii	91,425	38.7	141,324	59.8	3,469	1.5					49,899
Idaho	165,369	56.8	89,273	30.7	36,541	12.6					76,096
Illinois	2,174,774	47.1	2,039,814	44.2	390,958	8.5	13,878	.3	325		134,960
Indiana	1,067,885	50.3	806,659	38.0	243,108	11.5			5,909	.3	261,226
Iowa	619,106	53.0	476,699	40.8	66,422	5.7	241		5,463	.5	142,407
Kansas	478,674	54.8	302,996	34.7	88,921	10.2			2,192	.3	175,678
Kentucky	462,411	43.8	397,541	37.7	193,098	18.3			2,843	.3	64,870
Louisiana	257,535	23.5	309,615	28.2	530,300	48.3					220,685
Maine	169,254	43.1	217,312	55.3	6,370	1.6					48,058
Maryland	517,995	41.9	538,310	43.6	178,734	14.5					20,315
Massachusetts	766,844	32.9	1,469,218	63.0	87,088	3.7	6,180	.3	2,422	.1	702,374
Michigan	1,370,665	41.5	1,593,082	48.2	331,968	10.0	1,762	.1	8,773	.3	222,417
Minnesota	658,643	41.5	857,738	54.0	68,931	4.3	285		2,909	.2	199,095
Mississippi	88,516	13.5	150,644	23.0	415,349	63.5					264,705
Missouri	811,932	44.9	791,444	43.7	206,126	11.4					20,488
Montana	138,835	50.6	114,117	41.6	20,015	7.3			1,437	.5	24,718
Nebraska	321,163	59.8	170,784	31.8	44,904	8.4					150,379
Nevada	73,188	47.5	60,598	39.3	20,432	13.3					12,590
New Hampshire	154,903	52.1	130,589	43.9	11,173	3.8			633	.2	24,314
New Jersey	1,325,467	46.1	1,264,206	44.0	262,187	9.1	6,784	.2	16,751	.6	61,261
New Mexico	169,692	51.9	130,081	39.8	25,737	7.9			1,771	.5	39,611
New York	3,007,932	44.3	3,378,470	49.8	358,864	5.3	8,432	.1	36,368	.5	370,538
North Carolina	627,192	39.5	464,113	29.2	496,188	31.3					131,004
North Dakota	138,669	55.9	94,769	38.2	14,244	5.8			200	.1	43,900
Ohio	1,791,014	45.2	1,700,586	43.0	467,495	11.8	120		483		90,428
Oklahoma	449,697	47.7	301,658	32.0	191,731	20.3					148,039
Oregon	408,433	49.8	358,866	43.8	49,683	6.1			2,640	.3	49,567
Pennsylvania	2,090,017	44.0	2,259,403	47.6	378,582	8.0	4,977	.1	14,947	.3	169,386
Rhode Island	122,359	31.8	246,518	64.0	15,678	4.1			383		124,159
South Carolina	254,062	38.1	197,486	29.6	215,430	32.3					38,632
South Dakota	149,841	53.3	118,023	42.0	13,400	4.8					31,818
Tennessee	472,592	37.9	351,233	28.1	424,792	34.0					47,800
Texas	1,227,844	39.9	1,266,804	41.1	584,269	19.0			489		38,960
Utah	238,728	56.5	156,665	37.1	26,906	6.4			269	.1	82,063
Vermont	85,142	52.8	70,255	43.5	5,104	3.2			903	.6	14,887
Virginia	590,319	43.4	442,387	32.5	320,272	23.6	4,671	.3	2,281	.2	147,932
Washington	588,510	45.2	616,037	47.3	96,990	7.4	491		2,319	.2	27,527
West Virginia	307,555	40.8	374,091	49.6	72,560	9.6					66,536
Wisconsin	809,997	47.9	748,804	44.3	127,835	7.6	1,338	.1	3,564	.2	61,193
Wyoming	70,927	55.8	45,173	35.5	11,105	8.7					25,754
Totals	31,785,148	43.42	31,274,503	42.72	9,901,151	13.53	52,591	.07	189,977	.26	

1. For breakdown of "Other" vote, see minor candidate vote totals, p. 127.
2. Figures from Richard M. Scammon, America Votes 8 (Washington, 1970), p. 26.
3. Ibid., p. 433.

1972 Presidential Election

Total Popular Votes: 77,727,590
Nixon's Plurality: 17,998,388

STATE	RICHARD M. NIXON (Republican) Votes	%	GEORGE S. MCGOVERN (Democrat) Votes	%	JOHN G. SCHMITZ (American) Votes	%	BENJAMIN SPOCK (People's) Votes	%	OTHER[1] Votes	%	PLURALITY
Alabama[2]	728,701	72.4	256,923	25.5	11,928	1.1			8,559	.9	471,778
Alaska	55,349	58.1	32,967	34.6	6,903	7.3					22,382
Arizona	402,812	61.6	198,540	30.4	21,208	3.3			30,945	4.7	204,272
Arkansas	448,541	68.9	199,892	30.7	2,887	.4					248,649
California	4,602,096	55.0	3,475,847	41.5	232,554	2.8	55,167	.7	2,198		1,126,249
Colorado	597,189	62.6	329,980	34.6	17,269	1.8	2,403	.3	7,043	.8	267,209
Connecticut	810,763	58.6	555,498	40.1	17,239	1.3			777	.1	255,265
Delaware	140,357	59.6	92,283	39.2	2,638	1.1			238	.1	48,074
D.C.[3]	35,226	21.6	127,627	78.1					568	.3	92,401
Florida	1,857,759	71.9	718,117	27.8					7,407	.3	1,139,642
Georgia	881,490	75.3	289,529	24.7							591,961
Hawaii	168,933	62.5	101,433	37.5							67,500
Idaho	199,384	64.2	80,826	26.0	28,869	9.3	903	.3	397	.1	118,558
Illinois	2,788,179	59.0	1,913,472	40.5	2,471	.1			19,114	.4	874,707
Indiana	1,405,154	66.1	708,568	33.3			4,544	.2	7,263	.3	696,586
Iowa	706,207	57.6	496,206	40.5	22,056	1.8			1,475	.1	210,001
Kansas	619,812	67.7	270,287	29.5	21,808	2.4			4,188	.5	349,525
Kentucky	676,446	63.4	371,159	34.8	17,627	1.7	1,118	.1	1,149	.1	305,287
Louisiana[4]	686,852	66.0	298,142	28.6	44,127	4.2			12,169	1.2	388,710
Maine	256,458	61.5	160,584	38.5							95,874
Maryland	829,305	61.3	505,781	37.4	18,726	1.4					323,524
Massachusetts	1,112,078	45.2	1,332,540	54.2	2,877	.1	101		11,160	.5	220,462
Michigan	1,961,721	56.2	1,459,435	41.8	63,321	1.8			5,848	.2	502,286
Minnesota	898,269	51.6	802,346	46.1	31,407	1.8	2,805	.2	6,825	.4	95,923
Mississippi	505,125	78.2	126,782	19.6	11,598	1.8			2,458	.4	378,343
Missouri	1,154,058	62.3	698,531	37.7							455,527
Montana	183,976	57.9	120,197	37.9	13,430	4.2					63,779
Nebraska	406,298	70.5	169,991	29.5							236,307
Nevada	115,750	63.7	66,016	36.3							49,734
New Hampshire	213,724	64.0	116,435	34.9	3,386	1.0			510	.2	97,289
New Jersey	1,845,502	61.6	1,102,211	36.8	34,378	1.2	5,355	.2	9,783	.3	743,291
New Mexico	235,606	61.1	141,084	36.6	8,767	2.3			474	.1	94,522
New York	4,192,778	57.3	2,951,084	40.3					17,968	.3	1,241,694
North Carolina	1,054,889	69.5	438,705	28.9	25,018	1.7					616,184
North Dakota	174,109	62.1	100,384	35.8	5,646	2.0			375	.1	73,725
Ohio	2,441,827	59.6	1,558,889	38.1	80,067	2.0			14,004	.3	882,938
Oklahoma	759,025	73.7	247,147	24.0	23,728	2.3					511,878
Oregon	486,686	52.5	392,760	42.3	46,211	5.0			2,289	.3	93,926
Pennsylvania	2,714,521	59.1	1,796,951	39.1	70,593	1.5			10,040	.2	917,570
Rhode Island	220,383	53.0	194,645	46.8					729	.2	25,738
South Carolina	477,044	70.8	186,824	27.7	10,075	1.5			17		290,220
South Dakota	166,476	54.2	139,945	45.5					994	.3	26,531
Tennessee	813,147	67.7	357,293	29.8	30,373	2.5			369		455,854
Texas	2,298,896	66.2	1,154,289	33.3	6,039	.2			12,057	.4	1,144,607
Utah	323,643	67.6	126,284	26.4	28,549	6.0					197,359
Vermont	117,149	62.9	68,174	36.6			1,010	.5			48,975
Virginia	988,493	67.8	438,887	30.1	19,721	1.4			9,918	.7	549,606
Washington	837,135	56.9	568,334	38.6	58,906	4.0	2,644	.2	3,828	.3	68,801
West Virginia	484,964	63.6	277,435	36.4							207,529
Wisconsin	989,430	53.4	810,174	43.7	47,525	2.6	2,701	.2	3,060	.1	179,256
Wyoming	100,464	69.0	44,358	30.5	748	.5					56,106
Totals	**47,170,179**	**60.69**	**29,171,791**	**37.53**	**1,090,673**	**1.40**	**78,751**	**.10**	**216,196**	**.28**	

1. For breakdown of "other" vote, see minor candidate vote totals, p. 128.
2. Figures from Richard Scammon *America Votes 10* (Washington, 1973), p. 25.
3. Ibid. p. 415.
4. Ibid., p. 156.

1976 Presidential Election

Total Popular Votes: 81,555,889
Carter's Plurality: 1,682,970

STATE	JIMMY CARTER (Democrat) Votes	%	GERALD R. FORD (Republican) Votes	%	EUGENE J. McCARTHY (Independent) Votes	%	ROGER MacBRIDE (Libertarian) Votes	%	OTHER[1] Votes	%	PLURALITY
Alabama	659,170	55.7	504,070	42.6	99	—	1,481	0.1	18,030	1.5	155,100
Alaska	44,058	35.7	71,555	57.9			6,785	5.5	1,176	1.0	27,497
Arizona	295,602	39.8	418,642	56.4	19,229	2.6	7,647	1.0	1,599	0.2	123,040
Arkansas	498,604	65.0	267,903	34.9	639	0.1			389	0.1	230,701
California	3,742,284	47.6	3,882,244	49.3	58,412	0.7	56,388	0.7	127,789	1.6	139,960
Colorado	460,353	42.6	584,367	54.0	26,107	2.4	5,330	0.5	5,397	0.5	124,014
Connecticut	647,895	46.9	719,261	52.1	3,759	0.3	209	—	10,402	0.8	71,366
Delaware	122,596	52.0	109,831	46.6	2,437	1.0			970	0.4	12,765
D.C.	137,818	81.6	27,873	16.5			274	0.2	2,665	1.7	109,945
Florida	1,636,000	51.9	1,469,531	46.6	23,643	0.8	103	—	21,354	0.7	166,469
Georgia	979,409	66.7	483,743	33.0	991	0.1	175	—	3,140	0.2	495,666
Hawaii	147,375	50.6	140,003	48.1			3,923	1.3			7,372
Idaho	126,549	36.8	204,151	59.3	1,194	0.3	3,558	1.0	8,619	2.5	77,602
Illinois	2,271,295	48.1	2,364,269	50.1	55,939	1.2	8,057	0.2	19,354	0.4	92,974
Indiana	1,014,714	45.7	1,183,958	53.3					21,690	1.0	169,244
Iowa	619,931	48.5	632,863	49.5	20,051	1.6	1,452	0.1	5,009	0.4	12,932
Kansas	430,421	44.9	502,752	52.5	13,185	1.4	3,242	0.3	8,245	0.9	72,331
Kentucky	615,717	52.8	531,852	45.6	6,837	0.6	814	0.1	11,922	1.0	83,865
Louisiana	661,365	51.7	587,446	46.0	6,588	0.5	3,325	0.3	19,715	1.5	73,919
Maine	232,279	48.1	236,320	48.9	10,874	2.3	11	—	3,732	0.8	4,041
Maryland	759,612	52.8	672,661	46.7	4,541	0.3	255	—	2,828	0.2	86,951
Massachusetts	1,429,475	56.1	1,030,276	40.4	65,637	2.6	135	—	22,035	0.9	399,199
Michigan	1,696,714	46.4	1,893,742	51.8	47,905	1.3	5,406	0.1	9,982	0.3	197,028
Minnesota	1,070,440	54.9	819,395	42.0	35,490	1.8	3,529	0.2	21,077	1.1	251,045
Mississippi	381,309	49.6	366,846	47.7	4,074	0.5	2,788	0.4	14,344	1.9	14,463
Missouri	998,387	51.1	927,443	47.5	24,029	1.2			3,741	0.2	70,944
Montana	149,259	45.4	173,703	52.8					5,772	1.8	24,444
Nebraska	233,692	38.5	359,705	59.2	9,409	1.5	1,482	0.2	3,380	0.6	126,013
Nevada	92,479	45.8	101,273	50.2			1,519	0.8	6,605	3.3	8,794
New Hampshire	147,635	43.5	185,935	54.7	4,095	1.2	936	0.3	1,017	0.3	38,300
New Jersey	1,444,653	47.9	1,509,688	50.1	32,717	1.1	9,449	0.3	17,965	0.6	65,035
New Mexico	201,148	48.1	211,419	50.5	1,161	0.3	1,110	0.3	3,571	0.9	10,271
New York	3,389,558	51.9	3,100,791	47.5	4,303	0.1	12,197	0.2	27,321	0.4	288,767
North Carolina	927,365	55.2	741,960	44.2	780	—	2,219	0.1	6,590	0.4	185,405
North Dakota	136,078	45.8	153,470	51.6	2,952	1.0	253	0.1	4,435	1.5	17,392
Ohio	2,011,621	48.9	2,000,505	48.7	58,258	1.4	8,961	0.2	32,528	0.8	11,116
Oklahoma	532,442	48.7	545,708	50.0	14,101	1.3					13,266
Oregon	490,407	47.6	492,120	47.8	40,207	3.9			7,142	0.7	1,713
Pennsylvania	2,328,677	50.4	2,205,604	47.7	50,584	1.1			35,922	0.8	123,073
Rhode Island	227,636	55.4	181,249	44.1	479	0.1	715	0.2	1,091	0.3	46,387
South Carolina	450,807	56.2	346,149	43.1	289	—	53	—	5,285	0.7	104,658
South Dakota	147,068	48.9	151,505	50.4			1,619	0.5	486	0.2	4,437
Tennessee	825,879	55.9	633,969	42.9	5,004	0.3	1,375	0.1	10,118	0.7	191,910
Texas	2,082,319	51.1	1,953,300	48.0	20,118	0.5	189	—	15,958	0.4	129,019
Utah	182,110	33.6	337,908	62.4	3,907	0.7	2,438	0.5	14,835	2.7	155,798
Vermont	80,954	43.1	102,085	54.4	4,001	2.1			725	0.4	21,131
Virginia	813,896	48.0	836,554	49.3			4,648	0.3	41,996	2.5	22,658
Washington	717,323	46.1	777,732	50.0	36,986	2.4	5,042	0.3	18,451	1.2	60,409
West Virginia	435,914	58.0	314,760	41.9	113	—	16	—	161	—	121,154
Wisconsin	1,040,232	49.4	1,004,987	47.8	34,943	1.7	3,814	0.2	20,199	1.0	35,245
Wyoming	62,239	39.8	92,717	59.3	624	0.4	89	0.1	674	0.4	30,478
Totals	**40,830,763**	**50.1**	**39,147,793**	**48.0**	**756,691**	**0.9**	**173,011**	**0.2**	**647,631**	**0.8**	

1. For breakdown of "Other" vote, see minor candidate vote totals, p. 128.

1980 Presidential Election

Total Popular Vote: 86,513,296
Reagan's Plurality: 8,417,992

STATE	RONALD REAGAN (Republican)		JIMMY CARTER (Democrat)		JOHN B. ANDERSON (Independent)		ED CLARK (Libertarian)		OTHER[1]		PLURALITY
	Votes	%	Votes	%	Votes	%	Votes	%	Votes	%	
Alabama	654,192	48.8	636,730	47.5	16,481	1.2	13,318	1.0	21,238	1.5	17,462
Alaska	86,112	54.4	41,842	26.4	11,156	7.0	18,479	11.7	805	0.5	44,270
Arizona	529,688	60.6	246,843	28.2	76,952	8.8	18,784	2.2	1,678	0.2	282,845
Arkansas	403,164	48.1	398,041	47.5	22,468	2.7	8,970	1.1	4,939	0.6	5,123
California	4,524,835	52.7	3,083,652	35.9	739,832	8.6	148,434	1.7	90,657	1.1	1,441,197
Colorado	652,264	55.0	368,009	31.1	130,633	11.0	25,744	2.2	7,800	0.7	284,291
Connecticut	677,210	48.2	541,732	38.5	171,807	12.2	8,570	0.6	6,966	0.5	135,478
Delaware	111,252	47.2	105,754	44.8	16,288	6.9	1,974	0.9	632	0.2	5,498
D.C.	23,313	13.4	130,231	74.9	16,131	9.3	1,104	0.6	3,110	1.8	107,568
Florida	2,046,951	55.5	1,419,475	38.5	189,692	5.2	30,524	0.8	285	0.0	627,476
Georgia	654,168	41.0	890,955	55.8	36,055	2.2	15,627	1.0	112	0.0	236,565
Hawaii	130,112	42.9	135,879	44.8	32,021	10.6	3,269	1.1	2,006	0.6	5,767
Idaho	290,699	66.4	110,192	25.2	27,058	6.2	8,425	1.9	1,470	0.3	180,507
Illinois	2,358,094	49.7	1,981,413	41.7	346,754	7.3	38,939	0.8	24,566	0.5	376,636
Indiana	1,255,656	56.0	844,197	37.6	111,639	5.0	19,627	0.9	24,479	0.5	411,459
Iowa	676,026	51.3	508,672	38.6	115,633	8.8	13,123	1.0	4,207	0.3	167,354
Kansas	566,812	57.8	326,150	33.3	68,231	7.0	14,470	1.5	4,132	0.4	240,662
Kentucky	635,274	49.0	617,417	47.7	31,127	2.4	5,531	0.4	6,278	0.5	18,857
Louisiana	792,853	51.2	708,453	45.8	26,345	1.7	8,240	0.5	12,700	0.8	84,400
Maine	238,522	45.6	220,974	42.3	53,327	10.2	5,119	1.0	5,069	0.9	17,548
Maryland	680,606	44.2	726,161	47.1	119,537	7.8	14,192	0.9			45,555
Massachusetts	1,056,223	41.8	1,053,800	41.7	382,539	15.2	22,038	0.9	10,028	0.4	3,829
Michigan	1,915,225	49.0	1,661,532	42.5	275,223	7.0	41,597	1.1	16,148	0.4	253,693
Minnesota	873,268	42.6	954,173	46.5	174,997	8.5	31,593	1.5	17,885	0.9	80,906
Mississippi	441,089	49.4	429,281	48.1	12,036	1.4	5,465	0.6	4,749	0.5	11,808
Missouri	1,074,181	51.2	931,182	44.3	77,920	3.7	14,422	0.7	2,119	0.1	142,999
Montana	206,814	56.8	118,032	32.4	29,281	8.1	9,825	2.7			88,782
Nebraska	419,214	65.6	166,424	26.0	44,854	7.0	9,041	1.4			253,086
Nevada	155,017	62.5	66,666	26.9	17,651	7.1	4,358	1.8	4,193	1.7	88,351
New Hampshire	221,705	57.7	108,864	28.4	49,693	12.9	2,064	0.5	1,664	0.5	112,841
New Jersey	1,546,557	52.0	1,147,364	38.6	234,632	7.9	20,652	0.6	26,479	0.9	399,193
New Mexico	250,779	55.0	167,826	36.8	29,459	6.5	4,365	0.9	3,808	0.8	82,953
New York	2,893,831	46.7	2,728,372	44.0	467,801	7.5	52,648	0.8	59,307	1.0	165,459
North Carolina	915,018	49.3	875,635	47.2	52,800	2.9	9,677	0.5	2,703	0.1	39,383
North Dakota	193,695	64.2	79,189	26.3	23,640	7.8	3,743	1.2	1,278	0.5	114,506
Ohio	2,206,545	51.5	1,752,414	40.9	254,472	5.9	49,033	1.2	21,139	0.5	454,131
Oklahoma	695,570	60.5	402,026	35.0	38,284	3.3	13,828	1.2			293,544
Oregon	571,044	48.3	456,890	38.7	112,389	9.5	25,838	2.2	15,355	1.3	114,154
Pennsylvania	2,261,872	49.6	1,937,540	42.5	292,921	6.4	33,263	0.7	43,693	0.8	324,332
Rhode Island	154,793	37.2	198,342	47.7	59,819	14.4	2,458	0.6	660	0.1	43,549
South Carolina	441,841	49.4	430,385	48.2	14,153	1.6	5,139	0.6	2,177	0.2	11,456
South Dakota	198,343	60.5	103,855	31.7	21,431	6.5	3,824	1.2	250	0.1	94,488
Tennessee	787,761	48.7	783,051	48.4	35,991	2.2	7,116	0.4	3,697	0.3	4,710
Texas	2,510,705	55.3	1,881,147	41.4	111,613	2.5	37,643	0.8	528	0.0	629,558
Utah	439,687	72.8	124,266	20.6	30,284	5.0	7,156	1.2	2,759	0.4	315,421
Vermont	94,628	44.4	81,952	38.4	31,761	14.9	1,900	0.9	3,058	1.4	12,676
Virginia	989,609	53.0	752,174	40.3	95,418	5.1	12,821	0.7	16,010	0.9	237,435
Washington	865,244	49.7	650,193	37.3	185,073	10.6	29,213	1.7	12,671	0.7	215,051
West Virginia	334,206	45.3	367,462	49.8	31,691	4.3	4,356	0.6			33,256
Wisconsin	1,088,845	47.9	981,584	43.2	160,657	7.1	29,135	1.3	13,000	0.5	107,261
Wyoming	110,700	62.6	49,427	28.0	12,072	6.8	4,514	2.6			61,273
Totals	**43,901,812**	**50.7**	**35,483,820**	**41.0**	**5,719,722**	**6.6**	**921,188**	**1.1**	**486,754**	**6.0**	

1. For breakdown of "Other" vote, see minor candidate vote totals, p. 129.

Popular Returns: Minor Candidates and Parties

This section contains popular vote returns for all minor candidates and parties that were aggregated in the columns labeled "Other" in the tables of presidential election returns.

The source for these data, except for 1976, 1980 and where indicated by a footnote, is the Historical Archive of the Inter-University Consortium for Political Research (ICPR). For 1976 and 1980 the source was Scammon's *America Votes 12* and *14*. Footnotes are on page 130.

The material is presented in the following order:
- Year of presidential election.
- Name of candidate and party, if available from the ICPR data. "Unknown" is used where ICPR sources indicated votes but neither candidate nor a party.
- State name, votes and per cent. Statewide percentages were calculated to two decimal places and rounded to one place. Thus, 0.05 per cent is listed as 0.1 per cent.
- Nationwide vote totals and per cent. Totals and percentages were calculated only where a candidate or party received votes in more than one state. Percentages were calculated to three decimal places and rounded to two.

1824

Unpledged Republican
Massachusetts: 6,616 votes, 15.7 per cent of Mass. vote.

Unknown:
Connecticut: 1,188 votes, 11.2 per cent; Indiana: 7; Massachusetts: 4,753, 11.3; Missouri: 33, 1.0; North Carolina: 256, 0.7; Rhode Island: 200, 8.5.

1828

Unknown:
Alabama: 4 votes; Connecticut: 1,101, 5.7 per cent; Maine: 89, 0.3; Massachusetts: 3,226, 8.3; New Jersey: 8; North Carolina: 15; Rhode Island: 5, 0.1; Vermont: 120, 0.4.

1832

Unknown:
Illinois: 30 votes, 0.1 per cent; Massachusetts: 7,031, 10.4; Rhode Island: 6, 0.1; Vermont: 206, 0.6.

1836

Unknown:
Delaware: 5 votes, 0.1 per cent; Maine: 1,112, 2.9; Massachusetts: 45, 0.1; North Carolina: 1; Rhode Island: 1; Vermont: 65, 0.2; Virginia: 5.

1840

Unknown:
Delaware: 13 votes, 0.1 per cent; Indiana: 599, 0.5; Rhode Island: 136, 1.6; Vermont: 19.

1844

Unknown:
Delaware: 6 votes, 0.1 per cent; Illinois, 939, 0.9; Massachusetts: 1,106, 0.8; North Carolina: 2; Rhode Island: 5.

1848

Gerrit Smith (Liberty)
New York: 2,545 votes, 0.6 per cent of N.Y. vote.

In the ICPR data, the distinct party designations appearing in the original sources are preserved. Thus, in the ICPR returns for 1880, John W. Phelps received votes under the following 4 party designations: "Anti-Masonic" — California 5 votes, Illinois 150 votes and Pennsylvania 44 votes; "Anti-Secret" — Kansas 25 votes; "National American" — Michigan 312 votes and "American" — Rhode Island 4 votes and Wisconsin 91 votes.

In order to provide a single party designation for each minor candidate, Congressional Quarterly has aggregated under a single party designation the votes of minor candidates who are listed in the ICPR data as receiving votes under more than one party designation. The source for the designation is Svend Petersen's *A Statistical History of the American Presidential Elections* (Frederick Ungar, New York 1968) where Petersen gives a party designation. In the 1880 election cited above, Petersen lists John W. Phelps as an "American" party candidate. Where Petersen lists no party designation, Congressional Quarterly selected the party designation for a candidate which appeared most frequently in the ICPR returns.

Henry Clay (Clay Whig)
Illinois: 89 votes, 0.1 per cent of Ill. vote.

Unknown:
Alabama: 4 votes; Connecticut: 24; Massachusetts: 62, 0.1 per cent; North Carolina: 26; Rhode Island: 5, 0.1; Texas: 75, 0.4.

1852

Daniel Webster (Whig) [1]
Georgia: 5,324 votes, 8.5 per cent; Massachusetts: 1,670 votes, 1.3 per cent.
Totals: 6,994, .22%.

—Broome (Native American)
Massachusetts: 158 votes, 0.1 per cent; New Jersey: 738, 0.9; Pennsylvania: 1,670, 0.4.
Totals: 2,566, 0.08%.

George Michael Troup (Southern Rights) [2]
Alabama: 2,205 votes, 5.0 per cent; Georgia: 126, 0.2.
Totals: 2,331 votes, 0.07%.

Unknown:
California: 56 votes, 0.1 per cent; Connecticut: 12; Iowa: 139, 0.4; North Carolina: 60, 0.1; Texas: 10, 0.1.

1856

Unknown:
California: 14 votes; Delaware: 9, 0.1 per cent; Massachusetts: 3,006, 1.8; Ohio, 148.

1860

Gerrit Smith (Union)
Illinois: 35 votes; Ohio: 136.

Unknown:
California: 15 votes; Massachusetts: 328, 0.2 per cent; Minnesota: 17, 0.1.

1864

E. Cheeseborough
Kansas: 543 votes, 2.5 per cent of Kan. vote.

Unknown:
Kansas: 112 votes, 0.5 per cent; Massachusetts: 6; Minnesota: 26, 0.1; Oregon: 5.

1868

S. J. Crawford
Kansas: 1 vote.

C. B. Lines
Kansas: 1 vote.

Walter Ross
Kansas: 1 vote.

Unknown:
Alabama: 6 votes; Massachusetts: 26; New Hampshire: 11.

1872

James Black (Prohibition)
Michigan: 1,271 votes, 0.6 per cent; Ohio: 2,100, 0.4.
Totals: 3,371, 0.05%

George W. Slocum
Iowa: 424 votes, 0.2 per cent of Iowa vote.

James Baird Weaver
Iowa: 309 votes, 0.1 per cent of Iowa vote.

William Palmer
Kansas: 440 votes, 0.4 per cent of Kan. vote.

Liberal Republican Elector
Iowa: 10,447 votes, 4.8 per cent of Iowa vote.

Unknown:
Iowa: 209 votes, 0.1 per cent; Kansas: 141, 0.1; Minnesota: 168, 0.2; New Hampshire: 313, 0.5; South Carolina: 259, 0.3.

1876

Green Clay Smith (Prohibition)
Connecticut: 374 votes, 0.3 per cent; Illinois: 141; Kansas: 110, 0.1; Michigan: 766, 0.2; New York: 2,369, 0.2; Ohio: 1,636, 0.3; Pennsylvania: 1,320, 0.2; Wisconsin: 27.
Totals: 6,743; 0.08%

James B. Walker (American)
Illinois: 177 votes; Kansas: 23; Michigan: 71; Ohio: 76; Pennsylvania: 83; Wisconsin: 29.
Totals: 459; 0.01%

Louis Brookwater
Iowa: 97 votes.

Communist
Wisconsin: 32 votes.

Unknown:
Alabama: 2 votes; California: 19; Connecticut: 26; Iowa: 423, 0.1 per cent; Kansas: 5; Kentucky: 2,998, 1.2; Maine: 828, 0.7; Massachusetts: 779, 0.3; New Hampshire: 93, 0.1; Texas: 46; Vermont: 114, 0.2; Wisconsin: 1,607, 0.6.

1880

Neal Dow (Prohibition)
California: 54 votes; Connecticut: 409, 0.3 per cent; Illinois: 440, 0.1; Kansas: 10; Kentucky: 233, 0.1; Maine: 92, 0.1; Massachusetts: 682, 0.2; Michigan: 938, 0.3; Minnesota: 286, 0.2; New Hampshire: 180, 0.2; New Jersey: 191, 0.1; New York: 1,517, 0.1; Ohio: 2,613, 0.4; Pennsylvania: 1,940, 0.2; Rhode Island: 20, 0.1; Wisconsin: 69.
Totals 9,674, 0.11%

John W. Phelps (American)
California: 5 votes; Illinois: 150; Kansas: 25; Michigan: 312, 0.1 per cent; Pennsylvania: 44; Rhode Island: 4; Wisconsin: 91.
Totals 631, 0.01%

A. C. Brewer (Independent Democrat)
Arkansas: 322 votes, 0.3 per cent of Ark. vote.

W. Pitt Norris
Iowa: 433 votes, 0.1 per cent of Iowa vote.

H. Scott Howells
Iowa: 159 votes, 0.1 per cent of Iowa vote.

Unknown:
Arkansas: 1,221 votes, 1.1 per cent; California: 70; Colorado: 14; Connecticut: 39; Iowa: 472, 0.2; Maine: 139, 0.1; Massachusetts: 117; Mississippi: 677, 0.6; Rhode Island: 1; South Carolina: 36.

1884

Unknown:
Alabama: 72 votes, 0.1 per cent; California: 329, 0.2; Florida: 118, 0.2; Iowa: 1,297, 0.3; Kansas: 468, 0.2; Maine: 6; Massachusetts: 2; New Jersey: 28; Oregon: 35, 0.1; South Carolina: 1,237, 1.3; Vermont: 27, 0.1.

1888

Robert H. Cowdrey (United Labor)
Illinois: 150 votes; New York: 519; Oregon: 351; 0.6 per cent.
Totals 1,020, 0.01%

Socialist Labor
New York: 2,068 votes, 0.2 per cent.
Totals 2,068, 0.02%

James Langdon Curtis (American)
California: 1,591 votes, 0.6 per cent; Pennsylvania: 24.
Totals: 1,615, 0.01%

E.W. Perry
Iowa: 399 votes, 0.1 per cent of Iowa vote.

Unknown:
California: 1,442 votes, 0.6 per cent; Colorado: 177, 0.2; Delaware: 1; Iowa: 157; Kansas: 937, 0.3; Maine: 16; Massachusetts: 60; New Hampshire: 58, 0.1; North Carolina: 37; Oregon: 53, 0.1; Rhode Island: 7; South Carolina: 437, 0.6; Vermont: 35, 0.1.

1892

Simon Wing (Socialist Labor)
Connecticut: 333 votes, 0.2 per cent; Massachusetts: 649, 0.2; New Jersey: 1,337, 0.4; New York: 17,956, 1.3; Pennsylvania: 888, 0.1.
Totals: 21,163; 0.18%

Unknown:
Arkansas: 1,267 votes, 0.9 per cent; Delaware: 13; Georgia: 2,345, 1.1 Maine: 4; Massachusetts: 3; Michigan: 925, 0.2; Rhode Island: 3; South Carolina: 72, 0.1; Texas: 4,086, 1.0; Vermont: 10; Wyoming: 29, 0.2.

1896

Charles Horatio Matchett (Socialist Labor)
California: 1,611 votes, 0.5 per cent; Colorado: 159, 0.1; Connecticut: 1,223, 0.7; Illinois: 1,147, 0.1; Indiana: 324, 0.1; Iowa: 453, 0.1; Maryland: 587, 0.2; Massachusetts: 2,112, 0.5; Michigan: 293, 0.1; Minnesota: 954, 0.3; Missouri: 599, 0.1; Nebraska: 186, 0.1; New Hampshire: 228, 0.3; New Jersey: 3,985, 1.1; New York: 17,667, 1.2; Ohio: 1,165, 0.1; Pennsylvania: 1,683, 0.1; Rhode Island: 558, 1.0; Virginia: 108; Wisconsin: 1,314, 0.3.
Totals: 36,356; 0.26%

Charles Eugene Bentley (National Prohibition)
Arkansas: 892 votes, 0.6 per cent; California: 1,047, 0.4; Colorado: 386, 0.2; Illinois: 793, 0.1; Indiana: 2,267, 0.4; Iowa: 352, 0.1; Kansas: 620, 0.2; Maryland: 136, 0.1; Michigan: 1,816, 0.3; Missouri: 292; Nebraska: 797, 0.4; New Hampshire: 49, 0.1; New Jersey: 5,614, 1.5; North Carolina: 222, 0.1; Ohio: 2,716, 0.3; Pennsylvania: 870, 0.1; Washington: 148, 0.2; Wisconsin: 346, 0.1.
Totals: 19,363; 0.14%

W. C. Douglass

North Carolina: 51 votes.

Unknown:

California: 4 votes; Connecticut: 4; Georgia: 47; Massachusetts: 20; Michigan: 1,073, 0.2 per cent; North Carolina: 321, 0.1; North Dakota: 12; Rhode Island: 5.

1900

Wharton Barker (Populist)

Alabama: 4,188 votes, 2.6 per cent; Arkansas: 972, 0.8; Colorado: 333, 0.2; Florida: 1,143, 2.9; Georgia: 4,568, 3.8; Idaho: 445, 0.8; Illinois: 1,141, 0.1; Indiana: 1,438, 0.2; Iowa: 615, 0.1; Kentucky: 1,961, 0.4; Michigan: 889, 0.2; Mississippi: 1,642, 2.8; Missouri: 4,244; 0.6; Nebraska: 1,104, 0.5; New Jersey: 669, 0.2; North Carolina: 798, 0.3; North Dakota: 109, 0.2; Ohio: 251; Oregon: 269, 0.3; Pennsylvania: 638, 0.1; South Dakota: 340, 0.4; Tennessee: 1,322, 0.5; Texas: 20,565, 4.9; Vermont: 367, 0.7; Virginia: 63; West Virginia: 246, 0.1; Wyoming: 20, 0.1.

Totals: 50,340; 0.36%

Joseph F. Malloney (Socialist Labor)

California: 7,554 votes, 2.5 per cent; Colorado: 654, 0.3; Connecticut: 908, 0.5; Illinois: 1,374, 0.1; Indiana: 663, 0.1; Iowa: 259, 0.1; Kentucky: 390, 0.1; Maryland: 382, 0.1; Massachusetts: 2,599, 0.6; Michigan: 830, 0.2; Minnesota: 1,329, 0.4: Missouri: 1,296, 0.2; Montana: 119, 0.2; New Jersey: 2,074, 0.5; New York: 12,622, 0.8; Ohio: 1,688, 0.2; Pennsylvania: 2,936, 0.3; Rhode Island: 1,423, 2.5; Texas: 162; Utah: 102, 0.1; Virginia: 167, 0.1; Washington: 866, 0.8; Wisconsin: 503, 0.1.

Totals: 40,900; 0.29%

Seth Hockett Ellis (Union Reform)

Arkansas: 341 votes, 0.3 per cent; Illinois: 672, 0.1; Indiana: 254; Maryland: 142, 0.1; Ohio: 4,284, 0.4.

Totals: 5,693; 0.04%

Jonah Fitz Randolph Leonard (United Christian)

Illinois: 352 votes; Iowa: 166.
Totals: 518.

E. W. Perrin

Arkansas: 27 votes.

W. J. Palmer

Colorado: 26 votes.

Edward Waldo Emerson

Massachusetts: 342 votes, 0.1 per cent of Mass. vote.

G. W. Pape

Vermont: 1 vote.

S. W. Cook

Wyoming: 21 votes, 0.1 per cent of Wyo. vote.

Anti-Imperialist

Connecticut: 45 votes.

Unknown:

Connecticut: 10 votes; Louisiana: 4; Massachusetts: 191, 0.1; New Hampshire: 16; Utah: 9; Vermont: 4.

1904

Thomas Edward Watson (Populist)

Alabama: 5,051 votes, 4.6 per cent; Arkansas: 2,326, 2.0; Colorado: 824, 0.3; Connecticut: 495, 0.3; Delaware: 51, 0.1; Florida: 1,605, 4.2; Georgia: 22,635, 17.3; Idaho: 352, 0.5; Illinois: 6,725, 0.6; Indiana: 2,444, 0.4; Iowa: 2,207, 0.5; Kansas: 6,253, 1.9; Kentucky: 2,521, 0.6; Maine: 337, 0.4; Maryland: 1; Massachusetts: 1,294, 0.3; Michigan: 1,145, 0.2; Minnesota: 2,103, 0.7; Mississippi: 1,499, 2.6; Missouri: 4,226, 0.7; Montana: 1,531, 2.4; Nebraska: 20,518, 9.1; Nevada: 344, 2.8; New Hampshire: 82, 0.1; New Jersey: 3,705, 0.9; New York: 7,459, 0.5; North Carolina: 819, 0.4; Ohio: 1,392, 0.1; Oregon: 746, 0.8; South

Dakota: 1,240, 1.2; Tennessee: 2,491, 1.0; Texas: 8,062, 3.5; Washington: 669, 0.5; West Virginia: 339, 0.1; Wisconsin: 560, 0.1.

Totals: 114,051; 0.84%

Charles Hunter Corregan (Socialist Labor)

Colorado: 335 votes, 0.1 per cent; Connecticut: 583, 0.3; Illinois: 4,698, 0.4; Indiana: 1,598, 0.2; Kentucky: 596, 0.1; Massachusetts: 2,359, 0.5; Michigan: 1,018, 0.2; Minnesota: 974, 0.3; Missouri: 1,674, 0.3; Montana: 213, 0.3; New Jersey: 2,380, 0.6; New York: 9,122, 0.6; Ohio: 2,635, 0.3; Pennsylvania: 2,211, 0.2; Rhode Island: 488, 0.7; Texas: 431, 0.2; Washington: 1,592, 1.1; Wisconsin: 249, 0.1.

Totals: 33,156; 0.25%

Austin Holcomb (Continental)

Illinois: 826 votes, 0.1 per cent of Ill. vote.

Thomas O. Clark

Maryland: 4 votes.

Unknown:

California: 333 votes, 0.1 per cent; Connecticut: 11; Massachusetts: 5; New Hampshire: 1; Vermont: 1.

1908

Thomas L. Hisgen (Independence)

Alabama: 497 votes, 0.5 per cent; Arkansas: 286, 0.2; California: 4,278, 1.1; Connecticut: 728, 0.4; Delaware: 29, 0.1; Florida: 553, 1.1; Georgia: 76, 0.1; Idaho: 124, 0.1; Illinois: 7,724, 0.7; Indiana: 514, 0.1; Iowa: 404, 0.1; Kansas: 68; Kentucky: 200; Louisiana: 77, 0.1; Maine: 700, 0.7; Maryland: 485; 0.2; Massachusetts: 19,235, 4.2; Michigan: 734, 0.1; Minnesota: 424, 0.1; Missouri: 392, 0.1; Montana: 493, 0.7; Nevada: 436, 1.8; New Hampshire: 584, 0.7; New Jersey: 2,916, 0.6; New York: 35,817, 2.2; North Dakota: 43, 0.1; Ohio: 439; Oregon: 289, 0.3; Pennsylvania: 1,057, 0.1; Rhode Island: 1,105, 1.5; South Carolina: 46, 0.1; South Dakota: 88, 0.1; Tennessee: 332, 0.1; Texas: 106; Utah: 92, 0.1; Vermont: 804, 1.5; Virginia: 51; Washington: 248, 0.1; Wyoming: 63, 0.2.

Totals: 82,537; 0.55%

Thomas Edward Watson (Populist)

Alabama: 1,576 votes, 1.5 per cent; Arkansas: 987, 0.7; Florida: 1,946, 3.9; Georgia: 16,687, 12.6; Illinois: 633, 0.1; Indiana: 1,193, 0.2; Iowa: 261, 0.1; Kentucky: 333, 0.1; Mississippi: 1,276, 1.9; Missouri: 1,165, 0.2; Ohio: 162; Tennessee: 1,092, 0.4; Texas: 960, 0.3; Virginia: 105, 0.1.

Totals: 28,376; 0.19%

August Gillhaus (Socialist Labor)

Connecticut: 608 votes, 0.3 per cent; Illinois: 1,680, 0.2; Indiana: 643, 0.1; Kentucky: 405, 0.1; Massachusetts: 1,011, 0.2; Michigan: 1,085, 0.2; Missouri: 867, 0.1; New Jersey: 1,196, 0.3; New York: 3,877, 0.2; Ohio: 721, 0.1; Pennsylvania: 1,224, 0.1; Rhode Island: 183, 0.3; Texas: 175, 0.1; Virginia: 25; Wisconsin: 318; 0.1.

Totals: 14,018; 0.09%

Daniel Braxton Turney (United Christian)

Illinois: 400 votes; Michigan: 61.

S. H. Lasiter

Colorado: 1 vote.

B. J. McGrue

Colorado: 1 vote.

Edwin H. Lentz

New Hampshire: 8 votes.

Edward Clark

North Carolina: 13 votes.

Republican (Davidson Faction)

Alabama: 987 votes; 0.9 per cent of Ala. vote.

Unknown:

California: 28 votes; Connecticut: 4, Massachusetts: 9; Vermont: 29, 0.1 per cent; Wisconsin: 2.

1912

Eugene W. Chafin (Prohibition)

Arizona: 265 votes, 1.1 per cent; Arkansas: 908, 0.7; California: 23,366, 3.5; Colorado: 5,063, 1.9; Connecticut: 2,068, 1.1; Delaware: 620, 1.3; Florida: 1,854, 3.7; Georgia: 149, 0.1; Idaho: 1,536, 1.5; Illinois: 15,710, 1.4; Indiana: 19,249, 2.9; Iowa: 8,440, 1.7; Kentucky: 3,253, 0.7; Maine: 947, 0.7; Maryland: 2,244, 1.0; Massachusetts: 2,753, 0.6; Michigan: 8,794, 1.6; Minnesota: 7,886, 2.4; Missouri: 5,380, 0.8; Montana: 32; Nebraska: 3,383, 1.4; New Hampshire: 535, 0.6; New Jersey: 2,936, 0.7; New York: 19,455, 1.2; North Carolina: 118, 0.1; North Dakota: 1,243, 1.4; Ohio: 11,511, 1.1; Oklahoma: 2,195, 0.9; Oregon: 4,360, 3.2; Pennsylvania: 19,525, 1.6; Rhode Island: 616, 0.8; South Dakota: 3,910, 3.4; Tennessee: 832, 0.3; Texas: 1,701, 0.6; Vermont: 1,094, 1.7; Virginia: 709, 0.5; Washington: 9,810, 3.0; West Virginia: 4,517, 1.7; Wisconsin: 8,584, 2.2; Wyoming: 421, 1.0.

Totals: 207,972; 1.38%

Arthur E. Reimer (Socialist Labor)

Colorado: 475 votes, 0.2 per cent; Connecticut: 1,260, 0.7; Illinois: 4,066, 0.4; Indiana: 3,130, 0.5; Kentucky: 1,055, 0.2; Maryland: 322, 0.1; Massachusetts: 1,102, 0.2; Michigan: 1,239, 0.2; Minnesota: 2,212; 0.7; Missouri: 1,778, 0.3; New Jersey: 1,396, 0.3; New York: 4,273, 0.3; Ohio: 2,630, 0.3; Pennsylvania: 706, 0.1; Rhode Island: 236, 0.3; Texas: 430, 0.1; Utah: 510, 0.5; Virginia: 50; Washington: 1,872, 0.6; Wisconsin: 632, 0.2.

Totals: 29,374; 0.2%

Independent

Alabama: 5 votes.

Unknown

California: 4,417, 0.7 per cent; Connecticut: 6; Kansas: 63; Massachusetts: 1; South Carolina: 55, 0.1; Wisconsin: 9.

1916

Arthur E. Reimer (Socialist Labor)

Connecticut: 606 votes, 0.3 per cent; Illinois: 2,488, 0.1; Indiana: 1,659, 0.2; Iowa: 460, 0.1; Kentucky: 332, 0.1; Maryland: 756, 0.3; Massachusetts: 1,096, 0.2; Michigan: 831, 0.1; Minnesota: 468, 0.1; Missouri: 903, 0.1; Nebraska: 624, 0.2; New Jersey: 855, 0.2; New York: 2,666, 0.2; Pennsylvania: 419; Rhode Island: 180, 0.2; Utah: 144, 0.1; Virginia: 67; Washington: 730, 0.2.

Totals: 15,284; 0.08%

Progressive [3]

Colorado: 409 votes, 0.1 per cent; Georgia: 20,692, 12.9; Indiana: 3,898, 0.5; Iowa: 1,793, 0.4; Kentucky: 129; Louisiana: 6,349, 6.8; Minnesota: 290, 0.1; Mississippi: 520, 0.6; Montana: 338, 0.2; Oklahoma: 234, 0.1; Oregon: 310, 0.1; South Carolina: 162, 0.3; Utah: 110, 0.1

Totals 35,234; 0.19%

Unknown:

California: 187 votes; Massachusetts: 6; South Carolina: 258, 0.4 per cent; Vermont: 10.

1920

Aaron Sherman Watkins (Prohibition) [4]

Alabama: 766 votes, 0.3 per cent; California: 25,085, 2.7; Colorado: 2,807, 1.0; Connecticut: 1,771; 0.5; Delaware: 986, 1.0; Florida: 5,124; 3.5; Idaho: 32; Illinois: 11,216, 0.5; Indiana: 13,462, 1.1; Iowa: 4,197, 0.5; Kentucky: 3,250, 0.4; Michigan: 9,510, 0.9; Minnesota: 11,489, 1.6; Missouri: 5,152, 0.4; Nebraska: 5,947, 1.6; New Jersey: 4,674, 0.5; New York: 19,653, 0.7; North Carolina: 17; Oregon: 3,595, 1.5; Pennsylvania: 42,696, 2.3; Rhode Island: 510,

0.3; South Dakota: 900, 0.5; Vermont: 762, 0.9; Virginia: 826, 0.4; Washington: 3,790, 1.0; West Virginia: 1,526, 0.3; Wisconsin: 8,648, 1.2.

Totals: 188,391, 0.7%

James Edward Ferguson (American)

Texas: 47,812 votes, 9.8 per cent.

William W. Cox (Socialist Labor)

Connecticut: 1,491 votes, 0.4 per cent; Illinois: 3,471, 0.2; Iowa: 982, 0.1; Maryland: 1,178, 0.3; Massachusetts: 3,583, 0.4; Michigan: 2,450, 0.2; Minnesota: 5,828, 0.8; Missouri: 1,587, 0.1; New Jersey: 923, 0.1; New York: 4,841, 0.2; Oregon: 1,515, 0.6; Pennsylvania: 753; Rhode Island: 495, 0.3; Washington: 1,321, 0.3.

Totals: 30,418; 0.11%

Robert Colvin Macauley (Single Tax)

Delaware: 39 votes; Illinois: 774; Indiana: 566; Maine: 310, 0.2 per cent; Michigan: 425; New Jersey: 517, 0.1; Ohio: 2,153, 0.1; Pennsylvania: 806; Rhode Island: 100, 0.1.

Totals: 5,690; 0.02%

Black and Tan Republican

Texas: 27,198, 5.6 per cent.

Independent Republican

Louisiana: 342 votes, 0.3 percent.

Insurgent Referendum

South Carolina: 366 votes, 0.6 per cent.

Unknown:

California: 587 votes, 0.1 per cent; Iowa: 6; Kansas: 75; Maryland: 8; Massachusetts: 24; Nebraska: 90; Ohio: 294; Pennsylvania: 27; Vermont: 56, 0.1.

1924

Frank T. Johns (Socialist Labor)

Connecticut: 1,373 votes, 0.3 per cent; Illinois: 2,334, 0.1; Kentucky: 1,512, 0.2; Maine: 406, 0.2; Maryland: 987, 0.3; Massachusetts: 1,668, 0.2; Minnesota: 1,855, 0.2; Missouri: 1,066, 0.1; New Jersey: 819, 0.1; New York: 9,928, 0.3; Ohio: 3,025, 0.2; Oregon: 908, 0.3; Pennsylvania: 634; Rhode Island: 268, 0.1; Vermont: 3; Virginia: 189, 0.1; Washington: 982, 0.2; Wisconsin: 411, 0.1.

Totals: 28,368, 0.1%

William Zebulon Foster (Communist)

Illinois: 2,622 votes, 0.1 per cent; Indiana: 987, 0.1; Iowa: 4,037, 0.4; Massachusetts: 2,634, 0.2; Michigan: 5,330, 0.5; Minnesota: 4,427, 0.5; Montana: 370, 0.2; New Jersey: 1,540, 0.1; New York: 8,244, 0.3; North Dakota: 370, 0.2; Pennsylvania: 2,735, 0.1; Rhode Island: 289, 0.1; Washington: 736, 0.2; Wisconsin: 3,759, 0.5.

Totals: 38,080; 0.13%

Gilbert Owen Nations (American)

Arkansas: 10 votes; Florida: 2,315, 2.1 per cent; Kentucky: 1,334, 0.2; New Jersey: 358; Pennsylvania: 13,035, 0.6; Tennessee: 100; Washington: 5,991; 1.4; West Virginia: 1,072, 0.2.

Totals: 24,215; 0.08%.

William J. Wallace (Commonwealth Land)

Delaware: 16 votes; Illinois: 421; Kentucky: 247; Missouri: 165; New Jersey: 219; Ohio: 1,246, 0.1 per cent; Pennsylvania: 296; Rhode Island: 38; Wisconsin: 271.

Totals: 2,919; 0.01%

Andrew Gump

South Carolina: 1 vote.

Socialist

Oklahoma: 5,134 votes, 1.0 percent.

Unknown:

California: 122 votes; Iowa: 445, 0.1 per cent; Kansas: 3; Louisiana: 4,063, 3.3; Massachusetts: 2; Vermont: 2.

1928

Verne L. Reynolds (Socialist Labor)

Connecticut: 622 votes, 0.1 per cent; Illinois: 1,812, 0.1; Indiana: 645, 0.1; Iowa: 230; Kentucky: 354; Maryland: 906, 0.2; Massachusetts: 772, 0.1; Michigan: 799, 0.1; Minnesota: 1,921, 0.2; Missouri: 342; New Jersey: 488; New York: 4,211, 0.1; Ohio: 1,515, 0.1; Oregon: 1,564, 0.5; Pennsylvania: 382; Rhode Island: 416, 0.2; Virginia: 180, 0.1; Washington: 4,068, 0.8; Wisconsin: 381.

Totals: 21,608; 0.6%

William Frederick Varney (Prohibition)

California: 14,394 votes, 0.8 per cent; Indiana: 5,496, 0.4; Michigan: 2,728, 0.2; New Jersey: 154; Ohio: 3,556, 0.1; Pennsylvania: 3,875, 0.1; Vermont: 338, 0.3; West Virginia: 1,703, 0.3; Wisconsin: 2,245, 0.2.

Totals: 34,489; 0.09%.

Frank Elbridge Webb (Farmer Labor)

Colorado: 1,092 votes, 0.3 per cent; Iowa: 3,088, 0.3; Oklahoma: 1,283, 0.2; South Dakota: 927, 0.4.

Totals: 6,390; 0.02%.

Benjamin Gitlow

California: 104 votes.

H. Morgan

California: 6 votes.

W. O. Ligon

Mississippi: 524 votes, 0.4 per cent of Miss. vote.

Z. A. Rogers

Mississippi: 264 votes, 0.2 per cent of Miss. vote.

Unknown:

California: 151 votes; Iowa: 2; Massachusetts: 4; Pennsylvania: 14; Vermont: 9.

1932

William David Upshaw (Prohibition)

Alabama: 13 votes; California: 20,637, 0.9 per cent; Colorado: 1,928, 0.4; Georgia: 1,125, 0.4; Illinois: 6,388, 0.2; Indiana: 10,399, 0.7; Iowa: 2,111, 0.2; Kentucky: 2,263; 0.2; Massachusetts: 1,142, 0.1; Michigan: 2,893, 0.2; Missouri: 2,429, 0.2; New Jersey: 757, 0.1; Ohio: 7,421, 0.3; Pennsylvania: 11,369, 0.4; Rhode Island: 183, 0.1; South Dakota: 463, 0.2; Tennessee: 1,998, 0.5; Virginia: 1,843, 0.6; Washington: 1,540, 0.3; West Virginia: 2,342, 0.3; Wisconsin: 2,672, 0.2.

Totals: 81,916; 0.21%

William Hope Harvey (Liberty)

Arkansas: 952 votes, 0.4 per cent; California: 9,827, 0.4; Idaho: 4,660, 2.5; Michigan: 217; Montana: 1,461, 0.7; New Mexico: 389, 0.3; North Dakota: 1,817, 0.7; South Dakota: 3,333, 1.2; Texas: 235; Washington: 30,308, 4.9.

Totals: 53,199, 0.13%

Verne L. Reynolds (Socialist Labor)

Colorado: 427 votes, 0.1 per cent; Connecticut: 2,287, 0.4; Illinois: 3,638, 0.1; Indiana: 2,070, 0.1; Kentucky: 1,400, 0.1; Maine: 255, 0.1; Maryland: 1,036, 0.2; Massachusetts: 2,668, 0.2; Michigan: 1,401, 0.1; Minnesota: 770, 0.1; Missouri: 404; New Jersey: 1,054, 0.1; New York: 10,339, 0.2; Ohio: 1,968, 0.1; Oregon: 1,730, 0.5; Pennsylvania: 659; Rhode Island: 433, 0.2; Washington: 996, 0.2; Wisconsin: 493.

Totals: 34,028; 0.09%

Jacob Sechler Coxey (Farmer Labor)

Colorado: 469 votes, 0.1 per cent; Iowa: 1,094, 0.1; Michigan: 137; Minnesota: 5,731, 0.6.

Totals: 7,431; 0.02%

John Zahnd (National)

Indiana: 1,615 votes, 0.1 per cent of Ind. vote.

James R. Cox (Jobless)

Pennsylvania: 726 votes; Virginia: 15.
Totals: 741.

Arizona Progressive Democrat

Arizona: 9 votes.

Independent

Louisiana: 533 votes, 0.2 per cent of La. vote.

Jacksonian

Texas: 152 votes.

Populist

South Carolina: 4 votes.

Unknown:

Iowa: 4 votes; Massachusetts: 71; Pennsylvania: 53; Vermont: 2.

1936

Earl Russell Browder (Communist)[5]

Alabama: 678 votes, 0.3 per cent; Arkansas: 167, 0.1; California: 10,877, 0.4; Colorado: 497, 0.1; Connecticut: 1,193, 0.2; Delaware: 51; Indiana: 1,090, 0.1; Iowa: 506; Kentucky: 210; Maine: 257, 0.1; Maryland: 915, 0.2; Massachusetts: 2,930, 0.2; Michigan: 3,384, 0.2; Minnesota: 2,574, 0.2; Missouri: 417; Montana: 385, 0.2; New Hampshire: 193, 0.1; New Jersey: 1,595, 0.1; New Mexico: 43; New York: 35,609, 0.6; North Dakota: 360, 0.1; Ohio: 5,251, 0.2; Pennsylvania: 4,061, 0.1; Rhode Island: 411, 0.1; Tennessee: 326, 0.1; Texas: 253; Utah: 280, 0.1; Vermont: 405, 0.3; Virginia: 98; Washington: 1,907, 0.3; Wisconsin: 2,197, 0.2; Wyoming: 91, 0.1.

Totals: 79,211; 0.17%

David Leigh Colvin (Prohibition)[5]

Alabama: 719 votes, 0.3 per cent; Arizona: 384, 0.3; California: 12,917, 0.5; Georgia: 660, 0.2; Illinois: 3,438, 0.1; Iowa: 1,182, 0.1; Kentucky: 952, 0.1; Maine: 334, 0.1 ; Massachusetts: 1,032, 0.1; Michigan: 579; Missouri: 908, 0.1; Montana: 224, 0.1; New Jersey: 916, 0.1; New Mexico: 61; North Dakota: 197, 0.1; Oklahoma: 1,328, 0.2; Pennsylvania: 6,687, 0.2; Tennessee: 634, 0.1; Texas: 519, 0.1; Utah: 43; Virginia: 594, 0.2; Washington: 1,041, 0.2; West Virginia: 1,173, 0.1; Wisconsin: 1,071, 0.1; Wyoming: 75, 0.1.

Totals: 37,668; 0.08%

John W. Aiken (Socialist Labor)[5]

Colorado: 327 votes, 0.1 per cent; Connecticut: 1,228, 0.2; Illinois: 1,924, 0.1; Iowa: 252; Kentucky: 310; Maine: 129; Maryland: 1,305, 0.2; Massachusetts: 1,305, 0.1; Michigan: 600; Minnesota: 961, 0.1; Missouri: 292; New Jersey: 349; Oregon: 500, 0.1; Pennsylvania: 1,424; Rhode Island: 929, 0.3; Virginia: 36; Washington: 362, 0.1; Wisconsin: 557.

Totals: 12,790; 0.03%

William Dudley Pelley (Christian)

Washington: 1,598 votes, 0.2 per cent of Wash. vote.

Independent Republican

Delaware: 3,222, 2.5 per cent of Del. vote.

Unknown:

Iowa: 4 votes; Louisiana: 93; Massachusetts: 11; Michigan: 5; Oregon: 108; Vermont: 137, 0.1 per cent.

1940

Earl Russell Browder (Communist)

Alabama: 509 votes, 0.2 per cent; California: 13,586, 0.4; Colorado: 378, 0.1; Connecticut: 1,091, 0.1; Idaho: 276, 0.1; Iowa: 1,524, 0.1; Maine: 411, 0.1; Maryland: 1,274, 0.2; Massachusetts: 3,806, 0.2; Michigan: 2,834, 0.1; Minnesota: 2,711, 0.2; Montana: 489, 0.2; New Jersey: 8,814, 0.5; Oregon: 191; Pennsylvania: 4,519, 0.1; Rhode Island: 239, 0.1; Texas: 215; Utah: 191, 0.1; Vermont: 411, 0.3; Virginia: 72; Washington: 2,626, 0.3; Wisconsin: 2,381, 0.2.

Totals: 48,548; 0.1%

John W. Aiken (Socialist Labor)

Connecticut: 971 votes, 0.1 per cent; Indiana: 706; Iowa: 452; Maryland: 657, 0.1; Massachusetts: 1,492, 0.1; Michigan: 795; Minnesota: 2,553, 0.2; Missouri: 209; New Jersey: 446; Oregon: 2,487, 0.5; Pennsylvania: 1,518; Virginia: 48; Washington: 667, 0.1; Wisconsin: 1,882, 0.1.

Totals: 14,883, 0.03%

Alfred Knutson (Independent)

North Dakota: 545 votes, 0.2 per cent of N.D. vote.

Independent

Louisiana: 108 votes.

Unknown:

California: 262 votes; Georgia: 14; Maryland: 9; Massachusetts: 12; Michigan: 4; Pennsylvania: 827; Vermont: 11.

1944

Edward A. Teichert (Socialist Labor)

California: 180 votes; Connecticut: 1,220, 0.2 per cent; Illinois: 9,677, 0.2; Iowa: 193; Kentucky: 317; Maine: 335, 0.1; Massachusetts: 2,780, 0.1; Michigan: 1,264, 0.1; Minnesota: 3,176, 0.3; Missouri: 220; New Jersey: 6,939, 0.4; New York: 14,352, 0.2; Pennsylvania: 1,789, 0.1; Virginia: 90; Washington: 1,645, 0.2; Wisconsin: 1,002, 0.1.

Totals: 45,179; 0.09%

Gerald L. K. Smith (America First)

Michigan: 1,530 votes, 0.1 per cent; Texas: 250.
Totals: 1,780

Darlington Hoopes (Socialist)

California: 1,408 votes.

Anla A. Albaugh

California: 147 votes.

Independent

Louisiana: 69 votes.

Independent Democrat

Georgia: 3,373 votes, 1.0 per cent of Ga. vote.

Southern Democrat

South Carolina: 7,799, 7.5 per cent of S.C. vote.

Texas Regulars

Texas: 135,411, 11.8 per cent of Texas vote.

Unknown:

California: 326 votes; Massachusetts: 266; Michigan: 6; Vermont: 14.

1948

Norman M. Thomas (Socialist)

Arkansas: 1,037 votes, 0.4 per cent; California: 3,459, 0.1; Colorado: 1,678, 0.3; Connecticut: 6,964, 0.8; Delaware: 250, 0.2; Georgia: 3; Idaho: 332, 0.2; Illinois: 11,522, 0.3; Indiana: 2,179, 0.1; Iowa: 1,829, 0.2; Kansas: 2,807, 0.4; Kentucky: 1,284, 0.2; Maryland: 2,941, 0.5; Michigan: 6,063, 0.3; Minnesota: 4,646, 0.4; Missouri: 2,222, 0.1; Montana: 695, 0.3; New Hampshire: 86; New Jersey: 10,521, 0.5; New Mexico: 80; New York: 40,879, 0.7; North Dakota: 1,000, 0.5; Oregon: 5,051, 1.0; Pennsylvania: 11,325, 0.3; Rhode Island: 429, 0.1; South Carolina: 1; Tennessee: 1,288, 0.2; Texas: 874, 0.1; Vermont: 584, 0.5; Virginia: 726, 0.2; Washington: 3,534, 0.4; Wisconsin: 12,547, 1.0; Wyoming: 137, 0.1.

Totals: 138,973; 0.29%

Claude A. Watson (Prohibition)

Alabama: 1,026 votes, 0.5 per cent, Arizona: 786, 0.4; Arkansas: 1; California: 16,926, 0.4; Delaware: 343, 0.3; Georgia: 732, 0.2; Idaho: 628, 0.3; Illinois: 11,959, 0.3; Indiana: 14,711, 0.9; Iowa: 3,382, 0.3; Kansas: 6,468, 0.8; Kentucky: 1,245, 0.2; Massachusetts: 1,663, 0.1; Michigan: 13,052, 0.6; Missouri: 8;

Montana: 429, 0.2; New Jersey: 10,593, 0.5; New Mexico: 124, 0.1; Pennsylvania: 10,538, 0.3; Texas: 2,758, 0.2; Washington: 6,117, 0.7.

Totals: 103,489; 0.21%

Edward A. Teichert (Socialist Labor)

Arizona: 121 votes, 0.1 per cent; California: 195; Colorado: 214; Connecticut: 1,184, 0.1; Delaware: 29; Illinois: 3,118, 0.1; Indiana: 763, 0.1; Iowa: 4,274, 0.4; Kentucky: 185; Massachusetts: 5,535, 0.3; Michigan: 1,263, 0.1; Minnesota: 2,525, 0.2; Missouri: 3; New Hampshire: 83; New Jersey: 3,354, 0.2; New Mexico: 49; New York: 2,729; Pennsylvania: 1,461; Rhode Island: 131; Virginia: 234, 0.1; Washington: 1,133, 0.1; Wisconsin: 399; Wyoming: 56, 0.1.

Totals: 29,038; 0.06%

Farrell Dobbs (Socialist Workers)

California: 133 votes; Colorado: 228; Connecticut: 606, 0.1 per cent; Iowa: 256; Michigan: 672; Minnesota: 606, 0.1; New Jersey: 5,825, 0.3; New York: 2,675; Pennsylvania: 2,133, 0.1; Utah: 74; Washington: 103; Wisconsin: 303.

Totals: 13,614, 0.03%

Gerald L. K. Smith

California: 42 votes.

John G. Scott

California: 6 votes.

John Maxwell

California: 4 votes.

Morgan Blake

Georgia: 1 vote.

Fielding L. Wright

Maryland: 2,294 votes, 0.4 per cent of Md. vote.

Dwight David Eisenhower

Missouri: 1 vote.

Unknown:

California: 761 votes; Illinois: 1,629; Iowa: 8; Louisiana: 10; Massachusetts: 634; Michigan: 1; Pennsylvania: 107; Vermont: 35.

1952

Eric Hass (Socialist Labor)

Arkansas: 1 vote; California: 273; Colorado: 352, 0.1 per cent; Connecticut: 535, 0.1; Delaware: 242, 0.1; Illinois: 9,363, 0.2; Indiana: 979, 0.1; Iowa: 139; Kentucky: 893, 0.1; Massachusetts: 1,957, 0.1; Michigan: 1,495, 0.1; Minnesota: 2,383, 0.2; Missouri: 169; New Jersey: 5,815, 0.2; New Mexico: 35; New York: 1,560; Pennsylvania: 1,377; Rhode Island: 83; Virginia: 1,160, 0.2; Washington: 633, 0.1; Wisconsin: 770, 0.1; Wyoming: 36.

Totals: 30,250; 0.05%

Darlington Hoopes (Socialist)

California: 206 votes; Colorado: 365, 0.1 per cent; Connecticut: 2,244, 0.2; Delaware: 20; Iowa: 219; Kansas: 530, 0.1; Missouri: 227; Montana: 159, 0.1; New Jersey: 8,593, 0.4; New York: 2,664; Pennsylvania: 2,698, 0.1; Vermont: 185, 0.1; Virginia: 504, 0.1; Washington: 254; Wisconsin: 1,157, 0.1; Wyoming: 40.

Totals: 20,065; 0.03%

Douglas MacArthur (Constitution)

Arkansas: 458 votes, 0.1 per cent; California: 3,504, 0.1; Colorado: 2,181, 0.4; Missouri: 535; New Mexico: 215, 0.1; North Dakota: 1,075, 0.4; Tennessee: 379; Texas: 1,563, 0.1; Washington: 7,290, 0.7.

Totals: 17,200; 0.03%

Farrell Dobbs (Socialist Worker)

Michigan: 655 votes; Minnesota: 618; New Jersey: 3,850, 0.2 per cent; New York: 2,212; Pennsylvania: 1,508; Washington: 119; Wisconsin: 1,350, 0.1.

Totals: 10,312; 0.02%

Henry Krajewski (Poor Man's)

New Jersey: 4,203 votes, 0.2 per cent of N.J. vote.

Unknown:

California: 3,578 votes, 0.1 per cent; Georgia: 1; Idaho: 23; Illinois: 448; Massachusetts: 69; Michigan: 3; New York: 178; Pennsylvania: 155; Vermont: 18.

1956

Harry Flood Byrd (States' Rights)[6]

Kentucky: 2,657 votes, 0.3 per cent of Ky. vote.

Enoch A. Holtwick (Prohibition)[6]

California: 11,119 votes, 0.2 per cent; Delaware: 400, 0.2; Indiana: 6,554, 0.3; Kansas: 3,048, 0.4; Kentucky: 2,145, 0.2; Massachusetts: 1,205, 0.1; Michigan: 6,923, 0.2; New Jersey: 9,147, 0.4; New Mexico: 607, 0.2; Tennessee: 789, 0.1.

Totals: 41,937; 0.07%

Farrell Dobbs (Socialist Workers)

California: 96 votes; Minnesota: 1,098, 0.1 per cent; New Jersey: 4,004, 0.2; Pennsylvania: 2,035; Wisconsin: 564.

Totals: 7,797; 0.01%

Darlington Hoopes (Socialist)

California: 123 votes; Colorado: 531, 0.1 per cent; Iowa: 192; Virginia: 444, 0.1; Wisconsin: 754, 0.1.

Totals: 2,044

Henry Krajewski (American Third Party)

New Jersey: 1,829 votes, 0.1 per cent of N.J. vote.

Gerald L. K. Smith

California: 11 votes.

Independent

Mississippi: 42,961, 17.3 per cent of Miss. vote.

Unpledged

Alabama: 20,323 votes, 4.1 per cent; Louisiana: 44,520, 7.2; South Carolina: 88,509, 29.5.

Unknown:

Alabama: 10 votes; California: 819; Florida: 1,542, 0.1 per cent; Georgia: 2,189, 0.3; Idaho: 16; Illinois: 56; Massachusetts: 341; Vermont: 39.

1960

Rutherford L. Decker (Prohibition)

California: 21,706 votes, 0.3 per cent; Delaware: 284, 0.1; Indiana: 6,746, 0.3; Kansas: 4,138, 0.5; Massachusetts: 1,633, 0.1; Michigan: 2,029, 0.1; Montana: 456, 0.2; New Mexico: 777, 0.3; Tennessee: 2,450, 0.2; Texas: 3,868, 0.2.

Totals: 44,087; 0.06%

Orval E. Faubus (National States Rights)[7]

Alabama: 4,367 votes, 0.8 per cent; Arkansas: 28,952, 6.8; Delaware: 354, 0.2; Louisiana: 169,572, 21.0; Tennessee: 11,296, 1.1.

Totals: 209,314; 0.3%

Farrell Dobbs (Socialist Workers)

Colorado: 563 votes, 0.1 per cent; Iowa: 634, 0.1; Michigan: 4,347, 0.1; Minnesota: 3,077, 0.2; Montana: 391, 0.1; New Jersey: 11,402, 0.4; New York: 14,319, 0.2; North Dakota: 158, 0.1; Pennsylvania: 2,678, 0.1; Utah: 100; Washington: 705, 0.1; Wisconsin: 1,792, 0.1.

Totals: 40,166; 0.06%

Charles Loten Sullivan (Constitutional)

Texas: 18,170 votes, 0.8 per cent.
Total: 0.03%

J. Bracken Lee (Conservative)

New Jersey: 8,708 votes, 0.3 per cent.
Total: 0.01%

C. Benton Coiner (Virginia Conservative)

Virginia: 4,204 votes, 0.5 per cent of Va. vote.

Lar Daly (Tax Cut)

Michigan: 1,767 votes, 0.1 per cent of Mich. vote.

Clennon King (Independent Afro-American Unity)

Alabama: 1,485 votes, 0.3 per cent of Ala. vote.

Merritt B. Curtis (Constitution)

Washington: 1,401 votes, 0.1 per cent of Wash. vote.

T. Coleman Andrews

Maryland: 2 votes.

Barry Goldwater

Maryland: 1 vote.

Stuart Symington

South Carolina: 1 vote.

Independent American

Michigan: 539 votes.

Unknown:

Alabama: 231 votes; Georgia: 245; Illinois: 15; Massachusetts: 31; Oregon: 959, 0.1 per cent; Pennsylvania: 440; Texas: 175; Vermont: 7.

1964

E. Harold Munn (Prohibition)

California: 305 votes; Colorado: 1,355, 0.2 per cent; Delaware: 425, 0.2; Indiana: 8,266, 0.4; Iowa: 1,902, 0.2; Kansas: 5,393, 0.6; Massachusetts: 3,735, 0.2; Michigan: 669; Montana: 499, 0.2; New Mexico: 543, 0.2; North Dakota: 174, 0.1.

Totals: 23,266; 0.03%

John Kasper (National States Rights)

Arkansas: 2,965 votes, 0.5 per cent; Kentucky: 3,469, 0.3; Montana: 519, 0.2.

Totals: 6,953; 0.01%

Joseph B. Lightburn (Constitution)

Texas: 5,060 votes, 0.2 per cent.
Total: 0.01%

James Hensley (Universal Party)

California: 19 votes.

George C. Wallace

Georgia: 60 votes.

Richard B. Russell

Georgia: 50 votes.

Unpledged Democrat

Alabama: 210,732 votes, 30.6 per cent of Ala. vote.

Unknown:

Alabama: 1 vote; California: 5,401, 0.1 per cent; Connecticut: 1,313, 0.1; Georgia: 85; Illinois: 62; Iowa: 118; Massachusetts: 159; Michigan: 145; New York: 268; Oregon: 2,509, 0.3; Pennsylvania: 2,531, 0.1; South Carolina: 8; Tennessee: 34; Vermont: 20.

1968

Dick Gregory (Peace and Freedom)

California: 3,230 votes; Colorado: 1,393, 0.2 per cent; New Jersey: 8,084, 0.3; New York: 24,517, 0.4; Ohio: 372; Pennsylvania: 7,821, 0.2; Virginia: 1,680, 0.1.

Totals: 47,097, 0.06%

Fred Halstead (Socialist Workers)

Arizona: 85 votes; Colorado: 235; Indiana: 1,293, 0.1 per cent; Iowa: 3,377, 0.3; Kentucky: 2,843, 0.3; Michigan: 4,099, 0.1; Minnesota: 807, 0.1; Montana: 457, 0.2; New Hampshire: 104; New Jersey: 8,667, 0.3; New Mexico: 252, 0.1; New York: 11,851, 0.2;

North Dakota: 128, 0.1; Ohio: 69; Pennsylvania: 4,862, 0.1; Rhode Island: 383, 0.1; Utah: 89; Vermont: 295, 0.2; Washington: 272; Wisconsin: 1,222, 0.1.

Totals: 41,390; 0.06%

Eldridge Cleaver (Peace and Freedom)

Arizona: 217 votes; Iowa: 1,332, 0.1 per cent; Michigan: 4,585, 0.1; Minnesota: 933, 0.1; Washington: 1,669, 0.1.

Totals: 8,736; 0.01%

Eugene McCarthy

Arizona: 2,751 votes, 0.6 per cent; California: 20,721, 0.3; Minnesota: 584; Oregon: 1,496, 0.2.

Totals: 25,552; 0.03%

E. Harold Munn (Prohibition)

Alabama: 3,814 votes, 0.4 per cent; California: 59; Colorado: 275; Indiana: 4,616, 0.2; Iowa: 362; Kansas: 2,192, 0.3; Massachusetts: 2,369, 0.1; Michigan: 60: Montana: 510, 0.2; North Dakota: 38; Ohio: 19; Virginia: 601.

Totals: 14,915; 0.02%

Ventura Chavez (People's Constitution)

New Mexico: 1,519 votes, 0.5 per cent of N.M. vote.

Charlene Mitchell (Communist)

California: 260 votes; Minnesota: 415; Ohio: 23; Washington: 378.

James Hensley (Universal)

Iowa: 142 votes.

Richard K. Troxell (Constitution)

North Dakota: 34 votes.

Kent M. Soeters (Berkeley Defense Group)

California: 17 votes.

Nelson A. Rockefeller

Oregon: 69 votes.

American Independent Democrat

Alabama: 10,518 votes; 1.0 per cent of Ala. vote.

New Party

New Hampshire: 421 votes, 0.1 per cent; Vermont: 579, 0.4.

New Reform

Montana: 470 votes, 0.2 per cent of Mont. vote.

Peace and Freedom

California: 27,707 votes, 0.4 per cent; Utah: 180.

Totals: 27,887 votes; 0.04%

Unknown:

Colorado: 948 votes, 0.1 per cent; Connecticut: 1,300, 0.1; Georgia: 173; Illinois: 325; Iowa: 250; Massachusetts: 53; Michigan: 29; Minnesota: 170; New Hampshire: 108; Oregon: 1,075, 0.1; Pennsylvania: 2,264, 0.1; Texas: 489; Vermont: 29; Wisconsin: 2,342, 0.1.

1972

Linda Jenness (Socialist Workers)

California: 574 votes; Colorado: 666, 0.1 per cent; Idaho: 397, 0.1; Iowa: 488; Kentucky: 685, 0.1; Massachusetts: 10,600, 0.4; Michigan: 1,603, 0.1; Minnesota: 940, 0.1; Mississippi: 2,458, 0.4; New Hampshire: 368, 0.1; New Jersey: 2,233, 0.1; New Mexico: 474, 0.1; North Dakota: 288, 0.1; Pennsylvania: 4,639, 0.1; Rhode Island: 729, 0.2; South Dakota: 994, 0.3; Texas: 8,664, 0.3; Washington: 623.

Totals: 37,423; 0.05%

Louis Fisher (Socialist Labor)

California: 197 votes; Colorado: 4,361, 0.5 per cent; Illinois: 12,344, 0.3; Indiana: 1,688, 0.1; Iowa: 195; Massachusetts: 129; Michigan: 2,437, 0.1; Minnesota: 4,261, 0.2; New Jersey: 4,544, 0.2; New York: 4,530, 0.1; Ohio: 7,107, 0.2; Virginia: 9,918, 0.7; Washington: 1,102, 0.1; Wisconsin: 998, 0.1.

Totals: 53,811, 0.07%

Gus Hall (Communist)

California: 373 votes; Colorado: 432, 0.1 per cent; Illinois: 4,541, 0.1; Iowa: 272; Kentucky: 464; Massachusetts: 46; Michigan: 1,210; Minnesota: 662; New Jersey: 1,263; New York: 5,641, 0.1; North Dakota: 87; Ohio: 6,437, 0.2; Pennsylvania: 2,686, 0.1; Washington: 566; Wisconsin: 663.

Totals: 25,343; 0.03%

E. Harold Munn (Prohibition)[8]

Alabama: 8,559 votes, 0.9 per cent; California: 53; Colorado: 467, 0.1; Delaware: 238, 0.1; Kansas: 4,188, 0.5.

Totals: 12,818; 0.02%

John Hospers (Libertarian)

California: 980 votes; Colorado: 1,111, 0.1 per cent; Massachusetts: 43; Washington: 1,537, 0.1.

Totals: 3,671

John V. Mahalchik (America First)

New Jersey: 1,743 votes, 0.1 per cent of N.J. vote.

Gabriel Green (Universal)

California: 21 votes; Iowa: 199.

John Beno

Colorado: 6 votes.

Evelyn Reed (Socialist Workers)

Indiana: 5,575 votes, 0.3 per cent; New York: 7,797, 0.1; Wisconsin: 506.

Totals: 13,878; 0.02%

Edward A. Wallace

Ohio: 460 votes.

Socialist Worker

Arizona: 30,945, 4.7 per cent; Louisiana: 12,169, 1.2.

Unknown:

Connecticut: 777 votes, 0.1 per cent; Florida; 7,407, 0.3; Illinois: 2,229, 0.1; Iowa: 321; Massachusetts: 342; Michigan: 598; Minnesota: 962, 0.1; New Hampshire: 142; Oregon: 2,289, 0.3; Pennsylvania: 2,715, 0.1; South Carolina: 17; Tennessee: 369; Texas: 3,393, 0.1; Wisconsin: 893, 0.1; District of Columbia: 568, 0.3.

1976

Lester Maddox (American Independent)

Alabama: 9,198 votes, 0.8 per cent; Arizona: 85; California: 51,098, 0.6; Connecticut: 7,101, 0.5; Georgia: 1,071, 0.1; Idaho: 5,935, 1.7; Kansas: 2,118, 0.2; Kentucky: 2,328, 0.2; Louisiana: 10,058, 0.8; Maine: 8; Maryland: 171; Mississippi: 4,861, 0.6; Nebraska: 3,380, 0.6; Nevada: 1,497, 0.7; New Jersey: 7,716, 0.3; New Mexico: 31; New York: 97; North Dakota: 269, 0.1; Ohio: 15,529, 0.4; Pennsylvania: 25,344, 0.5; Rhode Island: 1; South Carolina: 1,950, 0.2; Tennessee: 2,303, 0.2; Texas: 41; Utah: 1,162, 0.2; Washington: 8,585, 0.6; West Virginia: 12; Wisconsin: 8,552, 0.4; Wyoming: 30.

Totals: 170,531; 0.2%

Thomas J. Anderson (American)

Alabama: 70 votes; Arizona: 564, 0.1 per cent; Arkansas: 389, 0.1; California: 4,565, 0.1; Colorado: 397; Connecticut: 155; Delaware: 645, 0.3; Florida: 21,325, 0.7; Georgia: 1,168, 0.1; Idaho: 493, 0.1; Illinois: 387; Indiana: 14,048, 0.6; Iowa: 3,040, 0.2; Kansas: 4,724, 0.5; Kentucky: 8,308, 0.7; Maine: 28; Maryland:

321; Massachusetts: 7,555, 0.3; Minnesota: 13,592, 0.7; Mississippi: 6,678, 0.9; Montana: 5,772, 1.8; New Mexico: 106; New York: 451; North Carolina: 5,607, 0.3; North Dakota: 3,796, 1.3; Oregon: 1,035, 0.1; Rhode Island: 24; South Carolina: 2,996, 0.4; Tennessee: 5,769, 0.4; Texas: 11,442, 0.3; Utah: 13,284, 2.5; Virginia: 16,686, 1.0; Washington: 5,046, 0.3; West Virginia: 17; Wyoming: 290, 0.2.

Totals: 160,773; 0.2%.

Peter Camejo (Socialist Workers)

Alabama: 1 vote; Arizona: 928, 0.1 per cent; California: 17,259, 0.2; Colorado: 1,126, 0.1; Connecticut: 42; District of Columbia: 545, 0.3; Georgia: 43; Idaho: 14; Illinois: 3,615, 0.1; Indiana: 5,695, 0.3; Iowa: 267; Kentucky: 350; Louisiana: 2,240, 0.2; Maine: 1; Maryland: 261; Massachusetts: 8,138, 0.3; Michigan: 1,804; Minnesota: 4,149, 0.2; Mississippi: 2,805, 0.4; New Hampshire: 161; New Jersey: 1,184; New Mexico: 2,462, 0.6; New York: 6,996, 0.1; North Dakota: 43; Ohio: 4,717, 0.1; Pennsylvania: 3,009, 0.1; Rhode Island: 462, 0.1; South Carolina: 8; South Dakota: 168, 0.1; Texas: 1,723; Utah: 268; Vermont, 430, 0.2; Virginia: 17,802, 1.0; Washington: 905, 0.1; West Virginia: 2; Wisconsin: 1,691, 0.1.

Totals: 91,314, 0.1%

Gus Hall (Communist)

Alabama: 1,954 votes, 0.2 per cent; California: 12,766, 0.2; Colorado: 403; Connecticut: 186; District of Columbia: 219, 0.1; Georgia: 3; Idaho: 5; Illinois: 9,250, 0.2; Iowa: 554; Kentucky: 426; Louisiana: 7,417, 0.6; Maine: 14; Maryland: 68; Minnesota: 1,092, 0.1; New Jersey: 1,662, 0.1; New Mexico: 19; New York: 10,270, 0.2; North Dakota: 84; Ohio: 7,817, 0.2; Pennsylvania: 1,891; Rhode Island: 334, 0.1; South Carolina: 1; South Dakota: 318, 0.1; Tennessee: 547; Utah: 121; Washington: 817, 0.1; West Virginia: 5; Wisconsin: 749.

Totals: 58,992; 0.07%.

Margaret Wright (People's Party)

California: 41,731 votes, 0.5 per cent; Connecticut: 1; Idaho: 1; Maryland: 8; Massachusetts: 33; Michigan: 3,504, 0.1; Minnesota: 635; New Jersey: 1,044; Washington: 1,124, 0.1; Wisconsin: 943.

Totals: 49,024; 0.06%.

Lyndon H. LaRouche (U.S. Labor)

Alabama: 1 vote; Colorado: 567, 0.1 per cent; Connecticut: 1,789, 0.1; Delaware: 136, 0.1; District of Columbia: 157, 0.1; Georgia: 1; Idaho: 739, 0.2; Illinois: 2,018; Indiana: 1,947, 0.1; Iowa: 241; Kentucky: 510; Maryland: 21; Massachusetts: 4,922, 0.2; Michigan: 1,366; Minnesota: 543; New Hampshire: 186, 0.1; New Jersey: 1,550, 0.1; New Mexico: 1; New York: 5,413, 0.1; North Carolina: 755; North Dakota: 142; Ohio: 4,335, 0.1; Pennsylvania: 2,744, 0.1; South Carolina: 2; Tennessee: 512; Vermont: 196, 0.1; Virginia: 7,508, 0.4; Washington: 903, 0.1; Wisconsin: 738.

Totals: 40,043; 0.05%.

Benjamin C. Bubar (Prohibition)

Alabama: 6,669 votes, 0.6 per cent; California: 34; Colorado: 2,882, 0.3; Delaware: 103; Kansas: 1,403, 0.1; Maine: 3,495, 0.7; Maryland: 2; Massachusetts: 14; New Jersey: 554; New Mexico: 211, 0.1; North Dakota: 63; Ohio: 62; Tennessee: 442.

Totals: 15,934; 0.02%.

Jules Levin (Socialist Labor)

California: 222 votes; Colorado: 14; Connecticut: 1; Delaware: 86; Florida: 19; Georgia: 2; Illinois: 2,422, 0.1 per cent; Iowa: 167; Maine: 1; Maryland: 7; Massachusetts: 19; Michigan: 1,148; Minnesota: 370; New Hampshire: 66; New Jersey: 3,686, 0.1; New York: 28; Ohio: 68; Rhode Island: 188; Washington: 713; Wisconsin: 389.

Totals: 9,616; 0.01%.

Frank P. Zeidler (Socialist)

Connecticut: 5 votes; Florida: 8; Georgia: 2; Idaho: 2; Iowa: 234; Maryland: 16; Minnesota: 354; New Jersey: 469; New Mexico: 240, 0.1 per cent; New York: 14; North Dakota: 38; Washington: 358; Wisconsin: 4,298, 0.2.

Totals: 6,038; 0.01%.

Ernest L. Miller (Restoration)

California: 26 votes; Colorado: 6; Florida: 2; Georgia: 3; Maryland: 8; Tennessee: 316.

Totals: 361.

Frank Taylor (United American)

Arizona: 22 votes; California: 14.

Totals: 36.

Unknown

Alabama: 137 votes; Alaska: 1,176, 1.0 per cent; California: 74; Colorado: 2; Connecticut: 1,122, 0.1; District of Columbia: 1,944, 1.2; Georgia: 847, 0.1; Idaho: 1,430, 0.4; Illinois: 1,662; Iowa: 506; Maine: 185; Maryland: 1,945, 0.1; Massachusetts: 1,354, 0.1; Michigan: 2,160, 0.1; Minnesota: 342; Missouri: 3,741, 0.2; Nevada: 5,108, 2.5; New Hampshire: 604, 0.2; New Mexico: 501. 0.1; New York: 4,052, 0.1; North Carolina: 228; Oregon: 6,107, 0.6; Pennsylvania: 2,934, 0.1; Rhode Island: 82; South Carolina: 328; Tennessee: 229; Texas: 2,752, 0.1; Vermont: 99. 0.1; West Virginia: 125; Wisconsin: 2,839, 0.1; Wyoming: 354, 0.2.

Totals: 44,969; 0.06%.

1980

Barry Commoner (Citizens)

Alabama: 517 votes; Arizona: 551, 0.1 per cent; Arkansas: 2,345, 0.3; California: 61,063, 0.7; Colorado: 5,614, 0.5; Connecticut: 6,130, 0.4; Delaware, 103; District of Columbia: 1,826, 1.1; Georgia: 104; Hawaii: 1,548, 0.5; Illinois: 10,692, 0.2; Indiana: 4,852, 0.2; Iowa: 2,273, 0.2; Kentucky: 1,304, 0.1; Louisiana: 1,584, 0.1; Maine: 4,394, 0.8; Massachusetts: 2,056, 0.1; Michigan: 11,930, 0.3; Minnesota: 8,406, 0.4; Missouri: 573; New Hampshire: 1,320, 0.4; New Jersey: 8,203, 0.3; New Mexico: 2,202, 0.5; New York: 23,186, 0.4; North Carolina: 2,287, 0.1; North Dakota: 429, 0.2; Ohio: 8,564, 0.2; Oregon: 13,642, 1.2; Pennsylvania: 10,430, 0.2; Rhode Island: 67; Tennessee: 1,112, 0.1; Texas: 453; Utah: 1,009, 0.1; Vermont: 2,316, 1.1; Virginia: 14,024, 0.8; Washington: 9,403, 0.5; Wisconsin: 7,767, 0.3.

Totals: 234,279; 0.3%

Gus Hall (Communist)

Alabama: 1,629 votes, 0.1 per cent; Arizona, 25; Arkansas: 1,244, 0.1; California: 847; Colorado: 487; Delaware: 13; District of Columbia: 371; Florida: 123; Hawaii: 458, 0.2; Illinois: 9,711, 0.2; Indiana: 702; Iowa, 298; Kansas, 967, 0.1; Kentucky: 348; Maine: 591, 0.1; Michigan: 3,262, 0.1; Minnesota: 1,184, 0.1; Missouri: 26; New Hampshire: 129; New Jersey: 2,555, 0.1; New York: 7,414, 0.1; North Dakota: 93; Pennsylvania: 5,184, 0.1; Rhode Island: 218, 0.1; Tennessee: 503; Texas: 49; Utah: 139; Vermont: 118, 0.1; Washington: 834; Wisconsin: 772.

Totals: 45,023

John R. Rarick (American Independent)

Alabama: 15,010 votes, 1.1 per cent; California: 9,856, 0.1; Idaho: 1,057, 0.2; Kansas: 789, 0.1; Louisiana: 10,333, 0.7; Michigan: 5; South Carolina: 2,177, 0.2; Utah: 522, 0.1; Wisconsin: 1,519, 0.1.

Totals: 41,268

Clifton DeBerry (Socialist Workers)

Alabama: 1,303 votes, 0.1 per cent; Arizona: 1,100, 0.1; District of Columbia: 173, 0.1; Florida: 41; Illinois: 1,302, 0.1; Indiana: 610; Iowa:

244; Louisiana: 783, 0.1; Massachusetts: 5,143, 0.2; Minnesota: 711; Missouri: 1,515, 0.1; New Hampshire: 71; New York: 2,068; North Carolina: 416; North Dakota: 89; Pennsylvania: 20,291, 0.4; Rhode Island: 90; Tennessee: 490; Utah: 124; Vermont: 75; Virginia: 1,986, 0.1; Washington: 1,137, 0.1.

Totals: 38,737

Ellen McCormack (Right to Life)

Delaware: 3 votes; Kentucky: 4,233, 0.3 per cent; Missouri: 5; New Jersey: 3,927, 0.1; New York: 24,159, 0.4; Rhode Island: 1.

Totals: 32,327

Maureen Smith (Peace and Freedom)

California: 18,116 votes, 0.2 per cent.

Dierdre Griswold (Workers World)

California: 15 votes; Delaware: 3; District of Columbia: 52; Florida: 8; Georgia: 1; Illinois: 2,257; Massachusetts: 19; Michigan: 30; Minnesota: 698; Mississippi: 2,402, 0.3 per cent; New Hampshire: 76; New Jersey: 1,288; Ohio: 3,790, 0.1; Rhode Island: 77; Tennessee: 400; Texas: 11; Washington: 341; Wisconsin: 414.

Totals: 13,300

Benjamin C. Bubar (Statesman)

Alabama: 1,743 votes, 0.1 per cent; Arkansas: 1,350, 0.2; California: 36; Colorado, 1,180, 0.1; Delaware: 6; Iowa: 150; Kansas: 821, 0.1; Massachusetts: 34; Michigan: 9; New Mexico: 1,281, 0.3; North Dakota: 54; Ohio: 27; Tennessee: 521.

Totals: 7,212

David McReynolds (Socialist)

Alabama: 1,006 votes, 0.1 per cent; Florida: 116; Iowa: 534; Massachusetts: 62; Minnesota: 536; New Jersey: 1,973, 0.1; North Dakota: 82; Rhode Island: 170; Tennessee: 519; Vermont: 136, 0.1; Washington: 956, 0.1; Wisconsin: 808.

Totals: 6,895

Percy L. Greaves (American)

California: 87 votes: Delaware: 400, 0.2 per cent; Indiana: 4,750, 0.2; Iowa: 189; Michigan: 21; North Dakota: 235, 0.1; Utah: 965, 0.2.

Totals: 6,647

Andrew Pulley (Socialist Workers)

California: 231 votes; Colorado: 520; Delaware: 4; Georgia: 4; Kentucky: 393; Mississippi: 2,347, 0.3 per cent; New Jersey: 2,198, 0.1; New Mexico: 325, 0.1; South Dakota: 250, 0.1.

Totals: 6,271

Richard Congress (Socialist Workers)

Ohio: 4,029 votes, 0.1 per cent.

Kurt Lynen (Middle Class)

New Jersey: 3,694 votes, 0.1 per cent.

Bill Gahres (Down With Lawyers)

New Jersey: 1,718 votes, 0.1 per cent.

Frank W. Shelton (American)

Kansas: 1,555 votes, 0.2 per cent.

Harley McLain (Natural Peoples League)

North Dakota: 296, 0.1 per cent.

Unknown

Alaska: 857 votes, 0.5 per cent; California: 1,242, 0.2; Connecticut: 836, 0.1; Delaware: 101; District of Columbia: 690, 0.4; Georgia: 112; Illinois: 604; Iowa: 519; Maine: 84; Massachusetts: 2,382, 0.1; Michigan: 891; Minnesota: 6,139 (American Party, with no candidate specified), 0.3; Missouri: 604; Nevada: 4,193 (none of the above), 1.7; New Hampshire: 68; New Mexico: 734; New York: 1,064; Oregon: 1,713, 0.1; Rhode Island: 37; South Carolina: 376; Tennessee: 152; Vermont: 413, 0.2; Wisconsin: 1,337, 0.1.

Totals: 23,517

---

1. *Georgia figures for Webster obtained from Petersen, Svend, A Statistical History of the American Presidential Elections, Frederick Ungar, New York, 1963, 1968, p. 31.*

2. *Troup figures obtained from Petersen, ibid.*

3. *Iowa and Mississippi figures from Petersen, op. cit., p. 81. Petersen lists these votes, as well as Progressive votes in all other states, for Theodore Roosevelt. In the ICPR data for 1916, votes are listed for Progressive electors; Roosevelt's name does not appear. Since Roosevelt declined to be a candidate, Congressional Quarterly followed ICPR listing these votes as Progressive.*

4. *Florida figures for Watkins obtained from Petersen, op. cit., p. 83.*

5. *Maine figures for Browder, Colvin and Aiken obtained from Petersen, op. cit., p. 94.*

6. *Kentucky figures for Byrd and Holtwick obtained from Petersen, op. cit., p. 109.*

7. *Arkansas figures for Faubus obtained from Petersen, op. cit., p. 113.*

8. *Alabama figures for Munn obtained from Scammon, Richard M., America Votes (10), Congressional Quarterly, 1973, p. 28.*

The Electoral College

For almost two centuries, Americans have been electing their presidents through a unique method called the Electoral College. Conceived by the Founding Fathers as a compromise between electing presidents by Congress or by direct popular vote, the system has continued to function even while the United States has undergone radical transformation from an agricultural seaboard nation to a world power.

Under the Electoral College system, each state is entitled to electoral votes equal in number to its congressional delegation — i.e., the number of representatives from the state, plus two more for the state's two senators. Whichever party receives a plurality of the popular vote in a state usually wins that state's electoral votes. However, there have been numerous exceptions to that rule, including choosing of electors by district, statewide votes for each individual elector and selection of electors by state legislatures.

Constitutional Background

The method of selecting a president was the subject of long debate at the Constitutional Convention of 1787. Several plans were proposed and rejected before a compromise solution, which was modified only slightly in later years, was adopted (Article II, section I, Clause 2).

Facing the convention when it convened May 25 was the question of whether the chief executive should be chosen by direct popular election, by the Congress, by state legislatures or by intermediate electors. Direct election was opposed, because it was generally felt that the people lacked sufficient knowledge of the character and qualifications of possible candidates to make an intelligent choice. Many delegates also feared that the people of the various states would be unlikely to agree on a single person, usually casting their votes for favorite-son candidates well known to them.

The possibility of giving Congress the power to choose the president also received consideration. However, this plan was rejected, largely because of fear that it would jeopardize the principle of executive independence. Similarly, a plan favored by many delegates, to let state legislatures choose the president, was turned down because it was feared that the president might feel so indebted to the states as to allow them to encroach on federal authority.

Unable to agree on a plan, the convention on Aug. 31 appointed a "Committee of 11" to propose a solution to the problem. The committee on Sept. 4 suggested a compromise under which each state would appoint presidential electors equal to the total number of its representatives and senators. The electors, chosen in a manner set forth by each state legislature, would meet in their own states and each cast votes for two persons. The votes would be counted in Congress, with the candidate receiving a majority elected president and the second-highest candidate becoming vice president.

No distinction was made between ballots for president and vice president. Moreover, the development of national political parties and the nomination of tickets for president and vice president created further confusion in the electoral system. All the electors of one party tended to cast ballots for their two party nominees. But with no distinction between the presidential and vice presidential nominees, the danger arose of a tie vote between the two. That actually happened in 1800, leading to a change in the original electoral system with ratification of the 12th Amendment in 1804.

The committee's compromise plan constituted a great concession to the less populous states, since they were assured of three votes (two for their two senators and at least one for their representative) however small their populations might be. The plan also left important powers with the states by giving complete discretion to state legislatures to determine the method of choosing electors.

The only part of the committee's plan that aroused serious opposition was a provision giving the Senate the

Sources

Petersen, Svend. *A Statistical History of the American Presidential Elections.* New York: Frederick Ungar, 1968.

Schlesinger, Arthur M. Jr., ed. *History of American Presidential Elections.* 4 vols. New York: McGraw-Hill, 1971.

Stanwood, Edward. *A History of the Presidency, 1788-1916.* 2 vols. Boston: Houghton Mifflin, vol. 1, 1889; Vol. 2, 1916.

U.S. Bureau of the Census. *Historical Statistics of the United States, Colonial Times to 1957.* Washington, D.C.: U.S. Government Printing Office, 1960.

right to decide presidential elections in which no candidate received a majority of electoral votes. Some delegates feared that the Senate, which already had been given treaty ratification powers and the responsibility to "advise and consent" to all important executive appointments, might become too powerful. Therefore, a counterproposal was made and accepted to let the House decide in instances when the electors failed to give a majority of their votes to a single candidate. The interests of the small states were preserved by giving each state's delegation only one vote in the House on roll calls to elect a president.

The system adopted by the Constitutional Convention was a compromise born out of problems involved in diverse state voting requirements, the slavery problem, big- versus small-state rivalries and the complexities of the balance of power among different branches of the government. It also was apparently as close to a direct popular election as the men who wrote the Constitution thought possible and appropriate at the time.

The 12th Amendment

Only once since ratification of the Constitution has an amendment been adopted that substantially altered the method of electing the president. In the 1800 presidential election, the Democratic-Republican electors inadvertently caused a tie in the Electoral College by casting equal numbers of votes for Thomas Jefferson, whom they wished to be elected president, and Aaron Burr, whom they wished to elect vice president. The election was thrown into the House of Representatives and 36 ballots were required before Jefferson was finally elected president. The 12th Amendment, ratified in 1804, sought to prevent a recurrence of this incident by providing that the electors should vote separately for president and vice president. *(Text, appendix, p. 195)*

Other changes in the system evolved over the years. The authors of the Constitution, for example, had intended that each state should choose its most distinguished citizens as electors and that they would deliberate and vote as individuals in electing the president. But as strong political parties began to appear, the electors came to be chosen merely as representatives of the parties; independent voting by electors disappeared almost entirely.

Methods of Choosing Electors

In the early years of the Republic, states chose a variety of methods to select presidential electors. For the first presidential election, in 1789, four states held direct popular elections to choose their electors: Pennsylvania and Maryland (at large) and Virginia and Delaware (by district). In five states — Connecticut, Georgia, New Jersey, New York and South Carolina — the state legislatures were to make the choice.

Two states, New Hampshire and Massachusetts, adopted a combination of the legislative and popular methods. New Hampshire held a statewide popular vote for presidential electors with the stipulation that any elector would have to win a majority of the popular vote to be elected; otherwise, the Legislature would choose.

In Massachusetts, the arrangement was for the people in each congressional district to vote for the two persons they wanted to be presidential electors. From the two persons in each district having the highest number of votes,

the Legislature, by joint ballot of both houses, was to choose one. In addition, the Legislature was to choose two additional electors at large.

In a dispute between the two houses of the state Legislature in New York, that state failed to choose electors. The state Senate insisted on full equality with the Assembly (lower house); that is, the Senate wanted each house to take a separate ballot and to resolve any differences between them by agreement rather than by having one house impose its will on the other. The Assembly, on the other hand, wanted a joint ballot, on which the lower house's larger numbers would prevail, or it was willing to divide the electors with the Senate. The failure to compromise cost the state its vote in the first presidential election.

The 12th and 13th states — North Carolina and Rhode Island — had not ratified the Constitution by the time the electors were chosen, and so they did not participate.

Generally similar arrangements prevailed for the election of 1792. Massachusetts, while continuing the system of choosing electors by district, changed the system somewhat to provide for automatic election of any candidate for elector who received a majority of the popular vote. New Hampshire continued the system of popular election at large, but substituted a popular runoff election in place of legislative choice, if no candidate received a majority of the popular vote.

Besides Massachusetts and New Hampshire, electors were chosen in 1792 by popular vote in Maryland and Pennsylvania (at large) and Virginia and Kentucky (by district). State legislatures chose electors in Connecticut, Delaware, Georgia, New Jersey, New York, North Carolina, Rhode Island, South Carolina and Vermont.

By 1796 several changes had occurred. New Hampshire switched back to legislative choice for those electors who failed to receive a majority of the popular vote. Tennessee entered the Union (1796) with a unique system for choosing presidential electors: The state Legislature appointed three persons in each county, who in turn chose the presidential electors. Massachusetts retained the system used in 1792. Other states chose their electors as follows: popular vote, at large: Georgia, Pennsylvania; popular vote, by district: Kentucky, Maryland, North Carolina, Virginia; state legislature: Connecticut, Delaware, New Jersey, New York, Rhode Island, South Carolina, Vermont.

Political Parties and Electors: 1800

As political parties gained power, manipulation of the system of choosing electors became increasingly widespread. For example, in 1800 Massachusetts switched from popular voting to legislative selection of electors because of recent successes by the Democratic-Republican Party in that state. The Federalists, still in firm control of the Legislature, sought to secure the state's entire electoral vote for its presidential candidate, native son John Adams. New Hampshire did likewise.

Nor were the Democratic-Republicans innocent of this kind of political maneuver. In Virginia, where that party was in control, the Legislature changed the system for choosing electors from districts to a statewide at-large ballot. That way, the expected statewide Democratic-Republican majority could overcome Federalist control in some districts and garner a unanimous vote for Democratic-Republican presidential candidate Thomas Jefferson.

In Pennsylvania, the two houses of the state Legislature could not agree on legislation providing for popular ballots, the system used in the first three elections, so the Legislature itself chose the electors, dividing them between the parties.

In other changes in 1800, Rhode Island switched to popular election and Georgia reverted to legislative elections. The 16 states thus used the following methods of choosing presidential electors in 1800:

● By popular vote: Kentucky, Maryland, North Carolina (by district); Rhode Island, Virginia (at large).

● By the legislature: Connecticut, Delaware, Georgia, Massachusetts, New Hampshire, New Jersey, New York, Pennsylvania, South Carolina, Tennessee (indirectly, as in 1796), Vermont.

Trend to Winner-Take-All System

For the next third of a century, the states moved slowly but inexorably toward a standard system of choosing presidential electors — the statewide, winner-take-all popular ballot. The development of political parties resulted in the adoption of party slates of electors pledged to vote for the parties' presidential candidates. Each party organization saw a statewide ballot as being in its best interest, with the hope of sweeping in all its electors and preventing the opposition group from capitalizing on local areas of strength (which could result in winning only part of the electoral vote under the districting system).

From 1804 to 1832 there were three basic methods used by the states in choosing presidential electors — popular vote, at large; popular vote, by district; and election by the state legislature. The following list shows the changing methods of choosing presidential electors for each state from 1804 to 1932:

1804

Popular vote, at large: New Hampshire, New Jersey, Ohio, Pennsylvania, Rhode Island, Virginia.

Popular vote, by district: Kentucky, Maryland, Massachusetts, North Carolina.

State legislature: Connecticut, Delaware, Georgia, New York, South Carolina, Tennessee, Vermont.

1808

Popular vote, at large: New Hampshire, New Jersey, Ohio, Pennsylvania, Rhode Island, Virginia.

Popular vote, by district: Kentucky, Maryland, North Carolina, Tennessee.

State legislature: Connecticut, Delaware, Georgia, Massachusetts, New York, South Carolina, Vermont.

1812

Popular vote, at large: New Hampshire, Ohio, Pennsylvania, Rhode Island, Virginia.

Popular vote, by district: Kentucky, Maryland, Massachusetts, Tennessee.

State legislature: Connecticut, Delaware, Georgia, Louisiana, New Jersey, New York, North Carolina, South Carolina, Vermont.

1816

Popular vote, at large: New Hampshire, New Jersey, North Carolina, Ohio, Pennsylvania, Rhode Island, Virginia.

Popular vote, by district: Kentucky, Maryland, Tennessee.

State legislature: Connecticut, Delaware, Georgia, Indiana, Louisiana, Massachusetts, New York, South Carolina, Vermont.

1820

Popular vote, at large: Connecticut, Mississippi, New Hampshire, New Jersey, North Carolina, Ohio, Pennsylvania, Rhode Island, Virginia.

Popular vote, by district: Illinois, Kentucky, Maine, Maryland, Massachusetts, Tennessee.

State legislature: Alabama, Delaware, Georgia, Indiana, Louisiana, Missouri, New York, South Carolina, Vermont.

1824

Popular vote, at large: Alabama, Connecticut, Indiana, Massachusetts, Mississippi, New Hampshire, New Jersey, North Carolina, Ohio, Pennsylvania, Rhode Island, Virginia.

Popular vote, by district: Illinois, Kentucky, Maine, Maryland, Missouri, Tennessee.

State legislature: Delaware, Georgia, Louisiana, New York, South Carolina, Vermont.

1828

Popular vote, at large: Alabama, Connecticut, Georgia, Illinois, Indiana, Kentucky, Louisiana, Massachusetts, Mississippi, Missouri, New Hampshire, New Jersey, North Carolina, Ohio, Pennsylvania, Rhode Island, Vermont, Virginia.

Popular vote, by district: Maine, Maryland, New York, Tennessee.

State legislature: Delaware, South Carolina.

1832

Popular vote, at large: All states except Maryland and South Carolina.

Popular vote, by district: Maryland.

State legislature: South Carolina.

By 1836 Maryland switched to the system of choosing its electors statewide, by popular vote. This left only South Carolina selecting its electors through the state legislature. The state continued this practice through the election of 1860. Only after the Civil War was popular voting for presidential electors instituted in South Carolina.

Thus, since 1836 the statewide, winner-take-all popular vote for electors has been the almost universal practice. Exceptions include the following:

Massachusetts, 1848. Three slates of electors ran — Whig, Democratic and Free Soil — none of which received a majority of the popular vote. Under the law then in force, the state Legislature was to choose in such a case. It chose the Whig electors.

Florida, 1868. The state Legislature chose the electors.

Colorado, 1876. The state Legislature chose the electors because the state had just been admitted to the Union, had held state elections in August and did not want to go to the trouble and expense of holding a popular vote for the presidential election so soon thereafter.

Michigan, 1892. Republicans had been predominant in the state since the 1850s. However, in 1890 the Democrats managed to gain control of the Legislature and the governorship. They promptly enacted a districting system of choosing presidential electors in the expectation that the Democrats could carry some districts and thus win some electoral votes in 1892. The result confirmed their expectations, with the Republicans winning nine and the Democrats five electoral votes that year. But the Republicans soon regained control of the state and re-enacted the at-large system for the 1896 election.

Maine, 1972. In 1969 the Maine Legislature enacted a district system for choosing presidential electors. Two of the state's four electors were selected on the basis of the statewide vote, while the other two were determined by which party carried each of the state's two congressional districts. The system is still in force.

Historical Anomalies

The complicated and indirect system of electing the president has led to anomalies from time to time. In 1836, for example, the Whigs sought to take advantage of the electoral system by running different presidential candidates in different parts of the country. William Henry Harrison ran in most of New England, the mid-Atlantic states and the Midwest; Daniel Webster ran in Massachusetts; Hugh White of Tennessee ran in the South.

The theory was that each candidate could capture electoral votes for the Whig Party in the region where he was strongest. Then the Whig electors could combine on one candidate or, alternatively, throw the election into the House, whichever seemed to their advantage. However, the scheme did not work because Martin Van Buren, the Democratic nominee, captured a majority of the electoral vote.

Another quirk in the system surfaced in 1872. The Democratic presidential nominee, Horace Greeley, died between the popular vote and the meeting of the presidential electors. Thus the Democratic electors had no party nominee to vote for, and each was left to his own judgment. Forty-two of the 66 Democratic electors chose to vote for the Democratic governor-elect of Indiana, Thomas Hendricks. The rest of the electors split their votes among three other politicians: 18 for B. Gratz Brown of Missouri, the Democratic vice presidential nominee; two for Charles J. Jenkins of Georgia; and one for David Davis of Illinois. Three Georgia electors insisted on casting their votes for Greeley, but Congress refused to count them.

The provision that the Electoral College, not the people directly, is to choose the president has led to three presidents assuming the office even though they ran behind their opponents in the popular vote. In two of these instances — Republican Rutherford B. Hayes in 1876 and Republican Benjamin Harrison in 1888 — the winning candidate carried a number of key states by close margins, while losing other states by wide margins. In the third instance — Democratic-Republican John Quincy Adams in 1824 — the House chose the new president after no candidate had achieved a majority in the Electoral College.

Election by Congress

Congress under the Constitution has two key responsibilities relating to the election of the president and vice president. First, it is directed to receive and in joint session count the electoral votes certified by the states. Second, if no candidate has a majority of the electoral vote, the House of Representatives must elect the president and the Senate the vice president.

Although many of the framers of the Constitution

Methods of Selecting Electors: Sources

Information on the methods of selecting presidential electors for the period 1789-1836 appears in several sources, and the sources in a number of instances are in conflict. Among the sources are *Historical Statistics of the United States, Colonial Times to 1957*, prepared by the Bureau of the Census with the cooperation of the Social Science Research Council, published by the U.S. Government Printing Office, Washington, D.C., 1960; Edward Stanwood's *A History of the Presidency, 1788-1916*, Vol. I (Houghton Mifflin, Boston, 1889); Svend Petersen's *A Statistical History of the American Presidential Elections* (Frederick Ungar, New York, 1968); and Neil R. Peirce's *The People's President: the Electoral College in American History and the Direct Vote Alternative* (Simon & Schuster, New York, 1968).

Congressional Quarterly used the Census Bureau's *Historical Statistics of the United States* as its basic source. The chart on p. 681 of *Historical Statistics* presented the most detailed information of all the sources on the various methods used for choosing electors.

apparently thought that most elections would be decided by Congress, the House actually has chosen a president only twice, in 1801 and 1825. But a number of campaigns have been deliberately designed to throw elections into the House, where each state has one vote and a majority of states is needed to elect.

In modern times the formal counting of electoral votes has been largely a ceremonial function, but the congressional role can be decisive when votes are contested. The pre-eminent example is the Hayes-Tilden contest of 1876, when congressional decisions on disputed electoral votes from four states gave the election to Republican Rutherford B. Hayes despite the fact that Democrat Samuel J. Tilden had a majority of the popular vote. *(Tilden-Hayes election, p. 138)*

From the beginning, the constitutional provisions governing the selection of the president have had few defenders, and many efforts at Electoral College reform have been undertaken. Although prospects for reform seemed favorable after the close 1968 presidential election, the 91st Congress (1969-71) did not take final action on a proposed constitutional amendment that would have provided for direct popular election of the president and eliminated the existing provision for contingent election by the House. Reform legislation was reintroduced in the Senate during the 94th Congress (1975-77) and the 95th Congress (1977-79).

In addition to its role in electing the president, Congress bears responsibility in the related areas of presidential succession and disability. The 20th Amendment empowers Congress to decide what to do if the president-elect and the vice president-elect both fail to qualify by the date prescribed for commencement of their terms; it also gives Congress authority to settle problems arising from the death of candidates in cases where the election devolves upon Congress. Under the 25th Amendment, Congress has ultimate responsibility for resolving disputes over presidential disability. It also must confirm presidential nominations to fill a vacancy in the vice presidency.

Jefferson-Burr Deadlock

The election of 1800 was the first in which the contingent election procedures of the Constitution were put to the test and the president was elected by the House.

The Federalists, a declining but still potent political force, nominated John Adams for a second term and chose Charles Cotesworth Pinckney as his running mate. A Democratic-Republican congressional caucus chose Vice President Thomas Jefferson for president and Aaron Burr, who had been instrumental in winning the New York Legislature for the Democratic-Republicans earlier in 1800, for vice president.

The electors met in each state on Dec. 4, and the results gradually became known throughout the country: Jefferson and Burr, 73 electoral votes each; Adams, 65; Pinckney, 64; John Jay, 1. The Federalists had lost, but because the Democratic-Republicans had neglected to withhold one electoral vote from Burr, their presidential and vice presidential candidates were tied and the election was thrown into the House.

The lame-duck Congress, with a partisan Federalist majority, was still in office for the electoral count, and the possibilities for intrigue were only too apparent. After toying with and rejecting a proposal to block any election until March 4, when Adams' term expired, the Federalists decided to support Burr and thus elect a relatively pliant politician over a man they considered a "dangerous radical." Alexander Hamilton opposed this move. "I trust the Federalists will not finally be so mad as to vote for Burr," he wrote. "I speak with intimate and accurate knowledge of his character. His elevation can only promote the purposes of the desperate and the profligate. If there be a man in the world I ought to hate, it is Jefferson. With Burr I have always been personally well. But the public good must be paramount to every private consideration."

On Feb. 11, 1801, Congress met in joint session — with Jefferson, the outgoing vice president, in the chair — to count the electoral vote. This ritual ended, the House retired to its own chamber to elect a president. When the House met, it became apparent that the advice of Hamilton had been rejected. A majority of Federalists in the House insisted on backing Burr over Jefferson, the man they despised more. Indeed, if Burr had given clear assurances that he would run the country as a Federalist, he might have been elected. But Burr was unwilling to make those assurances; and, as one chronicler put it, "No one knows whether it was honor or a wretched indecision which gagged Burr's lips."

In all, there were 106 members of the House at the time, 58 Federalists and 48 Democratic-Republicans. If the ballots had been cast per capita, Burr would have been elected, but the Constitution provided that each state should cast a single vote and that a majority of states was necessary for election.

On the first ballot Jefferson received the votes of eight states, one short of a majority of the 16 states then in the Union. Six states backed Burr, while the representatives of Vermont and Maryland were equally divided, so they lost their votes. By midnight of the first day of voting, 19 ballots had been taken, and the deadlock remained.

In all, 36 ballots were taken before the House came to a decision on Feb. 17. Predictably, there were men who sought to exploit the situation for personal gain. Jefferson wrote: "Many attempts have been made to obtain terms and promises from me. I have declared to them unequivocally that I would not receive the Government on capitulation; that I would not go in with my hands tied."

The impasse was finally broken when Vermont and Maryland switched to support of Jefferson. Delaware and South Carolina also withdrew their support from Burr by casting blank ballots. The final vote: 10 states for Jefferson, four (all in New England) for Burr. Thus Jefferson became president, and Burr, under the Constitution as it then stood, automatically became vice president.

Federalist James A. Bayard of Delaware, who had played a key role in breaking the deadlock, wrote to Hamilton: "The means existed of electing Burr, but this required his cooperation. By deceiving one man (a great blockhead) and tempting two (not incorruptible), he might have secured a majority of the states. He will never have another chance of being president of the United States; and the little use he has made of the one which has occurred gives me but an humble opinion of the talents of an unprincipled man."

The Jefferson-Burr contest clearly illustrated the dangers of the double-balloting system established by the original Constitution, and pressure began to build for an amendment requiring separate votes for president and vice president. Congress approved the 12th Amendment in December 1803, and the states — acting with unexpected speed — ratified it in time for the 1804 election.

John Quincy Adams Election

The only other time a president was elected by the House of Representatives was in 1825. There were many contenders for the presidency in the 1824 election, but four predominated: John Quincy Adams, Henry Clay, William H. Crawford and Andrew Jackson. Crawford, secretary of the Treasury under Monroe, was the early front-runner, but his candidacy faltered after he suffered an incapacitating illness in 1823.

When the electoral votes were counted, Jackson had 99, Adams 84, Crawford 41 and Clay 37. With 18 of the 24 states choosing their electors by popular vote, Jackson also led in the popular voting, although the significance of the popular vote was open to challenge. Under the 12th Amendment, the names of the three top contenders — Jackson, Adams and the ailing Crawford — were placed before the House. Clay's support was vital to either of the two front-runners.

From the start, Clay apparently intended to support Adams as the lesser of two evils. But before the House voted, a great scandal erupted. A Philadelphia newspaper printed an anonymous letter alleging that Clay had agreed to support Adams in return for being made secretary of state. The letter alleged also that Clay would have been willing to make the same deal with Jackson. Clay immediately denied the charge and pronounced the writer of the letter "a base and infamous character, a dastard and a liar." But Jackson believed the charges and found his suspicions vindicated when Adams, after the election, did appoint Clay as secretary of state. 'Was there ever witnessed such a bare-faced corruption in any country before?" Jackson wrote to a friend.

When the House met to vote, Adams was supported by the six New England states and New York and, in large part through Clay's backing, by Maryland, Ohio, Kentucky, Illinois, Missouri and Louisiana. Thus a majority of 13 delegations voted for him — the bare minimum he needed for election, since there were 24 states in the Union at the time. The election was accomplished on the first ballot, but Adams took office under a cloud from which his administration never emerged.

Jackson's successful 1828 campaign made much of his contention that the House of Representatives had thwarted

Splitting of States' Electoral Votes . . .

Throughout the history of presidential elections, there have been numerous cases where a state's electoral votes have been divided between two candidates. The split electoral votes occurred for a variety of reasons.

Electoral Vote Splits, 1789-1836

Splits of a state's electoral votes cast for president before 1836 occurred for these reasons:

● For the first four presidential elections (1789-1800) held under Article II, section 1 of the Constitution, each elector cast two votes without designating which vote was for president and which for vice president. As a result, electoral votes for each state were often scattered among several candidates. The 12th Amendment, ratified in 1804, required electors to vote separately for president and vice president.

● The district system of choosing electors, in which different candidates each could carry several districts. This system is the explanation for the split electoral votes in Maryland in 1804, 1808, 1812, 1824, 1828 and 1832; North Carolina in 1808; Illinois in 1824; Maine in 1828, and New York in 1828.

● The selection of electors by the legislatures of some states. This system sometimes led to party factionalism or political deals that resulted in the choice of electors loyal to more than one candidate. This was the cause for the division of electoral votes in New York in 1808 and 1824, Delaware in 1824 and Louisiana in 1824.

● The vote of an individual elector for someone other than his party's candidate. This happened in New Hampshire in 1820 when one Democratic-Republican elector voted for John Quincy Adams instead of the party nominee, James Monroe.

Voting for Individual Electors

By 1836 all states with the exception of South Carolina, which selected its electors by the state legislature until after the Civil War, had established a system of statewide popular election of electors. The new system limited the frequency of electoral vote splits. Nevertheless, a few states still, on occasion, divided their electoral votes among different presidential candidates. This occurred because of the practice of listing on the ballot the names of all electors and allowing voters to cross off the names of any particular electors they did not like, or, alternatively, requiring voters to vote for each individual elector. In a close election, electors of different parties sometimes were chosen. An example occurred in California in 1880, when one Democratic elector ran behind the Republican thus:

Winning Votes	Party	Losing Electors	Party
80,443	Democratic	80,282	Republican
80,426	Democratic	80,252	Republican
80,420	Democratic	80,242	Republican
80,413	Democratic	80,228	Republican
80,348	Republican	79,885	Democratic

Other similar occurrences include the following:

New Jersey, 1860. Four Republican and three Douglas Democratic electors won.
California, 1892. Eight Democratic electors and one Republican won.

the will of the people by denying him the presidency in 1825 even though he had been the leader in popular and electoral votes.

Other Anomalies

On only one occasion has the Senate chosen the vice president. That was in 1837, when Van Buren was elected president with 170 of the 294 electoral votes while his vice presidential running mate, Richard M. Johnson, received only 147 electoral votes — one less than a majority. This discrepancy occurred because Van Buren electors from Virginia boycotted Johnson, reportedly in protest against his social behavior. The Senate elected Johnson, 33-16, over Francis Granger of New York, the runner-up in the electoral vote for vice president.

Although only two presidential elections actually have been decided by the House, a number of others — including those of 1836, 1856, 1860, 1892, 1948, 1960 and 1968 — could have been thrown into the House by only a small shift in the popular vote.

The threat of House election was most clearly evident in 1968, when Democrat George C. Wallace of Alabama ran as a strong third-party candidate. Wallace frequently asserted that he could win an outright majority in the Electoral College by the addition of key Midwestern and Moun-

tain states to his hoped-for base in the Deep South and border states. In reality, the Wallace campaign had a narrower goal: to win the balance of power in Electoral College voting, thus depriving either major party of the clear electoral majority required for election. Wallace made it clear that he would then expect one of the major party candidates to make concessions in return for enough votes from Wallace electors to win the election. Wallace indicated that he expected the election to be settled in the Electoral College and not in the House of Representatives. At the end of the campaign it was disclosed that Wallace had obtained written affidavits from all of his electors in which they promised to vote for Wallace "or whomsoever he may direct" in the Electoral College.

In response to the Wallace challenge, both major party candidates, Republican Richard M. Nixon and Democrat Hubert H. Humphrey, maintained that they would refuse to bargain with Wallace for his electoral votes. Nixon asserted that the House, if the decision rested there, should elect the popular-vote winner. Humphrey said the representatives should select "the president they believe would be best for the country." Bipartisan efforts to obtain advance agreements from House candidates to vote for the national popular-vote winner if the election should go to the House ended in failure. Neither Nixon nor Humphrey replied to suggestions that they pledge before the election

. . . Factionalism and 'Faithless Electors'

North Dakota, 1892. Two Fusionists (Democrats and Populists) and one Republican won. One of the Fusion electors voted for Democrat Grover Cleveland and the other voted for Populist James B. Weaver, while the Republican elector voted for Benjamin Harrison, thus splitting the state's electoral vote three ways.

Ohio, 1892. Twenty-two Republicans and one Democratic elector won.

Oregon, 1892. Three Republicans and one Populist with Democratic support won.

California, 1896. Eight Republicans and one Democratic elector won.

Kentucky, 1896. Twelve Republicans and one Democratic elector won.

Maryland, 1904. Seven Democratic electors and one Republican won.

Maryland, 1908. Six Democratic and two Republican electors won.

California, 1912. Eleven Progressive and two Democratic electors won.

West Virginia, 1916. Seven Republicans and one Democratic elector won.

The increasing use of voting machines and straight-ticket voting — where the pull of a lever or the marking of an "X" results in automatically casting a vote for every elector — led to the decline in split electoral votes.

'Faithless Electors'

Yet another cause for occasional splits in a state's electoral vote is the so-called "faithless elector." Legally, no elector is bound to vote for any particular candidate; he may cast his ballot for whom he chooses. But in reality, electors are almost always faithful to the candidate of the party with which they are affiliated.

However, sometimes in American political history an elector has broken ranks to vote for a candidate other than his party's. In 1796 a Pennsylvania Federalist elector voted for Democratic-Republican Thomas Jefferson instead of Federalist John Adams. And some historians and political scientists claim that three Democratic-Republican electors voted for Adams. However, the fluidity of political party lines at that early date, and the well-known personal friendship between Adams and at least one of the electors, makes the claim of their being "faithless electors" one of continuing controversy. In 1820 a New Hampshire Democratic-Republican elector voted for John Quincy Adams instead of the party nominee, James Monroe.

There was no further occurrence until 1948, when Preston Parks, a Truman elector in Tennessee, voted for Gov. Strom Thurmond of South Carolina, the States Rights Democratic Party (Dixiecrat) presidential nominee. Since then, there have been the following additional instances:

● In 1956, when W. F. Turner, a Stevenson elector in Alabama, voted for a local judge, Walter E. Jones.

● In 1960, when Henry D. Irwin, a Nixon elector in Oklahoma, voted for Sen. Harry F. Byrd, D-Va.

● In 1968, when Dr. Lloyd W. Bailey, a Nixon elector in North Carolina, voted for George C. Wallace, the American Independent Party candidate.

● In 1972, when Roger L. MacBride, a Nixon elector in Virginia, voted for John Hospers, the Libertarian Party candidate.

● In 1976, when Mike Padden, a Ford elector in the state of Washington, voted for former Gov. Ronald Reagan of California.

to swing enough electoral votes to the popular-vote winner to assure his election without help from Wallace.

In the end Wallace received only 13.5 percent of the popular vote and 46 electoral votes (including the vote of one Republican defector), all from Southern states. He failed to win the balance of power in the Electoral College which he had hoped to use to wring policy concessions from one of the major-party candidates. If Wallace had won a few border states, or if a few thousand more Democratic votes had been cast in Northern states barely carried by Nixon, thus reducing Nixon's electoral vote below 270, Wallace would have been in a position to bargain off his electoral votes or to throw the election into the House for final settlement.

The near success of the Wallace strategy provided dramatic impetus for electoral reform efforts in the 91st Congress.

Counting the Electoral Vote

Congress has mandated a variety of dates for the casting of popular votes, the meeting of the electors to cast ballots in the various states and the official counting of the electoral votes before both houses of Congress.

The Continental Congress made the provisions for the first election. On Sept. 13, 1788, the Congress directed that each state choose its electors on the first Wednesday in January 1789. It further directed these electors to cast their ballots on the first Wednesday in February 1789.

In 1792 the 2nd Congress passed legislation setting up a permanent calendar for choosing electors. Allowing some flexibility in dates, the law directed that states choose their electors within the 34 days preceding the first Wednesday in December of each presidential election year. Then the electors would meet in their various states and cast their ballots on the first Wednesday in December. On the second Wednesday of the following February, the votes were to be opened and counted before a joint session of Congress. Provision also was made for a special presidential election in case of the removal, death, resignation or disability of both the president and vice president.

Under that system, states chose presidential electors at various times. For instance, in 1840 the popular balloting for electors began in Pennsylvania and Ohio on Oct. 30 and ended in North Carolina on Nov. 12. South Carolina, the only state still choosing presidential electors through the state Legislature, appointed its electors on Nov. 26.

Congress modified the system in 1845, providing that each state choose its electors on the same day — the Tuesday next after the first Monday in November — a provision that still remains in force. Otherwise, the days for casting and counting the electoral votes remained the same.

The next change occurred in 1887, when Congress provided that electors were to meet and cast their ballots on the second Monday in January instead of the first Wednesday in December. Congress also dropped the provision for a special presidential election.

In 1934 Congress again revised the law. The new arrangements, still in force, directed the electors to meet on the first Monday after the second Wednesday in December. The ballots are opened and counted before Congress on Jan. 6 (the next day if Jan. 6 falls on a Sunday).

The Constitution states: "The President of the Senate shall, in the presence of the Senate and House of Representatives, open all the certificates, and the votes shall then be counted." It gives no guidance on disputed ballots.

Before counting the electoral votes in 1865, Congress adopted the 22nd Joint Rule, which provided that no electoral votes objected to in joint session could be counted except by the concurrent votes of both the Senate and House. The rule was pushed by congressional Republicans to ensure rejection of the electoral votes from the newly reconstructed states of Louisiana and Tennessee. Under this rule, Congress in 1873 also threw out the electoral votes of Louisiana and Arkansas and three from Georgia.

However, the rule lapsed at the beginning of 1876, when the Senate refused to readopt it because the House was in Democratic control. Thus, following the 1876 election, when it became apparent that for the first time the outcome of an election would be determined by decisions on disputed electoral votes, Congress had no rules to guide it.

Hayes-Tilden Contest

The 1876 campaign pitted Republican Rutherford B. Hayes against Democrat Samuel J. Tilden. Early election-night returns indicated that Tilden had been elected. He had won the swing states of Indiana, New York, Connecticut and New Jersey; those states plus his expected Southern support would give him the election. However, by the following morning it became apparent that if the Republicans could hold South Carolina, Florida and Louisiana, Hayes would be elected with 185 electoral votes to 184 for Tilden. But if a single elector in any of these states voted for Tilden, he would throw the election to the Democrats. Tilden led in the popular-vote count by more than a quarter million votes.

The situation was much the same in each of the three contested states. Historian Eugene H. Roseboom described it as follows: "The Republicans controlled the state governments and the election machinery, had relied upon the Negro masses for votes, and had practiced frauds as in the past. The Democrats used threats, intimidation, and even violence when necessary, to keep Negroes from the polls; and where they were in a position to do so they resorted to fraud also. The firm determination of the whites to overthrow carpetbag rule contributed to make a full and fair vote impossible; carpetbag hold on the state governments made a fair count impossible. Radical reconstruction was reaping its final harvest."

Both parties pursued the votes of the three states with a fine disregard for propriety or legality, and in the end double sets of elector returns were sent to Congress from all three. Oregon also sent two sets of returns. Although Hayes carried that state, the Democratic governor discovered that one of the Hayes electors was a postmaster and therefore ineligible to be an elector under the Constitution, so he certified the election of the top-polling Democratic elector. However, the Republican electors met, received the resignation of their ineligible colleague, then reappointed him to the vacancy since he had in the meantime resigned his postmastership.

Had the 22nd Joint Rule remained in effect, the Democratic House of Representatives could have objected to any of Hayes' disputed votes. But since the rule had lapsed, Congress had to find some new method of resolving electoral disputes. A joint committee was created to work out a plan, and the resulting Electoral Commission Law was approved by large majorities and signed into law Jan. 29, 1877 — only a few days before the date scheduled for counting the electoral votes.

The law, which applied only to the 1876 electoral vote count, established a 15-member electoral commission which was to have final authority over disputed electoral votes, unless both houses of Congress agreed to overrule it. The commission was to consist of five senators, five representatives and five Supreme Court justices. Each chamber was to select its own members of the commission, with the understanding that the majority party would have three members and the minority two. Four justices, two from each party, were named in the bill, and these four were to select the fifth. It was expected that they would choose Justice David Davis, who was considered a political independent, but he disqualified himself when the Illinois Legislature named him to a seat in the Senate. Justice Joseph P. Bradley, a Republican, then was named to the 15th seat on the commission. The Democrats supported his selection, because they considered him the most independent of the remaining justices, all of whom were Republicans. However, he was to vote with the Republicans on every dispute and thus assure the victory of Hayes.

The electoral count began in Congress Feb. 1 (moved up from the second Wednesday in February for this one election), and the proceedings continued until March 2. States were called in alphabetical order, and as each disputed state was reached, objections were raised to both the Hayes and Tilden electors. The question was then referred to the electoral commission, which in every case voted 8-7 for Hayes. In each case, the Democratic House rejected the commission's decision, but the Republican Senate upheld it, so the decision stood.

As the count went on, Democrats in the House threatened to launch a filibuster to block resumption of joint sessions so that the count could not be completed before Inauguration Day. The threat was never carried out, because of an agreement reached between the Hayes forces and Southern conservatives. The Southerners agreed to let the electoral count continue without obstruction. In return Hayes agreed that, as president, he would withdraw federal troops from the South, end Reconstruction and make other concessions. The Southerners, for their part, pledged to respect Negro rights, a pledge they did not carry out.

Thus, at 4 a.m. March 2, 1877, the president of the Senate was able to announce that Hayes had been elected president with 185 electoral votes, as against 184 for Tilden. Later that day Hayes arrived in Washington. The next evening he took the oath of office privately at the White House, because March 4 fell on a Sunday. His formal inauguration followed on Monday. The country acquiesced. Thus ended a crisis that could have resulted in civil war.

Not until 1887 did Congress enact permanent legislation on the handling of disputed electoral votes. The Electoral Count Act of that year gave each state final authority in determining the legality of its choice of electors and required a concurrent majority of both the Senate and House to reject any electoral votes. It also established procedures for counting electoral votes in Congress. *(Text, appendix, p. 196)*

Application of 1887 Law in 1969

The procedures relating to disputed electoral votes were utilized for the first time after the election of 1968. When Congress met in joint session Jan. 6, 1969, to count the electoral votes, Sen. Edmund S. Muskie, D-Maine, and Rep. James G. O'Hara, D-Mich., joined by six other senators and 37 other representatives, filed a written objection to the vote cast by a North Carolina elector, Dr. Lloyd W. Bailey of Rocky Mount, who had been elected as a Republican but chose to vote for George C. Wallace and Curtis LeMay, the presidential and vice presidential candidates of the American Independent Party, instead of Republicans Richard M. Nixon and Spiro T. Agnew.

Acting under the 1887 law, Muskie and O'Hara objected to Bailey's vote on the grounds that it was "not properly given" because a plurality of the popular votes in North Carolina were cast for Nixon-Agnew and the state's voters had chosen electors to vote for Nixon and Agnew only. Muskie and O'Hara asked that Bailey's vote not be counted at all by Congress.

The 1887 statute, incorporated in the U.S. Code, Title 3, Section 15, stipulated that "no electoral vote or votes from any state which shall have been regularly given by electors whose appointment has been lawfully certified ... from which but one return has been received shall be rejected, but the two Houses concurrently may reject the vote or votes when they agree that such vote or votes have not been so regularly given by electors whose appointment has been so certified." The statute did not define the term "regularly given," although at the time of its adoption chief concern centered on problems of dual sets of electoral vote returns from a state, votes cast on an improper day or votes disputed because of uncertainty about whether a state lawfully was in the Union on the day that the electoral vote was cast.

The 1887 statute provided that if written objection to any state's vote was received from at least one member of both the Senate and House, the two legislative bodies were to retire immediately to separate sessions, debate for two hours with a five-minute limitation on speeches, and that each chamber was to decide the issue by vote before resuming the joint session. The statute made clear that both the Senate and House had to reject a challenged electoral vote (or votes) for such action to prevail.

At the Jan. 6 joint session, in the House chamber with Senate President Pro Tempore Richard B. Russell, D-Ga., presiding, the counting of the electoral vote proceeded smoothly through the alphabetical order of states until the North Carolina result was announced, at which time O'Hara rose to announce filing of the complaint. The two houses then reassembled in joint session at which the results of the separate deliberations were announced and the count of the electoral vote by state proceeded without event. At the conclusion, Russell announced the vote and declared Nixon and Agnew elected.

Although Congress did not sustain the challenge to Bailey's vote, the case of the "faithless" elector led to increased pressure for changes in the procedures. However, no reforms had cleared Congress by early 1983.

Reform Proposals

Since Jan. 6, 1797, when Rep. William L. Smith, F-S.C., introduced in Congress the first proposed constitutional amendment for reform of the Electoral College system, hardly a session of Congress has passed without the introduction of one or more resolutions of this nature. But only one — the 12th Amendment, ratified in 1804 — ever has been approved.

In recent years, public interest in a change in the Electoral College system was spurred by the close 1960 and 1968 elections, by a series of Supreme Court rulings relating to apportionment and districting and by introduction of unpledged elector systems in the Southern states.

House Approval of Amendment

Early in 1969, President Nixon asked Congress to take prompt action on Electoral College reform. He said he would support any plan that would eliminate individual electors and distribute among the presidential candidates the electoral vote of every state and the District of Columbia in a manner more closely approximating the popular vote.

Later that year the House approved, 338-70, a resolution proposing a constitutional amendment to eliminate the Electoral College and to provide instead for direct popular election of the president and vice president. The measure set a minimum of 40 percent of the popular vote as sufficient for election and provided for a runoff election between the two top candidates for the presidency if no candidate received 40 percent. Under this plan the House of Representatives could no longer be called upon to select a president. The proposed amendment also authorized Congress to provide a method of filling vacancies caused by the death, resignation or inability of presidential nominees before the election and a method of filling post-election vacancies caused by the death of the president-elect or vice president-elect.

Nixon, who previously had favored a proportional plan of allocating each state's electoral votes, endorsed the House resolution and urged the Senate to adopt it. To become effective, the proposed amendment had to be approved by a two-thirds majority in both the Senate and House and be ratified by the legislatures of three-fourths of the states.

When the proposal reached the Senate floor in September 1970, small-state and Southern senators succeeded in blocking final action on it. The resolution was laid aside Oct. 5, after two unsuccessful efforts to cut off debate by invoking cloture.

Carter Endorsement of Plan

Another major effort to eliminate the Electoral College occurred in 1977, when President Carter included such a proposal in his election reform package, unveiled March 22.

Carter endorsed the amendment approved by the House in 1969, to replace the Electoral College with direct popular election of the president and vice president, and provide for a runoff if no candidate received at least 40 percent of the vote. Because the Senate was again seen as the major stumbling block, the House waited to see what the Senate would do before beginning any deliberation of its own.

After several months of deadlock, the Senate Judiciary Committee approved Sept. 15 the direct presidential election plan by a vote of 9 to 8. But Senate opponents of the measure promised another filibuster and the Senate leadership decided it could not spare the time or effort to try to break it. The measure was never brought to the floor and died when the 95th Congress adjourned in 1978.

On Jan. 15, 1979, the opening day of the 96th Congress, Sen. Birch Bayh, D-Ind., began another effort to abolish the Electoral College through a constitutional amendment. In putting off action in the previous Congress, Senate leaders had agreed to try for early action in the 96th.

A proposed constitutional amendment to abolish the Electoral College and elect the president by popular vote did reach the Senate floor in July 1979. The Senate voted in favor of the measure, 51-48 — 15 votes short of the required two-thirds majority of those present and voting needed to approve a constitutional amendment.

Supporters of the resolution blamed defections by several Northern liberals for the margin of defeat. Major Jewish and black groups extensively lobbied the Northern senators, arguing that the voting strength of black and Jewish voters is maximized under the Electoral College system because both groups are concentrated in urban areas of the large electoral vote states.

Presidential Disability

A decade of congressional concern over the question of presidential disability was eased in 1967 by ratification of the 25th Amendment to the Constitution. The amendment for the first time provided for continuity in carrying out the functions of the presidency in the event of presidential disability and for filling a vacancy in the vice presidency.

Congressional consideration of the problem of presidential disability had been prompted by President Eisenhower's heart attack in 1955. The ambiguity of the language of the disability clause (Article II, Section 1, Clause 5) of the Constitution had provoked occasional debate ever since the Constitutional Convention of 1787. But it had never been decided how far the term "disability" extended or who would be the judge of it.

Clause 5 provided that Congress should decide who was to succeed to the presidency in the event that both the president and the vice president died, resigned or became disabled. Congress enacted succession laws three times. By the Act of March 1, 1792, it provided for succession (after the vice president) of the president pro tempore of the Senate, then of the House Speaker; if those offices were vacant, states were to send electors to Washington to choose a new president.

That law stood until passage of the Presidential Succession Act of Jan. 19, 1886, which changed the line of succession to run from the vice president to the secretary of state, secretary of the Treasury and so on through the Cabinet in order of rank. Sixty-one years later, the Act of July 18, 1947 (still in force), placed the Speaker of the House and the president pro tempore of the Senate ahead of Cabinet officers in succession after the vice president.

Before ratification of the 25th Amendment in 1967, no procedures had been laid down to govern situations arising in the event of presidential incapacity or of a vacancy in the office of vice president. Two presidents had had serious disabilities — James A. Garfield, shot in 1881 and confined to his bed until he died 2½ months later, and Woodrow Wilson, who suffered a stroke in 1919. In each case the vice president did not assume any duties of the presidency for fear he would appear to be usurping the powers of that office. As for a vice presidential vacancy, the United States has been without a vice president 18 times for a total of 40 years through 1980, after the elected vice president succeeded to the presidency, died or resigned.

Ratification of the 25th Amendment established procedures that clarified these areas of uncertainty in the Constitution. The amendment provided that the vice president should become acting president under either one of two circumstances. If the president informed Congress that he was unable to perform his duties, the vice president would become acting president until the president could resume his responsibilities.

If the vice president and a majority of the Cabinet, or another body designated by Congress, found the president to be incapacitated, the vice president would become acting president until the president informed Congress that his disability had ended. Congress was given 21 days to resolve any dispute over the president's disability; a two-thirds vote of both chambers was required to overrule the president's declaration that he was no longer incapacitated.

Whenever a vacancy occurred in the office of the vice president, either by death, succession to the presidency or resignation, the president was to nominate a vice president, and the nomination was to be confirmed by a majority vote of both houses of Congress.

The proposed 25th Amendment was approved by the Senate and House in 1965. It took effect Feb. 10, 1967, after ratification by 38 states. *(Text, appendix, p. 197)*

Within only eight years, the power of the president to appoint a new vice president under the terms of the 25th Amendment was used twice. In 1973, when Vice President Agnew resigned, President Nixon nominated Gerald R. Ford as the new vice president. Ford was confirmed by both houses of Congress and sworn in Dec. 6, 1973. On Nixon's resignation Aug. 9, 1974, Ford succeeded to the presidency, becoming the first unelected president in American history. President Ford chose as his new vice president former Gov. Nelson A. Rockefeller of New York, who was sworn in Dec. 19, 1974.

With both the president and vice president holding office through appointment rather than election, members of Congress and the public expressed concern about the power of a president to, in effect, appoint his own successor. Accordingly, Sen. John O. Pastore, D-R.I., introduced a proposed constitutional amendment on Feb. 3, 1975, to provide for a special national election for president with more than one year remaining in a presidential term. Hearings were held before the Senate Judiciary Subcommittee on Constitutional Amendments but no action was taken on the measure.

Electoral College Votes, 1789-1980

Electoral votes cast for presidential candidates were listed in the *Senate Manual,* Washington, D.C., U.S. Government Printing Office, 1979, pp. 779-812. 1980 figures are from Richard M. Scammon, *America Votes 14* (Washington, D.C., Elections Research Center, 1981). Total electoral votes for each state were compiled from a chart of each apportionment of the House of Representatives, published in the *Biographical Directory of the American Congress,* Washington, D.C., U.S. Government Printing Office, 1971, p. 47.

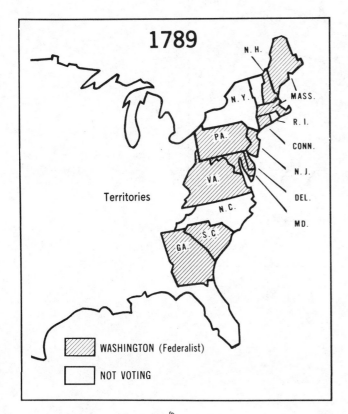

Electoral Votes 1789-1800

Under Article II, section 1 of the Constitution, each presidential elector had two votes and was required to cast each vote for a different person. The person receiving the highest number of votes from a majority of electors was elected president; the person receiving the second highest total became vice president. Since there were 69 electors in 1789, Washington's 69 votes constituted a unanimous election. After ratification of the 12th Amendment in 1804, electors were required to designate which of their two votes was for president and which was for vice president. The Electoral College tables on pages 141 to 144 show *all* electoral votes cast in the elections of 1789, 1792, 1796 and 1800, the charts for 1804 and thereafter show electoral votes cast only for president. For electoral votes totals for vice president, see table page 185.

States	Electoral Votes[6]	Washington	Adams	Jay	Harrison	Rutledge	Hancock	Clinton	Huntington	Milton	Armstrong	Lincoln	Telfair
Connecticut[1]	(14)	7	5	-	-	-	-	-	2	-	-	-	-
Delaware	(6)	3	-	3	-	-	-	-	-	-	-	-	-
Georgia[1]	(10)	5	-	-	-	-	-	-	-	2	1	1	1
Maryland[2]	(16)	6	-	-	6	-	-	-	-	-	-	-	-
Massachusetts	(20)	10	10	-	-	-	-	-	-	-	-	-	-
New Hampshire	(10)	5	5	-	-	-	-	-	-	-	-	-	-
New Jersey[1]	(12)	6	1	5	-	-	-	-	-	-	-	-	-
New York[3]	(16)	-	-	-	-	-	-	-	-	-	-	-	-
North Carolina[4]	(14)	-	-	-	-	-	-	-	-	-	-	-	-
Pennsylvania[1]	(20)	10	8	-	-	-	2	-	-	-	-	-	-
Rhode Island[4]	(6)	-	-	-	-	-	-	-	-	-	-	-	-
South Carolina[1]	(14)	7	-	-	-	6	1	-	-	-	-	-	-
Virginia[5]	(24)	10	5	1	-	-	1	3	-	-	-	-	-
Totals		69	34	9	6	6	4	3	2	2	1	1	1

1. For explanation of split electoral votes, see p. 136.
2. Two Maryland electors did not vote.
3. Not voting. For explanation, see p. 132.
4. Not voting because had not yet ratified Constitution.
5. Two Virginia electors did not vote. For explanation of split electoral votes, see p. 136.
6. Two vots for each elector, see text above.

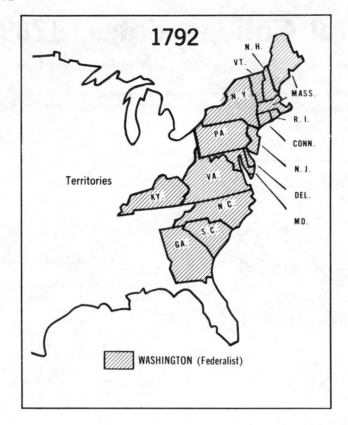

States	Electoral Votes[3]	Washington	Adams	Clinton	Jefferson	Burr
Connecticut	(18)	9	9	-	-	-
Delaware	(6)	3	3	-	-	-
Georgia	(8)	4	-	4	-	-
Kentucky	(8)	4	-	-	4	-
Maryland[1]	(20)	8	8	-	-	-
Massachusetts	(32)	16	16	-	-	-
New Hampshire	(12)	6	6	-	-	-
New Jersey	(14)	7	7	-	-	-
New York	(24)	12	-	12	-	-
North Carolina	(24)	12	-	12	-	-
Pennsylvania[2]	(30)	15	14	1	-	-
Rhode Island	(8)	4	4	-	-	-
South Carolina[2]	(16)	8	7	-	-	1
Vermont[1]	(8)	3	3	-	-	-
Virginia	(42)	21	-	21	-	-
Totals	**(270)**	**132**	**77**	**50**	**4**	**1**

1. *Two Maryland electors and one Vermont elector did not vote.*
2. *For explanation of split electoral votes, see p. 136.*
3. *Two votes for each elector, see text p. 141.*

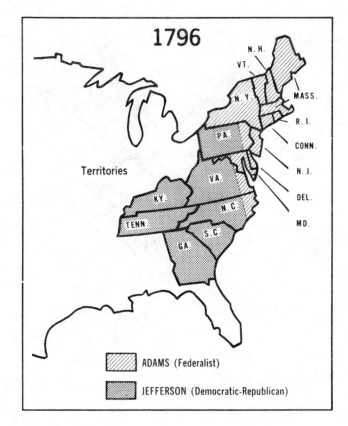

ADAMS (Federalist)

JEFFERSON (Democratic-Republican)

States	Electoral Votes[2]	J. Adams	Jefferson	T. Pinckney	Burr	S. Adams	Ellsworth	Clinton	Jay	Iredell	Henry	Johnston	Washington	C. Pinckney
Connecticut[1]	(18)	9	-	4	-	-	-	-	5	-	-	-	-	-
Delaware	(6)	3	-	3	-	-	-	-	-	-	-	-	-	-
Georgia	(8)	-	4	-	-	-	-	4	-	-	-	-	-	-
Kentucky	(8)	-	4	-	4	-	-	-	-	-	-	-	-	-
Maryland[1]	(20)	7	4	4	3	-	-	-	-	-	2	-	-	-
Massachusetts[1]	(32)	16	-	13	-	1	-	-	-	-	-	2	-	-
New Hampshire	(12)	6	-	-	-	-	6	-	-	-	-	-	-	-
New Jersey	(14)	7	-	7	-	-	-	-	-	-	-	-	-	-
New York	(24)	12	-	12	-	-	-	-	-	-	-	-	-	-
North Carolina[1]	(24)	1	11	1	6	-	-	-	-	3	-	-	1	1
Pennsylvania[1]	(30)	1	14	2	13	-	-	-	-	-	-	-	-	-
Rhode Island	(8)	4	-	-	-	-	4	-	-	-	-	-	-	-
South Carolina	(16)	-	8	8	-	-	-	-	-	-	-	-	-	-
Tennessee	(6)	-	3	-	3	-	-	-	-	-	-	-	-	-
Vermont	(8)	4	-	4	-	-	-	-	-	-	-	-	-	-
Virginia[1]	(42)	1	20	1	1	15	-	3	-	-	-	-	1	-
Totals	**(276)**	**71**	**68**	**59**	**30**	**15**	**11**	**7**	**5**	**3**	**2**	**2**	**2**	**1**

1. For explanation of split electoral votes, see p. 136.
2. Two votes for each elector, see text p. 141.

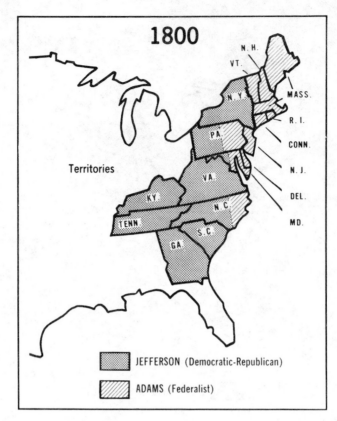

States	Electoral Votes[2]	Jefferson[3]	Burr[3]	Adams	Pinckney	Jay
Connecticut	(18)	-	-	9	9	-
Delaware	(6)	-	-	3	3	-
Georgia	(8)	4	4	-	-	-
Kentucky	(8)	4	4	-	-	-
Maryland[1]	(20)	5	5	5	5	-
Massachusetts	(32)	-	-	16	16	-
New Hampshire	(12)	-	-	6	6	-
New Jersey	(14)	-	-	7	7	-
New York	(24)	12	12	-	-	-
North Carolina[1]	(24)	8	8	4	4	-
Pennsylvania[1]	(30)	8	8	7	7	-
Rhode Island[1]	(8)	-	-	4	3	1
South Carolina	(16)	8	8	-	-	-
Tennessee	(6)	3	3	-	-	-
Vermont	(8)	-	-	4	4	-
Virginia	(42)	21	21	-	-	-
Totals	**(276)**	**73**	**73**	**65**	**64**	**1**

1. For explanation of split electoral votes, see p. 136.
2. Two votes for each elector, see text p. 141.
3. For explanation and result of tie vote, see p. 136.

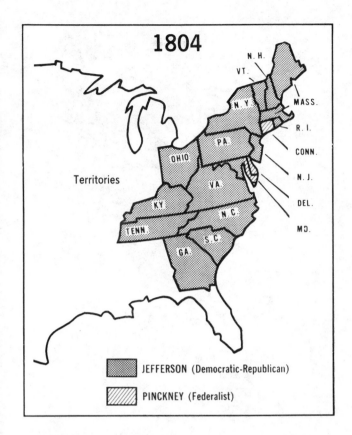

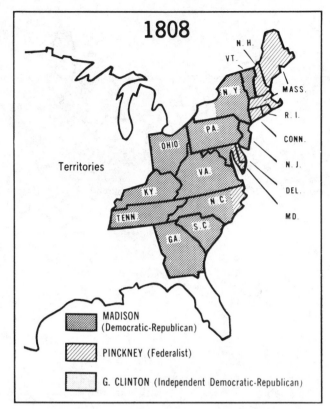

States	Electoral Votes	Jefferson	Pinckney
Connecticut	(9)	-	9
Delaware	(3)	-	3
Georgia	(6)	6	-
Kentucky	(8)	8	-
Maryland[1]	(11)	9	2
Massachusetts	(19)	19	-
New Hampshire	(7)	7	-
New Jersey	(8)	8	-
New York	(19)	19	-
North Carolina	(14)	14	-
Ohio	(3)	3	-
Pennsylvania	(20)	20	-
Rhode Island	(4)	4	-
South Carolina	(10)	10	-
Tennessee	(5)	5	-
Vermont	(6)	6	-
Virginia	(24)	24	-
Totals	**(176)**	**162**	**14**

States	Electoral Votes	Madison	Pinckney	Clinton
Connecticut	(9)	-	9	-
Delaware	(3)	-	3	-
Georgia	(6)	6	-	-
Kentucky[1]	(8)	7	-	-
Maryland[2]	(11)	9	2	-
Massachusetts	(19)	-	19	-
New Hampshire	(7)	-	7	-
New Jersey	(8)	8	-	-
New York[2]	(19)	13	-	6
North Carolina[2]	(14)	11	3	-
Ohio	(3)	3	-	-
Pennsylvania	(20)	20	-	-
Rhode Island	(4)	-	4	-
South Carolina	(10)	10	-	-
Tennessee	(5)	5	-	-
Vermont	(6)	6	-	-
Virginia	(24)	24	-	-
Totals	**(176)**	**122**	**47**	**6**

1. For explanation of split electoral votes, see p. 136.

1. One Kentucky elector did not vote.
2. For explanation of split electoral votes, see p. 136.

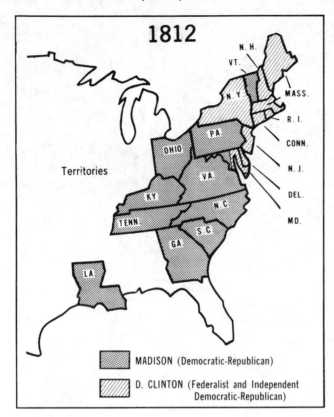

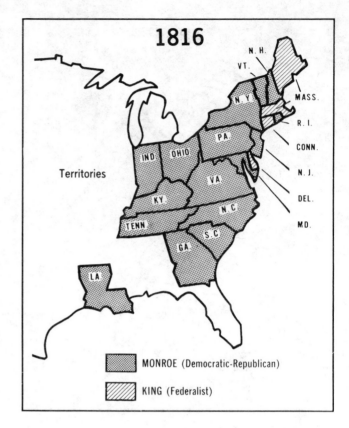

States	Electoral Votes	Madison	Clinton
Connecticut	(9)	-	9
Delaware	(4)	-	4
Georgia	(8)	8	-
Kentucky	(12)	12	-
Louisiana	(3)	3	-
Maryland[1]	(11)	6	5
Massachusetts	(22)	-	22
New Hampshire	(8)	-	8
New Jersey	(8)	-	8
New York	(29)	-	29
North Carolina	(15)	15	-
Ohio[2]	(8)	7	-
Pennsylvania	(25)	25	-
Rhode Island	(4)	-	4
South Carolina	(11)	11	-
Tennessee	(8)	8	-
Vermont	(8)	8	-
Virginia	(25)	25	-
Totals	**(218)**	**128**	**89**

States	Electoral Votes	Monroe	King
Connecticut	(9)	-	9
Delaware[1]	(4)	-	3
Georgia	(8)	8	-
Indiana	(3)	3	-
Kentucky	(12)	12	-
Louisiana	(3)	3	-
Maryland[1]	(11)	8	-
Massachusetts	(22)	-	22
New Hampshire	(8)	8	-
New Jersey	(8)	8	-
New York	(29)	29	-
North Carolina	(15)	15	-
Ohio	(8)	8	-
Pennsylvania	(25)	25	-
Rhode Island	(4)	4	-
South Carolina	(11)	11	-
Tennessee	(8)	8	-
Vermont	(8)	8	-
Virginia	(25)	25	-
Totals	**(221)**	**183**	**34**

1. For explanation of split electoral votes, see p. 136.
2. One Ohio elector did not vote.

1. One Delaware and three Maryland electors did not vote.

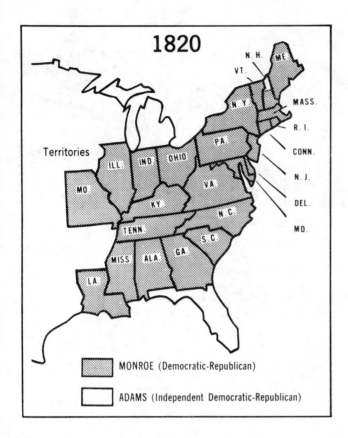

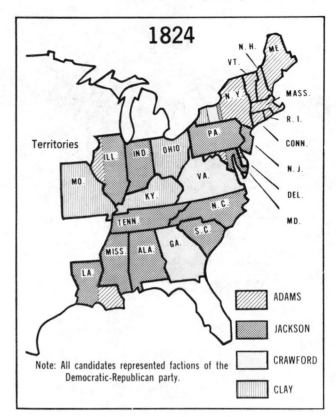

States	Electoral Votes	Monroe	Adams
Alabama	(3)	3	-
Connecticut	(9)	9	-
Delaware	(4)	4	-
Georgia	(8)	8	-
Illinois	(3)	3	-
Indiana	(3)	3	-
Kentucky	(12)	12	-
Louisiana	(3)	3	-
Maine	(9)	9	-
Maryland	(11)	11	-
Massachusetts	(15)	15	-
Mississippi [1]	(3)	2	-
Missouri	(3)	3	-
New Hampshire [2]	(8)	7	1
New Jersey	(8)	8	-
New York	(29)	29	-
North Carolina	(15)	15	-
Ohio	(8)	8	-
Pennsylvania [1]	(25)	24	-
Rhode Island	(4)	4	-
South Carolina	(11)	11	-
Tennessee [1]	(8)	7	-
Vermont	(8)	8	-
Virginia	(25)	25	-
Totals	**(235)**	**231**	**1**

1. One elector each from Mississippi, Pennsylvania and Tennessee did not vote.
2. For explanation of split electoral votes, see p. 136.

States	Electoral Votes	Jackson	Adams	Crawford	Clay
Alabama	(5)	5	-	-	-
Connecticut	(8)	-	8	-	-
Delaware [1]	(3)	-	1	2	-
Georgia	(9)	-	-	9	-
Illinois [1]	(3)	2	1	-	-
Indiana	(5)	5	-	-	-
Kentucky	(14)	-	-	-	14
Louisiana [1]	(5)	3	2	-	-
Maine	(9)	-	9	-	-
Maryland [1]	(11)	7	3	1	-
Massachusetts	(15)	-	15	-	-
Mississippi	(3)	3	-	-	-
Missouri	(3)	-	-	-	3
New Hampshire	(8)	-	8	-	-
New Jersey	(8)	8	-	-	-
New York [1]	(36)	1	26	5	4
North Carolina	(15)	15	-	-	-
Ohio	(16)	-	-	-	16
Pennsylvania	(28)	28	-	-	-
Rhode Island	(4)	-	4	-	-
South Carolina	(11)	11	-	-	-
Tennessee	(11)	11	-	-	-
Vermont	(7)	-	7	-	-
Virginia	(24)	-	-	24	-
Totals	**(261)**	**99** [2]	**84**	**41**	**37**

1. For explanation of split electoral votes, see p. 136.
2. As no candidate received a majority of the electoral votes, the election was decided by the House of Representatives, see p. 137.

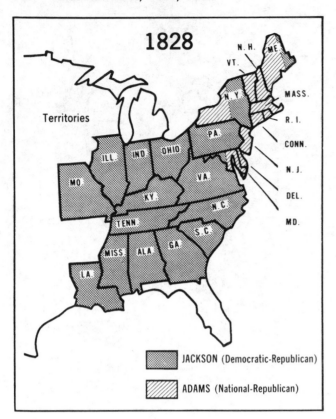

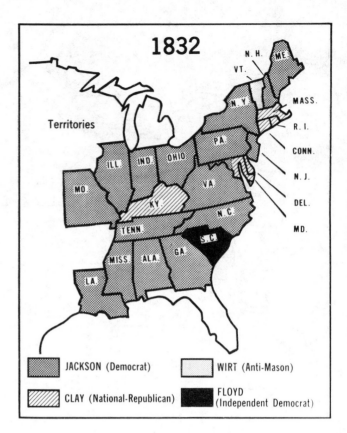

States	Electoral Votes	Jackson	Adams
Alabama	(5)	5	-
Connecticut	(8)	-	8
Delaware	(3)	-	3
Georgia	(9)	9	-
Illinois	(3)	3	-
Indiana	(5)	5	-
Kentucky	(14)	14	-
Louisiana	(5)	5	-
Maine[1]	(9)	1	8
Maryland[1]	(11)	5	6
Massachusetts	(15)	-	15
Mississippi	(3)	3	-
Missouri	(3)	3	-
New Hampshire	(8)	-	8
New Jersey	(8)	-	8
New York[1]	(36)	20	16
North Carolina	(15)	15	-
Ohio	(16)	16	-
Pennsylvania	(28)	28	-
Rhode Island	(4)	-	4
South Carolina	(11)	11	-
Tennessee	(11)	11	-
Vermont	(7)	-	7
Virginia	(24)	24	-
Totals	**(261)**	**178**	**83**

1. For explanation of split electoral votes, see p. 136.

States	Electoral Votes	Jackson	Clay	Floyd	Wirt
Alabama	(7)	7	-	-	-
Connecticut	(8)	-	8	-	-
Delaware	(3)	-	3	-	-
Georgia	(11)	11	-	-	-
Illinois	(5)	5	-	-	-
Indiana	(9)	9	-	-	-
Kentucky	(15)	-	15	-	-
Louisiana	(5)	5	-	-	-
Maine	(10)	10	-	-	-
Maryland[1]	(10)	3	5	-	-
Massachusetts	(14)	-	14	-	-
Mississippi	(4)	4	-	-	-
Missouri	(4)	4	-	-	-
New Hampshire	(7)	7	-	-	-
New Jersey	(8)	8	-	-	-
New York	(42)	42	-	-	-
North Carolina	(15)	15	-	-	-
Ohio	(21)	21	-	-	-
Pennsylvania	(30)	30	-	-	-
Rhode Island	(4)	-	4	-	-
South Carolina	(11)	-	-	11	-
Tennessee	(15)	15	-	-	-
Vermont	(7)	-	-	-	7
Virginia	(23)	23	-	-	-
Totals	**(288)**	**219**	**49**	**11**	**7**

1. Two Maryland electors did not vote. For explanation of split electoral votes, see p. 136.

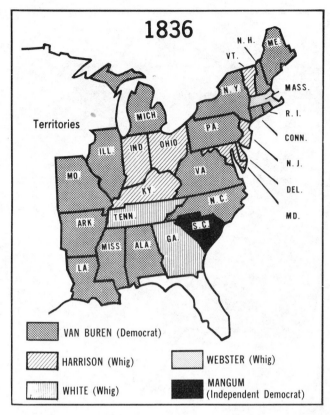

1836

Territories

VAN BUREN (Democrat)

HARRISON (Whig)

WHITE (Whig)

WEBSTER (Whig)

MANGUM (Independent Democrat)

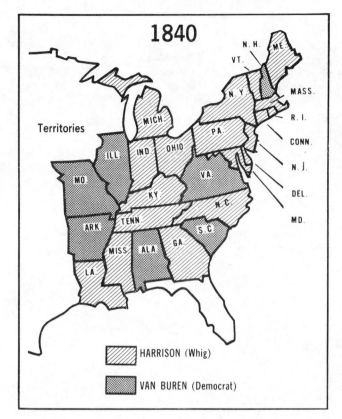

1840

Territories

HARRISON (Whig)

VAN BUREN (Democrat)

States	Electoral Votes	Van Buren	Harrison[1]	White[1]	Webster[1]	Mangum
Alabama	(7)	7	-	-	-	-
Arkansas	(3)	3	-	-	-	-
Connecticut	(8)	8	-	-	-	-
Delaware	(3)	-	3	-	-	-
Georgia	(11)	-	-	11	-	-
Illinois	(5)	5	-	-	-	-
Indiana	(9)	-	9	-	-	-
Kentucky	(15)	-	15	-	-	-
Louisiana	(5)	5	-	-	-	-
Maine	(10)	10	-	-	-	-
Maryland	(10)	-	10	-	-	-
Massachusetts	(14)	-	-	-	14	-
Michigan	(3)	3	-	-	-	-
Mississippi	(4)	4	-	-	-	-
Missouri	(4)	4	-	-	-	-
New Hampshire	(7)	7	-	-	-	-
New Jersey	(8)	-	8	-	-	-
New York	(42)	42	-	-	-	-
North Carolina	(15)	15	-	-	-	-
Ohio	(21)	-	21	-	-	-
Pennsylvania	(30)	30	-	-	-	-
Rhode Island	(4)	4	-	-	-	-
South Carolina	(11)	-	-	-	-	11
Tennessee	(15)	-	-	15	-	-
Vermont	(7)	-	7	-	-	-
Virginia	(23)	23	-	-	-	-
Totals	**(294)**	**170**	**73**	**26**	**14**	**11**

States	Electoral Votes	Harrison	Van Buren
Alabama	(7)	-	7
Arkansas	(3)	-	3
Connecticut	(8)	8	-
Delaware	(3)	3	-
Georgia	(11)	11	-
Illinois	(5)	-	5
Indiana	(9)	9	-
Kentucky	(15)	15	-
Louisiana	(5)	5	-
Maine	(10)	10	-
Maryland	(10)	10	-
Massachusetts	(14)	14	-
Michigan	(3)	3	-
Mississippi	(4)	4	-
Missouri	(4)	-	4
New Hampshire	(7)	-	7
New Jersey	(8)	8	-
New York	(42)	42	-
North Carolina	(15)	15	-
Ohio	(21)	21	-
Pennsylvania	(30)	30	-
Rhode Island	(4)	4	-
South Carolina	(11)	-	11
Tennessee	(15)	15	-
Vermont	(7)	7	-
Virginia	(23)	-	23
Totals	**(294)**	**234**	**60**

1. For explanation of three Whig presidential candidates, see p. 134.

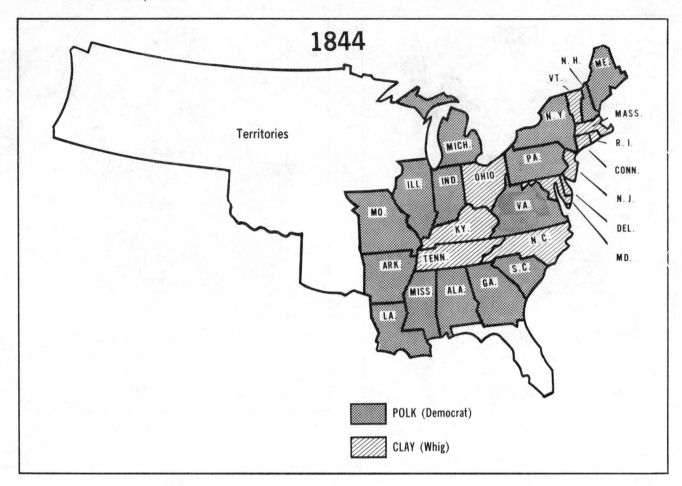

States	Electoral Votes	Polk	Clay
Alabama	(9)	9	-
Arkansas	(3)	3	-
Connecticut	(6)	-	6
Delaware	(3)	-	3
Georgia	(10)	10	-
Illinois	(9)	9	-
Indiana	(12)	12	-
Kentucky	(12)	-	12
Louisiana	(6)	6	-
Maine	(9)	9	-
Maryland	(8)	-	8
Massachusetts	(12)	-	12
Michigan	(5)	5	-
Mississippi	(6)	6	-
Missouri	(7)	7	-
New Hampshire	(6)	6	-
New Jersey	(7)	-	7
New York	(36)	36	-
North Carolina	(11)	-	11
Ohio	(23)	-	23
Pennsylvania	(26)	26	-
Rhode Island	(4)	-	4
South Carolina	(9)	9	-
Tennessee	(13)	-	13
Vermont	(6)	-	6
Virginia	(17)	17	-
Totals	**(275)**	**170**	**105**

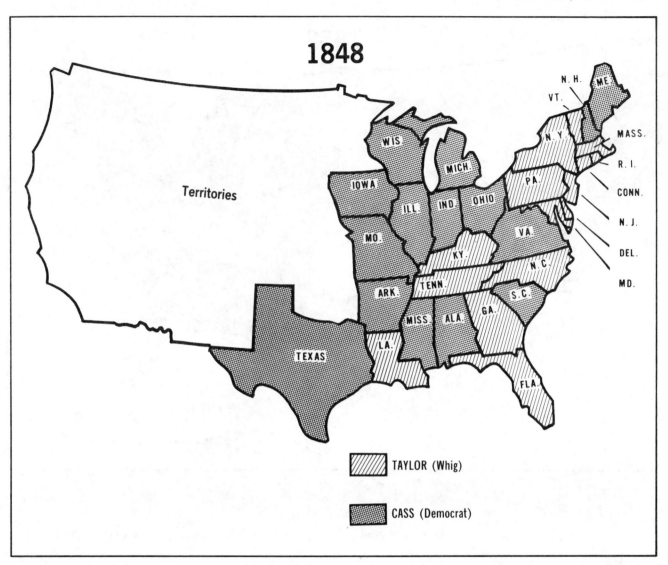

1848

Territories

TAYLOR (Whig)

CASS (Democrat)

States	Electoral Votes	Taylor	Cass	States	Electoral Votes	Taylor	Cass
Alabama	(9)	-	9	Mississippi	(6)	-	6
Arkansas	(3)	-	3	Missouri	(7)	-	7
Connecticut	(6)	6	-	New Hampshire	(6)	-	6
Delaware	(3)	3	-	New Jersey	(7)	7	-
Florida	(3)	3	-	New York	(36)	36	-
Georgia	(10)	10	-	North Carolina	(11)	11	-
Illinois	(9)	-	9	Ohio	(23)	-	23
Indiana	(12)	-	12	Pennsylvania	(26)	26	-
Iowa	(4)	-	4	Rhode Island	(4)	4	-
Kentucky	(12)	12	-	South Carolina	(9)	-	9
Louisiana	(6)	6	-	Tennessee	(13)	13	-
Maine	(9)	-	9	Texas	(4)	-	4
Maryland	(8)	8	-	Vermont	(6)	6	-
Massachusetts	(12)	12	-	Virginia	(17)	-	17
Michigan	(5)	-	5	Wisconsin	(4)	-	4
				Totals	**(290)**	**163**	**127**

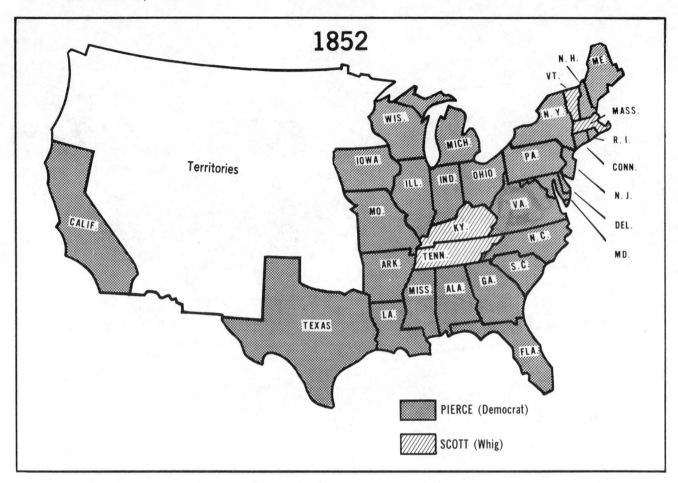

1852

Territories

PIERCE (Democrat)

SCOTT (Whig)

States	Electoral Votes	Pierce	Scott	States	Electoral Votes	Pierce	Scott
Alabama	(9)	9	-	Mississippi	(7)	7	-
Arkansas	(4)	4	-	Missouri	(9)	9	-
California	(4)	4	-	New Hampshire	(5)	5	-
Connecticut	(6)	6	-	New Jersey	(7)	7	-
Delaware	(3)	3	-	New York	(35)	35	-
Florida	(3)	3	-	North Carolina	(10)	10	-
Georgia	(10)	10	-	Ohio	(23)	23	-
Illinois	(11)	11	-	Pennsylvania	(27)	27	-
Indiana	(13)	13	-	Rhode Island	(4)	4	-
Iowa	(4)	4	-	South Carolina	(8)	8	-
Kentucky	(12)	-	12	Tennessee	(12)	-	12
Louisiana	(6)	6	-	Texas	(4)	4	-
Maine	(8)	8	-	Vermont	(5)	-	5
Maryland	(8)	8	-	Virginia	(15)	15	-
Massachusetts	(13)	-	13	Wisconsin	(5)	5	-
Michigan	(6)	6	-	**Totals**	**(296)**	**254**	**42**

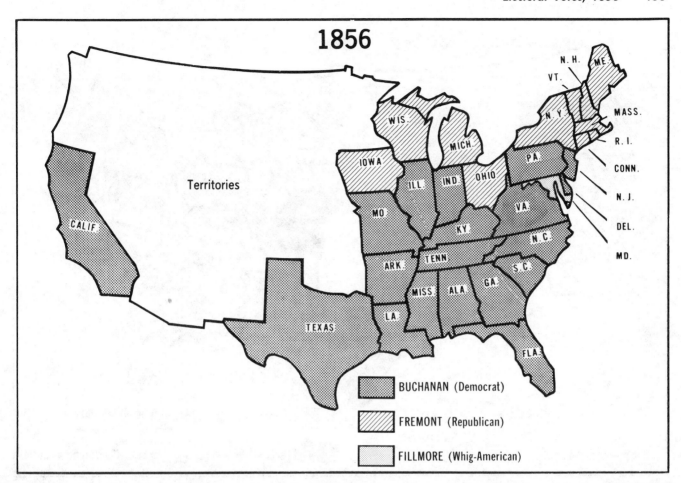

1856

BUCHANAN (Democrat)

FREMONT (Republican)

FILLMORE (Whig-American)

States	Electoral Votes	Buchanan	Fremont	Fillmore
Alabama	(9)	9	-	-
Arkansas	(4)	4	-	-
California	(4)	4	-	-
Connecticut	(6)	-	6	-
Delaware	(3)	3	-	-
Florida	(3)	3	-	-
Georgia	(10)	10	-	-
Illinois	(11)	11	-	-
Indiana	(13)	13	-	-
Iowa	(4)	-	4	-
Kentucky	(12)	12	-	-
Louisiana	(6)	6	-	-
Maine	(8)	-	8	-
Maryland	(8)	-	-	8
Massachusetts	(13)	-	13	-
Michigan	(6)	-	6	-
Mississippi	(7)	7	-	-
Missouri	(9)	9	-	-
New Hampshire	(5)	-	5	-
New Jersey	(7)	7	-	-
New York	(35)	-	35	-
North Carolina	(10)	10	-	-
Ohio	(23)	-	23	-
Pennsylvania	(27)	27	-	-
Rhode Island	(4)	-	4	-
South Carolina	(8)	8	-	-
Tennessee	(12)	12	-	-
Texas	(4)	4	-	-
Vermont	(5)	-	5	-
Virginia	(15)	15	-	-
Wisconsin	(5)	-	5	-
Totals	**(296)**	**174**	**114**	**8**

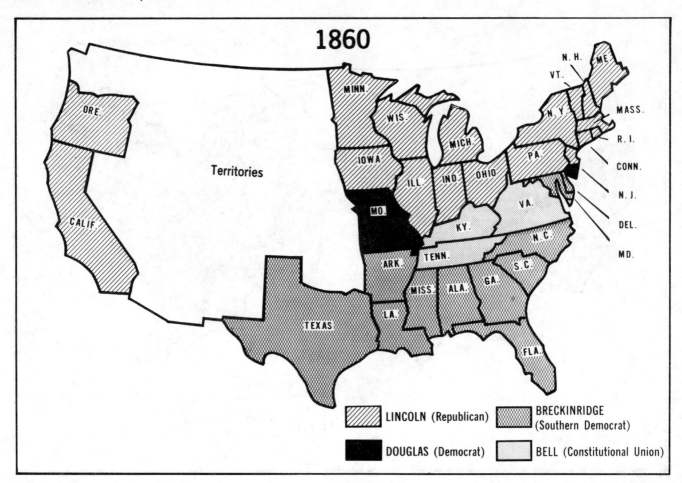

1860

LINCOLN (Republican)

DOUGLAS (Democrat)

BRECKINRIDGE (Southern Democrat)

BELL (Constitutional Union)

States	Electoral Votes	Lincoln	Breckinridge	Bell	Douglas	States	Electoral Votes	Lincoln	Breckinridge	Bell	Douglas
Alabama	(9)	-	9	-	-	Mississippi	(7)	-	7	-	-
Arkansas	(4)	-	4	-	-	Missouri	(9)	-	-	-	9
California	(4)	4	-	-	-	New Hampshire	(5)	5	-	-	-
Connecticut	(6)	6	-	-	-	New Jersey[1]	(7)	4	-	-	3
Delaware	(3)	-	3	-	-	New York	(35)	35	-	-	-
Florida	(3)	-	3	-	-	North Carolina	(10)	-	10	-	-
Georgia	(10)	-	10	-	-	Ohio	(23)	23	-	-	-
Illinois	(11)	11	-	-	-	Oregon	(3)	3	-	-	-
Indiana	(13)	13	-	-	-	Pennsylvania	(27)	27	-	-	-
Iowa	(4)	4	-	-	-	Rhode Island	(4)	4	-	-	-
Kentucky	(12)	-	-	12	-	South Carolina	(8)	-	8	-	-
Louisiana	(6)	-	6	-	-	Tennessee	(12)	-	-	12	-
Maine	(8)	8	-	-	-	Texas	(4)	-	4	-	-
Maryland	(8)	-	8	-	-	Vermont	(5)	5	-	-	-
Massachusetts	(13)	13	-	-	-	Virginia	(15)	-	-	15	-
Michigan	(6)	6	-	-	-	Wisconsin	(5)	5	-	-	-
Minnesota	(4)	4	-	-	-	**Totals**	**(303)**	**180**	**72**	**39**	**12**

1. For explanation of split electoral votes, see p. 136.

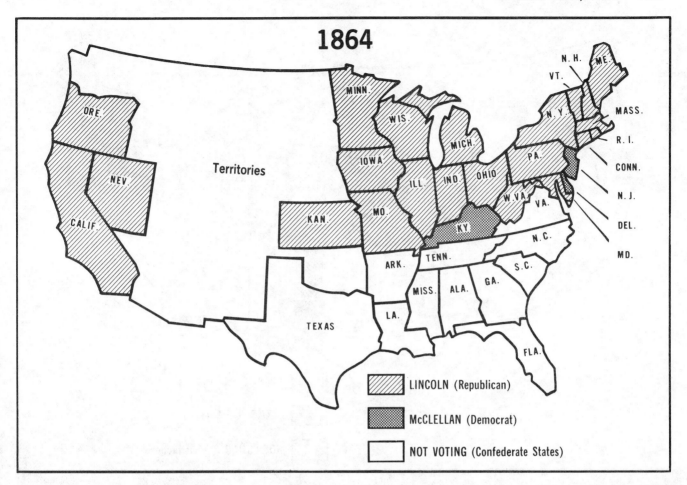

1864

LINCOLN (Republican)

McCLELLAN (Democrat)

NOT VOTING (Confederate States)

States[1]	Electoral Votes	Lincoln	McClellan	States[1]	Electoral Votes	Lincoln	McClellan
California	(5)	5	-	Missouri	(11)	11	-
Connecticut	(6)	6	-	Nevada[2]	(3)	2	-
Delaware	(3)	-	3	New Hampshire	(5)	5	-
Illinois	(16)	16	-	New Jersey	(7)	-	7
Indiana	(13)	13	-	New York	(33)	33	-
Iowa	(8)	8	-	Ohio	(21)	21	-
Kansas	(3)	3	-	Oregon	(3)	3	-
Kentucky	(11)	-	11	Pennsylvania	(26)	26	-
Maine	(7)	7	-	Rhode Island	(4)	4	-
Maryland	(7)	7	-	Vermont	(5)	5	-
Massachusetts	(12)	12	-	West Virginia	(5)	5	-
Michigan	(8)	8	-	Wisconsin	(8)	8	-
Minnesota	(4)	4	-	**Totals**	**(234)**	**212**	**21**

1. Eleven southern states—*Alabama, Arkansas, Florida, Georgia, Louisiana, Mississippi, North Carolina, South Carolina, Tennessee, Texas and Virginia had seceded from the Union and did not vote.*
2. *One Nevada elector did not vote.*

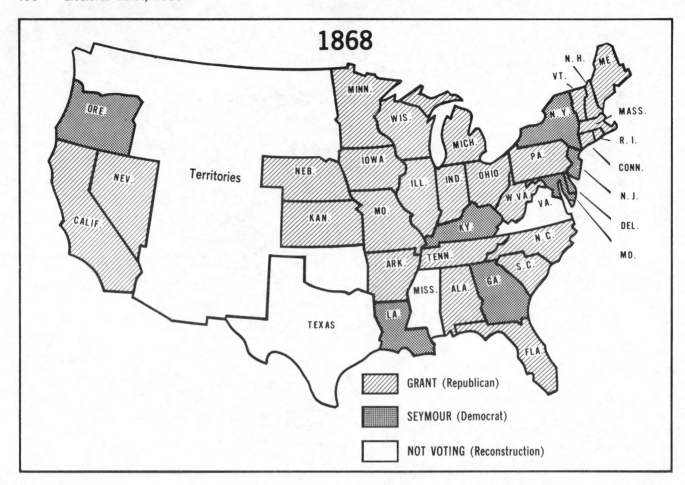

States [1]	Electoral Votes	Grant	Seymour	States [1]	Electoral Votes	Grant	Seymour
Alabama	(8)	8	-	Missouri	(11)	11	-
Arkansas	(5)	5	-	Nebraska	(3)	3	-
California	(5)	5	-	Nevada	(3)	3	-
Connecticut	(6)	6	-	New Hampshire	(5)	5	-
Delaware	(3)	-	3	New Jersey	(7)	-	7
Florida	(3)	3	-	New York	(33)	-	33
Georgia	(9)	-	9	North Carolina	(9)	9	-
Illinois	(16)	16	-	Ohio	(21)	21	-
Indiana	(13)	13	-	Oregon	(3)	-	3
Iowa	(8)	8	-	Pennsylvania	(26)	26	-
Kansas	(3)	3	-	Rhode Island	(4)	4	-
Kentucky	(11)	-	11	South Carolina	(6)	6	-
Louisiana	(7)	-	7	Tennessee	(10)	10	-
Maine	(7)	7	-	Vermont	(5)	5	-
Maryland	(7)	-	7	West Virginia	(5)	5	-
Massachusetts	(12)	12	-	Wisconsin	(8)	8	-
Michigan	(8)	8	-				
Minnesota	(4)	4	-	**Totals**	**(294)**	**214**	**80**

1. *Mississippi, Texas and Virginia were not yet readmitted to the Union and did not participate in the election.*

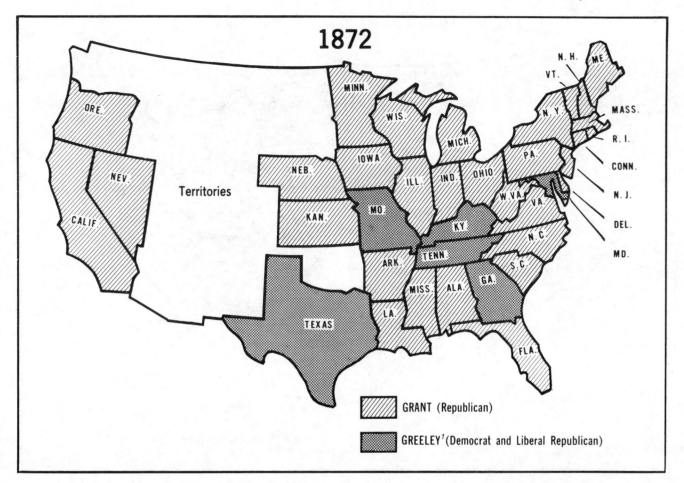

States	Electoral Votes	Grant	Hendricks[1]	Brown[1]	Jenkins[1]	Davis[1]	States	Electoral Votes	Grant	Hendricks[1]	Brown[1]	Jenkins[1]	Davis[1]
Alabama	(10)	10	-	-	-	-	**Nebraska**	(3)	3	-	-	-	-
Arkansas[2]	(6)	-	-	-	-	-	**Nevada**	(3)	3	-	-	-	-
California	(6)	6	-	-	-	-	**New Hampshire**	(5)	5	-	-	-	-
Connecticut	(6)	6	-	-	-	-	**New Jersey**	(9)	9	-	-	-	-
Delaware	(3)	3	-	-	-	-	**New York**	(35)	35	-	-	-	-
Florida	(4)	4	-	-	-	-	**North Carolina**	(10)	10	-	-	-	-
Georgia[3]	(11)	-	-	6	2	-	**Ohio**	(22)	22	-	-	-	-
Illinois	(21)	21	-	-	-	-	**Oregon**	(3)	3	-	-	-	-
Indiana	(15)	15	-	-	-	-	**Pennsylvania**	(29)	29	-	-	-	-
Iowa	(11)	11	-	-	-	-	**Rhode Island**	(4)	4	-	-	-	-
Kansas	(5)	5	-	-	-	-	**South Carolina**	(7)	7	-	-	-	-
Kentucky	(12)	-	8	4	-	-	**Tennessee**	(12)	-	12	-	-	-
Louisiana[2]	(8)	-	-	-	-	-	**Texas**	(8)	-	8	-	-	-
Maine	(7)	7	-	-	-	-	**Vermont**	(5)	5	-	-	-	-
Maryland	(8)	-	8	-	-	-	**Virginia**	(11)	11	-	-	-	-
Massachusetts	(13)	13	-	-	-	-	**West Virginia**	(5)	5	-	-	-	-
Michigan	(11)	11	-	-	-	-	**Wisconsin**	(10)	10	-	-	-	-
Minnesota	(5)	5	-	-	-	-							
Mississippi	(8)	8	-	-	-	-							
Missouri	(15)	-	6	8	-	1	**Totals**	(366)	286	42	18	2	1

1. For explanation of Democratic electoral vote, cast after Greeley's death, see p. 134.
2. Congress refused to accept electoral votes of Arkansas and Louisiana because of disruptive conditions during Reconstruction.
3. Three Georgia electoral votes cast for Greeley were not counted.

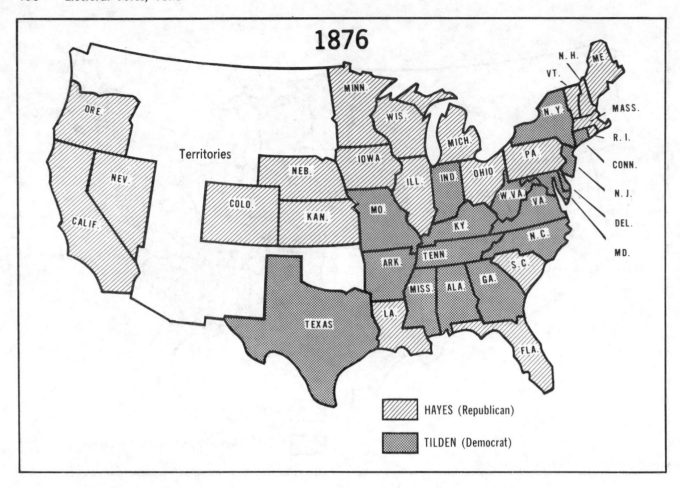

1876

HAYES (Republican)

TILDEN (Democrat)

States	Electoral Votes	Hayes	Tilden	States	Electoral Votes	Hayes	Tilden
Alabama	(10)	-	10	Missouri	(15)	-	15
Arkansas	(6)	-	6	Nebraska	(3)	3	-
California	(6)	6	-	Nevada	(3)	3	-
Colorado	(3)	3	-	New Hampshire	(5)	5	-
Connecticut	(6)	-	6	New Jersey	(9)	-	9
Delaware	(3)	-	3	New York	(35)	-	35
Florida[1]	(4)	4	-	North Carolina	(10)	-	10
Georgia	(11)	-	11	Ohio	(22)	22	-
Illinois	(21)	21	-	Oregon[1]	(3)	3	-
Indiana	(15)	-	15	Pennsylvania	(29)	29	-
Iowa	(11)	11	-	Rhode Island	(4)	4	-
Kansas	(5)	5	-	South Carolina[1]	(7)	7	-
Kentucky	(12)	-	12	Tennessee	(12)	-	12
Louisiana[1]	(8)	8	-	Texas	(8)	-	8
Maine	(7)	7	-	Vermont	(5)	5	-
Maryland	(8)	-	8	Virginia	(11)	-	11
Massachusetts	(13)	13	-	West Virginia	(5)	-	5
Michigan	(11)	11	-	Wisconsin	(10)	10	-
Minnesota	(5)	5	-	**Totals**	**(369)**	**185**	**184**
Mississippi	(8)	-	8				

1. *For explanation of disputed electoral votes of Florida, Louisiana, Oregon and South Carolina, see p. 138.*

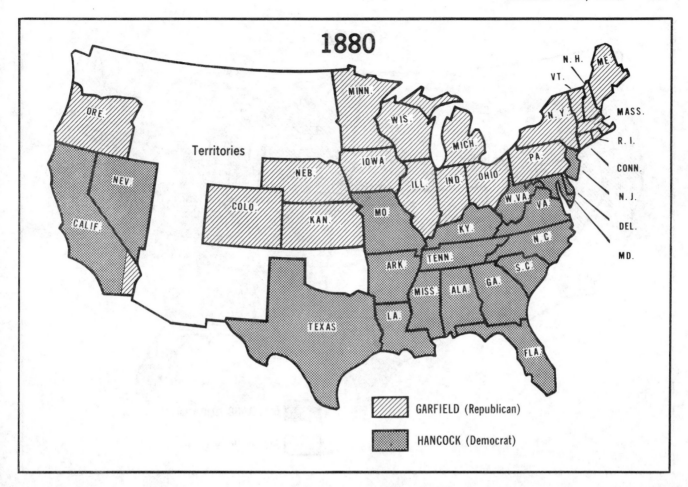

1880

| | GARFIELD (Republican) |
| | HANCOCK (Democrat) |

States	Electoral Votes	Garfield	Hancock	States	Electoral Votes	Garfield	Hancock
Alabama	(10)	-	10	Mississippi	(8)	-	8
Arkansas	(6)	-	6	Missouri	(15)	-	15
California[1]	(6)	1	5	Nebraska	(3)	3	-
Colorado	(3)	3	-	Nevada	(3)	-	3
Connecticut	(6)	6	-	New Hampshire	(5)	5	-
Delaware	(3)	-	3	New Jersey	(9)	-	9
Florida	(4)	-	4	New York	(35)	35	-
Georgia	(11)	-	11	North Carolina	(10)	-	10
Illinois	(21)	21	-	Ohio	(22)	22	-
Indiana	(15)	15	-	Oregon	(3)	3	-
Iowa	(11)	11	-	Pennsylvania	(29)	29	-
Kansas	(5)	5	-	Rhode Island	(4)	4	-
Kentucky	(12)	-	12	South Carolina	(7)	-	7
Louisiana	(8)	-	8	Tennessee	(12)	-	12
Maine	(7)	7	-	Texas	(8)	-	8
Maryland	(8)	-	8	Vermont	(5)	5	-
Massachusetts	(13)	13	-	Virginia	(11)	-	11
Michigan	(11)	11	-	West Virginia	(5)	-	5
Minnesota	(5)	5	-	Wisconsin	(10)	10	-
				Totals	**(369)**	**214**	**155**

1. For explanation of split electoral votes, see p. 136.

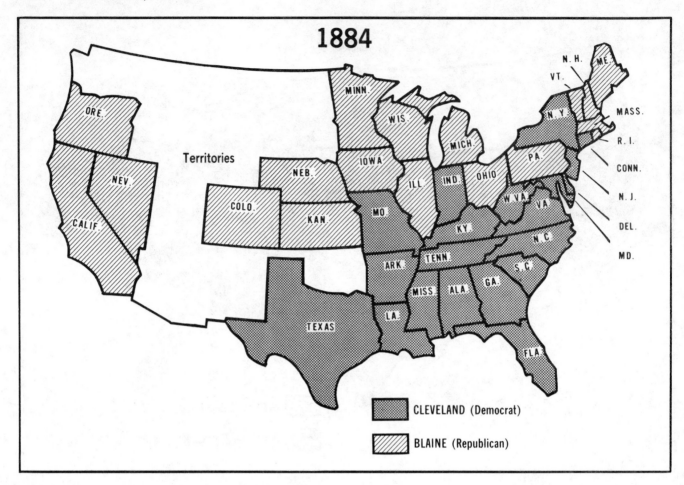

1884

CLEVELAND (Democrat)

BLAINE (Republican)

States	Electoral Votes	Cleveland	Blaine	States	Electoral Votes	Cleveland	Blaine
Alabama	(10)	10	-	Mississippi	(9)	9	-
Arkansas	(7)	7	-	Missouri	(16)	16	-
California	(8)	-	8	Nebraska	(5)	-	5
Colorado	(3)	-	3	Nevada	(3)	-	3
Connecticut	(6)	6	-	New Hampshire	(4)	-	4
Delaware	(3)	3	-	New Jersey	(9)	9	-
Florida	(4)	4	-	New York	(36)	36	-
Georgia	(12)	12	-	North Carolina	(11)	11	-
Illinois	(22)	-	22	Ohio	(23)	-	23
Indiana	(15)	15	-	Oregon	(3)	-	3
Iowa	(13)	-	13	Pennsylvania	(30)	-	30
Kansas	(9)	-	9	Rhode Island	(4)	-	4
Kentucky	(13)	13	-	South Carolina	(9)	9	-
Louisiana	(8)	8	-	Tennessee	(12)	12	-
Maine	(6)	-	6	Texas	(13)	13	-
Maryland	(8)	8	-	Vermont	(4)	-	4
Massachusetts	(14)	-	14	Virginia	(12)	12	-
Michigan	(13)	-	13	West Virginia	(6)	6	-
Minnesota	(7)	-	7	Wisconsin	(11)	-	11
				Totals	**(401)**	219	182

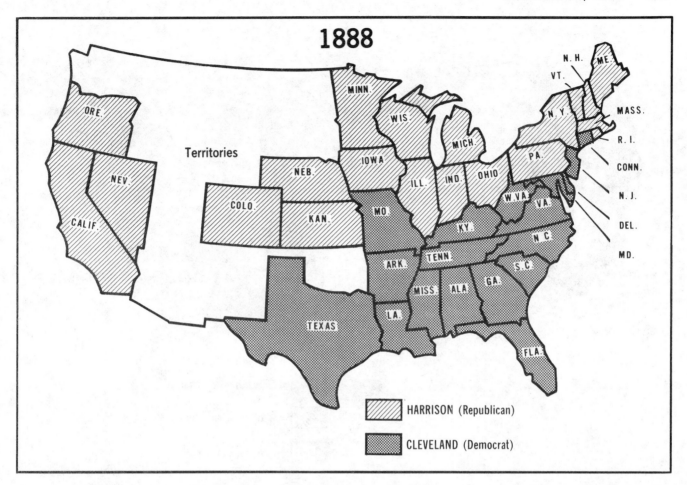

1888

HARRISON (Republican)

CLEVELAND (Democrat)

States	Electoral Votes	Harrison	Cleveland	States	Electoral Votes	Harrison	Cleveland
Alabama	(10)	-	10	Mississippi	(9)	-	9
Arkansas	(7)	-	7	Missouri	(16)	-	16
California	(8)	8	-	Nebraska	(5)	5	-
Colorado	(3)	3	-	Nevada	(3)	3	-
Connecticut	(6)	-	6	New Hampshire	(4)	4	-
Delaware	(3)	-	3	New Jersey	(9)	-	9
Florida	(4)	-	4	New York	(36)	36	-
Georgia	(12)	-	12	North Carolina	(11)	-	11
Illinois	(22)	22	-	Ohio	(23)	23	-
Indiana	(15)	15	-	Oregon	(3)	3	-
Iowa	(13)	13	-	Pennsylvania	(30)	30	-
Kansas	(9)	9	-	Rhode Island	(4)	4	-
Kentucky	(13)	-	13	South Carolina	(9)	-	9
Louisiana	(8)	-	8	Tennessee	(12)	-	12
Maine	(6)	6	-	Texas	(13)	-	13
Maryland	(8)	-	8	Vermont	(4)	4	-
Massachusetts	(14)	14	-	Virginia	(12)	-	12
Michigan	(13)	13	-	West Virginia	(6)	-	6
Minnesota	(7)	7	-	Wisconsin	(11)	11	-
				Totals	**(401)**	**233**	**168**

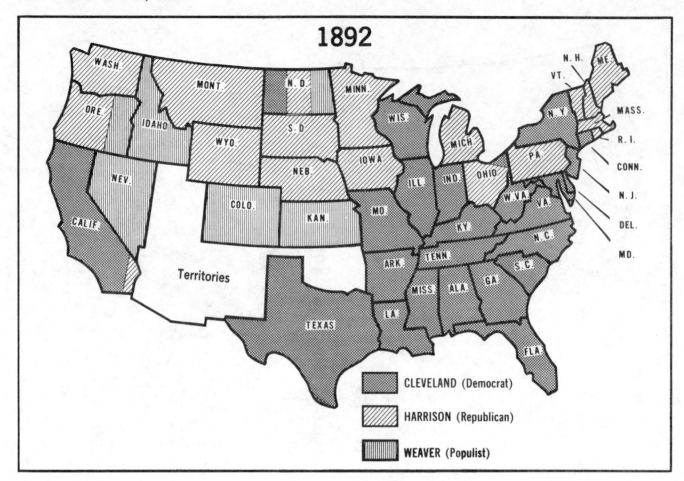

1892

CLEVELAND (Democrat)

HARRISON (Republican)

WEAVER (Populist)

States	Electoral Votes	Cleveland	Harrison	Weaver	States	Electoral Votes	Cleveland	Harrison	Weaver
Alabama	(11)	11	-	-	Montana	(3)	-	3	-
Arkansas	(8)	8	-	-	Nebraska	(8)	-	8	-
California[1]	(9)	8	1	-	Nevada	(3)	-	-	3
Colorado	(4)	-	-	4	New Hampshire	(4)	-	4	-
Connecticut	(6)	6	-	-	New Jersey	(10)	10	-	-
Delaware	(3)	3	-	-	New York	(36)	36	-	-
Florida	(4)	4	-	-	North Carolina	(11)	11	-	-
Georgia	(13)	13	-	-	North Dakota[1]	(3)	1	1	1
Idaho	(3)	-	-	3	Ohio[1]	(23)	1	22	-
Illinois	(24)	24	-	-	Oregon[1]	(4)	-	3	1
Indiana	(15)	15	-	-	Pennsylvania	(32)	-	32	-
Iowa	(13)	-	13	-	Rhode Island	(4)	-	4	-
Kansas	(10)	-	-	10	South Carolina	(9)	9	-	-
Kentucky	(13)	13	-	-	South Dakota	(4)	-	4	-
Louisiana	(8)	8	-	-	Tennessee	(12)	12	-	-
Maine	(6)	-	6	-	Texas	(15)	15	-	-
Maryland	(8)	8	-	-	Vermont	(4)	-	4	-
Massachusetts	(15)	-	15	-	Virginia	(12)	12	-	-
Michigan[1]	(14)	5	9	-	Washington	(4)	-	4	-
Minnesota	(9)	-	9	-	West Virginia	(6)	6	-	-
Mississippi	(9)	9	-	-	Wisconsin	(12)	12	-	-
Missouri	(17)	17	-	-	Wyoming	(3)	-	3	-
					Totals	**(444)**	**277**	**145**	**22**

1. For explanation of split electoral votes, see p. 136.

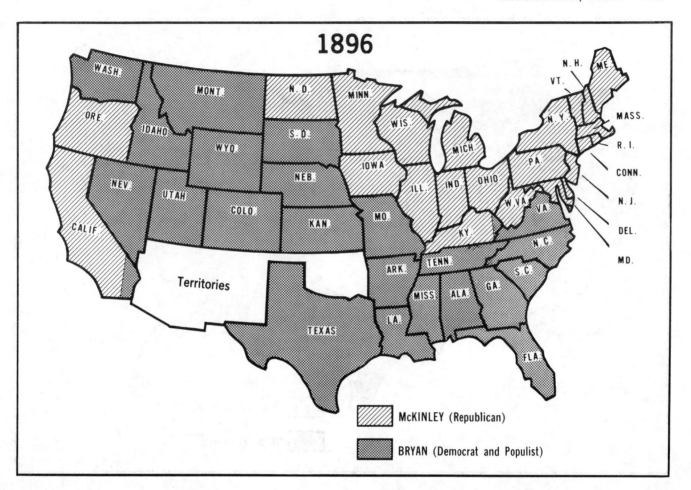

1896

McKINLEY (Republican)

BRYAN (Democrat and Populist)

States	Electoral Votes	McKinley	Bryan	States	Electoral Votes	McKinley	Bryan
Alabama	(11)	-	11	Nebraska	(8)	-	8
Arkansas	(8)	-	8	Nevada	(3)	-	3
California[1]	(9)	8	1	New Hampshire	(4)	4	-
Colorado	(4)	-	4	New Jersey	(10)	10	-
Connecticut	(6)	6	-	New York	(36)	36	-
Delaware	(3)	3	-	North Carolina	(11)	-	11
Florida	(4)	-	4	North Dakota	(3)	3	-
Georgia	(13)	-	13	Ohio	(23)	23	-
Idaho	(3)	-	3	Oregon	(4)	4	-
Illinois	(24)	24	-	Pennsylvania	(32)	32	-
Indiana	(15)	15	-	Rhode Island	(4)	4	-
Iowa	(13)	13	-	South Carolina	(9)	-	9
Kansas	(10)	-	10	South Dakota	(4)	-	4
Kentucky[1]	(13)	12	1	Tennessee	(12)	-	12
Louisiana	(8)	-	8	Texas	(15)	-	15
Maine	(6)	6	-	Utah	(3)	-	3
Maryland	(8)	8	-	Vermont	(4)	4	-
Massachusetts	(15)	15	-	Virginia	(12)	-	12
Michigan	(14)	14	-	Washington	(4)	-	4
Minnesota	(9)	9	-	West Virginia	(6)	6	-
Mississippi	(9)	-	9	Wisconsin	(12)	12	-
Missouri	(17)	-	17	Wyoming	(3)	-	3
Montana	(3)	-	3	**Totals**	**(447)**	**271**	**176**

1. For explanation of split electoral votes, see p. 136.

1900

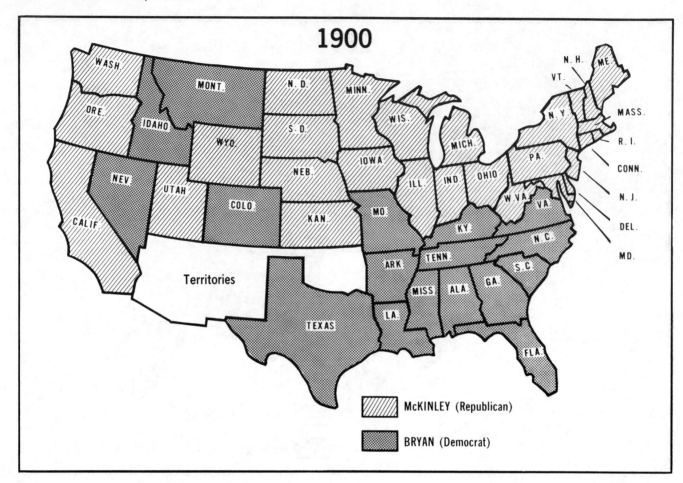

McKINLEY (Republican)

BRYAN (Democrat)

States	Electoral Votes	McKinley	Bryan	States	Electoral Votes	McKinley	Bryan
Alabama	(11)	-	11	Nebraska	(8)	8	-
Arkansas	(8)	-	8	Nevada	(3)	-	3
California	(9)	9	-	New Hampshire	(4)	4	-
Colorado	(4)	-	4	New Jersey	(10)	10	-
Connecticut	(6)	6	-	New York	(36)	36	-
Delaware	(3)	3	-	North Carolina	(11)	-	11
Florida	(4)	-	4	North Dakota	(3)	3	-
Georgia	(13)	-	13	Ohio	(23)	23	-
Idaho	(3)	-	3	Oregon	(4)	4	-
Illinois	(24)	24	-	Pennsylvania	(32)	32	-
Indiana	(15)	15	-	Rhode Island	(4)	4	-
Iowa	(13)	13	-	South Carolina	(9)	-	9
Kansas	(10)	10	-	South Dakota	(4)	4	-
Kentucky	(13)	-	13	Tennessee	(12)	-	12
Louisiana	(8)	-	8	Texas	(15)	-	15
Maine	(6)	6	-	Utah	(3)	3	-
Maryland	(8)	8	-	Vermont	(4)	4	-
Massachusetts	(15)	15	-	Virginia	(12)	-	12
Michigan	(14)	14	-	Washington	(4)	4	-
Minnesota	(9)	9	-	West Virginia	(6)	6	-
Mississippi	(9)	-	9	Wisconsin	(12)	12	-
Missouri	(17)	-	17	Wyoming	(3)	3	-
Montana	(3)	-	3	**Totals**	**(447)**	**292**	**155**

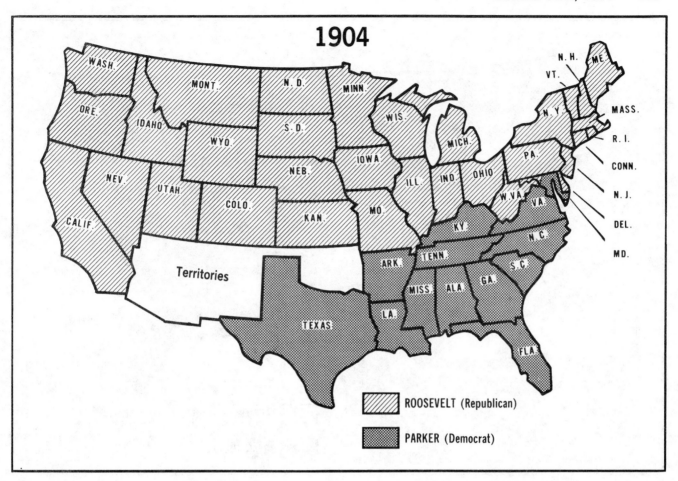

1904

ROOSEVELT (Republican)

PARKER (Democrat)

States	Electoral Votes	Roosevelt	Parker	States	Electoral Votes	Roosevelt	Parker
Alabama	(11)	-	11	Nebraska	(8)	8	-
Arkansas	(9)	-	9	Nevada	(3)	3	-
California	(10)	10	-	New Hampshire	(4)	4	-
Colorado	(5)	5	-	New Jersey	(12)	12	-
Connecticut	(7)	7	-	New York	(39)	39	-
Delaware	(3)	3	-	North Carolina	(12)	-	12
Florida	(5)	-	5	North Dakota	(4)	4	-
Georgia	(13)	-	13	Ohio	(23)	23	-
Idaho	(3)	3	-	Oregon	(4)	4	-
Illinois	(27)	27	-	Pennsylvania	(34)	34	-
Indiana	(15)	15	-	Rhode Island	(4)	4	-
Iowa	(13)	13	-	South Carolina	(9)	-	9
Kansas	(10)	10	-	South Dakota	(4)	4	-
Kentucky	(13)	-	13	Tennessee	(12)	-	12
Louisiana	(9)	-	9	Texas	(18)	-	18
Maine	(6)	6	-	Utah	(3)	3	-
Maryland[1]	(8)	1	7	Vermont	(4)	4	-
Massachusetts	(16)	16	-	Virginia	(12)	-	12
Michigan	(14)	14	-	Washington	(5)	5	-
Minnesota	(11)	11	-	West Virginia	(7)	7	-
Mississippi	(10)	-	10	Wisconsin	(13)	13	-
Missouri	(18)	18	-	Wyoming	(3)	3	-
Montana	(3)	3	-	**Totals**	**(476)**	**336**	**140**

1. For explanation of split electoral votes, see p. 136.

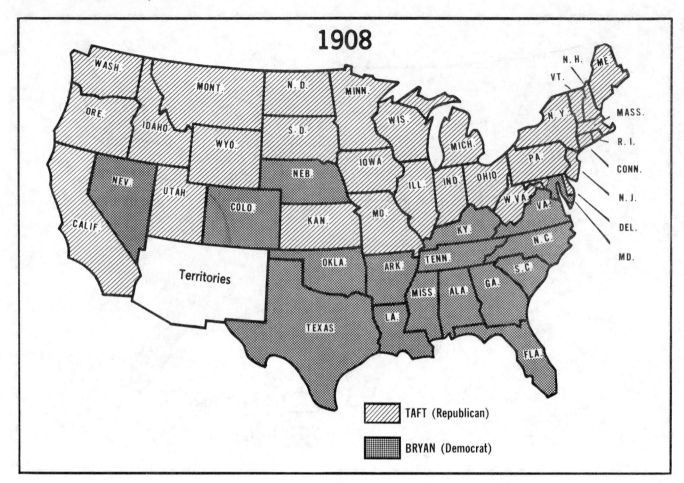

1908

TAFT (Republican)

BRYAN (Democrat)

States	Electoral Votes	Taft	Bryan	States	Electoral Votes	Taft	Bryan
Alabama	(11)	-	11	Nebraska	(8)	-	8
Arkansas	(9)	-	9	Nevada	(3)	-	3
California	(10)	10	-	New Hampshire	(4)	4	-
Colorado	(5)	-	5	New Jersey	(12)	12	-
Connecticut	(7)	7	-	New York	(39)	39	-
Delaware	(3)	3	-	North Carolina	(12)	-	12
Florida	(5)	-	5	North Dakota	(4)	4	-
Georgia	(13)	-	13	Ohio	(23)	23	-
Idaho	(3)	3	-	Oklahoma	(7)	-	7
Illinois	(27)	27	-	Oregon	(4)	4	-
Indiana	(15)	15	-	Pennsylvania	(34)	34	-
Iowa	(13)	13	-	Rhode Island	(4)	4	-
Kansas	(10)	10	-	South Carolina	(9)	-	9
Kentucky	(13)	-	13	South Dakota	(4)	4	-
Louisiana	(9)	-	9	Tennessee	(12)	-	12
Maine	(6)	6	-	Texas	(18)	-	18
Maryland[1]	(8)	2	6	Utah	(3)	3	-
Massachusetts	(16)	16	-	Vermont	(4)	4	-
Michigan	(14)	14	-	Virginia	(12)	-	12
Minnesota	(11)	11	-	Washington	(5)	5	-
Mississippi	(10)	-	10	West Virginia	(7)	7	-
Missouri	(18)	18	-	Wisconsin	(13)	13	-
Montana	(3)	3	-	Wyoming	(3)	3	-
				Totals	**(483)**	321	162

1. For explanation of split electoral votes, see p. 136.

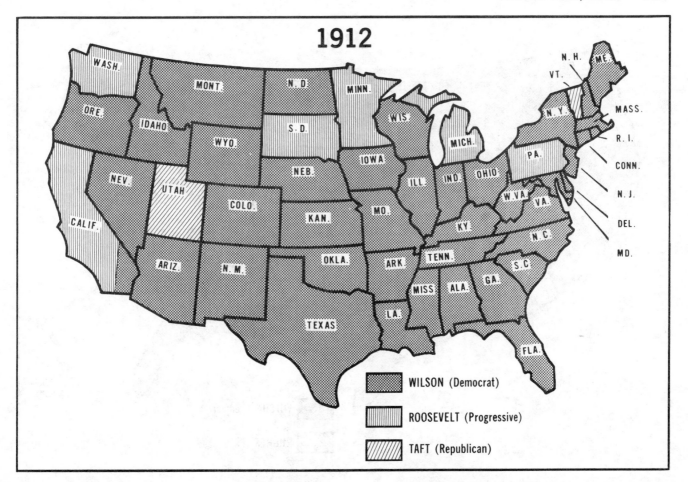

1912

- WILSON (Democrat)
- ROOSEVELT (Progressive)
- TAFT (Republican)

States	Electoral Votes	Wilson	Roosevelt	Taft	States	Electoral Votes	Wilson	Roosevelt	Taft
Alabama	(12)	12	-	-	Nebraska	(8)	8	-	-
Arizona	(3)	3	-	-	Nevada	(3)	3	-	-
Arkansas	(9)	9	-	-	New Hampshire	(4)	4	-	-
California[1]	(13)	2	11	-	New Jersey	(14)	14	-	-
Colorado	(6)	6	-	-	New Mexico	(3)	3	-	-
Connecticut	(7)	7	-	-	New York	(45)	45	-	-
Delaware	(3)	3	-	-	North Carolina	(12)	12	-	-
Florida	(6)	6	-	-	North Dakota	(5)	5	-	-
Georgia	(14)	14	-	-	Ohio	(24)	24	-	-
Idaho	(4)	4	-	-	Oklahoma	(10)	10	-	-
Illinois	(29)	29	-	-	Oregon	(5)	5	-	-
Indiana	(15)	15	-	-	Pennsylvania	(38)	-	38	-
Iowa	(13)	13	-	-	Rhode Island	(5)	5	-	-
Kansas	(10)	10	-	-	South Carolina	(9)	9	-	-
Kentucky	(13)	13	-	-	South Dakota	(5)	-	5	-
Louisiana	(10)	10	-	-	Tennessee	(12)	12	-	-
Maine	(6)	6	-	-	Texas	(20)	20	-	-
Maryland	(8)	8	-	-	Utah	(4)	-	-	4
Massachusetts	(18)	18	-	-	Vermont	(4)	-	-	4
Michigan	(15)	-	15	-	Virginia	(12)	12	-	-
Minnesota	(12)	-	12	-	Washington	(7)	-	7	-
Mississippi	(10)	10	-	-	West Virginia	(8)	8	-	-
Missouri	(18)	18	-	-	Wisconsin	(13)	13	-	-
Montana	(4)	4	-	-	Wyoming	(3)	3	-	-
					Totals	**(531)**	**435**	**88**	**8**

1. For explanation of split electoral votes, see p. 136.

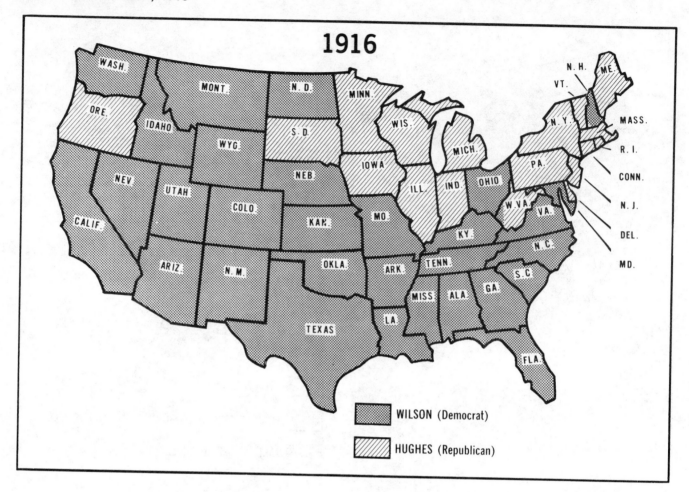

1916

WILSON (Democrat)

HUGHES (Republican)

States	Electoral Votes	Wilson	Hughes	States	Electoral Votes	Wilson	Hughes
Alabama	(12)	12	-	Nebraska	(8)	8	-
Arizona	(3)	3	-	Nevada	(3)	3	-
Arkansas	(9)	9	-	New Hampshire	(4)	4	-
California	(13)	13	-	New Jersey	(14)	-	14
Colorado	(6)	6	-	New Mexico	(3)	3	-
Connecticut	(7)	-	7	New York	(45)	-	45
Delaware	(3)	-	3	North Carolina	(12)	12	-
Florida	(6)	6	-	North Dakota	(5)	5	-
Georgia	(14)	14	-	Ohio	(24)	24	-
Idaho	(4)	4	-	Oklahoma	(10)	10	-
Illinois	(29)	-	29	Oregon	(5)	-	5
Indiana	(15)	-	15	Pennsylvania	(38)	-	38
Iowa	(13)	-	13	Rhode Island	(5)	-	5
Kansas	(10)	10	-	South Carolina	(9)	9	-
Kentucky	(13)	13	-	South Dakota	(5)	-	5
Louisiana	(10)	10	-	Tennessee	(12)	12	-
Maine	(6)	-	6	Texas	(20)	20	-
Maryland	(8)	8	-	Utah	(4)	4	-
Massachusetts	(18)	-	18	Vermont	(4)	-	4
Michigan	(15)	-	15	Virginia	(12)	12	-
Minnesota	(12)	-	12	Washington	(7)	7	-
Mississippi	(10)	10	-	West Virginia[1]	(8)	1	7
Missouri	(18)	18	-	Wisconsin	(13)	-	13
Montana	(4)	4	-	Wyoming	(3)	3	-
				Totals	**(531)**	**277**	**254**

1. *For explanation of split electoral votes, see p. 136.*

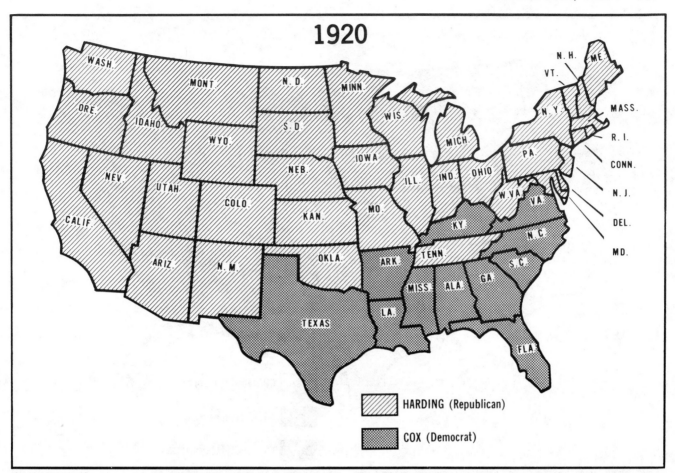

1920

HARDING (Republican)

COX (Democrat)

States	Electoral Votes	Harding	Cox	States	Electoral Votes	Harding	Cox
Alabama	(12)	-	12	Nebraska	(8)	8	-
Arizona	(3)	3	-	Nevada	(3)	3	-
Arkansas	(9)	-	9	New Hampshire	(4)	4	-
California	(13)	13	-	New Jersey	(14)	14	-
Colorado	(6)	6	-	New Mexico	(3)	3	-
Connecticut	(7)	7	-	New York	(45)	45	-
Delaware	(3)	3	-	North Carolina	(12)	-	12
Florida	(6)	-	6	North Dakota	(5)	5	-
Georgia	(14)	-	14	Ohio	(24)	24	-
Idaho	(4)	4	-	Oklahoma	(10)	10	-
Illinois	(29)	29	-	Oregon	(5)	5	-
Indiana	(15)	15	-	Pennsylvania	(38)	38	-
Iowa	(13)	13	-	Rhode Island	(5)	5	-
Kansas	(10)	10	-	South Carolina	(9)	-	9
Kentucky	(13)	-	13	South Dakota	(5)	5	-
Louisiana	(10)	-	10	Tennessee	(12)	12	-
Maine	(6)	6	-	Texas	(20)	-	20
Maryland	(8)	8	-	Utah	(4)	4	-
Massachusetts	(18)	18	-	Vermont	(4)	4	-
Michigan	(15)	15	-	Virginia	(12)	-	12
Minnesota	(12)	12	-	Washington	(7)	7	-
Mississippi	(10)	-	10	West Virginia	(8)	8	-
Missouri	(18)	18	-	Wisconsin	(13)	13	-
Montana	(4)	4	-	Wyoming	(3)	3	-
				Totals	**(531)**	**404**	**127**

1924

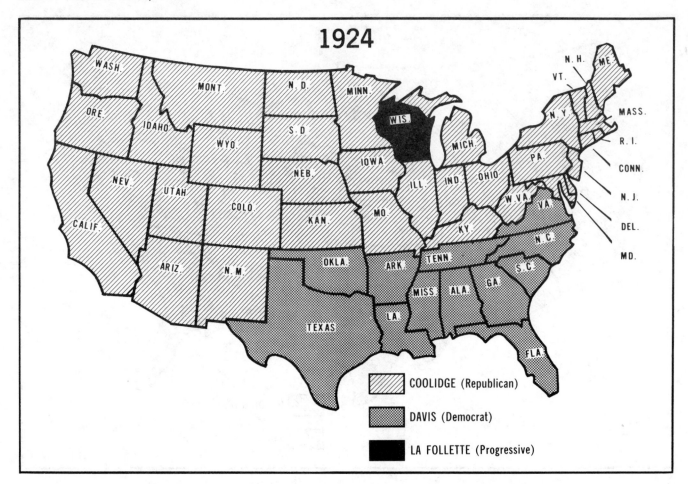

COOLIDGE (Republican)

DAVIS (Democrat)

LA FOLLETTE (Progressive)

States	Electoral Votes	Coolidge	Davis	La Follette	States	Electoral Votes	Coolidge	Davis	La Follette
Alabama	(12)	-	12	-	Nebraska	(8)	8	-	
Arizona	(3)	3	-	-	Nevada	(3)	3	-	-
Arkansas	(9)	-	9	-	New Hampshire	(4)	4	-	-
California	(13)	13	-	-	New Jersey	(14)	14	-	-
Colorado	(6)	6	-	-	New Mexico	(3)	3	-	-
Connecticut	(7)	7	-	-	New York	(45)	45	-	-
Delaware	(3)	3	-	-	North Carolina	(12)	-	12	-
Florida	(6)	-	6	-	North Dakota	(5)	5	-	-
Georgia	(14)	-	14	-	Ohio	(24)	24	-	-
Idaho	(4)	4	-	-	Oklahoma	(10)	-	10	-
Illinois	(29)	29	-	-	Oregon	(5)	5	-	-
Indiana	(15)	15	-	-	Pennsylvania	(38)	38	-	-
Iowa	(13)	13	-	-	Rhode Island	(5)	5	-	-
Kansas	(10)	10	-	-	South Carolina	(9)	-	9	-
Kentucky	(13)	13	-	-	South Dakota	(5)	5	-	-
Louisiana	(10)	-	10	-	Tennessee	(12)	-	12	-
Maine	(6)	6	-	-	Texas	(20)	-	20	-
Maryland	(8)	8	-	-	Utah	(4)	4	-	-
Massachusetts	(18)	18	-	-	Vermont	(4)	4	-	-
Michigan	(15)	15	-	-	Virginia	(12)	-	12	-
Minnesota	(12)	12	-	-	Washington	(7)	7	-	-
Mississippi	(10)	-	10	-	West Virginia	(8)	8	-	-
Missouri	(18)	18	-	-	Wisconsin	(13)	-	-	13
Montana	(4)	4	-	-	Wyoming	(3)	3	-	-
					Totals	**(531)**	**382**	**136**	**13**

1928

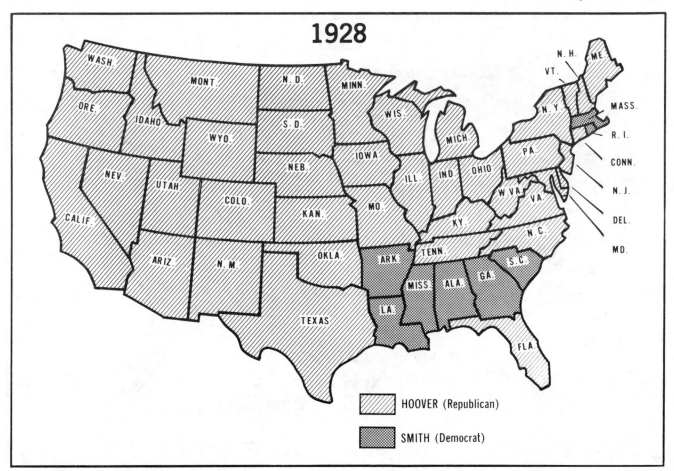

HOOVER (Republican)

SMITH (Democrat)

States	Electoral Votes	Hoover	Smith	States	Electoral Votes	Hoover	Smith
Alabama	(12)	-	12	Nebraska	(8)	8	-
Arizona	(3)	3	-	Nevada	(3)	3	-
Arkansas	(9)	-	9	New Hampshire	(4)	4	-
California	(13)	13	-	New Jersey	(14)	14	-
Colorado	(6)	6	-	New Mexico	(3)	3	-
Connecticut	(7)	7	-	New York	(45)	45	-
Delaware	(3)	3	-	North Carolina	(12)	12	-
Florida	(6)	6	-	North Dakota	(5)	5	-
Georgia	(14)	-	14	Ohio	(24)	24	-
Idaho	(4)	4	-	Oklahoma	(10)	10	-
Illinois	(29)	29	-	Oregon	(5)	5	-
Indiana	(15)	15	-	Pennsylvania	(38)	38	-
Iowa	(13)	13	-	Rhode Island	(5)	-	5
Kansas	(10)	10	-	South Carolina	(9)	-	9
Kentucky	(13)	13	-	South Dakota	(5)	5	-
Louisiana	(10)	-	10	Tennessee	(12)	12	-
Maine	(6)	6	-	Texas	(20)	20	-
Maryland	(8)	8	-	Utah	(4)	4	-
Massachusetts	(18)	-	18	Vermont	(4)	4	-
Michigan	(15)	15	-	Virginia	(12)	12	-
Minnesota	(12)	12	-	Washington	(7)	7	-
Mississippi	(10)	-	10	West Virginia	(8)	8	-
Missouri	(18)	18	-	Wisconsin	(13)	13	-
Montana	(4)	4	-	Wyoming	(3)	3	-
				Totals	**(531)**	**444**	**87**

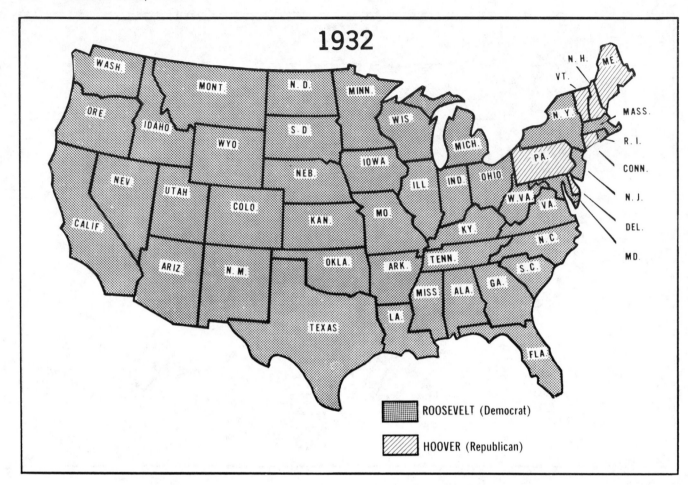

1932

ROOSEVELT (Democrat)

HOOVER (Republican)

States	Electoral Votes	Roosevelt	Hoover
Alabama	(11)	11	-
Arizona	(3)	3	-
Arkansas	(9)	9	-
California	(22)	22	-
Colorado	(6)	6	-
Connecticut	(8)	-	8
Delaware	(3)	-	3
Florida	(7)	7	-
Georgia	(12)	12	-
Idaho	(4)	4	-
Illinois	(29)	29	-
Indiana	(14)	14	-
Iowa	(11)	11	-
Kansas	(9)	9	-
Kentucky	(11)	11	-
Louisiana	(10)	10	-
Maine	(5)	-	5
Maryland	(8)	8	-
Massachusetts	(17)	17	-
Michigan	(19)	19	-
Minnesota	(11)	11	-
Mississippi	(9)	9	-
Missouri	(15)	15	-
Montana	(4)	4	-

States	Electoral Votes	Roosevelt	Hoover
Nebraska	(7)	7	-
Nevada	(3)	3	-
New Hampshire	(4)	-	4
New Jersey	(16)	16	-
New Mexico	(3)	3	-
New York	(47)	47	-
North Carolina	(13)	13	-
North Dakota	(4)	4	-
Ohio	(26)	26	-
Oklahoma	(11)	11	-
Oregon	(5)	5	-
Pennsylvania	(36)	-	36
Rhode Island	(4)	4	-
South Carolina	(8)	8	-
South Dakota	(4)	4	-
Tennessee	(11)	11	-
Texas	(23)	23	-
Utah	(4)	4	-
Vermont	(3)	-	3
Virginia	(11)	11	-
Washington	(8)	8	-
West Virginia	(8)	8	-
Wisconsin	(12)	12	-
Wyoming	(3)	3	-
Totals	**(531)**	**472**	**59**

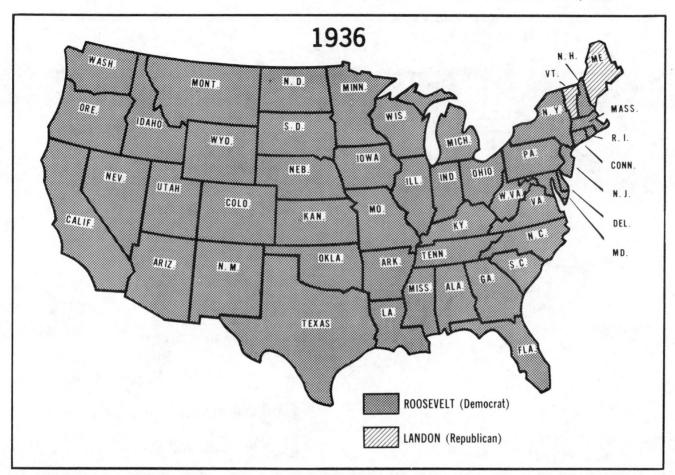

1936

◼ ROOSEVELT (Democrat)

▨ LANDON (Republican)

States	Electoral Votes	Roosevelt	Landon	States	Electoral Votes	Roosevelt	Landon
Alabama	(11)	11	-	Nebraska	(7)	7	-
Arizona	(3)	3	-	Nevada	(3)	3	-
Arkansas	(9)	9	-	New Hampshire	(4)	4	-
California	(22)	22	-	New Jersey	(16)	16	-
Colorado	(6)	6	-	New Mexico	(3)	3	-
Connecticut	(8)	8	-	New York	(47)	47	-
Delaware	(3)	3	-	North Carolina	(13)	13	-
Florida	(7)	7	-	North Dakota	(4)	4	-
Georgia	(12)	12	-	Ohio	(26)	26	-
Idaho	(4)	4	-	Oklahoma	(11)	11	-
Illinois	(29)	29	-	Oregon	(5)	5	-
Indiana	(14)	14	-	Pennsylvania	(36)	36	-
Iowa	(11)	11	-	Rhode Island	(4)	4	-
Kansas	(9)	9	-	South Carolina	(8)	8	-
Kentucky	(11)	11	-	South Dakota	(4)	4	-
Louisiana	(10)	10	-	Tennessee	(11)	11	-
Maine	(5)	-	5	Texas	(23)	23	-
Maryland	(8)	8	-	Utah	(4)	4	-
Massachusetts	(17)	17	-	Vermont	(3)	-	3
Michigan	(19)	19	-	Virginia	(11)	11	-
Minnesota	(11)	11	-	Washington	(8)	8	-
Mississippi	(9)	9	-	West Virginia	(8)	8	-
Missouri	(15)	15	-	Wisconsin	(12)	12	-
Montana	(4)	4	-	Wyoming	(3)	3	-
				Totals	**(531)**	**523**	**8**

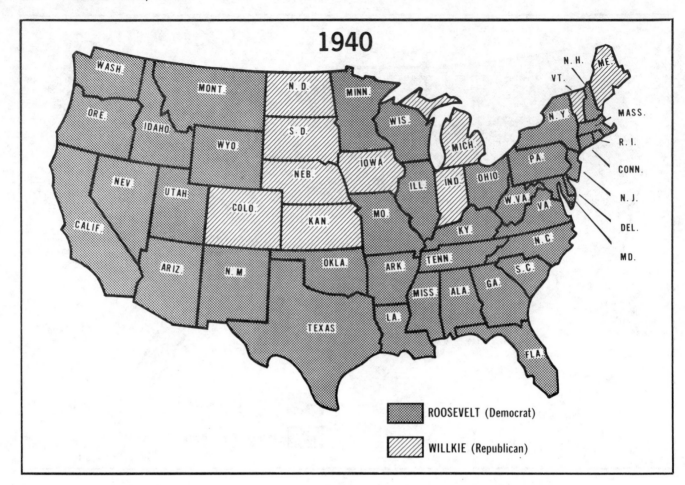

1940

ROOSEVELT (Democrat)

WILLKIE (Republican)

States	Electoral Votes	Roosevelt	Willkie	States	Electoral Votes	Roosevelt	Willkie
Alabama	(11)	11	-	Nebraska	(7)	-	7
Arizona	(3)	3	-	Nevada	(3)	3	-
Arkansas	(9)	9	-	New Hampshire	(4)	4	-
California	(22)	22	-	New Jersey	(16)	16	-
Colorado	(6)	-	6	New Mexico	(3)	3	-
Connecticut	(8)	8	-	New York	(47)	47	-
Delaware	(3)	3	-	North Carolina	(13)	13	-
Florida	(7)	7	-	North Dakota	(4)	-	4
Georgia	(12)	12	-	Ohio	(26)	26	-
Idaho	(4)	4	-	Oklahoma	(11)	11	-
Illinois	(29)	29	-	Oregon	(5)	5	-
Indiana	(14)	-	14	Pennsylvania	(36)	36	-
Iowa	(11)	-	11	Rhode Island	(4)	4	-
Kansas	(9)		9	South Carolina	(8)	8	-
Kentucky	(11)	11	-	South Dakota	(4)	-	4
Louisiana	(10)	10	-	Tennessee	(11)	11	-
Maine	(5)	-	5	Texas	(23)	23	-
Maryland	(8)	8	-	Utah	(4)	4	-
Massachusetts	(17)	17	-	Vermont	(3)	-	3
Michigan	(19)	-	19	Virginia	(11)	11	-
Minnesota	(11)	11	-	Washington	(8)	8	-
Mississippi	(9)	9	-	West Virginia	(8)	8	-
Missouri	(15)	15	-	Wisconsin	(12)	12	-
Montana	(4)	4	-	Wyoming	(3)	3	-
				Totals	**(531)**	**449**	**82**

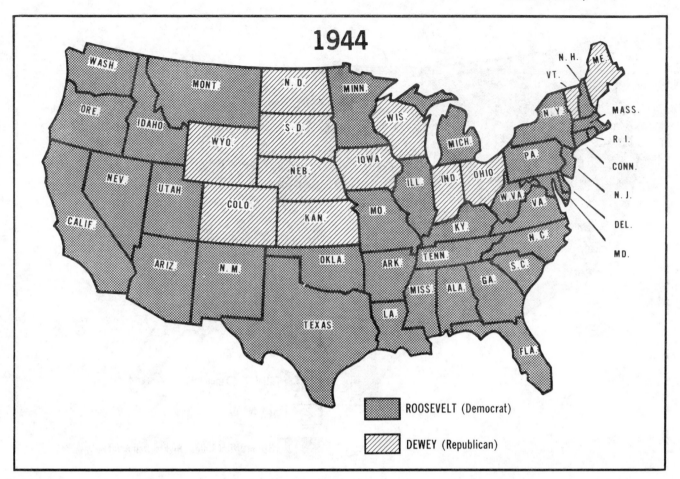

1944

ROOSEVELT (Democrat)

DEWEY (Republican)

States	Electoral Votes	Roosevelt	Dewey	States	Electoral Votes	Roosevelt	Dewey
Alabama	(11)	11	-	Nebraska	(6)	-	6
Arizona	(4)	4	-	Nevada	(3)	3	-
Arkansas	(9)	9	-	New Hampshire	(4)	4	-
California	(25)	25	-	New Jersey	(16)	16	-
Colorado	(6)	-	6	New Mexico	(4)	4	-
Connecticut	(8)	8	-	New York	(47)	47	-
Delaware	(3)	3	-	North Carolina	(14)	14	-
Florida	(8)	8	-	North Dakota	(4)	-	4
Georgia	(12)	12	-	Ohio	(25)	-	25
Idaho	(4)	4	-	Oklahoma	(10)	10	-
Illinois	(28)	28	-	Oregon	(6)	6	-
Indiana	(13)	-	13	Pennsylvania	(35)	35	-
Iowa	(10)	-	10	Rhode Island	(4)	4	-
Kansas	(8)	-	8	South Carolina	(8)	8	-
Kentucky	(11)	11	-	South Dakota	(4)	-	4
Louisiana	(10)	10	-	Tennessee	(12)	12	-
Maine	(5)	-	5	Texas	(23)	23	-
Maryland	(8)	8	-	Utah	(4)	4	-
Massachusetts	(16)	16	-	Vermont	(3)	-	3
Michigan	(19)	19	-	Virginia	(11)	11	-
Minnesota	(11)	11	-	Washington	(8)	8	-
Mississippi	(9)	9	-	West Virginia	(8)	8	-
Missouri	(15)	15	-	Wisconsin	(12)	-	12
Montana	(4)	4	-	Wyoming	(3)	-	3
				Totals	**(531)**	**432**	**99**

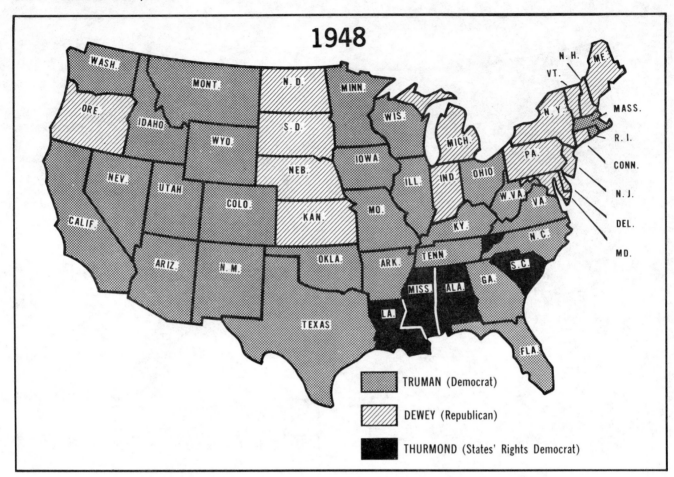

1948

TRUMAN (Democrat)

DEWEY (Republican)

THURMOND (States' Rights Democrat)

States	Electoral Votes	Truman	Dewey	Thurmond	States	Electoral Votes	Truman	Dewey	Thurmond
Alabama	(11)	-	-	11	Nebraska	(6)	-	6	-
Arizona	(4)	4	-	-	Nevada	(3)	3	-	-
Arkansas	(9)	9	-	-	New Hampshire	(4)	-	4	-
California	(25)	25	-	-	New Jersey	(16)	-	16	-
Colorado	(6)	6	-	-	New Mexico	(4)	4	-	-
Connecticut	(8)	-	8	-	New York	(47)	-	47	-
Delaware	(3)	-	3	-	North Carolina	(14)	14	-	-
Florida	(8)	8	-	-	North Dakota	(4)	-	4	-
Georgia	(12)	12	-	-	Ohio	(25)	25	-	-
Idaho	(4)	4	-	-	Oklahoma	(10)	10	-	-
Illinois	(28)	28	-	-	Oregon	(6)	-	6	-
Indiana	(13)	-	13	-	Pennsylvania	(35)	-	35	-
Iowa	(10)	10	-	-	Rhode Island	(4)	4	-	-
Kansas	(8)	-	8	-	South Carolina	(8)	-	-	8
Kentucky	(11)	11	-	-	South Dakota	(4)	-	4	-
Louisiana	(10)	-	-	10	Tennessee [1]	(12)	11	-	1
Maine	(5)	-	5	-	Texas	(23)	23	-	-
Maryland	(8)	-	8	-	Utah	(4)	4	-	-
Massachusetts	(16)	16	-	-	Vermont	(3)	-	3	-
Michigan	(19)	-	19	-	Virginia	(11)	11	-	-
Minnesota	(11)	11	-	-	Washington	(8)	8	-	-
Mississippi	(9)	-	-	9	West Virginia	(8)	8	-	-
Missouri	(15)	15	-	-	Wisconsin	(12)	12	-	-
Montana	(4)	4	-	-	Wyoming	(3)	3	-	-
					Totals	**(531)**	**303**	**189**	**39**

1. For explanation of split electoral votes, see p. 136.

1952

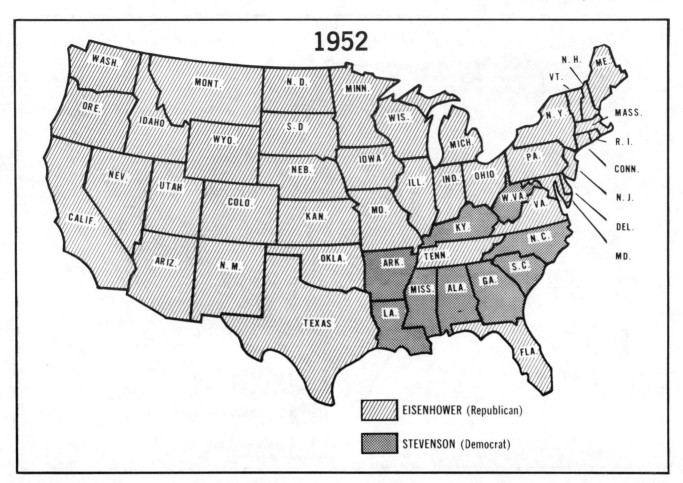

EISENHOWER (Republican)

STEVENSON (Democrat)

States	Electoral Votes	Eisenhower	Stevenson	States	Electoral Votes	Eisenhower	Stevenson
Alabama	(11)	-	11	Nebraska	(6)	6	-
Arizona	(4)	4	-	Nevada	(3)	3	-
Arkansas	(8)	-	8	New Hampshire	(4)	4	-
California	(32)	32	-	New Jersey	(16)	16	-
Colorado	(6)	6	-	New Mexico	(4)	4	-
Connecticut	(8)	8	-	New York	(45)	45	-
Delaware	(3)	3	-	North Carolina	(14)	-	14
Florida	(10)	10	-	North Dakota	(4)	4	-
Georgia	(12)	-	12	Ohio	(25)	25	-
Idaho	(4)	4	-	Oklahoma	(8)	8	-
Illinois	(27)	27	-	Oregon	(6)	6	-
Indiana	(13)	13	-	Pennsylvania	(32)	32	-
Iowa	(10)	10	-	Rhode Island	(4)	4	-
Kansas	(8)	8	-	South Carolina	(8)	-	8
Kentucky	(10)	-	10	South Dakota	(4)	4	-
Louisiana	(10)	-	10	Tennessee	(11)	11	-
Maine	(5)	5	-	Texas	(24)	24	-
Maryland	(9)	9	-	Utah	(4)	4	-
Massachusetts	(16)	16	-	Vermont	(3)	3	-
Michigan	(20)	20	-	Virginia	(12)	12	-
Minnesota	(11)	11	-	Washington	(9)	9	-
Mississippi	(8)	-	8	West Virginia	(8)	-	8
Missouri	(13)	13	-	Wisconsin	(12)	12	-
Montana	(4)	4	-	Wyoming	(3)	3	-
				Totals	**(531)**	**442**	**89**

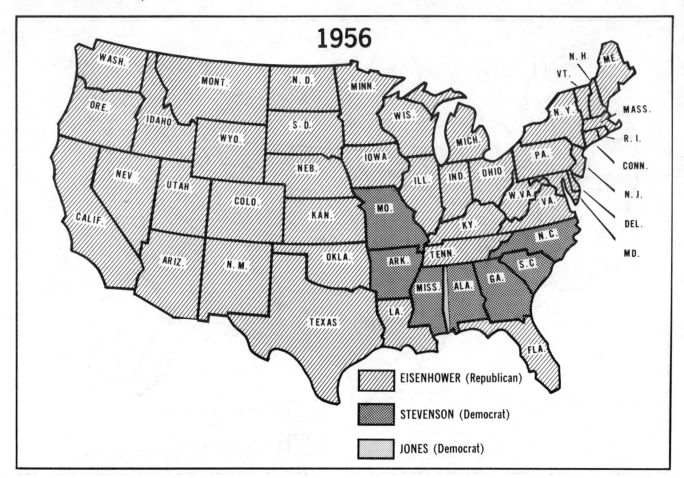

1956

	EISENHOWER (Republican)
	STEVENSON (Democrat)
	JONES (Democrat)

States	Electoral Votes	Eisenhower	Stevenson	Jones	States	Electoral Votes	Eisenhower	Stevenson	Jones
Alabama[1]	(11)	-	10	1	Nebraska	(6)	6	-	-
Arizona	(4)	4	-	-	Nevada	(3)	3	-	-
Arkansas	(8)	-	8	-	New Hampshire	(4)	4	-	-
California	(32)	32	-	-	New Jersey	(16)	16	-	-
Colorado	(6)	6	-	-	New Mexico	(4)	4	-	-
Connecticut	(8)	8	-	-	New York	(45)	45	-	-
Delaware	(3)	3	-	-	North Carolina	(14)	-	14	-
Florida	(10)	10	-	-	North Dakota	(4)	4	-	-
Georgia	(12)	-	12	-	Ohio	(25)	25	-	-
Idaho	(4)	4	-	-	Oklahoma	(8)	8	-	-
Illinois	(27)	27	-	-	Oregon	(6)	6	-	-
Indiana	(13)	13	-	-	Pennsylvania	(32)	32	-	-
Iowa	(10)	10	-	-	Rhode Island	(4)	4	-	-
Kansas	(8)	8	-	-	South Carolina	(8)	-	8	-
Kentucky	(10)	10	-	-	South Dakota	(4)	4	-	-
Louisiana	(10)	10	-	-	Tennessee	(11)	11	-	-
Maine	(5)	5	-	-	Texas	(24)	24	-	-
Maryland	(9)	9	-	-	Utah	(4)	4	-	-
Massachusetts	(16)	16	-	-	Vermont	(3)	3	-	-
Michigan	(20)	20	-	-	Virginia	(12)	12	-	-
Minnesota	(11)	11	-	-	Washington	(9)	9	-	-
Mississippi	(8)	-	8	-	West Virginia	(8)	8	-	-
Missouri	(13)	-	13	-	Wisconsin	(12)	12	-	-
Montana	(4)	4	-	-	Wyoming	(3)	3	-	-
					Totals	**(531)**	**457**	**73**	**1**

1. For explanation of split electoral votes, see p. 136.

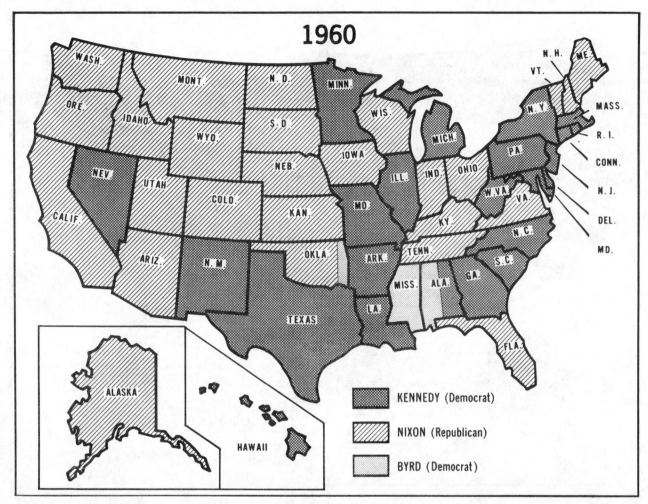

1960

KENNEDY (Democrat)

NIXON (Republican)

BYRD (Democrat)

States	Electoral Votes	Kennedy	Nixon	Byrd	States	Electoral Votes	Kennedy	Nixon	Byrd
Alabama[1]	(11)	5	-	6	Montana	(4)	-	4	-
Alaska	(3)	-	3	-	Nebraska	(6)	-	6	-
Arizona	(4)	-	4	-	Nevada	(3)	3	-	-
Arkansas	(8)	8	-	-	New Hampshire	(4)	-	4	-
California	(32)	-	32	-	New Jersey	(16)	16	-	-
Colorado	(6)	-	6	-	New Mexico	(4)	4	-	-
Connecticut	(8)	8	-	-	New York	(45)	45	-	-
Delaware	(3)	3	-	-	North Carolina	(14)	14	-	-
Florida	(10)	-	10	-	North Dakota	(4)	-	4	-
Georgia	(12)	12	-	-	Ohio	(25)	-	25	-
Hawaii	(3)	3	-	-	Oklahoma[1]	(8)	-	7	1
Idaho	(4)	-	4	-	Oregon	(6)	-	6	-
Illinois	(27)	27	-	-	Pennsylvania	(32)	32	-	-
Indiana	(13)	-	13	-	Rhode Island	(4)	4	-	-
Iowa	(10)	-	10	-	South Carolina	(8)	8	-	-
Kansas	(8)	-	8	-	South Dakota	(4)	-	4	-
Kentucky	(10)	-	10	-	Tennessee	(11)	-	11	-
Louisiana	(10)	10	-	-	Texas	(24)	24	-	-
Maine	(5)	-	5	-	Utah	(4)	-	4	-
Maryland	(9)	9	-	-	Vermont	(3)	-	3	-
Massachusetts	(16)	16	-	-	Virginia	(12)	-	12	-
Michigan	(20)	20	-	-	Washington	(9)	-	9	-
Minnesota	(11)	11	-	-	West Virginia	(8)	8	-	-
Mississippi	(8)	-	-	8	Wisconsin	(12)	-	12	-
Missouri	(13)	13	-	-	Wyoming	(3)	-	3	-
					Totals	**(537)**	**303**	**219**	**15**

1. For explanation of split electoral votes, see p. 136.

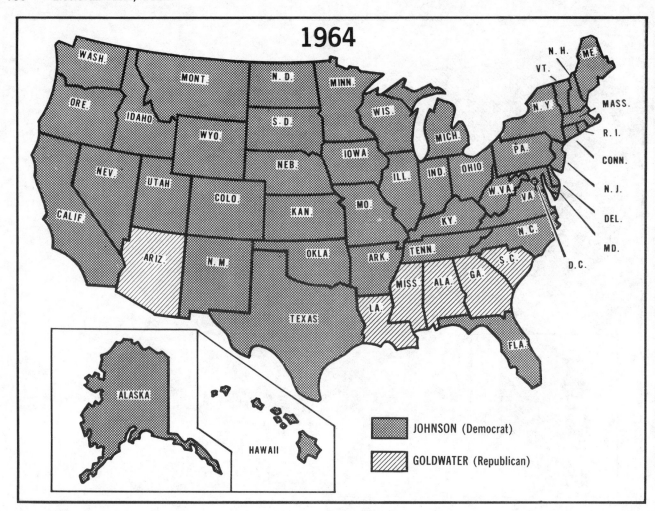

1964

JOHNSON (Democrat)

GOLDWATER (Republican)

States	Electoral Votes	Johnson	Goldwater	States	Electoral Votes	Johnson	Goldwater
Alabama	(10)	-	10	Montana	(4)	4	-
Alaska	(3)	3	-	Nebraska	(5)	5	-
Arizona	(5)	-	5	Nevada	(3)	3	-
Arkansas	(6)	6	-	New Hampshire	(4)	4	-
California	(40)	40	-	New Jersey	(17)	17	-
Colorado	(6)	6	-	New Mexico	(4)	4	-
Connecticut	(8)	8	-	New York	(43)	43	-
Delaware	(3)	3	-	North Carolina	(13)	13	-
District of Columbia	(3)	3	-	North Dakota	(4)	4	-
Florida	(14)	14	-	Ohio	(26)	26	-
Georgia	(12)	-	12	Oklahoma	(8)	8	-
Hawaii	(4)	4	-	Oregon	(6)	6	-
Idaho	(4)	4	-	Pennsylvania	(29)	29	-
Illinois	(26)	26	-	Rhode Island	(4)	4	-
Indiana	(13)	13	-	South Carolina	(8)	-	8
Iowa	(9)	9	-	South Dakota	(4)	4	-
Kansas	(7)	7	-	Tennessee	(11)	11	-
Kentucky	(9)	9	-	Texas	(25)	25	-
Louisiana	(10)	-	10	Utah	(4)	4	-
Maine	(4)	4	-	Vermont	(3)	3	-
Maryland	(10)	10	-	Virginia	(12)	12	-
Massachusetts	(14)	14	-	Washington	(9)	9	-
Michigan	(21)	21	-	West Virginia	(7)	7	-
Minnesota	(10)	10	-	Wisconsin	(12)	12	-
Mississippi	(7)	-	7	Wyoming	(3)	3	-
Missouri	(12)	12	-	**Totals**	**(538)**	**486**	**52**

1968

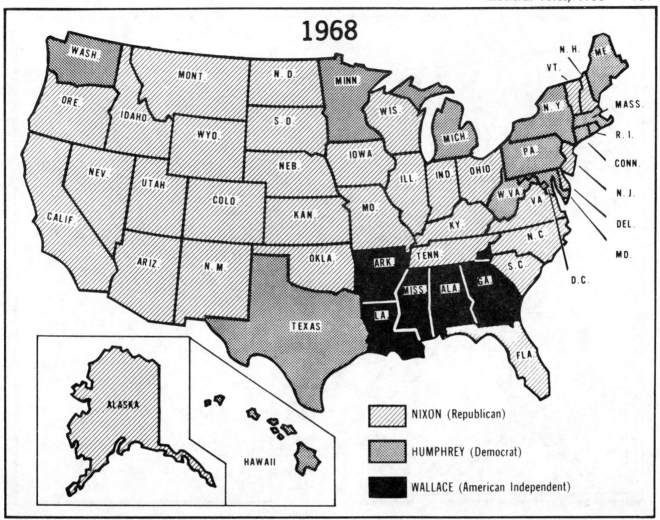

	NIXON (Republican)
	HUMPHREY (Democrat)
	WALLACE (American Independent)

States	Electoral Votes	Nixon	Humphrey	Wallace
Alabama	(10)	-	-	10
Alaska	(3)	3	-	-
Arizona	(5)	5	-	-
Arkansas	(6)	-	-	6
California	(40)	40	-	-
Colorado	(6)	6	-	-
Connecticut	(8)	-	8	-
Delaware	(3)	3	-	-
District of Columbia	(3)	-	3	-
Florida	(14)	14	-	-
Georgia	(12)	-	-	12
Hawaii	(4)	-	4	-
Idaho	(4)	4	-	-
Illinois	(26)	26	-	-
Indiana	(13)	13	-	-
Iowa	(9)	9	-	-
Kansas	(7)	7	-	-
Kentucky	(9)	9	-	-
Louisiana	(10)	-	-	10
Maine	(4)	-	4	-
Maryland	(10)	-	10	-
Massachusetts	(14)	-	14	-
Michigan	(21)	-	21	-
Minnesota	(10)	-	10	-
Mississippi	(7)	-	-	7
Missouri	(12)	12	-	-
Montana	(4)	4	-	-
Nebraska	(5)	5	-	-
Nevada	(3)	3	-	-
New Hampshire	(4)	4	-	-
New Jersey	(17)	17	-	-
New Mexico	(4)	4	-	-
New York	(43)	-	43	-
North Carolina[1]	(13)	12	-	1
North Dakota	(4)	4	-	-
Ohio	(26)	26	-	-
Oklahoma	(8)	8	-	-
Oregon	(6)	6	-	-
Pennsylvania	(29)	-	29	-
Rhode Island	(4)	-	4	-
South Carolina	(8)	8	-	-
South Dakota	(4)	4	-	-
Tennessee	(11)	11	-	-
Texas	(25)	-	25	-
Utah	(4)	4	-	-
Vermont	(3)	3	-	-
Virginia	(12)	12	-	-
Washington	(9)	-	9	-
West Virginia	(7)	-	7	-
Wisconsin	(12)	12	-	-
Wyoming	(3)	3	-	-
Totals	**(538)**	**301**	**191**	**46**

1. For explanation of split electoral votes, see p. 136.

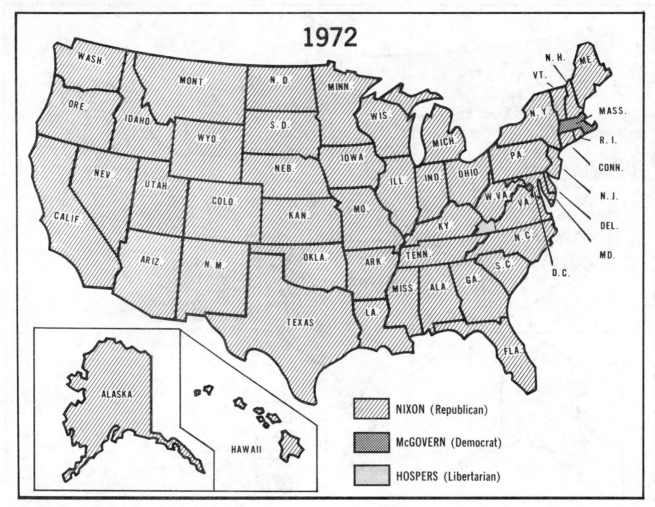

1972

	NIXON (Republican)
	McGOVERN (Democrat)
	HOSPERS (Libertarian)

States	Electoral Votes	Nixon	McGovern	Hospers
Alabama	(9)	9	-	-
Alaska	(3)	3	-	-
Arizona	(6)	6	-	-
Arkansas	(6)	6	-	-
California	(45)	45	-	-
Colorado	(7)	7	-	-
Connecticut	(8)	8	-	-
Delaware	(3)	3	-	-
District of Columbia	(3)	-	3	-
Florida	(17)	17	-	-
Georgia	(12)	12	-	-
Hawaii	(4)	4	-	-
Idaho	(4)	4	-	-
Illinois	(26)	26	-	-
Indiana	(13)	13	-	-
Iowa	(8)	8	-	-
Kansas	(7)	7	-	-
Kentucky	(9)	9	-	-
Louisiana	(10)	10	-	-
Maine	(4)	4	-	-
Maryland	(10)	10	-	-
Massachusetts	(14)	-	14	-
Michigan	(21)	21	-	-
Minnesota	(10)	10	-	-
Mississippi	(7)	7	-	-
Missouri	(12)	12	-	-
Montana	(4)	4	-	-
Nebraska	(5)	5	-	-
Nevada	(3)	3	-	-
New Hampshire	(4)	4	-	-
New Jersey	(17)	17	-	-
New Mexico	(4)	4	-	-
New York	(4)	41	-	-
North Carolina	(13)	13	-	-
North Dakota	(3)	3	-	-
Ohio	(25)	25	-	-
Oklahoma	(8)	8	-	-
Oregon	(6)	6	-	-
Pennsylvania	(27)	27	-	-
Rhode Island	(4)	4	-	-
South Carolina	(8)	8	-	-
South Dakota	(4)	4	-	-
Tennessee	(10)	10	-	-
Texas	(26)	26	-	-
Utah	(4)	4	-	-
Vermont	(3)	3	-	-
Virginia[1]	(12)	11	-	1
Washington	(9)	9	-	-
West Virginia	(6)	6	-	-
Wisconsin	(11)	11	-	-
Wyoming	(3)	3	-	-
Totals	(538)	520	17	1

1. *For explanation of split electoral votes, see p. 136.*

1976

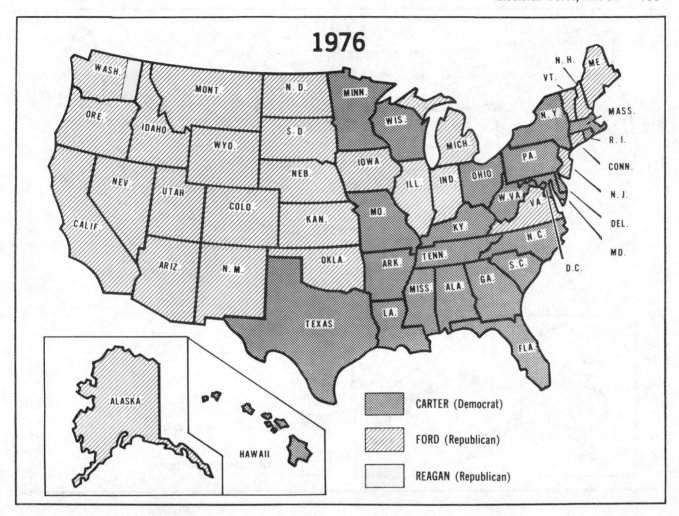

CARTER (Democrat)

FORD (Republican)

REAGAN (Republican)

ALASKA

HAWAII

States	Electoral Votes	Carter	Ford	Reagan
Alabama	(9)	9	-	-
Alaska	(3)	-	3	-
Arizona	(6)	-	6	-
Arkansas	(6)	6	-	-
California	(45)	-	45	-
Colorado	(7)	-	7	-
Connecticut	(8)	-	8	-
Delaware	(3)	3	-	-
District of Columbia	(3)	3	-	-
Florida	(17)	17	-	-
Georgia	(12)	12	-	-
Hawaii	(4)	4	-	-
Idaho	(4)	-	4	-
Illinois	(26)	-	26	-
Indiana	(13)	-	13	-
Iowa	(8)	-	8	-
Kansas	(7)	-	7	-
Kentucky	(9)	9	-	-
Louisiana	(10)	10	-	-
Maine	(4)	-	4	-
Maryland	(10)	10	-	-
Massachusetts	(14)	14	-	-
Michigan	(21)	-	21	-
Minnesota	(10)	10	-	-
Mississippi	(7)	7	-	-
Missouri	(12)	12	-	-
Montana	(4)	-	4	
Nebraska	(5)	-	5	-
Nevada	(3)	-	3	-
New Hampshire	(4)	-	4	-
New Jersey	(17)	-	17	-
New Mexico	(4)	-	4	-
New York	(41)	41	-	-
North Carolina	(13)	13	-	-
North Dakota	(3)	-	3	-
Ohio	(25)	25	-	-
Oklahoma	(8)	-	8	-
Oregon	(6)	-	6	-
Pennsylvania	(27)	27	-	-
Rhode Island	(4)	4	-	-
South Carolina	(8)	8	-	-
South Dakota	(4)	-	4	-
Tennessee	(10)	10	-	-
Texas	(26)	26	-	-
Utah	(4)	-	4	-
Vermont	(3)	-	3	-
Virginia	(12)	-	12	-
Washington[1]	(9)	-	8	1
West Virginia	(6)	6	-	-
Wisconsin	(11)	11	-	-
Wyoming	(3)	-	3	-
Totals	**(538)**	**297**	**240**	**1**

1. For explanation of split electoral votes, see p. 136.

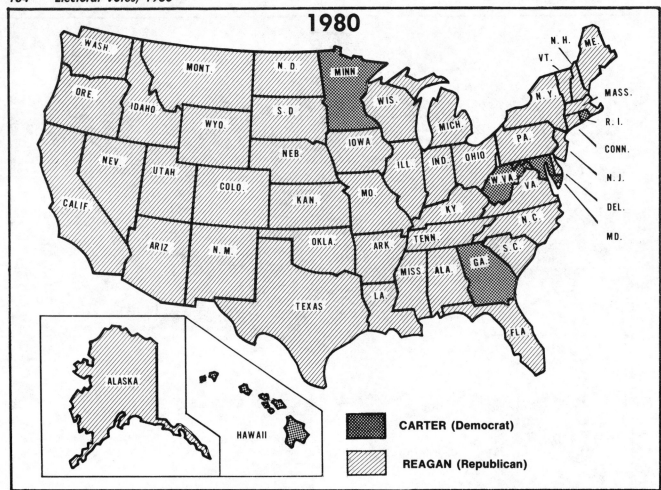

1980

CARTER (Democrat)

REAGAN (Republican)

States	Electoral Votes	Carter	Reagan	States	Electoral Votes	Carter	Reagan
Alabama	(9)	—	9	Montana	(4)	—	4
Alaska	(3)	—	3	Nebraska	(5)	—	5
Arizona	(6)	—	6	Nevada	(3)	—	3
Arkansas	(6)	—	6	New Hampshire	(4)	—	4
California	(45)	—	45	New Jersey	(17)	—	17
Colorado	(7)	—	7	New Mexico	(4)	—	4
Connecticut	(8)	—	8	New York	(41)	—	41
Delaware	(3)	—	3	North Carolina	(13)	—	13
District of Columbia	(3)	3	—	North Dakota	(3)	—	3
Florida	(17)	—	17	Ohio	(25)	—	25
Georgia	(12)	12	—	Oklahoma	(8)	—	8
Hawaii	(4)	4	—	Oregon	(6)	—	6
Idaho	(4)	—	4	Pennsylvania	(27)	—	27
Illinois	(26)	—	26	Rhode Island	(4)	4	—
Indiana	(13)	—	13	South Carolina	(8)	—	8
Iowa	(8)	—	8	South Dakota	(4)	—	4
Kansas	(7)	—	7	Tennessee	(10)	—	10
Kentucky	(9)	—	9	Texas	(26)	—	26
Louisiana	(10)	—	10	Utah	(4)	—	4
Maine	(4)	—	4	Vermont	(3)	—	3
Maryland	(10)	10	—	Virginia	(12)	—	12
Massachusetts	(14)	—	14	Washington	(9)	—	9
Michigan	(21)	—	21	West Virginia	(6)	6	—
Minnesota	(10)	10	—	Wisconsin	(11)	—	11
Mississippi	(7)	—	7	Wyoming	(3)	—	3
Missouri	(12)	—	12	**Totals**	**538**	**49**	**489**

Electoral Votes for Vice President, 1804-1980

The following list gives the electoral votes for vice president from 1804 to 1980. Unless indicated by a *footnote*, the state-by-state breakdown of electoral votes for each vice presidential candidate was the same as for his party's presidential candidate. These state-by-state votes are given in the section on presidential electoral votes *(pp. 141-84)*.

Electoral Votes 1789-1800

Prior to 1804, under Article II, Section 1 of the Constitution, each elector cast two votes — each vote for a different person. The electors did not distinguish between votes for president and vice president. The candidate receiving the second highest total became vice president. The 12th Amendment, ratified in 1804, required electors to vote separately for president and vice president. *(Electoral votes for 1789, 1792, 1796 and 1800, pp. 141-44)*

Candidates

In some cases persons have received electoral votes although they had never been formally nominated. The word *candidate* is used in this section to designate persons receiving electoral votes.

Sources: Votes and Parties

The *Senate Manual* (U.S. Government Printing Office, 1977) was the source used for vice presidential electoral votes.

For political party designation, the basic source was *A Statistical History of the American Presidential Elections* (Frederick Ungar, New York, 1968) by Svend Petersen; Petersen gives the party designation of *presidential candidates only*. Congressional Quarterly adopted Petersen's party designations for the running mates of presidential candidates. To supplement Petersen, Congressional Quarterly consulted the *Biographical Directory of the American Congress, 1774-1971*, U.S. Government Printing Office, 1971; the *Dictionary of American Eiography*, Charles Scribner's, New York, 1928-1936; the *Encyclopedia of American Biography*, Harper and Row, New York, 1974 and *Who Was Who in America, 1607-1968*, Marquis Co., Chicago, 1943-1968.

Year	Candidate	Electoral Votes
1804	George Clinton (Democratic-Republican)	162
	Rufus King (Federalist)	14
1808	George Clinton (Democratic-Republican)[1]	113
	John Langdon (Democratic-Republican)	9
	James Madison (Democratic-Republican)	3
	James Monroe (Democratic-Republican)	3
	Rufus King (Federalist)	47
1812	Elbridge Gerry (Democratic-Republican)[2]	131
	Jared Ingersoll (Federalist)	86
1816	Daniel D. Tompkins (Democratic-Republican)	183
	John E. Howard (Federalist)[3]	22
	James Ross (Federalist)	5
	John Marshall (Federalist)	4
	Robert G. Harper (Federalist)	3
1820	Daniel D. Tompkins (Democratic-Republican)[4]	218
	Richard Rush (Democratic-Republican)	1
	Richard Stockton (Federalist)	8
	Daniel Rodney (Federalist)	4
	Robert G. Harper (Federalist)	1
1824	John C. Calhoun (Democratic-Republican)[5]	182
	Nathan Sanford (Democratic-Republican)	30
	Nathaniel Macon (Democratic-Republican)	24
	Andrew Jackson (Democratic-Republican)	13
	Martin Van Buren (Democratic-Republican)	9
	Henry Clay (Democratic-Republican)	2
1828	John C. Calhoun (Democratic-Republican)[6]	171

Year	Candidate	Electoral Votes
	William Smith (Independent Democratic-Republican)	7
	Richard Rush (National Republican)	83
1832	Martin Van Buren (Democratic)[7]	189
	William Wilkins (Democratic)	30
	Henry Lee (Independent Democratic)	11
	John Sergeant (National Republican)	49
	Amos Ellmaker (Anti-Masonic)	7
1836	Richard M. Johnson (Democratic)[8]	147
	William Smith (Independent Democratic)	23
	Francis Granger (Whig)	77
	John Tyler (Whig)	47
1840	John Tyler (Whig)	234
	Richard M. Johnson (Democratic)[9]	48
	L. W. Tazewell (Democratic)	11
	James K. Polk (Democratic)	1
1844	George M. Dallas (Democratic)	170
	Theodore Frelinghuysen (Whig)	105
1848	Millard Fillmore (Whig)	163
	William O. Butler (Democratic)	127
1852	William R. King (Democratic)	254
	William A. Graham (Whig)	42
1856	John C. Breckinridge (Democratic)	174
	William L. Dayton (Republican)	114
	Andrew J. Donelson (American)	8
1860	Hannibal Hamlin (Republican)	180
	Joseph Lane (Southern Democratic)	72
	Edward Everett (Constitutional Union)	39
	Herschel V. Johnson (Democratic)	12
1864	Andrew Johnson (Republican)	212
	George H. Pendleton (Democratic)	21
1868	Schuyler Colfax (Republican)	214
	Francis P. Blair (Democratic)	80
1872	Henry Wilson (Republican)	286
	Benjamin G. Brown (Democratic)[10]	47
	Alfred H. Colquitt (Democratic)	5
	John M. Palmer (Democratic)	3
	Thomas E. Bramlette (Democratic)	3
	William S. Groesbeck (Democratic)	1
	Willis B. Machen (Democratic)	1

	George W. Julian (Liberal Republican)	5
	Nathaniel P. Banks (Liberal Republican)	1
1876	William A. Wheeler (Republican)	185
	Thomas A. Hendricks (Democratic)	184
1880	Chester A. Arthur (Republican)	214
	William H. English (Democratic)	155
1884	Thomas A. Hendricks (Democratic)	219
	John A. Logan (Republican)	182
1888	Levi P. Morton (Republican)	233
	Allen G. Thurman (Democratic)	168
1892	Adlai E. Stevenson (Democratic)	277
	Whitelaw Reid (Republican)	145
	James G. Field (Populist)	22
1896	Garret A. Hobart (Republican)	271
	Arthur Sewall (Democratic)[11]	149
	Thomas E. Watson (Populist)	27
1900	Theodore Roosevelt (Republican)	292
	Adlai E. Stevenson (Democratic)	155
1904	Charles W. Fairbanks (Republican)	336
	Henry G. Davis (Democratic)	140
1908	James S. Sherman (Republican)	321
	John W. Kern (Democratic)	162
1912	Thomas R. Marshall (Democratic)	435
	Hiram W. Johnson (Progressive)	88
	Nicholas M. Butler (Republican)	8
1916	Thomas R. Marshall (Democratic)	277
	Charles W. Fairbanks (Republican)	254
1920	Calvin Coolidge (Republican)	404
	Franklin D. Roosevelt (Democratic)	127
1924	Charles G. Dawes (Republican)	382
	Charles W. Bryan (Democratic)	136
	Burton K. Wheeler (Progressive)	13
1928	Charles Curtis (Republican)	444
	Joseph T. Robinson (Democratic)	87

1932	John N. Garner (Democratic)	472
	Charles Curtis (Republican)	59
1936	John N. Garner (Democratic)	523
	Frank Knox (Republican)	8
1940	Henry A. Wallace (Democratic)	449
	Charles L. McNary (Republican)	82
1944	Harry S Truman (Democratic)	432
	John W. Bricker (Republican)	99
1948	Alben W. Barkley (Democratic)	303
	Earl Warren (Republican)	189
	Fielding L. Wright (States' Rights Democratic)	39
1952	Richard M. Nixon (Republican)	442
	John J. Sparkman (Democratic)	89
1956	Richard M. Nixon (Republican)	457
	Estes Kefauver (Democratic)	73
	Herman Talmadge (Democratic)	1
1960	Lyndon B. Johnson (Democratic)	303
	J. Strom Thurmond (Democratic)[12]	14
	Henry Cabot Lodge (Republican)	219
	Barry Goldwater (Republican)	1
1964	Hubert H. Humphrey (Democratic)	486
	William E. Miller (Republican)	52
1968	Spiro T. Agnew (Republican)	301
	Edmund S. Muskie (Democratic)	191
	Curtis E. LeMay (American Independent)	46
1972	Spiro T. Agnew (Republican)	520
	R. Sargent Shriver (Democratic)	17
	Theodora Nathan (Libertarian)	1
1976	Walter F. Mondale (Democratic)	297
	Robert J. Dole (Republican)[13]	241
1980	George Bush (Republican)	489
	Walter F. Mondale (Democratic)	49

1. New York cast 13 presidential electoral votes for Democratic-Republican James Madison and 6 votes for Clinton; for vice president, New York cast 13 votes for Clinton, 3 votes for Madison and 3 votes for Monroe.

Langdon received Ohio's three votes and Vermont's 6 votes.

2. The state-by-state vote for Gerry was the same as for Democratic-Republican presidential candidate Madison except for Massachusetts and New Hampshire. Massachusetts cast 2 votes for Gerry and 20 votes for Ingersoll; New Hampshire cast 1 vote for Gerry and 7 votes for Ingersoll.

3. Four Federalists received vice presidential electoral votes: Howard—Massachusetts, 22 votes; Ross—Connecticut, 5 votes; Marshall—Connecticut, 4 votes; Harper—Delaware, 3 votes.

4. The state-by-state vote for Tompkins was the same as for Democratic-Republican presidential candidate James Monroe except for Delaware, Maryland and Massachusetts. Delaware cast 4 votes for Rodney; Maryland cast 10 votes for Tompkins and one for Harper; Massachusetts cast 7 votes for Tompkins and 8 for Stockton.

New Hamsphire, which cast 7 presidential electoral votes for Monroe and 1 vote for John Quincy Adams, cast 7 vice presidential electoral votes for Tompkins and 1 vote for Rush.

5. The state-by-state vice presidential electoral vote was as follows:

Calhoun—Alabama, 5 votes; Delaware, 1 vote; Illinois, 3 votes; Indiana, 5 votes; Kentucky, 7 votes; Louisiana, 5 votes; Maine, 9 votes; Maryland, 10 votes; Massachusetts, 15 votes; Mississippi, 3 votes; New Hampshire, 7 votes; New Jersey, 8 votes; New York, 29 votes; North Carolina, 15 votes; Pennsylvania, 28 votes; Rhode Island, 3 votes; South Carolina, 11 votes; Tennessee, 11 votes; Vermont, 7 votes.

Sanford—Kentucky, 7 votes; New York, 7 votes; Ohio, 16 votes.

Macon—Virginia, 24 votes.

Jackson—Connecticut, 8 votes; Maryland, 1 vote; Missouri, 3 votes; New Hamphire, 1 vote.

Van Buren—Georgia, 9 votes.

Clay—Delaware, 2 votes.

6. The state-by-state vote for Calhoun was the same as for Democratic-Republican presidential candidate Jackson except for Georgia, which cast 2 votes for Calhoun and 7 votes for Smith.

7. The state-by-state vote for Van Buren was the same as for Democratic presidential candidate Jackson except for Pennsylvania which cast 30 votes for Wilkins.

South Carolina cast 11 presidential electoral votes for Independent Democratic presidential candidate Floyd and 11 votes for Independent Democratic vice presidential candidate Lee.

Vermont cast 7 presidential electoral votes for Anti-Masonic candidate Wirt and 7 vice presidential electoral votes for Wirt's running mate, Ellmaker.

8. The state-by-state vote for Johnson was the same as for Democratic presidential candidate Van Buren except that cast 23 votes for Smith.

Granger's state-by-state vote was the same as for Whig presidential candidate Harrison except for Maryland and Massachusetts. Maryland cast 10 presidential electoral votes for Harrison and 10 vice presidential votes for Tyler; Massachusetts cast 14

presidential electoral votes for Whig candidate Webster and 14 vice presidential votes for Granger.

Tyler received 11 votes from Georgia, 10 from Maryland, 11 from South Carolina and 15 from Tennessee.

No vice presidential candidate received a majority of the electoral vote. As a result, the Senate, for the only time in history, selected the vice president under the provisions of the 12th Amendment. Johnson was elected vice president by a vote of 33 to 16 for Granger.

9. The Democratic Party did not nominate a vice presidential candidate in 1840. Johnson's state-by-state vote was the same as for presidential candidate Van Buren except for South Carolina and Virginia.

South Carolina cast 11 votes for Tazewell.

Virginia cast 23 presidential electoral votes for Van Buren, 22 vice presidential votes for Johnson and 1 vice presidential vote for Polk.

10. Liberal Republican and Democratic presidential candidate Horace Greeley died Nov. 29, 1872. As a result, 18 electors pledged to Greeley cast their presidential electoral votes for Brown, Greeley's running mate.

The vice presidential vote was as follows:

Brown—Georgia, 5 votes; Kentucky, 8 votes; Maryland, 8 votes; Missouri, 6 votes; Tennessee, 12 votes; Texas, 8 votes.

Colquitt—Georgia, 5 votes.

Palmer—Missouri, 3 votes.

Bramlette—Kentucky, 3 votes.

Groesbeck—Missouri, 1 vote.

Machen—Kentucky, 1 vote.

Julian—Missouri, 5 votes.

Banks—Georgia, 1 vote.

11. The state-by-state vote for Sewell was the same as for Democratic-Populist candidate William Jennings Bryan except for the following states which cast electoral votes for Thomas E. Watson: Arkansas—3 votes; Louisiana—4 votes; Missouri—4 votes; Montana—1 vote; Nebraska—4 votes; North Carolina—5 votes; South Dakota—2 votes; Utah—1 vote; Washington—2 votes; Wyoming—1 vote.

12. Democratic electors carried Alabama's 11 electoral votes. Five of the electors were pledged to the national Democratic ticket of John F. Kennedy and Lyndon B. Johnson. Six electors ran unpledged and voted for Harry F. Byrd for president and Thurmond for vice president.

Mississippi's 8 electors voted for Byrd and Thurmond.

In Oklahoma, the Republican ticket of Richard M. Nixon and Henry Cabot Lodge carried the state, but one of the state's 8 electors voted for Byrd for president and Goldwater for vice president.

13. One Republican elector from the state of Washington cast his presidential electoral vote for Ronald Reagan instead of the Republican nominee, Gerald R. Ford. But he voted for Robert J. Dole, Ford's running mate, for vice president. Thus Dole received one more electoral vote than Ford.

Biographical Directory of Presidential and Vice Presidential Candidates

The names in the directory include all persons who have received electoral votes for president or vice president since 1789. Also included are a number of prominent third party candidates who received popular votes but no electoral votes. The material is organized as follows: Name, state(s) in the year(s) the individual received electoral votes, party or parties with which the individual was identified at the time(s) they received electoral votes, dates of birth and death (where applicable), major offices held, and the year(s) in which the person received electoral votes. For third party candidates who received no electoral votes, the dates indicate the year(s) in which they were candidates.

For the elections of 1789, 1792, 1796 and 1800 presidential electors did not vote separately for president and vice president. It was, therefore, difficult in many cases to determine whether an individual receiving electoral votes in these elections was a candidate for president or vice president. Where no determination could be made from the sources consulted by Congressional Quarterly, the year(s)

in which the individual received electoral votes is given with no specification as to whether the individual was a candidate for president or vice president.

The following sources were used: *Biographical Directory of the American Congress, 1774-1971*, U.S. Government Printing Office, 1971; *Dictionary of American Biography*, Charles Scribner's Sons, New York, 1928-36; *Encyclopedia of American Biography*, John A. Garraty editor, Harper and Row, New York, 1974; *Who's Who in American Politics*, 6th edition, 1977-78, edited by Jaques Cattell Press, R. R. Bowker Co., New York, 1977; *Who Was Who in America, 1607-1968*, Marquis Co., Chicago, 1943-68: Petersen, Svend, *A Statistical History of the American Presidential Elections*, Frederick Ungar Publishing Co., New York, 1968; Scammon, Richard M., *America Votes 10* (1972), Governmental Affairs Institute, Congressional Quarterly, Washington, 1973; *America Votes 12* (1976), Governmental Affairs Institute, Congressional Quarterly, Washington, 1977; *America Votes 14* (1980), Elections Research Center, Washington, 1981.

ADAMS, Charles Francis - Mass. (Free Soil) Aug. 18, 1807 - Nov. 21, 1886; House, 1859-61; Minister to Great Britain, 1861-68; Candidacy: VP - 1848.

ADAMS, John - Mass. (Federalist) Oct. 30, 1735 - July 4, 1826; Continental Congress, 1774; signer of Declaration of Independence, 1776; Minister to Great Britain, 1785; Vice President, 1789-97; President, 1797-1801; Candidacies: VP - 1789, 1792; P - 1796, 1800.

ADAMS, John Quincy - Mass. (Democratic-Republican, National Republican) July 11, 1767 - Feb. 23, 1848; Senate, 1803-08; Minister to Russia, 1809-14; Minister to Great Britain, 1815-17; Secretary of State, 1817-25; President, 1825-29; House, 1831-48; Candidacies: P - 1820, 1824, 1828.

ADAMS, Samuel - Mass. (Federalist) Sept. 27, 1722 - Oct. 2, 1803; Continental Congress, 1774-82; signer of Declaration of Independence; Governor, 1794-97; Candidacy: 1796.

AGNEW, Spiro Theodore - Md. (Republican) Nov. 9, 1918—; Governor, 1967-69; Vice President, 1969-73 (resigned Oct. 10, 1973); Candidacies: VP - 1968, 1972.

ANDERSON, John B. - Ill. (Republican, Independent) Feb. 15, 1922—; state's attorney, 1956-60; U.S. House, 1961-80. Candidacy: P - 1980.

ARMSTRONG, James - Pa. (Federalist) Aug. 29, 1748 - May 6, 1828; House, 1793-95; Candidacy: 1789.

ARTHUR, Chester Alan - N.Y. (Republican) Oct. 5, 1830 - Nov. 18, 1886; Collector, Port of N.Y., 1871-78; Vice President, 1881; President (succeeded James A. Garfield, who was assassinated) 1881-85; Candidacy: VP - 1880.

BANKS, Nathaniel Prentice - Mass. (Liberal Republican) Jan. 30, 1816 - Sept. 1, 1894; House, 1853-57, 1865-73, 1875-79, 1889-91; Governor, 1858-61; Candidacy: VP - 1872.

BARKLEY, Alben William - Ky. (Democratic) Nov. 24, 1877 - April 30, 1956; House, 1913-27; Senate, 1927-49, 1955-56; Senate majority leader, 1937-47; Senate minority leader, 1947-49; Vice President, 1949-53; Candidacy: VP - 1948.

BELL, John - Tenn. (Constitutional Union) Feb. 15, 1797 - Sept. 10, 1869; House, 1827-41; House Speaker, 1834-35; Secretary of War, 1841; Senate, 1847-59; Candidacy: P - 1860.

BENSON, Allan Louis - N.Y. (Socialist) Nov. 6, 1871 - Aug. 19, 1940; Writer, editor; founder of *Reconstruction Magazine*, 1918; Candidacy: P - 1916.

BIDWELL, John - Calif. (Prohibition) Aug. 5, 1819 - April 4, 1900; California pioneer; Major in Mexican War; House, 1865-67; Candidacy: P - 1892.

BIRNEY, James Gillespie - N.Y. (Liberty) Feb. 4, 1792 - Nov. 25, 1857; Kentucky state legislature, 1816-17; Alabama state legislature, 1819-20; Candidacies: P - 1840, 1844.

BLAINE, James Gillespie - Maine (Republican) Jan. 31, 1830 - Jan. 27, 1893; House, 1863-76; House speaker, 1869-75; Senate, 1876-81; Secretary of State, 1881, 1889-92; President, first Pan American Congress, 1889; Candidacy: P - 1884.

BLAIR, Francis Preston Jr. - Mo. (Democratic) Feb. 19, 1821 - July 8, 1875; House, 1857-59, 1860, 1861-62, 1863-64; Senate, 1871-73; Candidacy: VP - 1868.

BRECKINRIDGE, John Cabell - Ky. (Democratic, Southern Democratic) Jan. 21, 1821 - May 17, 1875; House, 1851-55; Vice President, 1857-61; Senate, 1861; major general, Confederacy, 1861-65; Secretary of War, Confederacy, 1865; Candidacies: VP - 1856; P - 1860.

BRICKER, John William - Ohio (Republican) Sept. 6, 1893—; Attorney General of Ohio, 1933-37; Governor, 1939-45; Senate, 1947-59; Candidacy: VP - 1944.

BROWN, Benjamin Gratz - Mo. (Democratic) May 28, 1826 - Dec. 13, 1885; Senate, 1863-67; Governor, 1871-73; Candidacy: VP - 1872.

BRYAN, Charles Wayland - Neb. (Democratic) Feb. 10, 1867 - March 4, 1945;

Governor, 1923-25, 1931-35; Candidacy: VP - 1924.

BRYAN, William Jennings - Neb. (Democratic, Populist) March 19, 1860 - July 26, 1925; House, 1891-95; Secretary of State, 1913-15; Candidacies: P - 1896, 1900, 1908.

BUCHANAN, James - Pa. (Democratic) April 23, 1791 - June 1, 1868; House, 1821-31; Minister to Russia, 1832-34; Senate, 1834-45; Secretary of State, 1845-49; Minister to Great Britain, 1853-56; President, 1857-61; Candidacy: P - 1856.

BURR, Aaron - N.Y. (Democratic-Republican) Feb. 6, 1756 - Sept. 14, 1836; Attorney General of N.Y., 1789-90; Senate, 1791-97; Vice President, 1801-05; Candidacies: 1792, 1796, 1800.

BUSH, George - Texas (Republican) June 12, 1924—; House, 1967-70; ambassador to the United Nations, 1971-73; chairman of the Republican National Committee, 1973-74; head of the U.S. Liaison office in Peking, 1974-75; director of the Central Intelligence Agency, 1976-77; Vice President, 1981—; Candidacy, VP - 1980.

BUTLER, Nicholas Murray - N.Y. (Republican) April 2, 1862 - Dec. 7, 1947; president, Columbia University, 1901-45; president, Carnegie Endowment for International Peace, 1925-45; Candidacy: VP - 1912 (Substituted as candidate after Oct. 30, 1912, death of nominee James S. Sherman.)

BUTLER, William Orlando - Ky. (Democratic) April 19, 1791 - Aug. 6, 1880; House, 1839-43; Candidacy: VP-1848.

BYRD, Harry Flood - Va. (States' Rights Democratic. Independent Democratic) June 10, 1887 - Oct. 20, 1966; Governor, 1926-30; Senate, 1933-65; Candidacies: P - 1956, 1960.

CALHOUN, John Caldwell - S.C. (Democratic-Republican, Democratic) March 18, 1782-March 31, 1850; House, 1811-17; Secretary of War, 1817-25; Vice President, 1825-32; Senate, 1832-43, 1845-50; Secretary of State, 1844-45; Candidacies: VP - 1824, 1828.

CARTER, James Earl Jr. - Ga. (Democratic) Oct. 1, 1924—; state senate, 1963-67; Governor, 1971-75; President, 1977-81; Candidacy: P - 1976, 1980.

CASS, Lewis - Mich. (Democratic) Oct. 9, 1782 - June 17, 1866; Military and civil governor of Michigan Territory, 1813-31; Secretary of War, 1831-36; Minister to France, 1836-42; Senate, 1845-48, 1849-57; Secretary of State, 1857-60; Candidacy: P - 1848.

CLAY, Henry - Ky. (Democratic-Republican, National Republican, Whig) April 12, 1777-June 29, 1852; Senate, 1806-07, 1810-11, 1831-42, 1849-52; House, 1811-14, 1815-21, 1823-25; House Speaker, 1811-14, 1815-20, 1823-25; Secretary of State, 1825-29; Candidacies: P - 1824, 1832, 1844.

CLEVELAND, Stephen Grover - N.Y. (Democratic) March 18, 1837 - June 24, 1908; Mayor of Buffalo, 1882; Governor, 1883-85; President, 1885-89, 1893-97; Candidacies: P - 1884, 1888, 1892.

CLINTON, De Witt - N.Y. (independent Democratic-Republican, Federalist) March 2, 1769 - Feb. 11, 1828; Senate, 1802-03; Mayor of New York, 1803-07, 1810, 1811, 1813, 1814; Governor, 1817-23, 1825-28; Candidacy: P - 1812.

CLINTON, George - N.Y. (Democratic-Republican) July 26, 1739 - April 20, 1812; Continental Congress, 1775-76; Governor, 1777-95, 1801-04; Vice President, 1805-12; Candidacies: VP-1789, 1792, 1796, 1804, 1808.

COLFAX, Schuyler - Ind. (Republican) March 23, 1823 - Jan. 13, 1885; House, 1855-69; Speaker of the House, 1863-69; Vice President, 1869-73; Candidacy: VP - 1868.

COLQUITT, Alfred Holt - Ga. (Democratic) April 20, 1824 - March 26, 1894; House, 1853-55; Governor, 1877-82; Senate, 1883-94; Candidacy: VP - 1872.

COOLIDGE, Calvin - Mass. (Republican) July 4, 1872 - Jan. 5, 1933; Governor, 1919-21; Vice President, 1921-23; President, 1923-29; Candidacies: VP - 1920; P - 1924.

COX, James Middleton - Ohio (Democratic) March 31, 1870 - July 15, 1957; House, 1909-13; Governor, 1913-15, 1917-21; Candidacy: P - 1920.

CRAWFORD, William Harris - Ga. (Democratic-Republican) Feb. 24, 1772 - Sept. 15, 1834; Senate, 1807-13; President pro tempore of the Senate, 1812-13; Secretary of War, 1815-16; Secretary of the Treasury, 1816-25; Candidacy: P - 1824.

CURTIS, Charles - Kan. (Republican) Jan. 25, 1860 - Feb. 8, 1936; House, 1893-1907; Senate, 1907-13, 1915-29; President pro tempore, 1911; Vice President, 1929-33; Candidacies: VP - 1928, 1932.

DALLAS, George Mifflin - Pa. (Democratic) July 10, 1792 - Dec. 31, 1864; Senate, 1831-33; Minister to Russia, 1837-39; Vice President, 1845-49; Minister to Great Britain, 1856-61; Candidacy: VP - 1844.

DAVIS, David - Ill. (Democratic) March 9, 1815 - June 26, 1886; Associate Justice of the Supreme Court, 1862-77; Senate, 1877-83; Candidacy: P - 1872.

DAVIS, Henry Gassaway - W.Va. (Democratic) Nov. 16, 1823 - March 11, 1916; Senate, 1871-83; Chairman of Pan American Railway Committee, 1901-16; Candidacy: VP - 1904.

DAVIS, John William - W. Va. (Democratic) April 13, 1873 - March 24, 1955; House, 1911-13; Solicitor General, 1913-18; Ambassador to Great Britain, 1918-21; Candidacy: P - 1924.

DAWES, Charles Gates - Ill. (Republican) Aug. 27, 1865 - Apr. 23, 1951; U.S. Comptroller of the Currency, 1898-1901; first Director of the Bureau of the Budget, 1921-22; Vice President, 1925-29; Ambassador to Great Britain, 1929-32; Candidacy: VP - 1924.

DAYTON, William Lewis - N.J. (Republican) Feb. 17, 1807 - Dec. 1, 1864; Senate, 1842-51; Minister to France, 1861-64; Candidacy: VP - 1856.

DEBS, Eugene Victor - Ind. (Socialist) Nov. 5, 1855 - Oct. 20, 1926; Indiana legislature, 1885; president, American Railway Union, 1893-97; Candidacies: P - 1900, 1904, 1908, 1912, 1920.

DEWEY, Thomas Edmund - N.Y. (Republican) March 24, 1902 - March 16, 1971; District Attorney, New York County, 1937-41; Governor, 1943-55; Candidacies: P - 1944, 1948.

DOLE, Robert Joseph - Kan. (Republican) July 22, 1923—; House, 1961-69; Senate, 1969—; Candidacy: VP - 1976.

DONELSON, Andrew Jackson - Tenn. (American "Know-Nothing") Aug. 25, 1799 - June 26, 1871; Minister to Prussia, 1846-48; Minister to Germany, 1848-49; Candidacy: VP - 1856.

DOUGLAS, Stephen Arnold - Ill. (Democratic) April 23, 1813 - June 3, 1861; House, 1843-47; Senate, 1847-61; Candidacy: P - 1860.

EAGLETON, Thomas Francis - Mo. (Democratic) Sept. 4, 1929—; Attorney General of Missouri, 1961-65; Lieutenant Governor, 1965-68; Senate, 1968—; Candidacy: VP - 1972 (resigned from Democratic ticket July 31, replaced by R. Sargent Shriver Jr.)

EISENHOWER, Dwight David - N.Y., Pa. (Republican) Oct. 14, 1890 - March 28, 1969; General of U.S. Army, 1943-48; Army chief of staff, 1945-48; president of Columbia University, 1948-51; Commander of North Atlantic Treaty Organization, 1951-52; President, 1953-61; Candidacies: P - 1952, 1956.

ELLMAKER, Amos - Pa. (Anti-Masonic) Feb. 2, 1787 - Nov. 28, 1851; House, 1815; Attorney General of Pennsylvania, 1816-19, 1828-29; Candidacy: VP - 1832.

ELLSWORTH, Oliver - Conn. (Federalist) April 29, 1745 - Nov. 26, 1807; Continental Congress, 1777-84; Senate, 1789-96; Chief Justice of U.S. Supreme Court, 1796-1800; Minister to France, 1799; Candidacy: 1796.

ENGLISH, William Hayden - Ind. (Democratic) Aug. 27, 1822 - Feb. 7, 1896; House, 1853-61; Candidacy: VP - 1880.

EVERETT, Edward - Mass. (Constitutional Union) April 11, 1794 - Jan. 15, 1865; House, 1825-35; Governor, 1836-40; Minister to Great Britain, 1841-45; President of Harvard University, 1846-49; Secretary of State, 1852-53; Senate, 1853-54; Candidacy: VP- 1860.

FAIRBANKS, Charles Warren - Ind. (Republican) May 11, 1852 - June 4, 1918; Senate, 1897-1905; Vice President, 1905-09; Candidacies: VP - 1904, 1916.

FIELD, James Gaven - Va. (Populist) Feb. 24, 1826 - Oct. 12, 1901; major in the Confederate Army, 1861-65; Attorney General of Virginia, 1877-82; Candidacy: VP- 1892.

FILLMORE, Millard - N.Y. (Whig, (American "Know-Nothing") Jan. 7, 1800 - March 8, 1874; House, 1833-35, 1837-43; N.Y. Comptroller, 1847-49; Vice President, 1849-50; President, 1850-53; Candidates: VP - 1848; P - 1856.

FISK, Clinton Bowen - N.J. (Prohibition) Dec. 8, 1828 - July 9, 1890; Civil War brevet major general; founder Fisk University, 1866; member Board of Indian Commissioners, 1874, president, 1881-90; Candidacy: P - 1888.

FLOYD, John - Va. (Independent Democratic) April 24, 1783 - Aug. 17, 1837; House, 1817-29; Governor, 1830-34; Candidacy: P - 1832.

FORD, Gerald Rudolph Jr. - Mich. (Republican) July 14, 1913—; House, 1949-73; Vice President, 1973-74; President, 1974-77; Candidacy: P - 1976.

FRELINGHUYSEN, Theodore - N.J. (Whig) March 28, 1787 - April 12, 1862; Attorney General of New Jersey, 1817-29; Senate, 1829-35; president of Rutgers College, 1850-62; Candidacy: VP - 1844.

FREMONT, John Charles - Calif. (Republican) Jan. 21, 1813 - July 13, 1890; explorer and Army officer in West before 1847; Senate, 1850-51; Gover-

nor of Arizona Territory, 1878-81; Candidacy: P - 1856.

GARFIELD, James Abram - Ohio (Republican) Nov. 19, 1831 - Sept. 19, 1881; Major General in Union Army during Civil War; House, 1863-80; President, Mar. 4-Sept. 19, 1881; Candidacy: P - 1880.

GARNER, John Nance - Texas (Democratic) Nov. 22, 1868 - Nov. 7, 1967; House, 1903-33; Speaker of the House, 1931-33; Vice President, 1933-41; Candidacies: VP- 1932, 1936.

GERRY, Elbridge - Mass. (Democratic-Republican) July 17, 1744 - Nov. 23, 1814; Continental Congress, 1776-81, 1782-85; signer of Declaration of Independence; Constitutional Convention, 1787; House, 1789-93; Governor, 1810-12; Vice President, 1813-14; Candidacy: VP - 1812.

GOLDWATER, Barry Morris - Ariz. (Republican) Jan. 1, 1909—; Senate, 1953-65, 1969—; Candidacies: VP - 1960; P - 1964.

GRAHAM, William Alexander - N.C. (Whig) Sept. 5, 1804 - Aug. 11, 1875; Senate, 1840-43; Governor, 1845-49; Secretary of the Navy, 1850-52; Confederate Senate, 1864; Candidacy: VP - 1852.

GRANGER, Francis - N.Y. (Whig) Dec. 1, 1792 - Aug. 31, 1868; House, 1835-37, 1839-41, 1841-43; Postmaster General, 1841; Candidacy: VP - 1836.

GRANT, Ulysses Simpson - Ill. (Republican) April 27, 1822 - July 23, 1885; commander-in-chief, Union Army during Civil War; Secretary of War, 1867; President, 1869-77; Candidacies: P - 1868, 1872.

GREELEY, Horace - N.Y. (Liberal Republican, Democratic) Feb. 3, 1811 - Nov. 29, 1872; founder and editor, *New York Tribune,* 1841-72; House, 1848-49; Candidacy: P - 1872.

GRIFFIN, S. Marvin - Ga. (American Independent) Sept. 4, 1907—; Governor, 1955-59; Candidacy: VP - 1968.

GROESBECK, William Slocum - Ohio (Democratic) July 24, 1815 - July 7, 1897; House, 1857-59; delegate to International Monetary Conference in Paris, 1878; Candidacy: VP - 1872.

HALE, John Parker - N.H. (Free Soil) Mar. 31, 1806 - Nov. 19, 1873; House, 1843-45; Senate, 1847-53, 1855-65; Minister to Spain, 1865-69; Candidacy: P - 1852.

HAMLIN, Hannibal - Maine (Republican) Aug. 27, 1809 - July 4, 1891; House, 1843-47; Senate, 1848-57, 1857-61, 1869-81; Governor, Jan. 8-Feb. 20,

1857; Vice President, 1861-65; Candidacy: VP - 1860.

HANCOCK, John - Mass. (Federalist) Jan. 12, 1737 - Oct. 8, 1793; Continental Congress, 1775-80, 1785-86; president of Continental Congress, 1775-77; Governor, 1780-85, 1787-93; Candidacy: 1789.

HANCOCK, Winfield Scott - Pa. (Democratic) Feb. 14, 1824 - Feb. 9, 1886; Brigadier General, commander of II Army Corps, Civil War; Candidacy: P - 1880.

HARDING, Warren Gamaliel - Ohio (Republican) Nov. 2, 1865 - Aug. 2, 1923; Lieutenant Governor, 1904-05; Senate, 1915-21; President, 1921-23; Candidacy: P - 1920.

HARPER, Robert Goodloe - Md. (Federalist) Jan. 1765 - Jan. 14, 1825; House, 1795-1801; Senate, 1816; Candidacy: VP- 1816, 1820.

HARRISON, Benjamin - Ind. (Republican) Aug. 20, 1833-March 13, 1901; Union officer in Civil War; Senate, 1881-87; President, 1889-93; Candidacies: P - 1888, 1892.

HARRISON, Robert H. - Md. 1745 - 1790; chief justice General Court of Maryland, 1781; Candidacy: 1789.

HARRISON, William Henry - Ohio (Whig) Feb. 9, 1773 - April 4, 1841; delegate to Congress from the Northwest Territory, 1799-1800; Territorial Governor of Indiana, 1801-13; House, 1816-19; Senate, 1825-28; President, Mar. 4 - April 4, 1841; Candidacies: P - 1836, 1840.

HAYES, Rutherford Birchard - Ohio (Republican) Oct. 4, 1822 - Jan. 17, 1893; Major General in Union Army during Civil War; House, 1865-67; Governor, 1868-72, 1876-77; President, 1877-81; Candidacy: P - 1876.

HENDRICKS, Thomas Andrews - Ind. (Democratic) Sept. 7, 1819 - Nov. 25, 1885; House, 1851-55; Senate, 1863-69; Governor, 1873-77; Vice President, 1885; Candidacies: P - 1872; VP - 1876, 1884.

HENRY, John - Md. (Democratic-Republican) Nov. 1750 - Dec. 16, 1798; Continental Congress, 1778-81, 1784-87; Senate, 1789-97; Governor, 1797-98; Candidacy: 1796.

HOBART, Garret Augustus - N.J. (Republican) June 3, 1844 - Nov. 21, 1899; New Jersey senate, 1876-82; president of New Jersey senate, 1881-82; Republican National Committee, 1884-

96; Vice President, 1897-99; Candidacy: VP - 1896.

HOOVER, Herbert Clark - Calif. (Republican) Aug. 10, 1874 - Oct. 20, 1964; U.S. Food Administrator, 1917-19; Secretary of Commerce, 1921-28; President, 1929-33; chairman, Commission on Organization of the Executive Branch of Government, 1947-49. 1953-55; Candidacies: P - 1928, 1932.

HOSPERS, John - Calif. (Libertarian) June 9. 1918—; director of school of philosophy at University of Southern California; Candidacy: P - 1972.

HOWARD, John Eager - Md. (Federalist) June 4, 1752 - Oct. 12, 1827; Continental Congress, 1784-88; Governor, 1788-91; Senate, 1796-1803; Candidacy: VP-1816.

HUGHES, Charles Evans - N.Y. (Republican) April 11, 1862 - Aug. 27, 1948; Governor, 1907-10; Associate Justice of U.S. Supreme Court, 1910-16: Secretary of State, 1921-25; Chief Justice of U.S. Supreme Court, 1930-41; Candidacy: P - 1916.

HUMPHREY, Hubert Horatio Jr. - Minn. (Democratic) May 27, 1911 - Jan. 13, 1978; mayor of Minneapolis, 1945-48; Senate, 1949-64, 1971-78; Vice President, 1965-69; Candidacies: VP - 1964; P - 1968.

HUNTINGTON, Samuel - Conn., July 3, 1731 - Jan. 5, 1796; Continental Congress, 1776-84; president of Continental Congress, 1779-81, 1783; Governor, 1786-96; Candidacy: 1789.

INGERSOLL, Jared - Pa. (Federalist) Oct. 24. 1749 - Oct. 31, 1822; Continental Congress, 1780-81; Constitutional Convention, 1787; Candidacy: VP - 1812.

IREDELL, James - N.C. (Federalist) Oct. 5, 1751 - Oct. 20, 1799; Associate Justice of U.S. Supreme Court, 1790-99; Candidacy: 1796.

JACKSON, Andrew - Tenn. (Democratic-Republican, Democratic) March 15, 1767 - June 8, 1845; House, 1796-97; Senate, 1797-98; 1823-25; Territorial Governor of Florida, 1821; President, 1829-37; Candidacies: P - 1824, 1828, 1832.

JAY, John - N.Y.(Federalist) Dec. 12, 1745 - May 17, 1829; Continental Congress, 1774-77, 1778-79; president of Continental Congress, 1778-79; Minister to Spain, 1779; Chief Justice of U.S. Supreme Court, 1789-95; Governor, 1795-1801; Candidacies: 1789, 1796, 1800.

JEFFERSON, Thomas - Va. (Democratic-Republican) April 13, 1743 - July 4, 1826; Continental Congress, 1775-76, 1783-85; author and signer of Declaration of Independence, 1776; Governor, 1779-81; Minister to France, 1784-89, Secretary of State, 1789-93; Vice President, 1797-1801; President, 1801-09; Candidacies: VP - 1792; P - 1796, 1800, 1804.

JENKINS, Charles Jones - Ga. (Democratic) Jan. 6, 1805 - June 14, 1883; Governor, 1865-68; Candidacy: P - 1872.

JOHNSON, Andrew - Tenn. (Republican) Dec. 29, 1808 - July 31, 1875; House, 1843-53; Governor, 1853-57; Senate, 1857-62, 1875; Vice President, 1865; President, 1865-69; Candidacy: VP - 1864.

JOHNSON, Herschel Vespasian - Ga. (Democratic) Sept. 18, 1812 - Aug. 16, 1880; Senate, 1848-49; Governor, 1853-57; Senator in Confederate Congress, 1862-65; Candidacy: VP-1860.

JOHNSON, Hiram Warren - Calif. (Progressive) Sept. 2, 1866 - Aug. 6, 1945; Governor, 1911-17; Senate, 1917-45; Candidacy: VP- 1912.

JOHNSON, Lyndon Baines - Texas (Democratic) Aug. 27, 1908 - Jan. 22, 1973; House, 1937-49; Senate, 1949-61; Vice President, 1961-63; President, 1963-69; Candidacies: VP - 1960; P - 1964.

JOHNSON, Richard Mentor - Ky. (Democratic) Oct. 17, 1781 - Nov. 19, 1850; House, 1807-19, 1829-37; Senate, 1819-29; Vice President, 1837-41; Candidacies: VP - 1836, 1840.

JOHNSTON, Samuel - N.C. (Federalist) Dec. 15, 1733 - Aug. 18, 1816; Continental Congress, 1780-82; Senate, 1789-93; Candidacy: 1796.

JONES, Walter Burgwyn - Ala. (Independent Democratic) Oct. 16, 1888 - Aug. 1, 1963; Alabama legislature, 1919-20; Alabama circuit court judge, 1920-35; Presiding judge, 1935-63; Candidacy: P - 1956.

JULIAN, George Washington - Ind. (Free Soil, Liberal Republican) May 5, 1817 - July 7, 1899; House, 1849-51, 1861-71; Candidacies: VP - 1852, 1872.

KEFAUVER, Estes - Tenn. (Democratic) July 26, 1903 - Aug. 10, 1963; House, 1939-49; Senate, 1949-63; Candidacy: VP - 1956.

KENNEDY, John Fitzgerald - Mass. (Democratic) May 29, 1917 - Nov. 22, 1963; House, 1947-53; Senate, 1953-60; President, 1961-63; Candidacy: P - 1960.

KERN, John Worth - Ind. (Democratic) Dec. 20, 1849 - Aug. 17, 1917; Senate, 1911-17; Candidacy: VP - 1908.

KING, Rufus - N.Y. (Federalist) March 24, 1755 - April 29, 1827; Continental Congress, 1784-87; Constitutional Convention, 1787; Senate, 1789-96, 1813-25; Minister to Great Britain, 1796-1803, 1825-26; Candidacies: VP - 1804, 1808; P - 1816.

KING, William Rufus de Vane - Ala. (Democratic) April 7, 1786 - April 18, 1853; House, 1811-16; Senate, 1819-44, 1848-52; Minister to France, 1844-46; Vice President, March 4 - April 18, 1853; Candidacy: VP - 1852.

KNOX, Franklin - Ill. (Republican) Jan. 1, 1874 - April 28, 1944; Secretary of Navy, 1940-44; Candidacy: VP - 1936.

LA FOLLETTE, Robert Marion - Wis. (Progressive) June 14, 1855 - June 18, 1925; House, 1885-91; Governor, 1901-06; Senate, 1906-25; Candidacy: P - 1924.

LANDON, Alfred Mossman - Kan. (Republican) Sept. 9, 1887—; Governor, 1933-37; Candidacy: P - 1936.

LANE, Joseph - Ore. (Southern Democratic) Dec. 14, 1801 - April 19, 1881; Governor of Oregon Territory, 1849-50, May 16-19, 1853; House (Territorial Delegate), 1851-59; Senate, 1859-61; Candidacy: VP - 1860.

LANGDON, John - N.H. (Democratic-Republican) June 25, 1741 - Sept. 18, 1819; Continental Congress, 1775-1776, 1783; Governor, 1788-89; 1805-09, 1810-12; Senate, 1789-1801; first president pro tempore of Senate, 1789; Candidacies: VP - 1808.

LEE, Henry - Mass. (Independent Democratic) Feb. 4, 1782 - Feb. 6, 1867; Merchant and publicist; Candidacy: VP - 1832.

LeMAY, Curtis Emerson - Ohio (American Independent) Nov. 15, 1906—; Air Force Chief of Staff, 1961-65; Candidacy: VP - 1968.

LEMKE, William - N.D. (Union) Aug. 13, 1878 - May 30, 1950; House, 1933-41, 1943-50; Candidacy: P - 1936.

LINCOLN, Abraham - Ill. (Republican) Feb. 12, 1809 - April 15, 1865; House, 1847-49; President, 1861-65; Candidacies: P - 1860, 1864.

LINCOLN, Benjamin - Mass. (Federalist) Jan. 24, 1733 - May 9, 1810; Major

General in Continental Army, 1777-81; Secretary of War, 1781-83; Candidacy: 1789.

LODGE, Henry Cabot Jr. - Mass. (Republican) July 5, 1902—; Senate, 1937-44, 1947-53; Ambassador to United Nations, 1953-60; Ambassador to Republic of Vietnam, 1963-64, 1965-67; Candidacy: VP - 1960.

LOGAN, John Alexander - Ill. (Republican) Feb. 9, 1826 - Dec. 26, 1886; House, 1859-62, 1867-71; Senate, 1871-77, 1879-86; Candidacy: VP- 1884.

MACHEN, Willis Benson - Ky. (Democratic) April 10, 1810 - Sept. 29, 1893; Confederate Congress, 1861-65; Senate, 1872-73; Candidacy: VP- 1872.

MACON, Nathaniel - N.C. (Democratic-Republican) Dec. 17, 1757 - June 29, 1837; House, 1791-1815; Speaker of the House, 1801-07; Senate, 1815-28; Candidacy: VP- 1824.

MADISON, James - Va. (Democratic-Republican) March 16, 1751 - June 28, 1836; Continental Congress, 1780-83, 1786-88; Constitutional Convention, 1787; House, 1789-97; Secretary of State, 1801-09; President, 1809-17; Candidacies: P - 1808, 1812.

MANGUM, Willie Person - N.C. (Independent Democrat) May 10, 1792 - Sept. 7, 1861; House, 1823-26; Senate, 1831-36, 1840-53; Candidacy: P - 1836.

MARSHALL, John - Va. (Federalist) Sept. 24, 1755 - July 6, 1835; House 1799-1800; Secretary of State, 1800-01; Chief Justice of U.S. Supreme Court, 1801-35; Candidacy: VP - 1816.

MARSHALL, Thomas Riley - Ind. (Democratic) March 14, 1854 - June 1, 1925; Governor, 1909-13; Vice President, 1913-21; Candidacies: VP - 1912, 1916.

McCARTHY, Eugene Joseph - Minn. (Independent) March 29, 1916—; House, 1949-59; Senate, 1959-71; Candidacy: P - 1976.

McCLELLAN, George Brinton - N.J. (Democratic) Dec. 3, 1826 - Oct. 29, 1885; General-in-Chief of Army of the Potomac, 1861; Governor, 1878-81; Candidacy: P - 1864.

McGOVERN, George Stanley - S.D. (Democratic) July 19, 1922—; House, 1957-61; Senate, 1963-81; Candidacy: p - 1972.

McKINLEY, William Jr. - Ohio (Republican) Jan. 29, 1843 - Sept. 14, 1901; House, 1877 - May 27, 1884, 1885-91; Governor, 1892-96; President,

1897 - Sept. 14, 1901; Candidacies: P - 1896, 1900.

McNARY, Charles Linza - Ore. (Republican) June 12, 1874 - Feb. 25, 1944; state supreme court judge, 1913-15; Senate, 1917 - Nov. 5, 1918, Dec. 18, 1918 - 1944; Candidacy: VP - 1940.

MILLER, William Edward - N.Y. (Republican) March 22, 1914—; House, 1951-65; chairman of Republican National Committee, 1961-64; Candidacy: VP- 1964.

MILTON, John - Ga. ca. 1740 - ca. 1804, Secretary of State, Georgia, ca. 1778, 1781, 1783; Candidacy: 1789.

MONDALE, Walter Frederick - Minn. (Democratic) Jan. 5, 1928—; Senate, 1964-76; Vice President, 1977-81; Candidacy: VP - 1976, 1980.

MONROE, James - Va. (Democratic-Republican) April 28, 1758 - July 4, 1831; Senate, 1790-94; Minister to France, 1794-96, 1803; Minister to England, 1803-07; Governor, 1799-1802, 1811; Secretary of State, 1811-17; President, 1817-25; Candidacies: VP - 1808; P - 1816, 1820.

MORTON, Levi Parsons - N.Y. (Republican) May 16, 1824 - May 16, 1920; House, 1879-81; Minister to France, 1881-85; Vice President, 1889-93; Governor, 1895-97; Candidacy: VP - 1888.

MUSKIE, Edmund Sixtus - Maine (Democratic) March 28, 1914—; Governor, 1955-59; Senate, 1959-80; Secretary of State, 1980-81; Candidacy: VP - 1968.

NATHAN, Theodora Nathalia - Ore. (Libertarian) Feb. 9, 1923—; Broadcast journalist; National Judiciary Committee, Libertarian Party, 1972-75; Vice-chairperson, Oregon state Libertarian party, 1974-75; Candidacy: VP- 1972.

NIXON, Richard Milhous - Calif., N.Y. (Republican) Jan. 9, 1913—; House, 1947-50; Senate, 1950-53; Vice President, 1953-61; President, 1969-74; Candidacies: VP - 1952, 1956; P - 1960, 1968, 1972.

PALMER, John McAuley - Ill. (Democratic, National Democratic) Sept. 13, 1817 - Sept. 25, 1900; Governor, 1869-73; Senate, 1891-97; Candidacies: VP- 1872; P - 1896.

PARKER, Alton Brooks - N.Y. (Democratic) May 14, 1852 - May 10, 1926; Chief Justice of N.Y. Court of Appeals, 1898-1904; Candidacy: P - 1904.

PENDLETON, George Hunt - Ohio (Democratic) July 19, 1825 - Nov. 24,

1889; House, 1857-65; Senate, 1879-85; Minister to Germany, 1885-89; Candidacy: VP - 1864.

PIERCE, Franklin - N.H. (Democratic) Nov. 23, 1804 - Oct. 8, 1869; House, 1833-37; Senate, 1837-42; President, 1853-57; Candidacy: P - 1852.

PINCKNEY, Charles Cotesworth - S.C. (Federalist) Feb. 25, 1746 - Aug. 16, 1825; president, state senate, 1779, Minister to France, 1796; Candidacies: VP - 1800; P - 1804, 1808.

PINCKNEY, Thomas - S.C. (Federalist) Oct. 23, 1750 - Nov. 2, 1828; Governor, 1787-89; Minister to Great Britain, 1792-96; Envoy to Spain, 1794-95; House, 1797-1801; Candidacy: 1796.

POLK, James Knox - Tenn. (Democratic) Nov. 2, 1795 - June 15, 1849; House, 1825-39; Speaker, 1835-39; Governor, 1839-41; President, 1845-49; Candidacies: VP - 1840; P - 1844.

REAGAN, Ronald Wilson - Calif. (Republican) Feb. 6, 1911—; Governor, 1967-75; President, 1981—; Candidacy: P - 1976, 1980.

REID, Whitelaw - N.Y. (Republican) Oct. 27, 1837 - Dec. 15, 1912; Minister to France, 1889-92; Editor-in-chief, *New York Tribune,* 1872-1905; Candidacy: VP - 1892.

ROBINSON, Joseph Taylor - Ark. (Democratic) Aug. 26, 1872 - July 14, 1937; House, 1903-13; Governor, Jan. 16 - March 8, 1913; Senate, 1913-37; Senate minority leader, 1923-33; Senate majority leader, 1933-37; Candidacy: VP - 1928.

RODNEY, Daniel - Del. (Federalist) Sept. 10, 1764 - Sept. 2, 1846; Governor, 1814-17; House, 1822-23; Senate, 1826-27; Candidacy: VP - 1820.

ROOSEVELT, Franklin Delano - N.Y. (Democratic) Jan. 30, 1882 - April 12, 1945; Assistant Secretary of Navy, 1913-20; Governor, 1929-33; President, 1933-45; Candidacies: VP - 1920; P - 1932, 1936, 1940, 1944.

ROOSEVELT, Theodore - N.Y. (Republican, Progressive) Oct. 27, 1858 - Jan. 6, 1919; Governor, 1899-1901; Assistant Secretary of Navy, 1897-98; Vice President, March 4 - Sept. 14, 1901; President, 1901-09; Candidacies: VP - 1900; P - 1904, 1912.

ROSS, James - Pa. (Federalist) July 12, 1762 - Nov. 27, 1847; Senate, 1794-1803; Candidacy: VP- 1816.

RUSH, Richard - Pa. (Democratic-Republican, National-Republican) Aug.

29, 1780 - July 30, 1859; Attorney General, 1814-17; Minister to Great Britain, 1817-24; Secretary of Treasury, 1825-28; Candidacy: VP- 1820, 1828.

RUTLEDGE, John - S.C. (Federalist) Sept. 1739 - July 23, 1800; Continental Congress, 1774-76, 1782-83; Governor, 1779-82; Constitutional Convention, 1787; Associate Justice of U.S. Supreme Court, 1789-91; Candidacy: 1789.

SANFORD, Nathan - N.Y.(Democratic-Republican) Nov. 5, 1777 - Oct. 17, 1838; Senate, 1815-21, 1826-31; Candidacy: VP- 1824.

SCHMITZ, John George - Calif. (American Independent) Aug. 12, 1930—; House, 1970-73; Candidacy: P - 1972.

SCOTT, Winfield - N.J.(Whig) June 13, 1786 - May 29, 1866; General-in-chief of U.S. Army, 1841-61; Candidacy: P- 1852.

SERGEANT, John - Pa. (National-Republican) Dec. 5, 1779 - Nov. 23, 1852; House, 1815-23, 1827-29, 1837-41; Candidacy: VP - 1832.

SEWALL, Arthur - Maine (Democratic) Nov. 25, 1835 - Sept. 5, 1900; Democratic National Committee member, 1888-96; Candidacy: VP - 1896.

SEYMOUR, Horatio - N.Y. (Democratic) May 31, 1810 - Feb. 12, 1886; Governor, 1853-55, 1863-65; Candidacy: P - 1868.

SHERMAN, James Schoolcraft - N.Y. (Republican) Oct. 24, 1855 - Oct. 30, 1912; House, 1887-91, 1893-1909; Vice President, 1909-12; Candidacies: VP - 1908, 1912 (Died during 1912 campaign; Nicholas Murray Butler replaced Sherman on the Republican ticket.)

SHRIVER, Robert Sargent Jr. - Md. (Democratic) Nov. 9, 1915—; Director, Peace Corps, 1961-66; Director, Office of Economic Opportunity, 1964-68; Ambassador to France, 1968-70; Candidacy: VP - 1972 (Replaced Thomas F. Eagleton on Democratic ticket Aug. 8.)

SMITH, Alfred Emanuel - N.Y. (Democratic) Dec. 30, 1873 - Oct. 4, 1944; Governor, 1919-21, 1923-29; Candidacy: P - 1928.

SMITH, William - S.C., Ala. (Independent Democratic-Republican) Sept. 6, 1762 - June 26, 1840; Senate, 1816-23, 1826-31; Candidacies: VP - 1828, 1836.

SPARKMAN, John Jackson - Ala. (Democratic) Dec. 20, 1899—; House, 1937-46; Senate, 1946-79; Candidacy: VP - 1952.

STEVENSON, Adlai Ewing - Ill. (Democratic) Oct. 23, 1835 - June 14, 1914; House, 1875-77, 1879-81; Assistant Postmaster General, 1885-89; Vice President, 1893-97; Candidacies: VP - 1892, 1900.

STEVENSON, Adlai Ewing II - Ill. (Democratic) Feb. 5, 1900 - July 14, 1965; Assistant to the Secretary of Navy, 1941-44; Assistant to the Secretary of State, 1945; Governor, 1949-53; Ambassador to United Nations, 1961-65; Candidacies: P - 1952, 1956.

STOCKTON, Richard (Federalist) - N.J. April 17, 1764 - March 7, 1828; Senate, 1796-99; House, 1813-15; Candidacy: VP- 1820.

TAFT, William Howard - Ohio (Republican) Sept. 15, 1857 - March 8, 1930; Secretary of War, 1904-08; President, 1909-13; Chief Justice of U.S. Supreme Court, 1921-30; Candidacies: P - 1908, 1912.

TALMADGE, Herman Eugene - Ga. (Independent Democratic) Aug. 9, 1913—; Governor, 1947, 1948-55; Senate, 1957-81; Candidacy: VP - 1956.

TAYLOR, Glen Hearst - Idaho (Progressive) April 12, 1904—; Senate, 1945-51; Candidacy: VP- 1948.

TAYLOR, Zachary - La. (Whig) Nov. 24, 1784 - July 9, 1850; Major General, U.S. Army; President, 1849-50; Candidacy: P - 1848.

TAZEWELL, Littleton Waller - Va. (Democratic) Dec. 17, 1774 - May 6, 1860; House, 1800-01; Senate, 1824-32; Governor, 1834-36; Candidacy: VP - 1840.

TELFAIR, Edward - Ga.; 1735 - Sept. 17, 1807; Continental Congress, 1778-82, 1784-85, 1788-89; Governor, 1786, 1790-93; Candidacy: 1789.

THOMAS, Norman Mattoon - N.Y. (Socialist) Nov. 20, 1884 - Dec. 19, 1968; Presbyterian minister, 1911-31; author and editor; Candidacies: P - 1928, 1932, 1936, 1940, 1944, 1948.

THURMAN, Allen Granberry - Ohio (Democratic) Nov. 13, 1813 - Dec. 12, 1895; House, 1845-47; Ohio state supreme court, 1851-56; Senate, 1869-81; Candidacy: VP - 1888.

THURMOND, James Strom - S.C. (States' Rights Democrat, Democratic) Dec. 5, 1902—; Governor, 1947-51; Senate, 1954-56, 1956—; Candidacies: P - 1948; VP - 1960.

TILDEN, Samuel Jones - N.Y.(Democratic) Feb. 9, 1814 - Aug. 4, 1886; Governor, 1875-77; Candidacy: P - 1876.

TOMPKINS, Daniel D. - N.Y.(Democratic-Republican) June 21, 1774 - June 11, 1825; Governor, 1807-17; Vice President, 1817-25; Candidacies: VP - 1816, 1820.

TRUMAN, Harry S - Mo. (Democratic) May 8, 1884 - Dec. 26, 1972; Senate, 1935-45; Vice President, Jan. 20 - April 12, 1945; President, 1945-53; Candidacies: VP - 1944; P - 1948.

TYLER, John - Va. (Whig) March 29, 1790 - Jan. 18, 1862; Governor, 1825-27; Senate, 1827-36; Vice President, March 4 - April 4, 1841; President, 1841-45; Candidacies: VP - 1836, 1840.

VAN BUREN, Martin - N.Y. (Democratic, Free Soil) Dec. 5, 1782 - July 24, 1862; Senate, 1821-28; Governor, Jan. - March, 1829; Secretary of State, 1829-31; Vice President, 1833-37; President, 1837-41; Candidacies: VP - 1824, 1832; P - 1836, 1840, 1848.

WALLACE, George Corley - Ala. (American Independent) Aug. 25, 1919—; Governor, 1963-67, 1971-79, 1983—; Candidacy: P - 1968.

WALLACE, Henry Agard - Iowa (Democratic, Progressive) Oct. 7, 1888 - Nov. 18, 1965; Secretary of Agriculture, 1933-40; Vice President, 1941-45; Secretary of Commerce, 1945-46; Candidacies: VP - 1940; P - 1948.

WARREN, Earl - Calif. (Republican) March 19, 1891 - July 9, 1974; Governor, 1943-53; Chief Justice of U.S. Supreme Court, 1953-69; Candidacy: VP- 1948.

WASHINGTON, George - Va. (Federalist) Feb. 22, 1732 - Dec. 14, 1799; First and Second Continental Congresses, 1774, 1775; Commander-in-chief of armed forces, 1775-83; president of Constitutional Convention, 1787; President, 1789-97; Candidacies: P - 1789, 1792, 1796.

WATSON, Thomas Edward - Ga. (Populist) Sept. 5, 1856 - Sept. 26, 1922; House, 1891-93; Senate, 1921-22; Candidacies: VP - 1896; P - 1904, 1908.

WEAVER, James Baird - Iowa (Greenback, Populist) June 12, 1833 - Feb. 6, 1912; House, 1879-81, 1885-89; Candidacies: P - 1880, 1892.

WEBSTER, Daniel - Mass. (Whig) Jan. 18, 1782 - Oct. 24, 1852; House, 1813-17, 1823-27; Senate, 1827-41, 1845-50; Secretary of State, 1841-43, 1850-52; Candidacy: P - 1836.

WHEELER, Burton Kendall - Mont. (Progressive) Feb. 27, 1882 - Jan. 6,

1975; Senate, 1923-47; Candidacy: VP-1924.

WHEELER, William Almon - N.Y. (Republican) June 19, 1819 - June 4, 1887; House, 1861-63, 1869-77; Vice President, 1877-81; Candidacy: VP - 1876.

WHITE, Hugh Lawson - Tenn. (Whig) Oct. 30, 1773 - April 10, 1840; Senate, 1825-March 3, 1835, Oct. 6, 1835-1840; Candidacy: P - 1836.

WILKINS, William - Pa. (Democratic) Dec. 20, 1779 - June 23, 1865; Senate, 1831-34; Minister to Russia, 1834-35; House, 1843-44; Secretary of War, 1844-45; Candidacy: VP - 1832.

WILLKIE, Wendell Lewis - N.Y. (Republican) Feb. 18, 1892 - Oct. 8, 1944; Utility executive, 1933-40; Candidacy: P - 1940.

WILSON, Henry - Mass. (Republican) Feb. 16, 1812 - Nov. 22, 1875; Senate, 1855-73; Vice President, 1873-75; Candidacy: VP - 1872.

WILSON, Woodrow - N.J. (Democratic) Dec. 28, 1856 - Feb. 3, 1924; Governor, 1911-13; President, 1913-21; Candidacies: P - 1912, 1916.

WIRT, William - Md. (Anti-Masonic) Nov. 8, 1772 - Feb. 18, 1834; Attorney General, 1817-29; Candidacy: P - 1832.

WRIGHT, Fielding Lewis - Miss. (States' Rights Democratic) May 16, 1895 - May 4, 1956; Governor, 1946-52; Candidacy: VP - 1948.

Texts of Major Election Laws

Following are the texts of major election laws relating to presidential elections. Included are the constitutional provisions for selection of the president; the complete text of Title 3, section 15 of the U.S. Code, enacted originally in 1887, governing the counting of electoral votes in Congress; and the rules, reprinted from Hinds' *Precedents of the House of Representatives*, adopted by the House in 1825

for use in deciding the presidential election of 1824. They would provide a precedent for any future House election of a president, although the House could change them at will. Also included is the 25th Amendment to the Constitution, ratified Feb. 10, 1967, providing for presidential succession because of disability, removal or resignation and for filling a vacancy in the vice presidency.

Constitutional Provisions for Selection of the President

Article II

Section I. The executive Power shall be vested in a President of the United States of America. He shall hold his Office during the Term of four Years, and, together with the Vice President, chosen for the same term, be elected, as follows.

Each State shall appoint, in such Manner as the Legislature thereof may direct, a Number of Electors, equal to the whole Number of Senators and Representatives to which the State may be entitled in the Congress: but no Senator or Representative, or Person holding an Office of Trust or Profit under the United States, shall be appointed an Elector.

[The Electors shall meet in their respective States, and vote by Ballot for two Persons, of whom one at least shall not be an Inhabitant of the same State with themselves. And they shall make a List of all the Persons voted for, and of the Number of Votes for each; which List they shall sign and certify, and transmit sealed to the Seat of the Government of the United States, directed to the President of the Senate. The President of the Senate shall, in the Presence of the Senate and House of Representatives, open all the Certificates, and the Votes shall then be counted. The Person having the greatest Number of Votes shall be the President, if such Number be a Majority of the whole Number of Electors appointed; and if there be more than one who have such Majority, and have an equal Number of Votes, then the House of Representatives shall immediately chuse by Ballot one of them for President; and if no Person have a Majority, then from the five highest on the List the said House shall in like Manner chuse the President. But in chusing the President, the Votes shall be taken by States, the Representation from each State having one Vote; a quorum for this Purpose shall consist of a Member or Members from two thirds of the States, and a Majority of all the States shall be necessary to a Choice. In every Case, after the Choice of the President, the Person having the greatest Number of Votes of the Electors shall be the Vice President. But if there should remain two or more who have equal Votes, the Senate shall chuse from them by Ballot the Vice-President.]*

The Congress may determine the Time of chusing the Electors, and the Day on which they shall give their Votes; which Day shall be the same throughout the United States.

No person except a natural born Citizen, or a Citizen of the United States, at the time of the Adoption of this Constitution, shall be eligible to the Office of President; neither shall any Person be eligible to that Office who shall not have attained to the Age of thirty five Years, and been fourteen Years a Resident within the United States.

Amendment XII *(Ratified July 27, 1804)*

The Electors shall meet in their respective states and vote by ballot for President and Vice-President, one of whom, at least, shall not be an inhabitant of the same state with themselves; they shall name in their ballots the person voted for as President, and in distinct ballots the person voted for as Vice-President, and of the number of votes for lists of all persons voted for as President, and of all persons voted for as Vice-President, and of the number of votes for each, which lists they shall sign and certify, and transmit sealed to the seat of the government of the United States, directed to the President of the Senate; ...The person having the greatest number of votes for President, shall be the President, if such number be a majority of the whole number of Electors appointed; and if no person have such majority, then from the persons having the highest numbers not exceeding three on the list of those voted for as President, the House of Representatives shall choose immediately, by ballot, the President. But in choosing the President, the votes shall be taken by states, the representation from each state having one vote; a quorum for this purpose shall consist of a member or members from two-thirds of the states, and a majority of all the states shall be necessary to a choice. [And if the House of Representatives shall not choose a President whenever the right of choice shall devolve upon them, before the fourth day of March next following, then the Vice-President shall act as President, as in the case of the death or other constitutional disability of the President.—]† The person having the greatest number of votes as Vice-President, shall be the Vice-President, if such number be a majority of the whole number of Electors appointed, and if no person have a majority, then from the two highest numbers on the list, the Senate shall choose the Vice President; a quorum for the purpose shall consist of two-thirds of the whole number of Senators, and a majority of the whole number shall be necessary to a choice. But no person constitutionally ineligible to the office of President shall be eligible to that of Vice-President of the United States.

Amendment XX *(Ratified Jan. 23, 1933)*

Section 1. The terms of the President and Vice President shall end at noon on the 20th day of January....

Section 3. If, at the time fixed for the beginning of the term of the President, the President elect shall have died, the Vice President elect shall become President. If a President shall not have been chosen before the time fixed for the beginning of his term, or if the President elect shall have failed to qualify, then the Vice President elect shall act as President until a President shall have qualified; and the Congress may by law provide for the case wherein neither a President elect nor a Vice President elect shall have qualified, declaring who shall then act as President, or the manner in which one who is to act shall be selected, and such person shall act accordingly until a President or Vice President shall have qualified.

Section 4. The Congress may by law provide for the case of the death of any of the persons from whom the House of Representatives may choose a President whenever the right of choice shall have devolved upon them, and for the case of the death of any of the persons from whom the Senate may choose a Vice President whenever the right of choice shall have devolved upon them.

* Superseded by the 12th Amendment.
†Changed to Jan. 20 by the 20th Amendment, ratified in 1933.

Law for Counting Electoral Votes in Congress

Congress shall be in session on the sixth day of January succeeding every meeting of the electors. The Senate and House of Representatives shall meet in the Hall of the House of Representatives at the hour of 1 o'clock in the afternoon on that day, and the President of the Senate shall be their presiding officer. Two tellers shall be previously appointed on the part of the Senate and two on the part of the House of Representatives, to whom shall be handed, as they are opened by the President of the Senate, all the certificates and papers purporting to be certificates of the electoral votes, which certificates and papers shall be opened, presented, and acted upon in the alphabetical order of the States, beginning with the letter A; and said tellers, having then read the same in the presence and hearing of the two Houses, shall make a list of the votes as they shall appear from the said certificates; and the votes having been ascertained and counted according to the rules in this subchapter provided, the result of the same shall be delivered to the President of the Senate, who shall thereupon announce the state of the vote, which announcement shall be deemed a sufficient declaration of the persons, if any, elected President and Vice President of the United States, and, together with a list of votes, be entered on the Journals of the two Houses. Upon such reading of any such certificate or paper, the President of the Senate shall call for objections, if any. Every objection shall be made in writing, and shall state clearly and concisely, and without argument, the ground thereof, and shall be signed by at least one Senator and one Member of the House of Representatives before the same shall be received. When all objections so made to any vote or paper from a State shall have been received and read, the Senate shall thereupon withdraw, and such objections shall be submitted to the Senate for its decision; and the Speaker of the House of Representatives shall, in like manner, submit such objections to the House of Representatives for its decision; and no electoral vote or votes from any State which shall have been regularly given by electors whose appointment has been lawfully certified to according to section 6* of this title from which but one return has been received shall be rejected, but the two Houses concurrently may reject the vote or votes when they agree that such vote or votes have not been so regularly given by electors whose appointment has been so certified. If more than one return or paper purporting to be a return from a State shall have been received by the President of the Senate, those votes, and those only, shall be counted which shall have been regularly given by the electors who are shown by the determination mentioned in section 5† of this title to have been appointed, if the determination in said section provided for shall have been made, or by such successors or substitutes, in case of a vacancy in the board of electors so ascertained, as have been appointed to fill such vacancy in the mode provided by the laws of the State; but in case there shall arise the question which of two or more of such State authorities determining what electors have been appointed, as mentioned in section 5 of this title, is the lawful tribunal of such State, the votes regularly given of those electors, and those only, of such State shall be counted whose title as electors the two Houses, acting separately, shall concurrently decide is supported by the decision of such State so authorized by its law; and in such case of more than one return or paper purporting to be a return from a State, if there shall have been no such determination of the question in the State aforesaid, then those votes, and those only, shall be counted which the two Houses shall concurrently decide were cast by lawful electors appointed in accordance with the laws of the State, unless the two Houses, acting separately, shall concurrently decide such votes not to be the lawful votes of the legally appointed electors of such State. But if the two Houses shall disagree in respect of the counting of such votes, then, and in that case, the votes of the electors whose appointment shall have been certified by the executive of the State, under the seal thereof, shall be counted. When the two Houses have voted, they shall immediately again meet, and the presiding officer shall then announce the decision of the questions submitted. No votes or papers from any other State shall be acted upon until the objections previously made to the votes or papers from any State shall have been finally disposed of.

* Section 6 provides for certification of votes by electors by state Governors.
†Section 5 provides that if state law specifies a method for resolving disputes concerning the vote for Presidential electors, Congress must respect any determination so made by a state.

Presidential Election by the House

1. In the event of its appearing, on opening all the certificates, and counting the votes given by the electors of the several States for President, that no person has a majority of the votes of the whole number of electors appointed, the same shall be entered on the Journals of this House.

2. The roll of the House shall then be called by States; and, on its appearing that a Member or Members from two-thirds of the States are present, the House shall immediately proceed, by ballot, to choose a President from the persons having the highest numbers, not exceeding three, on the list of those voted for as President; and, in case neither of those persons shall receive the votes of a majority of all the states on the first ballot, the House shall continue to ballot for a President, without interruption by other business, until a President be chosen.

3. The doors of the Hall shall be closed during the balloting, except against the Members of the Senate, stenographers, and the officers of the House.

4. From the commencement of the balloting until an election is made no proposition to adjourn shall be received, unless on the motion of one State, seconded by States. The same rule shall be observed in regard to any motion to change the usual hour for the meeting of the House.

5. In balloting the following mode shall be observed, to wit:

The Representatives of each State shall be arranged and seated together, beginning with the seats at the right hand of the Speaker's chair, with the Members from the State of Maine; thence, proceeding with the Members from the States, in the order the States are usually named for receiving petitions* around the Hall of the House, until all are seated.

A ballot box shall be provided for each State.

The Representatives of each State shall, in the first instance, ballot among themselves, in order to ascertain the vote of their State; and they may, if necessary, appoint tellers of their ballots.

After the vote of each State is ascertained, duplicates thereof shall be made out; and in case any one of the persons from whom the choice is to be made shall receive a majority of the votes given, on any one balloting by the Representatives of a State, the name of that person shall be written on each of the duplicates; and in case the votes so given shall be divided so that neither of said persons shall have a majority of the whole number of votes given by such State, on any one balloting, then the word "divided" shall

be written on each duplicate.

After the delegation from each State shall have ascertained the vote of their State, the Clerk shall name the States in the order they are usually named for receiving petitions; and as the name of each is called the Sergeant-at-Arms shall present to the delegation of each two ballot boxes, in each of which shall be deposited, by some Representative of the State, one of the duplicates made as aforesaid of the vote of said State, in the presence and subject to the examination of all the Members from said State then present; and where there is more than one Representative from a State, the duplicates shall not both be deposited by the same person.

When the votes of the States are thus all taken in, the Sergeant-at-Arms shall carry one of said ballot boxes to one table and the other to a separate and distinct table.

One person from each State represented in the balloting shall be appointed by the Representatives to tell off said ballots; but, in case the Representatives fail to appoint a teller, the Speaker shall appoint.

The said tellers shall divide themselves into two sets, as nearly equal in number as can be, and one of the said sets of tellers shall proceed to count the votes in one of said boxes, and the other set the votes in the other box.

When the votes are counted by the different sets of tellers, the result shall be reported to the House; and if the reports agree, the same shall be accepted as the true votes of the States; but if the reports disagree, the States shall proceed, in the same manner as before, to a new ballot.

6. All questions arising after the balloting commences, requiring the decision of the House, which shall be decided by the House, voting per capita, to be incidental to the power of choosing a President, shall be decided by States without debate; and in case of an equal division of the votes of States, the question shall be lost.

7. When either of the persons from whom the choice is to be made shall have received a majority of all the States, the Speaker shall declare the same, and that that person is elected President of the United States.

8. The result shall be immediately communicated to the Senate by message, and a committee of three persons shall be appointed to inform the President of the United States and the President-elect of said election.

On February 9, 1825, the election of John Quincy Adams took place in accordance with these rules.

Petitions are no longer introduced in this way. This old procedure of calling the states beginning with Maine proceeded through the original 13 states and then through the remaining states in the order of their admission to the Union.

25th Amendment: Presidential Disability
(Ratified Feb. 10, 1967)

Section 1. In case of the removal of the President from office or of his death or resignation, the Vice President shall become President.

Section 2. Whenever there is a vacancy in the office of the Vice President, the President shall nominate a Vice President who shall take office upon confirmation by a majority vote of both Houses of Congress.

Section 3. Whenever the President transmits to the

President pro tempore of the Senate and the Speaker of the House of Representatives his written declaration that he is unable to discharge the powers and duties of his office, and until he transmits to them a written declaration to the contrary, such powers and duties shall be discharged by the Vice President as Acting President.

Section 4. Whenever the Vice President and a majority of either the principal officers of the executive departments or of such other body as Congress may by law provide, transmit to the President pro tempore of the Senate and the Speaker of the House of Representatives their written declaration that the President is unable to discharge the powers and duties of his office, the Vice President shall immediately assume the powers and duties of the office as Acting President.

Thereafter, when the President transmits to the President pro tempore of the Senate and the Speaker of the House of Representatives his written declaration that no inability exists, he shall resume the powers and duties of his office unless the Vice President and a majority of either the principal officers of the executive departments or of such other body as Congress may by law provide, transmit within four days to the President pro tempore of the Senate and the Speaker of the House of Representatives their written declaration that the President is unable to discharge the powers and duties of his office. Thereupon Congress shall decide the issue, assembling within forty-eight hours for that purpose if not in session. If the Congress, within twenty-one days after receipt of the latter written declaration, or, if Congress is not in session, within twenty-one days after Congress is required to assemble, determines by two-thirds vote of both houses that the President is unable to discharge the powers and duties of his office, the Vice President shall continue to discharge the same as Acting President; otherwise, the President shall resume the powers and duties of his office.

Selected Bibliography

Books

Abramson, Paul R., Aldrich, John H., and Rohde, David N. *Change and Continuity in the 1980 Elections*. Washington, D.C.: CQ Press, 1982.

Adamany, David. *Campaign Financing In America*. North Scituate, Mass.: Duxbury Press, 1972.

―――, and Agree, George E., eds. *Political Money: A Strategy for Campaign Financing in America*. Baltimore: Johns Hopkins University Press, 1975.

Alexander, Herbert E. *Campaign Money: Reform and Reality in the States*. New York: Free Press, 1976.

―――. *Financing Politics: Money, Elections and Political Reform*. Washington, D.C.: CQ Press; 2d edition, 1976.

―――. *Financing the 1968 Election*. Lexington, Mass.: D. C. Heath, 1971.

―――. *Financing the 1972 Election*. Lexington, Mass.: Lexington Books, 1976.

―――. *Financing the 1976 Election*. Washington, D.C.: CQ Press, 1979.

―――. *Money In Politics*. Washington, D.C.: Public Affairs Press, 1972.

―――. *Money, Politics and Public Reporting*. Princeton, N.J.: Citizens' Research Foundation, 1960.

―――. *Political Financing*. Minneapolis, Minn.: Burgess, 1973.

―――, and Lambert, Richard E., eds. *Political Finance: Reform and Reality*. Philadelphia, Pa.: American Academy of Political and Social Science, 1976.

Altschuler, Bruce E. *Keeping a Finger on the Public Pulse: Private Polling and Presidential Elections*. Westport, Conn.: Greenwood Press, 1982.

Asher, Herbert. *Presidential Elections and American Politics*. Homewood, Ill.: Dow Jones-Irwin, 1980.

Bain, Richard C., and Parris, Judith H. *Convention Decisions and Voting Records*. Washington, D.C.: Brookings Institution, 1973.

Barber, James D., ed. *Choosing the President*. Englewood Cliffs, N.J.: Prentice-Hall, 1974.

―――. James David. *The Pulse of Politics: Electing Presidents in the Media Age*. New York. W. W. Norton, 1980.

―――. *Race for the Presidency: The Media and the Nominating Process*. Englewood Cliffs, N.J.: Prentice-Hall, 1978.

Best, Judith. *The Case Against Direct Election of the President: A Defense of the Electoral College*. Ithaca, N.Y.: Cornell University Press, 1975.

Bickel, Alexander M. *The New Age of Political Reform: The Electoral College, the Convention and the Party*. New York: Harper & Row, 1968.

―――. *Reform and Continuity: The Electoral College, the Convention, and the Party System*. New York: Harper & Row, 1971.

Brams, Steven J. *The Presidential Election Game*. New Haven, Conn.: Yale University Press, 1978.

Brereton, Charles. *First Step to the White House: The New Hampshire Primary, 1952-1980*. Hampton, New Hampshire: The Wheelabrator Foundation Inc., 1979.

Burnham, Walter D. *Critical Elections and the Mainsprings of American Politics*. New York: Norton, 1970.

Caeser, James W. *Reforming the Reforms: A Critical Analysis of the Presidential Selection Process*. Cambridge, Mass.: Ballinger, 1982.

Campbell, Angus et al. *The American Voter*. New York: Wiley, 1960.

Chagall, David. *The New Kingmakers*. New York: Harcourt Brace Jovanovich, 1982.

Committee for Economic Development. *Financing a Better Election System*. New York: 1968.

Congressional Quarterly. *Candidates '80*. Washington, D.C.: 1980.

―――. *Congressional Districts in the 1970s*. 2d ed. Washington, D.C.: 1974.

―――. *Dollar Politics: The Issue of Campaign Spending*. Washington, D.C.: 1st ed, 1971; 2d ed, 1974; 3d ed, 1982.

―――. *Guide to 1976 Elections*. Washington, D.C.: 1977.

―――. *Guide to U.S. Elections*. Washington, D.C.: 1975.

―――. *National Party Conventions 1831-1976*. Washington, D.C.: 1979.

―――. *Politics in America*. Washington, D.C.: 1979.

Crotty, William J. *Political Reform and the American Experiment*. New York: Crowell, 1977.

David, Paul T. *The Politics of National Party Conventions*. Washington, D.C.: Brookings Institution, 1960.

Davis, James W. *Presidential Primaries: Road to the White House*. New York: Crowell, 1967.

―――. *Springboard to the White House: Presidential Primaries, How They Are Fought and Won*. New York: Thomas Y. Crowell, 1967.

De Vries, Walter, and Tarrance, Lance, Jr. *The Ticket-Splitter: A New Force in American Politics*. Grand Rapids, Mich.: Eerdmans Publishing Co., 1972.

Drew, Elizabeth. *American Journal: The Events of 1976*. New York: Random House, 1977.

―――. *Portrait of An Election: The 1980 Presidential Campaign*. New York: Simon & Schuster, 1981.

Dunn, Delmer D. *Financing Presidential Campaigns*. Washington, D.C.: Brookings Institution, 1972.

Fairlie, Henry. *The Parties: Republicans and Democrats in this Century*. New York: St. Martin's Press, 1978.

Ferguson, Thomas, and Rogers, Joel, eds. *The Hidden Election: Politics and Economics in the 1980 Presidential Campaign*. New York: Pantheon Books, 1981.

Fishel, Jeff. *Parties and Elections in an Anti-Party Age: American Politics and the Crisis of Confidence*. Bloomington: Indiana University Press, 1978.

Germond, Jack W., and Witcover, Jules. *Blue Smoke and Mirrors: How Reagan Won and Why Carter Lost the Election of 1980*. New York: Penguin Books, 1981.

Greenfield, Jeff. *The Real Campaign: How the Media Missed the Story of the 1980 Campaign*. New York: Summit Books, 1981.

Hadley, Arthur T. *The Empty Polling Booth*. Englewood Cliffs, N.J.: Prentice-Hall, 1978.

―――. *The Invisible Primary*. Englewood Cliffs, N.J.: Prentice-Hall, 1976.

Heard, Alexander E. *The Costs of Democracy*. Chapel Hill, N.C.: University of North Carolina Press, 1960.

Hess, Stephen. *The Presidential Campaign: The Leadership Selection Process After Watergate*. Washington, D.C.: Brookings Institution, 1978.

Johnson, Donald B., and Porter, Kirk H. *National Party Platforms*. 2 vols. Urbana, Ill.: University of Illinois Press, 1978.

Keech, William R., ed. *Winners Take All: Report of the Twentieth Century Task Force on Reform of the Presidential Election Process*. New York: Holmes & Meier, 1978.

Keech, William R., and Matthews, Donald R. *The Party's Choice: With An Epilogue on the 1976 Nominations*. Washington, D.C.: Brookings Institution, 1976.

Kessel, John. *Presidential Campaign Politics*. Homewood, Ill.: Dow Jones-Irwin, 1980.

Key, V. O. *Responsible Electorate: Rationality in Presidential Voting, 1936-1960*. Cambridge, Mass.: Harvard University Press, 1966.

Ladd, Everett C. *Where Have All the Voters Gone?* New York: W. W. Norton, 1978.

Ladd, Everett C., and Hadley, Charles D. *Transformation of the American Party System: Political Coalitions from the New Deal to the 1970s*. New York: W. W. Norton, 1978.

Lazarsfeld, Paul F. *The People's Choice: How the Voter Makes Up His Mind in a Presidential Campaign*. New York: Columbia University Press, 1968.

Lengle, James I. *Representation and Presidential Primaries: The Democratic Party in the Post-Reform Era.* Westport, Conn.: Greenwood Press, 1981.

Lipset, Seymour M., ed. *Emerging Coalitions in American Politics.* San Francisco: Institute for Contemporary Studies, 1978.

Littlewood, Thomas B. *The 1980 Carter-Kennedy Primary in Illinois.* Institute of Government and Public Affairs, University of Illinois, December 1981.

Longley, Lawrence D. *The Politics of Electoral College Reform.* New Haven, Conn.: Yale University Press, 1972.

Malbin, Michael J. *Parties, Interest Groups, and Campaign Finance Laws.* Washington, D.C.: American Enterprise Institute for Public Policy Research, 1980.

Matthews, Donald R., ed. *Perspectives on Presidential Selection.* Washington, D.C.: Brookings Institution, 1973.

Mazmanian, Daniel A. *Third Parties in Presidential Elections.* Washington, D.C.: Brookings Institution, 1974

Michener, James A. *Presidential Lottery: The Reckless Gamble In Our Electoral System.* New York: Random House, 1969.

Nichols, David. *Financing Elections: The Politics of an American Ruling Class.* New York: New Viewpoints, 1974.

Nie, Norman H., et al. *The Changing American Voter.* Cambridge, Mass.: Harvard University Press, 1976.

Novak, Michael. *Choosing Our King: Powerful Symbols In Presidential Politics.* New York: Macmillan, 1974.

Overacker, Louise. *Money in Elections.* New York: Arno Press, 1974.

_____. *The Presidential Primary.* New York: Arno Press, 1974.

Page, Benjamin I. *Choices and Echoes in Presidential Elections: Rational Man and Electoral Democracy.* Chicago: University of Chicago Press, 1978.

Parris, Judith H. *The Convention Problem: Issues in Reform of Presidential Procedures.* Washington, D.C.: Brookings Institution, 1972.

Peirce, Neal R. *The People's President: The Electoral College and the Emerging Consensus for a Direct Vote.* New York: Simon & Schuster, 1968.

Petersen, Svend. *A Statistical History of the American Presidential Elections.* New York: Frederick Ungar, 1968.

Phillips, Kevin P. *The Emerging Republican Majority.* New York: Arlington House, 1969.

Plissner, Martin, et al. eds. *Campaign '76.* New York: Arno Press, 1977.

Polsby, Nelson, and Wildavsky, Aaron. *Presidential Elections: Strategies of American Electoral Politics.* New York: Scribner, 1980.

Pomper, Gerald M. *Elections in America: Control and Influence in Democratic Politics.* New York: Dodd, Mead & Co., 1968.

_____. *Nominating the President: The Politics of Convention Choice.* Evanston, Ill.: Northwestern University Press, 1963.

_____. *Voters' Choice: Varieties of American Electoral Behavior.* New York: Dodd, Mead & Co., 1975.

Pomper, Marlene M., ed. *The Election of 1976: Reports and Interpretations.* New York: David McKay Co., 1977.

Ranney, Austin, ed. *The American Elections of 1980.* Washington, D.C.: American Enterprise Institute for Public Policy Research, 1981.

_____. *The Past and Future of Presidential Debates.* Washington, D.C.: American Enterprise Institute for Public Policy Research, 1979.

Roseboom, Eugene H. *History of Presidential Elections: From George Washington to Richard M. Nixon.* New York: Macmillan, 1970.

Runyon, John H. *Source Book of American Presidential Campaign and Election Statistics, 1948-1968.* New York: Frederick Ungar, 1971.

Sanford, Terry. *A Danger to Democracy: The Presidential Nominating Process.* Boulder, Colo.: Westview Press, 1981.

Sayre, Wallace S. *Voting for President: The Electoral College and the American Political System.* Washington, D.C.: Brookings Institution, 1970.

Scammon, Richard M., ed. *America at the Polls: A Handbook of American Presidential Election Statistics 1920-1964.* Pittsburgh, Pa.: University of Pittsburgh Press, 1965.

_____. *America Votes: A Handbook of Contemporary Election Statistics.* Washington, D.C.: Congressional Quarterly, 1956-.

Schlesinger, Arthur M. Jr., ed. *The Coming to Power: Critical Presidential Elections in American History.* New York: McGraw-Hill, 1972.

_____, ed. *History of American Presidential Elections.* 4 vols. New York: McGraw-Hill, 1971.

Schram, Martin. *Running for President 1976: The Carter Campaign.* Briarcliff Manor, New York: Stein & Day, 1977.

Singer, Aaron, ed. *Campaign Speeches of American Presidential Candidates, 1928-1972.* New York: Frederick Ungar, 1976.

Shoup, Laurence H. *The Carter Presidency and Beyond: Power and Politics in the 1980s.* Palo Alto, Calif.: Ramparts Press, 1980.

Stacks, John F. *Watershed: The Campaign for the Presidency, 1980.* New York: Times Books, 1981.

Stroud, Kandy. *How Jimmy Won: The Victory Campaign from Plains to the White House.* New York: William Morrow, 1977.

Thayer, George. *Who Shakes the Money Tree?* New York: Simon & Schuster, 1974.

Wallace, David. *First Tuesday.* Garden City, N.Y.: Doubleday, 1964.

Wayne, Stephen J. *The Road to the White House: The Politics of Presidential Elections.* New York: St. Martin's Press, 1980.

White, F. Clifton and Gill, William J. *Why Reagan Won: A Narrative History fo the Conservative Movement, 1964-1981.* Chicago, Ill.: Regenery Gateway, 1981.

White, Theodore H. *The Making of the President, 1960.* New York: Atheneum, 1961.

_____. *The Making of the President, 1964.* New York: Atheneum, 1965.

_____. *The Making of the President, 1968.* New York: Atheneum, 1969.

_____. *The Making of the President, 1972.* New York: Atheneum, 1973.

Winter, Ralph K. *Campaign Financing and Political Freedom.* Washington, D.C.: American Enterprise Institute for Public Policy Research, 1974.

Witcover, Jules. *Marathon: The Pursuit of the Presidency, 1972-1976.* New York: Viking Press, 1977.

Yunker, John H., and Longley, Lawrence D. *The Electoral College: Its Biases Newly Measured for the 1960s and 1970s.* Beverly Hills, Calif.: Sage Publications, 1976.

Zeidenstein, Harvey. *Direct Election of the President.* Lexington, Mass.: D. C. Heath, 1973.

Articles

Abramson, Paul R. "Class Voting in the 1976 Presidential Election." *Journal of Politics,* November 1978, pp. 1066-1072.

Alexander, Herbert E. "Financing American Politics." *Political Quarterly,* October/December 1974, pp. 439-448.

Axelrod, Robert. "Where the Votes Come From: An Analysis of Electoral Coalitions, 1952-1968." *American Political Science Review,* March 1972, pp. 15-17.

Bayh, Birch. "Electing a President: The Case for Direct Popular Election." *Harvard Journal on Legislation,* January 1969, pp. 1-12.

Biden, Joseph R., Jr. "Public Financing of Elections: Legislative Proposals and Constitutional Questions." *Northwestern University Law Review,* March/April 1974, pp. 1-70.

Black, Merle and Black, Earl. "Republican Party Development in the South: The Rise of the Contested Primary." *Social Science Quarterly,* December 1976, pp. 566-578.

Cronin, Thomas E. "Choosing a President." *Center Magazine,* September/October 1978, pp. 5-15.

Declerq, Eugene et al. "Voting in American Presidential Elections: 1952-1972." *American Politics Quarterly,* July 1975, pp. 222-246.

de Lesseps, Suzanne, "Electoral College Reform." *Editorial Re-*

search Reports, November 19, 1976, pp. 845-862.

Douglas, James. "Was Reagan's Victory a Watershed in American Politics?" *Political Quarterly,* April/June 1981, pp. 171-183.

Eshelman, Edwin D. "Congress and Electoral Reform: An Analysis of Proposals for Changing Our Method of Selecting a President." *Christian Century,* February 5, 1969, pp. 178-181.

Glantz, Stanton A. et al. "Election Outcomes: Whose Money Matters." *Journal of Politics,* November 1976, pp. 1033-1038.

Glen, Maxwell, "The PACs are Back, Richer and Wiser, to Finance the 1980 Elections." *National Journal,* November 24, 1979, pp. 1982-1984.

Goldstein, Joel H. "The Influence of Money on the Pre-Nomination Stage of the Presidential Selection Process: The Case of the 1976 Election." *Presidential Studies Quarterly,* Spring 1978, pp. 164-179.

Hardesty, Rex. "Elections '80: A Pivotal Decision for America." *American Federationist,* October 1980, pp. 1-5.

Hedlund, Ronald D. "Cross-Over Voting in a 1976 Open Presidential Primary." *Public Opinion Quarterly,* Winter 1977-1978, pp. 498-514.

Hodgson, Godfrey. "American Presidential and Party Politics: Changes in Spirit and Machine." *World Today,* September 1976, pp. 317-327.

Kirkpatrick, Samuel A. "American Electoral Behavior: Change and Stability." *American Politics Quarterly,* July 1975, pp. 219-352.

Ladd, Everett C. "The Brittle Mandate: Electoral Realignment and the 1980 Presidential Election." *Political Science Quarterly,* Spring 1982, pp. 1-25.

Lanouette, William J. "Complex Financing Laws Shape Presidential Campaign Strategies." *National Journal,* August 4, 1979, pp. 1281-1286.

Lechner, Alfred J. "Direct Election of the President: The Final Step in the Constitutional Evolution of the Right to Vote." *Notre Dame Lawyer,* October 1971, pp. 122-151.

Lengle, James I. "Divisive Presidential Primaries and Party Electoral Prospects, 1932-1976." *American Politics Quarterly,* July 1980, pp. 261-277.

Lobel, Martin. "Federal Control of Campaign Contributions." *Minnesota Law Review,* 1966, pp. 1-62.

McDonald, Kimberly. "The Impact of Political Action Committees." *Economic Forum,* Summer 1981, pp. 94-103.

"The Major Issues of the 1980 Campaign: Pro and Con." *Congressional Digest,* October 1980, pp. 225-256.

Mansfield, Harvey C. Jr. "The American Election: Towards Constitutional Democracy?" *Government and Opposition,* Winter 1981, pp. 3-18.

Menendez, Albert J. "Religion and Presidential Politics 1980." *Worldview,* November 1979, pp. 11-14.

———. "Religion at the Polls, 1980." *Church and State,* December 1980, pp. 15-18.

Mervin, David. "Personality and Ticket Splitting in U.S. Federal and Gubernatorial Elections, 1946-1972." *Political Studies,* September 1973, pp. 306-310.

Miller, Arthur H. "Partisanship Reinstated?" A Comparison of the 1972 and 1976 U.S. Presidential Elections." *British Journal of Political Science,* April 1978, pp. 129-152.

———. "Realignment in the 1980 Election." *Economic Outlook USA,* Autumn 1981, pp. 88-90.

———, and Wattenberg, Martin P. "The Politics from the Pulpit: Religiosity in the 1980 Elections." *Economic Outlook USA,* Summer 1982, pp. 61-64.

Olson, David M. "The Structure of Electoral Politics." *Journal of Politics,* May 1967, pp. 352-367.

Orren, Gary and Dionne, E. J. "The Next New Deal: Progressives and Democrats Won't Find It by Moving Right; a Second Look at the 1980 Election. . . ." *Working Papers for a New Society,* May/June 1981, pp. 24-35.

Pomper, Gerald M. "From Confusion to Clarity: Issues and American Voters, 1956-1968." *American Political Science Review,* June 1972, pp. 415-428.

"Pulpits and Politics, 1980." *Church and State,* November 1980.

Reiter, Howard L. "Why Is Turnout Down?" *Public Opinion Quarterly,* Fall 1979, pp. 297-311.

Roper, Burns W. "Making More Meaningful Choices: A Proposed New System for Selecting Presidential Candidates." *Freedom at Issue,* September/October 1980, pp. 3-5.

Shafer, Byron E. "Anti-Party Politics." *Public Interest,* Spring 1981, pp. 95-111.

Staats, Elmer B. "Impact of the Federal Election Campaign Act of 1971." *Annals of the American Academy of Political and Social Science,* May 1976, pp. 98-113.

Thomas, William V. "Choosing Presidential Candidates." *Editorial Research Reports,* June 6, 1980, pp. 407-424.

Tyler, Gus. "Gauging the Republican Tide: A New Age or An Interregnum?" *New Leader,* November 17, 1980, pp. 3-5.

Waldman, Loren K. "Liberalism of Congressmen and the Presidential Vote in Their District." *Midwest Journal of Political Science,* February 1967, pp. 73-85.

Walker, Jack. "Presidential Campaigns: Reforming the Reforms." *Wilson Quarterly,* Autumn 1981, pp. 88-101.

Ware, Alan. "The 1980 U.S. Elections: Party Revival or Continuing Party Decline?" *Parliamentary Affairs,* Spring 1981, pp. 174-190.

Weisberg, Harold, and Rusk, Jerrold. "Perceptions of Presidential Candidates: Implications for Electoral Change." *Midwest Journal of Political Science,* August 1972, pp. 388-410.

Wildavsky, Aaron. "The Three Party System-1980 and After." *Public Interest,* Summer 1981, pp. 47-57.

Zikmund, Joseph. "Suburban Voting in Presidential Elections: 1948-1964." *Midwest Journal of Political Science,* May 1968.

Documents

U.S. Congress. Clerk of the U.S. House of Representatives. *Statistics of the Presidential and Congressional Elections.* Washington, D.C.: Government Printing Office, 1981.

U.S. Congress. House. Committee on House Administration. *Presidential Matching Payments Regulations.* H. Doc. 96-57. 96th Cong., 1st sess. Washington, D.C.: Government Printing Office, 1979.

U.S. Congress. House. Committee on House Administration. *Presidential Primary Matching Payment Account: Revised Regulations.* H. Doc. 96-216. 96th Cong., 1st sess. Washington, D.C.: Government Printing Office, 1979.

U.S. Congress. House. Committee on House Administration. *The Presidential Campaign, 1976.* 2 vols. 95th Cong., 2d sess. Washington, D.C.: Government Printing Office, 1978.

U.S. Congress. Secretary of the U.S. Senate. *Nomination and Election of the President and Vice President of the United States Including the Manner of Selecting Delegates to National Political Conventions.* Washington, D.C.: Government Printing Office, 1980.

U.S. Congress. Senate. Committee on Rules and Administration. *Federal Election Campaign Act Amendments, 1979: Hearings, July 13, 1979.* 96th Cong., 1st sess. Washington, D.C.: Government Printing Office, 1979.

U.S. Congress. Senate. *Report of the Federal Election Commission Receipt and Use of Federal Funds by Candidates Who Accepted Public Financing for the 1980 Presidential Primary and General Elections.* H. Doc. 91-24, February 8, 1982. 97th Cong. 2d sess. Washington, D.C.: Government Printing Office, 1982.

U.S. Congress. Senate. Select Committee on Presidential Campaign Activities. *Election Reform: Basic References.* 93d Cong., 1st sess. Washington, D.C.: Government Printing Office, 1973.

U.S. Congress. Senate Library. *Factual Campaign Information.* Washington, D.C.: Government Printing Office, 1982.

U.S. Department of Commerce. Bureau of the Census. *Voter Participation.* Current Population Reports: Series P-20. Washington, D.C.: Government Printing Office, 19- .

U.S. Federal Election Commission. *FEC Annual Report.* Washington, D.C.: 1976-.

Index